ISRAEL VERSUS JIBRIL

ISRAEL VERSUS JIBRIL

THE THIRTY-YEAR WAR AGAINST A MASTER TERRORIST

SAMUEL M. KATZ

PARAGON HOUSE
New York

First edition, 1993

Published in the United States by

Paragon House
90 Fifth Avenue
New York, N.Y. 10011

Library of Congress Cataloging-in-Publication Data

Katz, Samuel M.
Israel versus Jibril : the thirty-year war against a master
terrorist / Samuel M. Katz.—1st ed.
p.   cm.
Includes bibliographical references and index.
1. Jibril, Ahmed.   2. Jabhah al-Sha' bīyah li-Tahrīr Filastīn-al—
Qiyādah al-' Āmmah.   3. Jewish-Arab relations—1973-   4. Terrorists—
Middle East—Biography.   I. Title.
DS119.7.J49K38   1993
956.94'0049274—dc20   92-34426
                                                          CIP

Manufactured in the United States of America

CONTENTS

PREFACE

CHRONICLING THE CAREER of one of the world's most effective and enigmatic terrorists and his organization, as well as looking into a nation's resolve to destroy it, is a most difficult task; after all, it is one in which many of the world's most capable intelligence agencies have come up short. Information is always sketchy. The statements of many people, from the terrorists themselves to those whose interests they represent to the men and women whose lifelong dedication is to hunt down these threats to law, order, and national security, are always laced with emotion, questionable assumptions, and the frustration that comes from knowing very little about the opposition, men and women to whom secrecy is a day-to-day religion. It is hoped that by sifting through the archives and government reports of several nations, through interviews and factual sources, the most accurate history of one man's war with one nation has been achieved. All opinions, however, are the author's own, and the Israel Ministry of Defense and the Israeli Defense Forces (IDF) are in no way connected with the production or conclusions of this book.

Researching a book of this kind, examining a man within an organization that by its nature is an enigma protected by an impenetrable veil of secrecy and an army of trained and eager gunmen, is a challenging task. Much of the information on which this book was based has come from overt sources, historical accounts, press reports, and other "open" areas where data can be gathered. A good deal of the information—and guidance—gathered for the completion of this project has come from intelligence sources on several continents who, for obvious reasons of security, have offered me insight into this topic in exchange for my keeping their anonymity.

I am in great debt to a great many people in the writing of this book— individuals who offered me their time, confidence, and expertise. Due to the extremely sensitive nature of the dirty profession of combating terrorism, many have requested absolute anonymity. Also, throughout the course of this book many Israeli security and military officials are identified only by the first initial in their name. This is a matter of state security dictated by the IDF Military Censor's Office, a ruling that has been strictly self-enforced. The reader should be informed that a security examination by the IDF Military Censor's Office is a basic responsibility imposed on all Israeli journalists and scholars, as well as anyone else working out of Israel. The office does not exist as a means to eliminate free thought or to silence political criticism. Rather, it is a mechanism employed to insure that classified material, from the identity of an intelligence agent to the unit designation of a paratrooper battalion, is not published. Only military and security items deemed classified are removed by the censor's pen—nothing else. Although many Westerners are offended by the dreaded "C" word of censorship, most Westerners are not forced to live their lives under the constant threat of full-scale war and terrorist attack.

I wish to thank a few friends and associates who offered invaluable assistance in the writing of this book; many, however, have wished to remain anonymous for the obvious reasons. I would like to offer a very heartfelt thanks to Yosef Argaman, the noted editor of the IDF weekly magazine *Bamachane*; Anat Kurz at the Jaffe Center for Strategic Study at Tel Aviv University; Joseph S. Bermudez, Jr.; Lee E. Russell; Dan David; Joe Ward; Major J.R. Vallance-Whitacre at the New York office of the U.S. Army Public Affairs; and the information offices at the Royal Danish Embassy in Washington, D.C. I would also like to thank my agent, Ethan Ellenberg, for all his assistance in seeing this project through; Alex Mazel and Hanni Katz for their generous help with the French and German translations; and Nissim Elyakim for all his generous and self-sacrificing help with logistics in Israel. Most important, I would like to thank my wife, Sigalit, for all her assistance, patience, hard work, understanding, and love.

Samuel M. Katz
Tel Aviv

INTRODUCTION

THE SWEEPING WINDS that followed Operation Desert Storm in early 1991 were meant to leave lasting change in the tumultuous and treacherous Middle East. The New World Order had dawned into the semblance of functional reality in an international campaign designed to defeat Iraqi strongman Saddam Hussein following his capture of Kuwait. The United States, a supporter of Iraq during its war with Iran, had assumed the vanguard in this elaborate campaign to liberate Kuwait from the Iraqi yoke and remove Iraqi military pressure from the ultrastrategic Saudi Arabian oil fields. To achieve this task, United States President George Bush had forged an odd, though cleverly assembled, inter-Arab coalition to make the destruction of one of the region's most tyrannical regimes politically acceptable to the masses back home. Standing behind the massive military might of the American war machine, the Saudis and Egyptians were quick to lead the anti-Arab "anti-Saddam" forces, but Syria, a police state run by a dictator equal in stature and brutality to Saddam Hussein, was quick to sign on to the coalition too. Although militarily the token Syrian force dispatched to the Saudi desert would have little impact on the course of the eventual fighting, their political value to the international coalition, especially its Arab members, was seen as vital.

There was a small string attached to this support from Damascus, however.

In exchange for Syrian participation in this international campaign, Israel could in no way become a combatant in the war; the thought of Syrian and Israeli forces joining forces to battle a common enemy—especially an Arab one—was too repugnant a thought, no matter how truly Byzantine, for Syrian President Hafaz al-Assad to contemplate. To keep Israel out of the war, even after the SCUD missiles began to fall on Tel Aviv, the United States had to make many precarious political promises and, in the case of American Patriot missile crews sent to

1

Israel, provide remarkable military support. Although attacked thirty-eight times by Iraqi missiles, Israel did not join in the fighting. President Bush's coalition had stood firm, and the entire region, it appears, has benefited from the humbling of Saddam Hussein.

Washington too would have its own demands as payback for leading the anti-Saddam coalition. To inaugurate the postwar New World Order, the United States pushed both Arabs and Israelis to attend a face-to-face peace conference. The time was ripe for delegates from Jerusalem to sit across the table from delegates from Syria, Egypt, and representatives from Jordan and the Palestinians. Both Israelis and Arabs were reluctant to talk peace but could not ignore the American demand. A neutral site had to be chosen. The Spanish capital of Madrid, with its shared history in the course of both Jewish and Arab history, served this purpose adequately.

The leaders of the Middle Eastern nations entered into their historic venture toward peace not in an embrace of goodwill, but under a veil of hermetic security. Throughout the conference, Spanish antiterrorist commandos from the famed *Grupo Especial de Operaciones* and *Unidad Especial de Intervencion* units were deployed to intercept any terrorist forces who wished to deter the slow march toward peace with a bloody statement of violence. Spanish vigilance was not just a precaution. As the Israeli and Arab delegations exchanged their terse conditions for coexistence, the region's true power brokers gathered in another world capital.

It was October 20, 1991, and a brisk autumn day in Tehran, the Iranian capital. Outside the grand parliament building in central Tehran, under the security umbrella of hundreds of heavily armed cleric-soldiers from the Iranian Revolutionary Guard sworn to martyr themselves in the defense of Islam, 400 representatives of the Who's Who of Arab and Islamic terror prepared their agenda for the future of their new world order: a declaration for an international holy war. They planned an eruption of hostilities that would drown out the cries for peace and eventually engulf the entire Middle East—as well as much of the remainder of the world—in an inescapable conflagration meant to last for decades and kill tens of thousands of people. Their first promised action would be to terminate all of the leaders participating in the Madrid Peace Conference, with the exception, of course, of Syria's President Assad.[1]

As the Israeli prime minister, Yitzhak Shamir, addressed his counterparts from Syria, Jordan, Egypt, and the Palestinians, the Iranian prime minister, Ayatollah ali Akbar Hashemi Rafsanjani, addressed *his* counterparts to inaugurate the first meeting of the forum called the Opposition Conference: the leaders of the world's most dangerous terrorist organizations assembled under the sparkle of opulence and the barrel of a gun to place the world in a dragnet of fear. Under the light of a gigantic Czech crystal chandelier, the men who have made international air travel a dangerous undertaking sat glued to their velvet draped seats as speaker after speaker preached from the podium promoting a deadly strategy to undermine the "treacherous" peace conference transpiring in the Spanish capital. In all, forty-five nations were represented at the gathering. Although men like Dr. George Habash, founder of the Popular Front for the Liberation of Palestine (PFLP), and Nayif Hawatmeh, commander of the Democratic Front for the Liberation of Palestine (DFLP), took their rightful places in the audience, the most important guest at the conference justly sat in the front row: Ahmed Jibril, the commander of one of the most lethal terrorist organizations to emerge on the international scene—the Popular Front for the Liberation of Palestine-General Command (PFLP-GC).

Even though there was much press coverage and fanfare to the Opposition Conference, Jibril's presence in Tehran was pure business. He was in Tehran to forge a military alliance between the hard-line Palestinian terrorist groups and the Iranian-supported Islamic fundamentalist movements in Iran, Lebanon, Jordan, Egypt, Algeria, Saudi Arabia, Turkey, and, of course, the Israeli-occupied territories of the West Bank and the Gaza Strip; it was an alliance Jibril had worked on since the summer of 1988, when, according to American intelligence reports, he accepted $10 million from the Iranians to blow an American airliner out of the sky.[2] As Jibril promised from the podium, "Such an alliance would bring one million Muslim warriors to bear against Israel and see the long-awaited destruction of the Jewish State and her supporters."[3] Nobody in Tehran, or Jerusalem for that matter, took Jibril's threats lightly. Abu Nidal might be the Arab world's most notorious terrorist, but Ahmed Jibril is its most lethal.

Until one fateful night over the Scottish hamlet of Lockerbie, the world had yet to hear much of this sixty-two-year-old native of Azur, a small Tel Aviv suburb. He was not a photogenic caricature of the Palestinian revolution, like Yasir Arafat, always availing himself of Third World conferences, television interview programs and the odd documentary; he was never the guest of Ted Koppel's *Nightline*. Jibril prefers the world of shadows, of decisive actions over rhetorical words, of cunning plots and deadly results over the promise of propaganda. Jibril, and the men and women he commands, are not frightened of meeting their most hated enemy head on in the field of battle. In fact, they cherish the confrontation with Israel's much-vaunted military—the more spectacular the operation the better—whether it is on the Lebanese shoreline or inside the unforgiving hell of a ravine in the Negev Desert. Unfortunately for Israel and the West, these battles have more often than not been fought on Jibril's terms.

For Israel—and the West—Ahmed Jibril's PFLP-GC presents the greatest of all terrorist threats. The State of Israel and Ahmed Jibril's PFLP-GC have been locked in an inescapable conflagration for more than twenty-three years. Few terrorist leaders have managed to strike consistently and incessantly at the heart of the Jewish State as has Jibril; his signature of technological efficiency and military precision adorns some of the most blood-chilling acts of carnage in the forty-three-year history of the Arab-Israeli conflict. From Qiryat Shmoneh in northern Galilee to the Night of the Hang Gliders and its aftermath, the eruption of the Intifadah; from the destruction of civilian airliners over the Swiss Alps and Scottish hamlets to hijackings and letter bombs; from kidnappings and hostage-taking to indiscriminate killings, Jibril has sworn a war of blood against the Jewish State and has seen it materialize. The perpetration of bold and bloody attacks against Israel—and its allies—is the PFLP-GC's principal ideology. In turn, Israel's defense establishment has dedicated much of its resources to bringing about Jibril's termination. Over the past two decades, the Israel Air Force has mounted hundreds of preemptive and retaliatory air raids against PFLP-GC positions in Lebanon; it has dispatched its finest combat units on spectacular commando raids meant to find, locate, and destroy Ahmed Jibril and his organization; and its three world-renowned intelligence services, the *Mossad* (the foreign espionage service), the *Shin Bet* (the counterintelligence and counterterrorist intelligence body), and *A'man* (military intelligence), have dedicated supreme efforts to destroying the PFLP-GC. Both sides have gone to unimaginable extremes in this deadly game of one-upsmanship, deploying the most bizarre tools of destruction against the other. Jibril has hidden bombs in record players and radios, and has used unsuspecting Western women to carry them onto passenger jets; he has delivered suicide-commandos into Israel by means of a hang glider, with deadly results. Israel too has tried extreme measures to destroy Jibril, launching the best units in the IDF's Order of Battle on what appear, to the layman, to be suicide raids in order to destroy the PFLP-GC warlord. They have even utilized kamikaze dogs carrying explosive packs on their backs to blow up the elusive terrorist chieftain in his underground bunker. The Israelis, the most powerful military force in the region, have failed in their most dire task.

Jibril remains at the forefront of the Palestinian holy war against the State of Israel. Israel's war with Ahmed Jibril and the PFLP-GC is a unique and unforgiving struggle that pits a nation of more than five million people against approximately one thousand determined and expertly trained men and women. Like other aspects of the Arab-Israeli struggle, the war between the PFLP-GC and Israel has also spilled out into the international arena, as well. The war between Israel and the PFLP-GC is a microcosm of the Arab-Israeli conflict, and yet it is a story of obsession—in Jibril's desire to strike at the nerve of the Jewish State and help see to its destruction, and in Israel's thirst for revenge and biblical justice against a few individuals who have made it their life's work to kill innocent civilians and undermine the security of a nation.[4] It is a struggle that dates back to the creation of the Palestinian refugee crisis in 1948 and, as events in the Middle East enter this most decisive decade of fanatic religious fundamentalism, it is a conflict that has only just begun.

CHAPTER ONE

MAKING THE WORLD AN UNSAFE PLACE

Rome, July 22, 1968. From all outward appearances, the hustle and bustle of Rome's Fiumicino International Airport could not have been farther removed from the conflict and bloodshed of the decade's most turbulent year. Thousands of passengers milled about the terminal, clutching suitcases and travel bags. Some money, a passport, and a good travel agent afforded a jet-age escape for the ordinary citizen—intercontinental distances were now only hour-long obstacles. The advent of affordable air travel had created a new, inalienable freedom for the citizens of the world. A global village had, indeed, been created. So, too, in the hours to come, would a global menace. The age of aerial terror was about to dawn.

THE PALESTINIANS too were part of that global village, and 1968 would prove to be a pivotal year for their aspirations and their yearnings for revenge. A year had passed since the epic Six-Day War of 1967, a conflict that had transformed Arab propaganda and bravado into a humiliating battlefield defeat. Egyptian President Gamal Abdel Nasser's public plea to push the Jewish State into the sea was a call sounded by every other Arab nation. His war against Israel would end the great injustice of 1948—the creation of the State of Israel—and correct history's displacement of nearly three million Palestinian refugees to a diaspora of squalor and misery. With a combined population of more than one hundred million people, the Arab world vastly outnumbered Israel, a country whose population at the time did not surpass

7

four million. With tremendous defense expenditures and the most modern and abundant supplies of weaponry the Soviet bloc could provide, the Arab states clearly outgunned Israel as well. Nevertheless, as the tides of war appeared to sweep across Israel and threaten its very existence in the spring and summer of 1967, Arab leaders told the Palestinians to pack up their belongings and be prepared to reclaim their homes.[1]

Israel, however, would strike first.

At 0745 hours on the morning of June 5, 1967, Israel launched its mighty Air Force on a preemptive strike against the air forces of Egypt, Syria, Jordan, and Iraq; in a matter of hours, more than five hundred Arab aircraft were destroyed, most of them on the ground. With absolute air superiority, Israeli ground forces were able to slam across the Sinai Desert and destroy much of Egypt's invincible army; it took the IDF less than seventy-two hours to capture the Sinai Desert and the Gaza Strip, and position itself along the Suez Canal. After being attacked by Jordanian forces, the IDF launched a counterstrike and recaptured the Holy City of Jerusalem and the West Bank from King Hussein. Syria and the Golan Heights were taken care of last. On June 9, Israel mounted a sweeping drive to capture the ultrastrategic volcanic plateau that had afforded Syrian gunners a deadly perch from which to lob artillery shells at the Israeli agricultural settlements around the Sea of Galilee. On June 10, the Arab armies surrendered as a humiliated and mauled entity. In six days of blood and fire, the Middle East was changed forever.

For the Palestinians, it was the second time in nineteen years that the glorious promises of their leaders had proved to be empty calls toward failure. Not only had the opportunity to destroy Israel been lost forever, but they would now be encountering a regional superpower—a one-time minuscule nation that now possessed strategic depth and the most powerful military in the area. The possibility of destroying Tel Aviv or liberating Haifa was transformed from an "about to happen certainty" into an unattainable fantasy, a mirage that epitomized the reality of their hopeless and tragic plight. The time for miracles had expired; so, too, had their reliance on the "other" Arabs for the promise of liberation. There needed to be a Palestinian revolution if liberation was ever to be achieved.

As far back as May 1964, when Ahmed Shuqairy's Palestine Liberation Organization (PLO), an umbrella group for all Palestinian political and military organizations, was announced in Cairo, it appeared as if the Palestinians had formed the nucleus of a military equation that would reclaim the land of Palestine from the Jews; it was, after all, Shuqairy, a veteran diplomat, who professed that the Palestinians would throw the "Jews into the sea."[2] Shuqairy was, however, a puppet of Egyptian President Nasser—a man who manipulated the Palestinians for his own nationalist policies. Shuqairy's power was eventually undermined by the small cadre of men who, as Palestinian workers in Kuwait, had created *el-Fatah*, an underground guerrilla movement that, unlike many of the Communist political organizations sprouting up in the various Arab capitals, preached Palestinian self-reliance in the armed struggle against Israel. Fatah's command triumvirate included Salah Khalef (Abu Iyad), Khalil al-Wazir,* and, of course, an engineer from Cairo whose image would personify the Palestinian revolution for three decades: Yasir Arafat's Fatah, as the organization would become known, followed a five-point doctrine that would guide the path toward Israel's annihilation: (1) The liberation of Palestine; (2) The use of armed struggle to attain this objective; (3) Reliance on Palestinian self-organization; (4) Cooperation with friendly Arab forces; and (5) Cooperation with friendly international forces.[3] With the help of the intelligence and military services of the Arab states, Arafat was slowly able to assemble the infrastructure of a guerrilla army that, it was hoped, would equal the success of the guerrilla armies of Communist China, North Korea, and North Vietnam. Arafat's desires were ambitious and, perhaps, premature. On January 1, 1965, Fatah perpetrated its first operation against Israel. An explosive device was planted along Israel's National Water Carrier near the Sea of Galilee. Although damage to the pipeline supplying much of Israel with its scarce water needs was minimal, Fatah was on the map.

As far as much of the Arab world was concerned, Fatah was mainstream. Its ideology resembled whichever nation-state, either Egypt or Syria, supported it at the time. In the years prior to the 1967 Six-Day War, Fatah guerrillas mounted numerous incursions into Israel—each attack against an isolated agricultural settlement usually resulted in Israeli civilian death and significant and immediate IDF retaliation. In fact, *fedayeen* (guerrilla) attacks emanating from Jordan resulted in Operation Shredder, a large-scale IDF paratroop raid against the town of

---

* Abu Iyad, the PLO's security chief and former secretive commander of the notorious Black September Organization, was assassinated in January 1991 by an Abu Nidal operative in a campaign of inter-Palestinian fratricide stemming from Saddam Hussein's invasion of Kuwait. Abu Jihad, the PLO's military commander responsible for special operations inside Israel, was assassinated, according to foreign reports, on April 16, 1988, by a joint force of Israeli commandos and Mossad agents in Tunis.

as-Samua, which was one of the turning points leading to full-scale war one year later.[4]

In Lebanon, however, a more radical element to the Palestine Liberation Organization had begun. Two Greek Orthodox Christian Palestinian physicians, Dr. George Habash and Dr. Wadi Haddad, had created the Arab Nationalists' Movement (ANM) and had been preaching the gospel of pan-Arabism to the students of the American University of Beirut, and in the meeting halls and cafes of the nearby Palestinian refugee camps. The two doctors were known to write nationalistic slogans on the backs of their medication prescriptions and dispense medical care for free to politically savvy patients.[5] Their struggle was not solely against Zionism, but against the diverse political aspirations of the Arab leaders: They hoped not only to one day liberate Palestine, but also to create an Arab state embracing the people from the Persian Gulf to the Atlantic Ocean.[6] Naturally pan-Arabism, especially when preached by the stateless Palestinians, was not viewed kindly in most Arab capitals, and much of the ANM's activities were conducted underground and amid a backdrop of Syrian and Egyptian competition for leadership in the Arab world. When Ahmed Shuqairy and Arafat's Fatah became credible and pronounced entities, Habash and Haddad formed a distinctive Palestinian branch of their ANM called the National Front for the Liberation of Palestine (NFLP); several reports indicate that it was Ahmed Jibril who had founded the NFLP in the early 1960s, as well as a distinctive military wing called *Shabab a-Tha'r* (Vengeance Youth) given the task of carrying out cross-border raids against Israel.[7] The first Vengeance Youth operation was carried out in the winter of 1965.

The Six-Day War had a sobering effect on the fledgling Palestinian liberation groups; the Arab defeat had revolutionized Habash's pan-Arab revolution. Habash painfully realized that the Arab states could not even defend themselves, let alone control the destiny of the Palestinians. Liberation depended on spectacular action and violence, and that required bringing the plight of the Palestinians to the hearts and souls of all the peoples of the world. Liberation also depended on Palestinian unity! In September 1967, Habash issued a plea to the other Palestinian groups to form under a general command—two groups, the Heroes of the Return and the Palestine Liberation Front, heeded the call. On December 11, 1967, the Popular Front for the Liberation of Palestine was created.[8] Unlike Arafat's Fatah, which accepted just about anybody into the organization and which particularly sought out the intellectually inferior volunteers who could carry a rifle or lob a grenade without asking too many questions, Habash recruited the most psychologically fit and ideologically secure individuals into the ranks of the PFLP. They needed to be highly intelligent, university educated if possible, and capable of operating decisively and violently in a range of military situations (they received extensive military instruction from various instructors), as well as being able to blend into the netherworld of a Western European city and lying low in a deep-cover sleeper cell. Simply put, Habash and his cohorts created the cadre of what the world knows today as the "terrorist." With the world as his battlefield, Habash's promise for spectacular and violent action would soon come true.

Although the PFLP would fight IDF forces in a protracted and extremely bloody conventional guerrilla campaign in the Jordan Valley desert and in the densely populated Gaza Strip, it would be in Rome that the world would first experience the new brand of warfare Habash had promised.

The thirty-five passengers waiting to board El Al Flight 426 to Tel Aviv on July 22, 1968, mainly Israeli tourists, were looking forward to being reunited with their families following a brief two-and-a-half-hour flight to Israel. Security that summer evening was nonexistent—the most pressing danger at Fiumicino International Airport was having one's wallet pickpocketed in the duty-free shop. At the departure gate, three men with Byzantine features also waited in line to board Flight 426; they had visited the duty-free counter and had burned-to-the-filter cigarettes fastened to their dry lips. The three were, indeed, Arabs but they aroused little suspicion. Not only were there hundreds of thousands of Arab citizens in Israel, but with the newly occupied territories of the West Bank and the Gaza Strip, nearly a million more Arabs had access to El Al's international routes. What could they possibly do to an airliner, anyway? After all, they were not wearing the checkered *kefiyeh* headdress and carrying submachine guns slung over their shoulders. Historically, the Palestinians had never done anything other than mount cross-border ambushes where civilians were killed. Many people in Israel, especially those in the intelligence community, which was resting on its laurels following the 1967 victory, thought the Arabs were not sophisticated enough to bring their war outside the boundaries of the region. Yet the three Arabs in their smart suits and neat ties appeared to be very respectable. George Habash's instructions to Ali Shafik Ahmed, the group's leader, better known by his nom de guerre

Captain Rifat,[9] was to look passive and incredibly ordinary. Habash had created an Arab warrior capable of striking anywhere in the world.

Just before midnight, Flight 426 lifted off into the dark Italian night. As the passengers unfastened their seat belts and began to relax, the three Arabs smoked their final cigarette, then sat trancelike in a state of silence while they prepared themselves mentally for the mission at hand. As the landing gear of the Boeing 707 retracted and the line at the lavatory grew, the three men left their seats quickly and raced toward the cockpit of the jet. First they fired a 9-mm bullet into the stomach of the flight's first officer, Maoz Poraz, and assumed control of the aircraft. *"Hem Chatfu Et Ha'Matos,"* ("They've hijacked the plane") a pretty young flight attendant with golden curls screamed in the first-class section. Her cries sent a shrill message to the horrified passengers.[10] El Al Flight 426 was being obliterated. Addressing the frightened travelers, Captain Rifat announced that the aircraft was now to be called *Liberation of Palestine*. It was ordered to change course toward Dar el-Beida Airport, near the Algerian capital of Algiers.

The hijacking was a turning point in the history of how wars in the second half of the twentieth century would be fought. For the next three weeks, the Israeli government struggled to come to grips with the fact that a few armed men had taken its citizens hostage and that the region's most powerful military force had no recourse.[11] The government of Israel, a nation that had professed never to negotiate with terrorists, eventually agreed to release sixteen Palestinian terrorists in Israeli jails in exchange for the El Al captives. Israeli Prime Minister Levi Eshkol vowed that the Algerian incident would be the last time his government would make a deal with terrorists.

In Beirut, glasses were raised and backs slapped at PFLP headquarters. Both Habash and Haddad shared in the exhilaration of their organization's monumental victory. By successfully hijacking an Israeli aircraft in Europe, the PFLP had simultaneously struck a decisive blow against Israel and against her European friends. Palestine was once again front-page news, and Israel's image had been critically humbled. "Revolutionary violence," a cornerstone of PFLP's edict, was proving a most successful strategy.

One man who did not share in the exuberance of Habash's victory was a thirty-year-old stout gentlemen who, with a penchant for colorful sports clothes, looked more like a schoolteacher on a Riviera holiday than a terrorist leader. The El Al hijacking, although a grand and revolutionary success, had displeased him, even though, as a PFLP senior operations officer, he had played a major part in the mission's execution.[12] The seizure of an aircraft and veiled threats to murder the hostages should the hijackers' demands not be met was a soft act of "ideologues" not courageous enough to pull the trigger at a man's head at close range, he thought. Palestine would never be liberated by the actions of academics and physicians playing highway robber with airliners. The young man felt disappointed and disheartened. It was time to start his own brand of revolutionary violence.

His name was Ahmed Jibril.

Ahmed Jibril was born in Yazur, a small village south of Tel Aviv and Jaffa, in 1937;* the town is now called Azur, and is a quiet Tel Aviv suburb known to most Israelis more for its spacious homes and crowded roadside restaurants than for being the birthplace of one of the world's most dangerous terrorists. Little information is available on Jibril's childhood, and even Western intelligence agencies have huge gaps in their computer data bases concerning Ahmed Jibril's formative years in what was at the time of his birth Palestine. In 1948, prior to the outbreak of the 1948 Israeli War of Independence, Jibril's family left Palestine and moved first to Jordan, then to Syria, where they settled in Quneitra, the capital city of the Golan Heights.[13] The town was a hotbed of Arab radicalism and the perfect backdrop for the formation of Jibril's militant political views.

In 1956, at the age of nineteen, Ahmed Jibril joined the ranks of the Syrian Army. He was a highly motivated soldier and a natural leader. In the racial and political nepotism of the Syrian Army, Jibril's rise through the ranks was a truly remarkable achievement for a Palestinian. He eventually reached the rank of captain in the engineering corps, more for his skills as a demolitions expert and bomb maker than for his conventional combat abilities.[14] Jibril might even have made a lifelong career in the Syrian military were it not for his expertise as a troublemaker. His revolutionary politics and loud, boisterous mannerisms when criticizing the regime in Damascus earned him powerful enemies. In 1958, at the time when Egypt and Syria unified to form the United Arab Republic, Jibril was ousted from the Syrian Army for his

---

* There is so little accurate and confirmed information on Ahmed Jibril that even his year of birth remains a point of mystery and speculation. Many accounts list his year of birth as 1929. Many reports also list his birthplace as Ramallah, a large city on the West Bank, and some accounts list him as not even being a Palestinian, claiming that he was born in Syria.

alleged, although never confirmed, Communist leanings.[15] Disgruntled and stateless, Jibril moved to Cairo, the mecca of Arab revolutionary politics and Palestinian nationalism, where he founded the underground guerrilla organization called the Palestine Liberation Front (PLF) along with Ali Nushnaq, Fadil Shukri Shruru, Ahmad Za'rur, Tahir Dablan, and cofounder Ahmed Bashnak, a Palestinian comrade from the Syrian Army.[16] Initially, the PLF's activities were simple: At night, Jibril's cohorts pasted flyers to street posts and walls declaring that the holy war against the Zionist enemy had now begun; during the day they recruited Palestinian students from Cairo University as foot soldiers in the holy armed struggle. Jibril's wife, Samira (known by her nom de guerre of Umm Faris, or Mother Courage), was named commander of the PLF's women's section. According to PFLP-GC sources, the purpose of Jibril's PLF was to "wage a war of nerves against Israel."[17] A war without boundaries would be Jibril's sole ideology in the years to follow.

Jibril soon made a name for himself in the Palestinian diaspora as a guerrilla-visionary who promised refugee-camp inhabitants that the destruction of Israel would happen any day. He was charismatic, confident, and capable. The fact that he achieved so respected a commission in the Syrian Army was proof that this young man was a unique representative of Palestinian martial skills. With some financial support from the Palestinian diaspora, he returned to Syria in 1961, following the split between Egypt and Syria and the end of the United Arab Republic, and reentered the Syrian military, this time, though, as part of the Syrian-controlled PLF. He spent much of his time conscripting Palestinian volunteers to mount raids against the north of Israel.

The relationship between the PLF and the regime in Damascus was the source of great trouble for Ahmed Jibril and a cornerstone of the inter-Palestinian rivalries that plague the PLO to this day. Syrian support for the PLF, or any other Palestinian group, was not an act of generosity, nor was it a moral responsibility of the Damascus regime to do its utmost to see through the Palestinian dream for the destruction of Israel. To the Syrians, the Palestinians were useful tools—the more dedicated to the destruction of Israel, the easier to manipulate. Even Ahmed Jibril, the notorious independent, fell into this trap. In 1963, Jibril and a small band of followers were sent to Egypt, under Syrian instructions, to work against Nasser's regime. The small group of Palestinians was quickly rounded up by the Egyptian secret police and briefly imprisoned before being deported to Beirut.[18] It is believed that Jibril's less than cordial treatment at the hands of the Egyptian *Mu-*

chabarat (secret service) interrogators, which is reported to have included severe torture sessions and routine beatings, molded his hatred toward the Egyptians and his view that they were paper tigers guilty of weakening and undermining the Palestinian cause. Jibril also despised the Palestinian groups that Cairo supported, especially Yasir Arafat's Fatah.

The Syrians viewed the fledgling Palestinian independence groups as troublesome political entities, and considered it a national security interest to monitor their activities and, if at all possible, control them.[19] In 1964, following the establishment of the PLO and the coming together of most of the splintered Palestinian political and guerrilla organizations, Syrian contact was first made with Fatah; the coincidence between Yasir Arafat's desire to advance the Palestinians' cause and Syria's ambition to increase its power and prestige in the Arab world created the basis for mutual cooperation that served both sides. Nevertheless, Syria was firmly in control of this relationship. Colonel Ahmed Swidarni, the brutal head of the notorious *Shu'ba al-Mukhabarat al-'Askariya* (Syrian military intelligence), was placed in charge of the Syrian Army liaison with the armed Palestinian groups. His office, the *Fara' Falistin* (Palestine Branch), supervised the recruitment of Palestinians for terrorist operations; even though Palestinians serving in the Syrian Army were *not* allowed to join the ranks of the guerrilla organizations, Palestinian civilians living in the refugee camps surrounding Damascus were actively recruited.[20] It also kept tabs, together with the highly secretive commando police (*al-Dabita al-Fida'iya*), on Palestinians disloyal to the Damascus regime, as well as subverted and sometimes liquidated key figures in Palestinian groups not in Syria's fold. Accordingly, the interrogation center of the Palestine Branch is one of the most brutal in all of Syria.[21]

Palestinian guerrillas were soon trained by Syrian Army officers, and Syrian Muchabarat officers trained the most capable and loyal Palestinian leaders in the art of covert and unconventional warfare. These efforts were assisted by the Eastern Bloc and the Soviet KGB, who viewed the eager and naive Palestinian fedayeen as the ideal vehicles for infiltrating the Arab world and inflicting pro-Soviet mayhem throughout the Middle East. (Recently declassified Russian documents show how ambitious Soviet intelligence sponsorship of the fledgling Palestinian terrorist movements actually was in the mid-1960's.) The Syrians, too, turned many of these Palestinian guerrilla officers into spies and sent them on espionage missions in other Arab nations. Under Syrian auspices, the Palestinians mounted hit-and-run raids against

Israeli frontier positions. The raids, usually run though Jordanian territory in order not to provoke Israeli retaliation against Syria, were ineffectual and did little to promote the Palestinian position. The Syrians managed to play the Palestinian cause with both ends toward the middle—manipulating its leaders, men, and objectives as a tool of Syrian policy. It was during this early period, between 1965 and 1966, that Ahmed Jibril's PLF distinguished itself as a unique and extremely violent entity in the Palestinian fold.

Jibril's military career had a great deal of influence on the PLF. Its members, recruited from the refugee camps and from Lebanon and Syria, were indoctrinated with an intensive military regimen—a mini-basic training of sorts where young guerrillas learned how to shine boots and press uniforms, salute properly, and parade for inspection.* The art of cold killing was also attended to with military precision. Syrian instructors, believed to have also included an international cast of experts from the Communist bloc, taught Jibril's faithful how to remove sentries with a knife or with the twisting pull of the garrote, how to execute a textbook-perfect military ambush, and how to plant explosives and sabotage sensitive fixed positions. From 1965 to 1967, the PLF and its various offshoots perpetrated dozens of attacks against Israeli frontier positions. The attacks were usually coordinated, cross-border assaults, conducted cautiously and close to the Syrian or Jordanian frontiers in order to ensure safe haven should the Israeli military respond in kind.

In 1966, PLF personnel, with Jibril's personal supervision, were also taught the art of assassination—although Israeli leaders would not be targeted. The Syrian Ba'athist coup of February 23, 1966, radically altered the Syrian-PLO relationship, as Damascus attempted, through Jibril, to force Yasir Arafat to become a Syrian puppet. In fact, the Syrians adopted the slogan "War and national liberation" as the cornerstone of their foreign and defense policy.[22] In exchange for permission to launch raids against Israel from Syrian territory, Arafat was forced to accept Jibril and the PLF into the fold of the Fatah Central Committee, the organization's governing body. Damascus also demanded that Arafat accept a Syrian Army officer, Captain Yusef Ourabi, to become one of the group's commanders. Jibril, however,

---

* Even today, in this age of barometric bombs, the PFLP-GC is still one of the few Palestinian groups to stress military fundamentals such as drills and uniforms. In their various training grounds in Syria and Lebanon, PFLP-GC members frequently parade for visiting dignitaries, presenting themselves as the vanguard of a Palestinian army on the verge of liberating their homeland.

found this arrangement distasteful—he is reported to hold a lifelong hatred of Arafat and wanted nothing to do with the self-professed president of the Palestinian revolution. Jibril withdrew his PLF legions from the Fatah fold and worked covertly to undermine Arafat's status. According to several unconfirmed reports, PLF gunmen assassinated several key Fatah leaders in Jordan and Syria in 1966. At Syria's behest, underground warfare had broken out in the Palestinian camp in a conflict described by one former Israeli intelligence officer as a "Syrian version of a Sicilian Mafia war."[23] The conflict would have permanent implications. Captain Ourabi was murdered by Fatah gunmen in February 1966 by a barrage of more than 100 bullets, and Arafat was briefly imprisoned by the Syrians. Ahmed Jibril, however, had earned his marker for the future struggle. He had become Syria's reliable man in the crux of the Palestinian movement.

According to several intelligence reports, Jibril was also Moscow's man in the Palestinian revolutionary movement. Jibril realized that the quickest path for entering into his full-scale war of nerves against the "Zionist Entity" was by allying his meager means with the sophisticated intelligence apparatus of the Soviet Komitet Gosudarstvemoy Bezopasnosti (KGB); he was the first Palestinian leader to possess a direct link with the Soviet intelligence and espionage community (the KGB and the Glavnoe Razvedyvateluoe Upravelenie [GRU]) since the early 1960's, and several PLF commanders were dispatched to the Soviet Union for "advanced guerrilla warfare and political subversion training.[24] Moscow saw in Jibril a man of decisive action. His rhetoric was supported by the ballistic might of firepower. From 1965 until the days prior to the Six-Day War, Jibril's men reportedly mounted nearly one hundred cross-border raids, actions characterized by their bold efficiency, which made them just right for Moscow's plans for the inevitable superpower struggle for control of the Middle East.

In October 1967, following the Six-Day War, Ahmed Jibril's PLF heeded the call of George Habash for Palestinian unity in the struggle against Israel and became one of the founding members of the Popular Front for the Liberation of Palestine. Jibril found promise in Habash's zeal and desire to bring the war against Israel outside the confines of the Middle East and to the doorsteps of its international supporters. As one of the senior operation planners in the Habash-Haddad circle, Jibril was instrumental in adding a professional, military edge to the PFLP's pan-Arabist and pseudointellectual version of Marxism. The PFLP's first public statement echoed Jibril's desire for conflict: "The only weapon left in the hands of the people is revolutionary violence."[25]

Just as Jibril's "marriage" to Arafat's Fatah ended in abrupt anger in 1966, so too did Jibril's split from the PFLP, in October 1968. Once again politics and infighting had crippled the Palestinian jihad against Israel.

On March 21, 1968, combined forces of Israeli paratroopers, reconnaissance commandos, and tank units crossed the Jordan River and attacked the Jordanian town of Karameh, a major training base for Arafat's Fatah guerrillas and sometimes called the Terrorist's Pentagon by Israeli intelligence and operations officers.* The Israeli attack (known, fittingly enough, as Operation Inferno)[27] was a retaliatory strike for a series of terrorist attacks against Jerusalem, Petach Tikva, Netanya, and the Beit Shean area, which had all originated from Karameh. Operation Inferno was designed as a one-shot thunderbolt destined to wipe out much of the Fatah in a decisive blow, but the Palestinians fought a determined defense in the desert abyss of the mountainous facilities; the Jordanian Army also took part in the fighting, launching a heavy tank and artillery barrage onto the besieged Palestinian facility. Even though the IDF managed to destroy much of Karameh (175 buildings), kill more than 200 Palestinian and Jordanian fighters, and capture 141 terrorists, the battle was considered by the Palestinian diaspora to be an Arab victory of historic proportions. Before being forced to withdraw into the labyrinth of caves in the Jordanian hills, the Palestinians had exacted a heavy toll on an Israeli Army that could ill-afford the casualties. In a battle that lasted a full day, twenty-eight Israeli troopers were killed, three were missing in action, and an additional ninety-one were seriously wounded. For the first time, the Palestinians gave as good as they got in a one-on-one battle. In a chaotic press conference in the rubble of a former Karameh command structure, Yasir Arafat, who had escaped the position by commandeering a motorcycle,[28] claimed Karameh to be the turning point—he displayed captured Israeli-produced Uzi 9-mm submachine guns as the spoils of war, and even King Hussein had an abandoned Israeli Centurion main battle tank—hit with a multitude of antitank rounds and severely charred—displayed in the main square of Amman, the Jordanian capital. Days after the implications of Karameh reached the Palestinian diaspora, thousands of young Palestinian men left their refugee-camp homes and volunteered to martyr their lives for Palestine as fedayeen warriors.

Yet Karameh was not a victory for all the Palestinians. Habash and

---

* According to Arab reports, the Israeli task force in Operation Inferno consisted of a remarkable ten thousand soldiers.[26]

Jibril also ran a training and recruitment center a few miles from Karameh, but they did not dispatch their men to lend a hand to the beleaguered Fatah defenders.[29] They had hunkered down inside their bunkers and, faithful to their guerrilla strategy, had avoided direct confrontation with the enemy. Many Arab leaders, especially Egyptian President Nasser, viewed the PFLP's policy of "disengagement" as nothing less than cowardice-inspired treason. Amid the great Karameh triumph, there was a fear that open fratricide would erupt between the various factions of the PLO. Jibril too viewed Habash's controversial order as treacherous. During a fund-raising visit to the oil-rich sheikhdom of Kuwait, Jibril vilified Habash and his politically elitist cohorts as "spineless warriors."[30] It was the beginning of the end of Habash's unified PFLP command.

At first Habash issued a series of published statements denouncing President Nasser's criticisms of the PFLP. Nasser followed suit by reiterating his displeasure with Habash. The round of accusations finally ended when Habash ordered his "lieutenant," Ahmed Jibril, to Cairo in late summer to mend some badly broken fences. Jibril saw this diplomatic mission as his golden opportunity to bring the PFLP around to his way of thinking. Jibril's brand of shuttle diplomacy worked. He convinced Nasser that inter-Arab division only benefited the Israelis, and that the entire Arab world must unite to defeat the Zionist enemy. After successfully bridging the gap between his direct leader and the leader of the Arab world, Jibril returned to Beirut.

But Habash's fortunes had already been decided in Damascus. In late March, Habash ventured to Syria in search of guns and ammunition— as well as a face-saving appearance to make up for the Karameh debacle. Syrian authorities quickly threw him in prison, where he was held until November, when he cut a deal with Damascus promising to tow the Syrian line more aggressively (in an operation created for outside world consumption, Wadi Haddad is reported to have sprung Habash from prison, employing PFLP commandos disguised as Syrian troopers).[31] Following a PFLP policy conference held in Habash's absence, in which Jibril's brand of politics and actions were not included in the front's policy, Ahmed Jibril decided to go it alone.*

In October 1968, he ordered his PLF faction out of the PFLP and

---

* Jibril's departure from the Habash camp was not a unilateral action. One of Jibril's key aides, Ahmed Za'rur, also broke with the PFLP to form a group known briefly as the Popular Front for the Liberation of Palestine-General Command (B), a pro-Nasser group that, with Egyptian support, eventually adopted the name Organization of Arab Palestine.[32]

created the *Al-Jabha ash-Sha'bi li-Tahrir Filastin—Al-Qiyada al'Amma*: the Popular Front for the Liberation of Palestine-General Command.[33] The group's headquarters were quickly set up in a nondescript building in the heart of the Rehan district in Damascus. The headquarters were protected by the Syrian Muchabarat and hand-picked PFLP-GC gunmen known for their fanatic loyalty to Jibril. A branch office, for special deniable purposes (should a major operation prove embarrassing to Damascus), was established in Beirut, as well. The PFLP-GC also used several other names, including the Popular Front for the Liberation of Palestine-General Command (A), and the al-Aqsa Fedayeen Front. Jibril's group was the fourth organization to join the PLO later that year.

Ahmed Jibril's PFLP-GC adopted a fitting emblem for its newfound organization: two crossed rifles with fixed bayonets covering all of Israel, including the West Bank (previously occupied by the Jordanians) and the Gaza Strip (previously occupied by Egypt), and adorned with the words "Return," "Combat," and "Liberation" in Arabic. The emblem, a symbol of Jibril's strategy, had one clear message: Bloodshed would be the constant of the day until all of Palestine was completely liberated. In fact, Jibril's sole ideology and modus operandi was military strength. The PFLP-GC possessed no unique ideology, national platform, or plans for a future Palestinian state. The sole objective of his organization was the violent destruction of the Jewish State in battle.[34] His time with Habash had convinced him that the Palestinians could not be bothered by the trivial trappings of politics, ideology, or governments in exiles. For the next seven years, Jibril would manage to steer clear of the state-sponsored battles that hampered the other Palestinian groups (his relationship with Syria was considered "special"). Jibril's group was as independent an armed group as could exist within the Palestinian community. He promised that independence would breed innovation. If this was, indeed, his show, Jibril would bring a brand-new element to Palestinian resistance. In a meeting with his lieutenants in Damascus, he vowed to revolutionize the Palestinian revolution.[35]

As the man vowing to be the sole military representative of the Palestinian revolution, Jibril's claims were more bravado than a statement of reality. The fledgling PFLP-GC started out with fewer than two hundred fighters, a very limited source of funds, and a lack of outside political support. Yet Ahmed Jibril enjoyed a reputation as a superior military officer. His promises of spectacular actions were looked upon by the young and disillusioned Palestinian youth of the refugee camps as exciting promises. Jibril was a man to be respected. He was a man to be feared. PFLP-GC headhunters soon ventured out to the refugee camps around Amman, Irbid, Damascus, Beirut, and the southern Lebanese camps around Damur, Sidon, and Tyre to seek out potential fighters and recruit them for his force.

His search would be extremely selective. Like Habash, Jibril sought out intellectuals capable of innovative thinking and operating abroad in what was called 'Amaliyyat Kharijiyya (External Operations), the subdivisions that would assume responsibility for expanding the Palestinian front in Europe into a full-scale battlefield. But like Arafat, Jibril also sought the simple person willing to take orders and fight—and die—for Palestine. After all, he wasn't forming an intellectual study group. He was creating the foundations of the Palestinian army, one where blowing up an Israeli installation abroad or sending a suicide squad to kill a Jewish settler in a kibbutz were separate but equal elements in the strategy for national liberation. Jibril's strategy of unleashing a special kind of war on Israel and her supporters was personified by the nom de guerre he chose for himself: Abu Jihad (Father Holy War, not to be confused with Khalil al-Wazir, assassinated in Tunis on April 16, 1988). To the world, however, he would be simply known as Jibril.[36]

CHAPTER TWO

THE TECHNOTERRORIST AND HIS LIEUTENANTS

ONE MAN, no matter how committed and talented, cannot wage a war by himself. For an organization like the Popular Front for the Liberation of Palestine-General Command to succeed in its mandate of humbling Israel into capitulation, it would need a highly capable officer cadre of committed lieutenants and a legion of highly trained warriors—the foot soldiers of a holy war of terrorism. There were three notable personalities Jibril attracted into his inner circle who would feature prominently in the years to come. The first was a young hired gun named Hafaz Mohammed Hussein Dalkamoni, a Sunni Moslem from a poor section of the Christian Arab town of Nazareth. Dalkamoni, one of the first young Palestinians recruited from the refugee camps and trained in the Yarmouk camp training facility, was an operative known for his fervent loyalty to Jibril. In October 1969, Jibril ordered Dalkamoni to lead a force of five commandos and conduct "massive sabotage" operations against the Galilee region of northern Israel. After leaving the group's staging base north of the Yarmouk refugee camp, Dalkamoni crossed into Jordanian territory, and then crossed the Jordan River into Israel. After evading several IDF patrols and crossing considerable stretches of inhospitable territory, Dalkamoni's squad succeeded in placing an explosive device next to a power line. The bomb detonated prematurely, however. The following morning, Israeli forces found several of Dalkamoni's men dead, and a mustached man bleeding profusely from his right leg, which he eventually lost.

Dalkamoni was tried in a military court on several counts of terrorism, and sentenced—seemingly—to two consecutive life terms in the maximum security Ashqelon prison in southern Israel.

Jibril's next lieutenant worthy of notice was Mohammed A'bbas Zaidan, a chubby and violent individual who adopted the nom de guerre Abu A'bbas. Born in the Galilee town of Safed in 1948,* A'bbas's family fled to the town of Aleppo, Syria, when fighting broke out in 1948; the family eventually moved to the sprawling Yarmouk refugee camp in Damascus. An insecure youth out to prove his worth, Abu A'bbas joined forces with Jibril in 1968, and soon raced up the ladder of command to become the PFLP-GC's operations chief.[1] Although the group lacked a vast human resource pool, both Jibril and A'bbas were expert in utilizing their personnel to maximize their numbers. A few hundred men in training camps in Jordan, Syria, and Lebanon would soon make their presence as felt as if they numbered in the thousands.

The third, and some say the most important person to follow Jibril in executing his *Jihad* (Holy War), was Marwan Kreeshat, a man known for one specific skill—bomb-making.[2] Kreeshat was born in Jordan in 1945. Jibril found him in 1968, and enlisted this fellow tinkerer and demolitions genius into his war of nerves even though Kreeshat was not a Palestinian and his loyalty to King Hussein appeared strong. Jibril offered Kreeshat a lucrative position inside the newly formed PFLP-GC as its chief bomb-maker and ordnance officer.

One means to make the PFLP-GC's bark louder than its bite was through technical innovativeness. Ahmed Jibril was the world's first "technoterrorist." An engineer by military training with the Syrian Army, Jibril's hobby was tinkering. He loved devices and gadgets and considered himself something of an inventor; according to several unconfirmed reports, he was the owner of a number of patents in Damascus. He quickly realized that technical parity with Israeli forces equalized the two factions on the battlefield. He ordered that each PFLP-GC squad operating in the field carry walkie-talkies and be linked, through field radios, to a command and control section situated at a forward position. He also helped develop and manufacture sophisticated detonation devices to be hidden inside load-bearing equipment where soldiers keep their gear. Should one of his commandos be captured alive, the device was to explode as Israeli soldiers removed the

---

* Much like Jibril, information concerning A'bbas's formative years remains shrouded in mystery. Although most reports list A'bbas as having been born in 1948, in Safed, several reports give 1941 as his birth year.

equipment.[3] For Jibril's men, there was no greater honor than to be martyred for the cause—especially if a few Zionist soldiers could be killed in the process.

Ahmed Jibril's love for tinkering was rivaled only by his obsession for airplanes. As a thinker and planner behind the PFLP's hijacking of El Al's Flight 426, Jibril's was one of the loudest voices in the decision to target an airplane. Why an airplane? Commercial airlines attract terrorists for both political and operational considerations; they are scepters of nationhood and are portable and extremely vulnerable targets.[4] Jibril, however, did not want to hijack aircrafts—he wanted to obliterate them. Jibril was not interested in a media circus and, in strategic terms, cared little one way or the other what the world thought of his campaign against Israel. Yet he was a pragmatist, and he realized that governments, especially the Ba'athist regime would not take kindly to the wrath of an international media blitz stemming from an operation gone bad. As a military officer with some sense of strategic proportion, Jibril realized that taking hostages on a world stage was risky business. The terrorist's resolve, as well as the impact of their revolutionary message, would become more diffuse with every hour the hostage ordeal dragged on. Eventually, one side was likely to cave in (usually the hostage-takers), and the plight of the captives would surely be covered by a sympathetic international media. Indeed, the Palestinians needed to strike at the heart of the Zionist Entity, but the attack would have to be a dagger in the heart, not a mere slap in the face.

After meeting with Kreeshat in late 1968, Jibril ordered the construction of a small, powerful explosive device that could bring an airliner down in midair. The bomb would need to be innocuous, and be able to be brought on board without too much difficulty. Following the July 22, 1968 hijacking of El Al Flight 426, security arrangements had been implemented in just about every airport in Europe. In his Damascus headquarters, Kreeshat began assembly of a prototype bomb that would, indeed, lead to an eruption of Jibril's long-anticipated full-scale guerrilla war with Israel.

From his bases in Syria, Jibril continued his war against Israel, but at the same time he expanded the scope of the PFLP-GC to include international operations. Through the Western Sector division of the organization, he established deep-cover sleeper cells throughout Europe—many belonged to pre-existing PFLP sleepers originally planted by Habash in 1968. Jibril's KGB contacts were instrumental in establishing the PFLP-GC's European Front. The East German foreign espionage service (the HVA) and the East German secret police (*Ministerium fur*

Sicherheitsdienst, or *MfS),* were among the first Eastern-bloc intelligence services to offer full support, logistic as well as manpower, to a Palestinian terrorist force; according to several reports, a heavily guarded PFLP-GC command, control, and communications center was established in an East Berlin neighborhood in early 1969.[5] Yet Jibril's PFLP-GC European headquarters were established in Sofia, the capital of Bulgaria, in early 1969.

Sofia was ideally suited for Jibril. It was close enough to central Europe, with such pro-Israeli nations as West Germany, Switzerland, and Holland, to serve as a staging ground for what was planned to be a campaign of spectacular operations, and yet it was deep enough behind the Iron Curtain to hamper the activities of the Western intelligence services—especially the Israeli Mossad. Jibril himself is reported to have purchased an apartment in a quaint section of Sofia, and his top lieutenants received advanced espionage and irregular warfare instruction from the Bulgarian secret service. Arms from the Bulgarian military were also secretly funneled to Jibril's training facilities in Syria. With East-bloc intelligence support, additional safe houses were rented and purchased throughout Western Europe with little difficulty.

With an established infrastructure in place to support a vast European network, Jibril labored to obtain official political support from the Arab nations. His relationship with Syria was already ironclad. In fact, Syrian intelligence agencies and military commands were involved with every aspect of the PFLP-GC's operational existence. Jibril routinely met with his counterparts in the Syrian defense and interior ministries in weekly briefing and debriefing sessions. Syrian intelligence officers were permanently attached to PFLP-GC installations, and Jibril did nothing without tacit approval from Damascus. Syrian control and involvement were so intense that one Israeli officer once wryly commented that "Jibril can't even pass gas without the Syrians getting wind of it."[6] In an emergency, Syrian diplomatic installations— and diplomatic credentials—could be made available.

Libya, too, became a PFLP-GC ally. On September 1, 1969, Muammar Qadaffi, a twenty-seven-year-old signal corps captain, led a bloodless coup that overthrew the monarchy of King Idris and established the new republic.[7] Qadaffi, a product of the tribal-minded guerrilla conflicts of the region, soon found alliances with the various Palestinian guerrilla groups. The most radical groups received more oil-revenue cash from Qadaffi. Ahmed Jibril was one of Qadaffi's most respected Palestinian leaders.

With the means and logistics for a grand strike available, all that

Jibril and his operational planners required was a target. Naturally, Jibril wanted to destroy an El Al aircraft in the air, but that would prove a difficult and ambitious, perhaps too ambitious, undertaking. Since the hijacking of Flight 426, security at El Al had been assumed by the well-trained and experienced operatives of the *Sherut Ha'Bitachon Ha'Klali* (General Security Services) Israel's counterintelligence and counterterrorist security force more commonly known as the Shin Bet. Following the hijacking of El Al Flight 426, heavily armed Shin Bet agents pursued an aggressive defense of all El Al installations, vowing to shoot it out with any terrorist squad rather than face another politically compromising situation.

Foreign governments, too, realized that it was in their best interests to safeguard El Al, as well as their own national carrier flights landing in and taking off from Israel. In airports throughout Western Europe, El Al takeoffs were escorted by paramilitary police armored cars, their turrets at the ready to eliminate any terrorist threat. Heavily armed policemen and soldiers, carrying submachine guns and wearing bulletproof vests, now roamed departure terminals. The vigilance was certainly warranted.

On December 26, 1968, a two-man squad from Dr. George Habash's PFLP launched an attack against El Al at Athens International Airport. The men, armed with automatic weapons and antipersonnel fragmentation grenades, had just disembarked from an Air France flight from Beirut and were walking on the tarmac to the immigration and customs checks when they broke free from the column of departing passengers and raced a hundred feet toward an El Al Boeing 707 about to take off for Paris carrying fifty-one passengers and crew.* In a few seconds of incessant fire, the plane was raked with hundreds of rounds of ammunition. For good measure, one terrorist hurled an incendiary device at the aircraft, causing its left engine to erupt in a tremendous fireball.[8] One Israeli passenger was killed, and a stewardess was seriously wounded. The operation was perpetrated, according to a PFLP spokesman in Beirut, in order to kill Israeli Air Force pilots being ferried home from training in the United States on the F-4 Phantom fighter-bomber; the fact that the aircraft attacked was heading away from Israel made such a claim incredible, however.

After this attack, Israel responded militarily. On the night of Decem-

---

* The Tel Aviv-Athens-Paris line has been an extremely popular target for Palestinian terrorists. On June 27, 1976, a four-man force from the Wadi Haddad Faction of the PFLP hijacked Air France Flight 139—the daily Tel Aviv-Athens-Paris route—to Entebbe, Uganda.

ber 28, 1968, reconnaissance paratroopers from *Sayeret Tzanhanim* (Paratroop Reconnaissance) and the ultrasecretive commando force *Sayeret Mat'kal* (General Staff Reconnaissance) used helicopters to mount a retaliatory strike against Arab civil aviation. The commandos landed at Beirut, staging ground for the PFLP hijackers/attackers, and proceeded to destroy thirteen aircraft belonging to Middle Eastern Airlines, the Lebanese national carrier. "Aviation terrorism," Israel declared, would carry an unbearable price.

The consequences of the PFLP's attacks on Israeli civil aviation were not lost to Ahmed Jibril. He did not want to commit to the type of operations where his men would be sacrificed in a gun battle with European security forces or El Al agents. Jibril knew that security forces were now mobilized and poised to fight back. On February 18, 1969, a four-man PFLP squad attacked El Al Flight 432, a Boeing 720, in Zurich's Kloten Airport. Before Swiss police could react, Mordechai Rachamim, an El Al security guard, burst open the door and began firing at the terrorists, killing one and wounding two others.[9] Jibril did not want to take hostages, and he did not want to commit an act that might "somehow" get back to Syria and spark a massive dose of Israeli military retaliation. Most important, he did not want to expose his handpicked legions of fighters to indiscriminate attacks that achieved little, if any, results. Jibril opted for quality over quantity—dramatic and lethal attacks over mere nuisances. The PFLP-GC's name would not appear in newspaper headlines every week, but its actions would spark international fear and concern.[10] With the support he was receiving from the KGB, StB (the Czech espionage service, which supplied Jibril with generous quantities of Semtex plastic explosives), the HVA, the MfS, and Bulgarian infrastructure, he could finally put Marwan Kreeshat's deadly skills to their ultimate use. After years of waiting, Jibril could implement his grand strategy. An attack against aviation that would make the PFLP operations seem like nothing more than impudent muscle flexing.

Ahmed Jibril's PFLP-GC viewed El Al and foreign airlines serving the Jewish State as one in the same. Since El Al security restrictions made the airline virtually invulnerable, attacks against European carriers would be easier. From a safe house in Sofia, Kreeshat experimented with a new type of explosive device that, if handled correctly in a particular type of operation, could destroy an airliner—in midair—without leaving telltale signs connecting the act to his group or to his state sponsors. The device centered around three principles: (a) it needed a foolproof timer that would explode while the aircraft was high in flight above a major body of water; (b) it needed to be smuggled on board the aircraft *without* the use of diplomatic pouches or the involvement of intelligence services or other foreign assistance; and, (c) the bomb had to be a reliable device that would, indeed, go off and bring down the airliner as it flew over the Mediterranean en route to Israel. Dead victims and wreckage at the bottom of the sea could not provide the authorities with any clues.

In the first weeks of January 1970, Marwan Kreeshat completed two small, and extremely potent, explosive devices with barometric detonation mechanisms, which were fitted into East German-produced transistor radios supplied by HVA agents. The air pressure, at a specific altitude believed to be 10,000 feet, would trigger a timing device, which would then detonate the small supply of plastic explosives centered in the bomb's core. The two devices were produced in the PFLP-GC's Sofia safe house and then smuggled to Western Europe.[11] The barometric/altimeter device was tested by four PFLP-GC operatives in West Germany who drove a simulator of the explosive package to the top of the 2,887-foot-high Feldberg mountain, the highest peak in the Taunnus mountain range northwest of Frankfurt.[12] Once the devices were deemed fully operational, they were packaged in ordinary brown paper airmail packages and, allegedly, mailed from a post office in Frankfurt; apparently the terrorists had hoped that the airmail packages might be placed—without a security check—on board an El Al flight.

The details of what actually led to the following events remain sketchy and speculative. The intelligence agencies of more than a dozen nations have yet to piece together the entire puzzle. The aftermath, however, leaves little room for the imagination.

In midafternoon on February 21, 1970, Captain Armand Etienne greeted passengers to Swissair Flight 330 in Zurich Airport for the four-and-a-half-hour flight to Lod Airport, in Israel. It was a rainy afternoon, but Captain Etienne reassured his passengers, all thirty-five of them, that it would be a pleasant flight to the Holy Land; the flight crew of twelve went to extra lengths to calm their anxious charges. Approximately fifteen minutes into the flight, as the jet roared to an altitude of 14,000 feet, an explosion rocked the rear luggage-hold area of the Coronado jet. It was a powerful blast but Etienne believed he could bring the aircraft safely back to Zurich. Calmly informing traffic controllers of what had just transpired, Etienne relied on years of flying experience to turn the hulking jet around and slowly decrease its altitude as smoke filled the rocking aircraft. Seconds later however, Etienne radioed

Zurich a final time. "We are crashing," he said. "Goodbye, everybody, goodbye."[13]

Swissair Flight 330 crashed in a heavily wooded forest in the Swiss canton of Aargau. Kreeshat's detonating device had apparently gone off prematurely, but the results were deadly enough: all forty-seven crew and passengers were killed in a crash site that was spread out over several miles. Only fifteen Israeli citizens were on board the aircraft. The rest were mainly Swiss and European nationals.

The barometric-triggered bomb had scored a bloody baptism of fire in a Swiss forest. Later that day, it was to make a curtain call.

The second of Kreeshat's bombs found its way on board an Austrian Airlines Caravelle jet traveling from Frankfurt to Vienna to Tel Aviv. Kreeshat's bomb did, indeed, explode once the aircraft reached an altitude of 10,000 feet, but it failed to trigger the incendiary demise of the aircraft. Instead, it just punched a two-foot hole through the rear cargo hold. The plane's pilot managed to bring the flight back to Frankfurt without serious damage or injury: The lives of thirty-eight passengers and crew were miraculously saved. Kreeshat's bomb had failed to do what it had been designed to do. Telltale evidence was even recovered. The remnants of the bomb were pulled from the jet, and forensic experts from West Germany, Austria, the United Kingdom, France, and, of course, Israel were summoned to study the device and prepare a strategy against this newly uncovered weapon. Jibril's failed bomb caused many a sleepless night in the headquarters of most of the world's counterintelligence agencies.

From a nondescript office in the Muslim section of Beirut, a PFLP-GC spokesman calling himself Abu Maryim broadcast a communiqué claiming responsibility for the destruction of the Swissair jet.[14]

February 21, 1970, was a day of red flags in most of the world's capitals. A man to be reckoned with had made a deadly debut onto the global stage. Israel had known of Ahmed Jibril for years—his file was rich and voluminous but he was known as a *military* threat, not an international player. A man trained in the Syrian Army officer corps, with little formal training in the art of international chaos, had done what the other Palestinian intellects, ideologues, and preachers had promised for so long but never managed to deliver.

In 1970, Jibril would reveal his versatility and prove that his war against Israel would be a conflict waged on many fronts.

Spring had quickly turned to summer in the hills of northern Galilee; the purple flowers that filled the hills had already turned tan and crisp from the fierce heat of the sun. The thick foliage had proved to be a major headache for the nearby farmers, but for the terrorists, it provided a godsend of natural camouflage. A small force of men could hide in the thick underbrush of weeds for several days without being noticed. They could monitor enemy movements and then attack at will. Moshav Avivim was one of the more isolated northern Israeli agricultural settlements, just a few dozen meters from the fortified Lebanese frontier. Avivim was also a target of particular interest to Ahmed Jibril.

In the early morning hours of May 20, 1970,[15] a squad of terrorists from the PFLP-GC crossed the heavily fortified Lebanese border and marched, through unforgiving terrain, toward a concealed position overlooking a stretch of road connecting Kibbutz Bar-Am and Moshav Avivim. The men, all wearing lizard-pattern camouflage fatigues, were connected by walkie-talkie to a central command center a few "kilometers" away in Lebanon and carried enough weaponry to hold off a platoon-size force for several hours. Besides their ubiquitous Soviet-produced AK-47 Kalashnikov 7.62-mm assault rifles and F-1 antipersonnel fragmentation grenades, these terrorists also carried several RPGs, a Soviet-produced infantry-held antitank rocket grenade that could penetrate the most heavily armored tanks and armored fighting vehicles. As the sun appeared and the darkened fields and hills were suddenly illuminated, the terrorists clutched their weapons and produced high-powered field glasses. Their target would be nearing soon.

The objective that sunny May morning was not an IDF patrol but rather a school bus filled with children from Moshav Avivim going to their school in Kibbutz Bar-Am, a few kilometers down the road. As the bus approached the winding dirt road, two terrorists quickly stood up, placing the slow-moving vehicle in the center of the RPG's sights. Each man took a deep breath and slowly released the air, then simultaneously pressed sharply on their trigger mechanisms. The cone-shaped antitank grenade burst through the air in a thunderous ballistic path and ripped through the thinly armored bus with unimaginable ferocity. The vehicle was turned immediately into a hellish fireball. The terrorists quickly grabbed their assault rifles and raked the burning bus with a sendoff barrage of 7.62-mm fire before escaping back across the frontier. The smoke from the burning bus could be seen for miles.

In all, eleven schoolchildren and three teachers were killed that morning; dozens more were critically burned or maimed for life.[16] It was, without doubt, the most horrific act of Palestinian terrorism yet to be perpetrated against Israel's precarious northern frontier. Many battle-hardened Israeli officers could not stomach the wanton ferocity and indiscriminate brutality of the close-quarters killing of so many children. Many people on the scene that day, including intelligence officers, vowed personal revenge against the men responsible for the outrage. The massacre of small children galvanized Israeli public opinion into a unified national yearning for revenge. Following the murderous assault on the school bus, Israeli Defense Minister Moshe Dayan viewed the carnage and declared with anger and promise as he gazed across the frontier at the Lebanese border, "If the government of Lebanon proclaims it is not its job to police its territory against terrorists, *we will do it!*"[17] So began the tumultuous cycle of bloodshed, kidnappings, and treachery involving Lebanon, Israel, and the PFLP-GC.

Jibril's bloody handiwork greatly frustrated the Israelis. The attack came exactly five days after a major IDF paratroop and armored force had conducted a major sweep of Palestinian terrorist positions in southern Lebanon (Operation Turmoil 2).[18] Further Israeli action, including bold and bloody air strikes, followed immediately, but the PFLP-GC was not a stationary target that the Israeli Air Force (IAF) could remove in a Mach.2 air raid. Israel could, indeed, exact bloody revenge, but against whom? Ahmed Jibril and his PFLP-GC was an entity as well as a state of mind. A single act of conventional military retribution could exact only a minimum of damage.

Ahmed Jibril had become a notorious celebrity in the shadowy world of Palestinian terrorism. With the PFLP-GC's newfound status earning Jibril great respect, the cycle of violence would only escalate.

CHAPTER THREE

THE YEARS OF MIRACLES, MISHAPS, AND MASSACRES

THE MASSACRE AT MOSHAV AVIVIM was seen as a breakthrough victory that elevated the PFLP-GC's prestige to a remarkable high. It was the kind of operation that struck fear and outrage into the hearts of Israel's citizens, the kind of exploit that transformed the Palestinian plight into a true war—a conflict that could only be won with the establishment of a Palestinian state in all of the land "illegally" occupied by Israel (the demands were to return all of British-mandate Palestine back to the Palestinians, even though that also included much of what is known today as Jordan). Jibril's stock in the Palestinian revolution had soared to grand levels, a feat all the more impressive considering that more than any other Palestinian leader, Jibril shunned media attention. A man known for his military expertise had blazed a path as a master terrorist. The year 1970 had begun quite well for Ahmed Jibril and the PFLP-GC. It would end disastrously for the Palestinians.

Since the end of the Six-Day War, the desert kingdom of Jordan had served the Palestinians as a convenient, protected, and elongated base of operations from which to strike against Israel. On the eastern bank of the Jordan River, inside a labyrinth of majestic and dominating hills, the various Palestinian liberation movements (Fatah, the PFLP, the DFLP,* as-Sa'iqa,** and the PFLP-GC) had set up training facilities,

---

* On February 22, 1969, Nayif Hawatmeh, a Jordanian-born revisionist Communist and ruthless terrorist leader, defected from the PFLP to create his own faction, the

intelligence-gathering posts, and staging ground from which the path toward an independent Palestine would be paved. Each Palestinian incursion across the dwindling waters of the River Jordan was usually met by vanguard elements of the IDF's *Hativat Ha'Biqa'a* (Jordan Valley Brigade), a force of reconnaissance paratroopers and indigenous Bedouin trackers that hunted down the infiltrators with merciless tenacity. Palestinian terror squads that managed to evade the sophisticated Israeli gauntlet (which included barbed wire fortifications, minefields, and electronic sensors), infiltrate into the web of safe houses and secretive cells of the West Bank, and eventually commit acts of terrorism inside Israel proper (or the Green Line, as it has become known), were sure to invite Israeli military retaliation against Jordan. If Israeli casualties were high, such as the November 22, 1968, car-bombing of Jerusalem's bustling Machane Yehuda market, in which eleven people were killed and sixty-eight people wounded, retaliation was sure to be massive. With its military badly mauled in the 1967 fighting, there was little King Hussein's rebuilding army could do but watch as Israeli warplanes and commando units attacked his kingdom at will. Many Jordanian civilians, innocent citizens who had the misfortune to live near a refugee camp, were killed or seriously hurt in these retaliatory operations. Supporting the plight of the Palestinians had become a supreme burden to the Hashemite Kingdom and a source of great tension.[3]

Throughout 1968, 1969, and the beginning of 1970, the *fedayeen* had provoked numerous acts of Israeli retaliation, especially paratroop or commando raids. These included Operation Remedy on March 21, 1968, an attack by a combined force of paratroopers and armored units against Jordanian positions south of the Dead Sea; Operation Iron, the December 2, 1968, destruction of two strategic bridges connecting Amman to the Red Sea port of Aqaba; Operation Cardinal, the November 17, 1969, attack against terrorist concentrations near Zarqa; Operation Wasp, the June 8, 1970, demolition of several buildings in and

---

Democratic Front for the Liberation of Palestine, a Marxist organization whose objectives included bringing about a North Korea-type brand of socialism to the entire Arab world.[1]

** As-Sa'iqa (Thunder and Lightning, also known as the Vanguards of the Liberation War, the Thunderbolt, and Eagles of the Palestinian Revolution), is the Syrian-controlled, Syrian-led, armed element of the Palestinian Ba'ath Party, whose primary objective is the establishment of a pro-Syrian Palestinian state.[2] In Jordan, it numbered approximately one thousand fighters.

around Karameh, as well as the planting of land mines on the Karameh-Amman road; and, Operation Cinnamon, the July 12, 1970, large-scale reconnaissance search-and-destroy operation on the eastern banks of the Dead Sea.[4] Israeli special forces forays were supported by incessant IAF aerial bombardments, mounted with virtual impunity over Jordanian air space.

Beyond Israel's exacerbation of Jordanian-Palestinian tensions, the Palestinian guerrillas, too, were contributing to their own demise in the Jordanian exile. Heavily armed, undisciplined, and drunk with the power of roaming a lawless state where they were answerable only to their local commanders, the fedayeen committed hundreds of acts of robbery, rape, and murder against Jordanian civilians. If Jordanian police or military forces attempted to intervene and restore order, the guerrillas would resort to deadly force. Before King Hussein could send in reinforcements to crush the armed dissension with brutal force, Arafat or Habash would usually contact Egyptian President Nasser who, in turn, would plead with King Hussein to show restraint. Hussein, dependent in many ways on Egyptian military might for his physical survival (as a check against Syrian ambitions), usually acquiesced.

Racial animosities between the Jordanians and the Palestinians also fueled the fires of violence. The largely Bedouin tribesmen who made up the Jordanian military held the urban Palestinians in great contempt. The educated Palestinians, who considered themselves to be the sophisticated elite of the Arab world with a permanent—and legitimate—chip on their shoulder, looked down upon the Hashemite Bedouins as primitive desert dwellers and rivals to their land and destiny.

A deadly situation of tensions and hatred pushed beyond the envelope of a Byzantine compromise worked out by tribal and national leaders. It was one that could not exist for much longer without the eruption of savage bloodshed.

King Hussein was under tremendous pressure to balance the reins of power, but he found himself overwhelmed by the Palestinian ministate that had sprung up inside his kingdom. By 1970, there were fifty-five Palestinian guerrilla bases spread out from the bottom of the Golan Heights plateau in the north to the hills surrounding Amman in the east, to a series of encampments along the Jordan River Valley.[5] The influx of so many fighters in a country of only two million people created enormous security problems. Palestinian forces openly carried their weapons into Jordan's principal cities, even carrying heavy guns in the vicinity of King Hussein's Amman palace. Yet perhaps the most unnerving element of the Palestinian ministate in Jordan was its Soviet-bloc influence, a presence and military dependence that began with the supply of weapons and ended with intelligence agents operating freely with the guerrilla force. The fact that these undermining Soviet, Syrian, Iraqi, and Egyptian influences—all heavily armed— were operating overtly inside a pro-Western monarchy, was a clear signal to King Hussein that there were plans to usurp his authority and terminate his family's historic reign of power.

The climax of this tension, however, did not begin in the desert hills of western Jordan, but rather in London, Amsterdam, Frankfurt, and Zurich, as George Habash introduced the world to Skyjack Sunday.

On Sunday, September 6, 1970, the PFLP mounted one of the most ambitious terrorist offensives ever attempted. To rebound from his past failures, and the defection of so many key figures from his ranks (especially Ahmed Jibril and Nayif Hawatmeh), and the recent (though still porous) security overhauls at most European airports, Habash dispatched his most trusted agents in a one-shot bid to prove to the world that the Palestinians meant business in bringing about a true international revolution. Skyjack Sunday was also designed to warn the Arab states that reaching any type of cease-fire with Israel would result in the outbreak of full-scale and uncontrolled terror. In fact, days earlier Egyptian President Nasser agreed to an American-sponsored cease-fire along the Suez Canal—a unilateral action that angered the Palestinians, especially Habash. In a few days, the operation and its brutal aftermath would prove just how correct Ahmed Jibril was in shying away from airline hijackings.

The first aircraft to be hijacked September 6 was a TWA flight en route from Frankfurt to New York; it was commandeered to Dawson's Airfield in the middle of the Jordanian desert near Zarqa. The second flight seized was a Swissair jet en route from Zurich to New York, and it too was taken to Dawson's Airfield.

A third aircraft supposed to have been hijacked that Sunday afternoon was an El Al jet en route from Amsterdam to New York; it was to have been seized by four terrorists. Leading this most difficult operation was Leila Khalid, the femme fatale of the Palestinian revolution and Wadi Haddad's reported mistress.[6] Ms. Khalid and two assistants were to seize the aircraft fifteen minutes after takeoff, but the operation was plagued by bad luck and mistiming from the beginning. First, two of the hijackers missed the flight altogether due to a tremendous traffic jam near the Dutch capital. * Second, Shin Bet security agents on board the aircraft reacted immediately to the announced hijacking and critically wounded one of the terrorists, a Puerto Rican named Patrick Arguello, with a volley of .22 caliber fire (Arguello eventually died of his wounds); Ms. Khalid was wrestled to the ground by an irate passenger and forcibly subdued. Finally, one of the passengers traveling on board that flight was Major-General Aharon Yariv, the A'man director. While it remains unclear to this day whether Major-General Yariv was armed or traveling with a bodyguard, a man with intimate knowledge of his nation's most closely guarded secrets was not about to allow himself to be diverted to Jordan or any other Arab country without a struggle. The aircraft was diverted to London, where Ms. Khalid and her accomplice were taken into British custody.

Less than seventy-two hours later, the PFLP hijacked a BOAC aircraft en route from Bombay to London and forced it to land at Dawson's Airfield (which had since been renamed Revolutionary Field), hoping that this final gesture would secure Ms. Khalid's immediate release. It worked. The British acquiesced immediately, and Ms. Khalid was flown back to Jordan, where she received a hero's welcome.

After some media play and the release of all the passengers from the four airliners (many of whom had been held inside the hellish confines of a fuselage, baking in the 120-degree heat of the desert sun), Habash ordered all four aircraft destroyed. The subsequent filmed destruction of explosive charges shattering the cockpit of each aircraft epitomized Palestinian arrogance in Jordan and proved to be the final straw in King Hussein's vast reserve of patience and tolerance. King Hussein was visiting a unit from the elite 40th Armored Brigade, an esteemed fighting force known for its fanatic loyalty to the monarchy, when he saw a bra hanging from the aerial of a tank. It was a clear indication that the Jordanian military was sick and tired of the Palestinians turning them into women.[7] The course of action for Jordan was clear: Fight back or eventually be destroyed.

On September 16, 1970, Hussein unleashed his Bedouin Army to rout the Palestinian guerrillas from Jordan. The carnage that lasted for the following two weeks became known in Palestinian vernacular as *Ailul al-Aswad*, a Black September. The fighting in the refugee camps

---

* In order not to risk angering Habash, the two men simply bought tickets on a Pan Am flight to New York, and moments after that plane's landing gear retracted for the trans-Atlantic journey, the aircraft was hijacked and flown to Cairo International Airport.

of Jordan, and in the city streets of Amman, Irbid, and Zarqa, surpassed all the imagined horrors of fratricide. Captured Jordanian soldiers were routinely tortured to death, and Jordanian tank soldiers were known to have tied the corpses of the Palestinian dead to the backs of their Centurion main battle tanks and Saladin armored cars, dragging them through refugee-camp alleyways in horrific displays of disrespect and deterrence. It appeared as if each side competed with the other to commit heinous atrocities to prisoners, wounded personnel, and civilians. The Syrians invaded northern Jordan in support of its Palestinian brethren, but the professional Jordanian military—especially tank-killing aircraft from the British-trained Royal Jordanian Air Force—proved too capable for the Syrians and the Palestinians. According to numerous reports, both the Israelis and the Americans made it clear to the Syrians (and the Soviets) that should Jordan be placed in a precarious military situation, both the IDF and the U.S. Sixth Fleet was poised to intervene in Jordan's defense.[8] It is interesting to note that many Palestinian guerrillas, including several dozen officers from the PFLP-GC, chose to cross the Jordan River and surrender to Israeli troops rather than incur the wrath of King Hussein's Bedouin legions and the Palestinians.

In a matter of weeks, the fedayeen were pushed out from their protective lairs and forced into an operational exile in Lebanon. The Palestinians suffered thousands of dead and wounded; their infrastructure had been decimated and Arab unity had been obliterated in the urban street-fighting of Amman. Egyptian President Nasser, the undisputed leader of the Arab world, suffered a fatal heart attack as a result of the enormous stress absorbed during the mediation efforts to end the Jordanian civil war.[9]

Every Palestinian liberation faction found itself weakened and in disarray following the Jordanian civil war, with one blatant exception—the PFLP-GC.

To many Palestinians, the tragic events of Black September rivaled even the creation of the State of Israel. But to Ahmed Jibril, Black September embodied every aspect of the Palestinian phenomenon his organization vowed to stay clear of: disastrous operations meant for media consumption rather than long-term military objectives, loss of operational and geopolitical focus, and the pandering to the whims of patron Arab states whose allegiance to the "cause" was suspect. He was determined to manipulate the bloody conflict's aftermath to his own advantage.

While many Palestinian leaders viewed Black September as a critical blow to the aspirations of the Palestinian people, Ahmed Jibril viewed its aftermath as his opportunity to cement the PFLP-GC as the cutting-edge force in the war against Israel. In fact, the events of Black September left Jibril stronger than ever. He had already moved much of his infrastructure to Lebanon and Syria following the creation of the PFLP-GC in 1968, and his training and operational network was left virtually unscathed by the Jordanian bloodbath. By 1971, when thousands of fighters from Fatah, the PFLP, and Nayif Hawatmeh's DFLP limped into Lebanon to establish a new full-scale front against Israel, Jibril was already conducting business as usual from across the Lebanese frontier in a well-established base of operations.[10] Throughout 1970 and 1971, the PFLP-GC perpetrated an effective war of attrition against Israel's northern frontier and the Golan Heights, where it performed an integral role in the Syrian effort to wage a war of nerves and attrition against the Israelis. The attacks never rivaled the bloody massacre near Moshav Avivim, but they did cause considerable loss of life and damage. Among the more notable PFLP-GC operations were the wounding of several children in Kibbutz Hanita by the planting of land mines; the killing of five civilians when a PFLP-GC land mine destroyed a vehicle near Ramat Magshimim; and the wounding of a small girl when a mine detonated in Kibbutz Bar-Am.[11]

Jibril was also making a name for himself on a different battlefield far from Israel's north. The Gaza Strip in 1970 was as close a copy to the American Wild West as could exist in the Middle East. Heavily armed Palestinian factions, mainly utilizing weapons left behind by the Egyptians in 1967, opened a deadly terrorist front against the residents of southern Israel. From the strip's eight refugee camps (Shati, Nutzirat, el-Burj, Mo'uzi, Dir el-Balach, Khan Yunis, Rafiah, and Jabalya) the terrorists were able to utilize the hundreds of caves and underground sewers of the strip for perfect hideouts and weapons caches; operating in small and compartmentalized cells, they were able to conduct their hit-and-run attacks with anonymity and impunity. Gaza became lawless and deadly, and the regular IDF units assigned to garrison the squalor found themselves incapable of combatting the terrorists. Attacks in the strip and against southern Israel became more brazen and deadlier each week, and the Israeli public, fearing a chaotic cancer growing in their soft underbelly, demanded a response.

Even though Jibril was separated from Gaza by hundreds of kilometers and numerous obstacles, he was able to issue orders to his men, which in the strip numbered approximately fifty hard-core operatives, through Radio El-Quds (Radio Jerusalem), the PFLP-GC station transmitting from Syria to the occupied territories.[12] According to various Israeli sources, Jibril's reputation in the Gaza Strip was great, a reputation backed by his abilities, ruthlessness, and willingness to resort to violence against fellow Palestinians. (According to Israeli journalist Yoram Binur in his book *My Enemy, My Self*, even the mention of the Jibril name still carries a formidable degree of intimidation power in the Gaza Strip to this day.)

Israeli Defense Minister Lieutenant-General (Res.) Moshe Dayan, outraged by the military's ineffectiveness against the guerrillas, called in the one man he confidently understood would be able to crush the "troubles": IDF OC Southern Command, Major-General Ariel "Arik" Sharon. The rambunctious general was brought into the campaign for his special talents and controversial methods in waging an irregular war; Sharon vowed to purify the strip *personally* and, with web gear and personal AK-47 in hand, Major-General Sharon commanded many forays himself. An ex-commando leader and founder of the infamous Unit 101 force of retaliatory counterterrorist warriors, Sharon employed a highly effective campaign of elite reconnaissance commando forces,* trained to operate as guerrillas under the most difficult and brutal conditions. Many of these fighters masqueraded as Arabs when operating in the field, and they attacked known terrorist locations at night. The conventional aspect of the fight was supported by a reinforced presence of Shin Bet agents to root out and terminate the terrorists.[13] One of Sharon's most potent weapons was the deployment of the *bishtril* (informants) to compromise well-established terrorist cells. Shin Bet agents turned to the counterintelligence agent's greatest source of information: criminals, profiteers, drug dealers, addicts, prostitutes, and pimps.[14] Payoffs included everything from cash rewards to, according to several reports, protection against rival criminal and terrorist groups. Against many of the Palestinian groups, this Israeli network of informants was highly successful, but they proved of limited value against the PFLP-GC. This failure was attributed in many cases to the fear of potential informants in betraying Jibril. Even Jibril's men who had been captured proved proud and stubborn

---

* These special forces included *Sayeret Shaked* (Almond Reconnaissance, Southern Command's recon unit); *Sayeret Tzanhanim* (Paratroop Reconnaissance); the conscript paratroop brigade recon force; *Sayeret Golani* (Golani Reconnaissance), the reconnaissance element of the 1st *Golani* Infantry Brigade and combat force, which would feature prominently in Israel's war against Ahmed Jibril in the years to come; and, according to foreign reports, *Sayeret Mat'kal* [General Staff Reconnaissance], the ultraelite top-secret intelligence-gathering/counterterrorist unit under the control of the IDF General Staff.

foes, tending not to crack under Shin Bet interrogation. Many were duly sentenced to long prison terms in Israel's maximum security facilities, where they soon blended into the growing terrorist prison population— an incarcerated legion over which Ahmed Jibril would yield remarkable influence.[15]

In Jibril's eyes, the battle for the Gaza Strip proved to be a primitive campaign. The world's first technoterrorist was determined to dazzle as he destroyed, not get bogged down in the trenches of a fight far removed from the spotlight and the crux of the Israeli consciousness. A military pragmatist, Jibril realized that he was outgunned, outmanned, and outmaneuvered in Gaza by Sharon's force of commandos and Shin Bet agents. He realized that Major-General Sharon might have won Gaza, but he couldn't "purify" the vast battlefield in Western Europe, nor could he keep El Al aircraft safe from Marwan Kreeshat's destructive genius.

It was time for the resumption of the aircraft offensive.

The PFLP-GC's destruction of Swissair Flight 330 succeeded in spreading fear among the traveling public in a manner Habash's hijackings could never accomplish. When faced with the choice, after all, anyone would rather be terrorized for a few hours in an Arab capital than be obliterated at 15,000 feet over a Swiss forest. The destruction of the Swissair jet, however, also alerted the Western European security services. Packages of significant size headed for Israel underwent greater scrutiny—sometimes even by X-ray machines—before being allowed a spot on board an aircraft. It would be extremely difficult to smuggle one of Kreeshat's bombs on board an aircraft again, but not impossible. If the mail wouldn't work, a human messenger would have to suffice.

Another PFLP-GC "innovation" was the employment of "mules," or unwitting human delivery systems, to carry an explosive device on to a plane, and then be blown up in the process. The men and women conducting day-to-day business for the international networks of the PFLP, *Fatah*, and the Popular Struggle Front (PSF)* needed to employ

---

* Founded in 1967 months before the Six-Day War by Bahjat Abu Gharbiyah and Major Fayez Hamdan, both disenchanted veterans of the Palestine Liberation Army, the PSF has been, throughout its history, allied to both Fatah and the pro-Syrian rejectionist fronts but has carried out several "independent" operations abroad, including a November 27, 1969, grenade attack against the El Al office in Athens; the April 24, 1970, bombings of the El Al office in Istanbul, and the Pan Am office in Izmir, Turkey; and the July 22, 1970, hijacking of an Olympic Airlines jet to Athens.[16]

completely dedicated personnel who were willing to sacrifice their lives for the cause. Hard-core revolutionaries tended to operate in a professional, though fanatic, manner; although trained to survive and persevere in a modern urban battlefield, they were trained that it was better to die in battle than be caught and disclose vital secrets during police or intelligence service interrogation. An organization's very survival depended on such secrets-to-the-grave security. Using a mule was a practical cradle-to-grave guarantee for operational security; the means for executing an operation was recruited and terminated in a matter of weeks. "Martyrdom" ensured that PFLP-GC operational secrets remained within Jibril's inner sanctum of lieutenants.

With a sexual revolution under way in the United States and Europe, finding a victim to be a mule would not be difficult. A young and handsome Middle Easterner circulating through the capitals of Europe with leftist political views and a hefty dose of cash would have little difficulty in finding a young woman who could be duped into unknowingly carrying an explosive device inside her luggage. The Arab male, proudly pronouncing the fact that he was a Palestinian, would promise to take the young girl to Israel to see his family. Because he was an Arab and considered El Al's ruthless security system an infringement of his civil dignities, *she* would fly El Al and he would meet her in the Holy Land at a later date. Naturally, the terrorist would give the young girl several gifts just prior to her departure to bring to his family.*

The Palestinian revolutionary and liberation movements had little trouble in sacrificing women for the cause; females were traditionally viewed with great contempt. *Palestinian* women, according to several reports, were inducted into the ranks of the terrorist movements only after they underwent a sexual indoctrination in the bed of one warlord or another. A popular song in the Palestinian training camps of Jordan and southern Lebanon in late 1970, loosely translated into English, went something like this:

---

* As will be seen later with the Syrian Air Force Intelligence's attempted midair bombing of El Al Flight 016 from London to Tel Aviv, this classic "false-flag terrorist" ploy has been the most successful trick in the terrorist's tradecraft play book. The use of European women purely as a "means" has not even escaped espionage fiction, including esteemed spy novelist John Le Carré, who examines this theme in great detail in his book *The Little Drummer Girl*, even though the novel's political line was clearly pro-Palestinian.

"Come here and let's play with your blouse
All the gang at your expense,
I wish your fiancé will get killed,
We'll pay for his funeral."[17]

European women were held in even lower esteem. They would make "inexpensive" martyrs for the cause.

On July 28, 1971, a young and extremely attractive Dutch woman* who shall be known simply as Jetti was driven to Rome's Fiumicino International Airport by her lover, a young and handsome Arab man, and proceeded toward the El Al check-in counter.[18] The line for Flight 426 to Tel Aviv was considerably longer than usual that brutally hot July evening. More than a hundred tired and nervous travelers clutched their luggage as they awaited the obligatory questioning by El Al's tenacious security staff, all Shin Bet-trained agents, who screened potential passengers before mechanical means, such as metal detectors and X-ray devices, could screen the ticketed passengers who held boarding cards. Through a series of deliberate questions—meant, of course, to elicit a deliberate response—the El Al security guard was supposed to provide a human intelligence barrier for the terrorist to cross before continuing with his mission, according to one former El Al security chief. The questions included: *Are these bags yours? Did you pack them yourself? Have the packed bags left your possession at any time? Has anyone given you anything, a parcel, a letter, or a gift, to give to anyone in Israel?* Should a passenger look wrong, sweat too much, not look straight into the eyes of the questioning agent, or appear in any way *suspicious* (being an Arab was a primary criterion), an extensive security examination was duly carried out on the passenger and his belongings. Passengers could even be strip-searched. If the targeted passenger refused this procedure, he was denied the right to fly El Al and, sometimes, he was even arrested. The entire procedure was meant to insure that the potential for harm did not board the aircraft and risk the lives of innocent passengers, even if it meant that an El Al jet took off several hours late.[19]

Jibril realized that the effectiveness of El Al's security apparatus was a formidable barrier, but he also realized that innocent travelers, or impressionable young women who believed in their hearts (manipulated by a false romantic passion) that their boyfriends could do no evil, could pass the human-agent gauntlet of questions with little difficulty.

---

* Her identity is protected for security reasons.

He also believed that Marwan Kreeshat could design a device of unique sophistication that even the best Shin Bet-trained agent would not succeed in uncovering. Jibril's theory was sound.

At the check-in counter, Jetti handed her ticket and Dutch passport to the reservation agent who, after a quick examination to see if the travel documents were forged, printed out her boarding pass. Before handing in her bags, however, she was questioned by the El Al security agent. Although one of her suitcases had been handed to her by her lover, filled with, ostensibly, gifts for his mother, she lied when asked if she had been given anything to take with her to Israel. While waiting to board the flight, the El Al security procedure had stirred some sinister suspicions in Jetti's heart, but human nature took over, and she decided to give her boyfriend the benefit of the doubt. She boarded the aircraft and settled into her aisle seat. As El Al Flight 426 gained altitude, however, the young Dutch woman began to tell her story to the woman in the next seat—an Israeli lady who, quite remarkably, understood quite a bit about Palestinian terrorists and their means of operation.[20] (Israeli travelers, conditioned through endless years of conflict and turmoil, were on the whole self-taught counterterrorist experts.) Alarmed, she contacted the flight attendant, who in turn raced toward the cockpit to inform the flight crew and an armed Shin Bet sky marshal.

El Al Flight 426 reached Tel Aviv safely on July 28. Little information has been made available by the Israeli government, El Al, or Italian security officials concerning the incident. It is known only that the suitcase Jetti had been handed contained a sophisticated false bottom holding a barometric-pressure explosive device.

Undaunted by this failure, Jibril tried once again. The next attempt was made in London—coincidentally, a major operational center for the Bulgarian intelligence services.

This time, the young Arab Romeo romanced a young Peruvian woman, a twenty-one-year-old South American beauty who shall be known as Dalia; he was known as Roberto, and told her he was a Brazilian of Arab decent. Abiding by the classic scenario, he romanced the young woman for several weeks, gaining her love, confidence, and body. Roberto, too, wanted the girl to meet some family in Israel, and bought her a round-trip airline ticket on El Al; after taking care of some business dealings in London, he was to join her in a week or so.[21]

On September 1, 1971, Dalia boarded El Al Flight 016, even though she had realized that her luggage had been switched prior to take-off. Nevertheless, she continued with her flight and, four-and-a-half hours later, the aircraft landed in Tel Aviv.

El Al and the people of Israel had been the recipients of divine intervention. Two bombs that could easily have destroyed the lives of more than four-hundred innocent civilians did not operate properly. On September 9, the Israeli government presented the two women at a press conference in Tel Aviv's Beit Sokolov journalist center. The women were not allowed to answer any questions or be photographed, but they told how they had been duped by Arab men to carry bags on the El Al flights. The anonymous Israeli security officials present at the eerie conference would not disclose how the bombs had been detected, or why they had failed to detonate and destroy the aircraft. They did, however, present both suitcases with their sophisticated bombs fully intact. Israeli intelligence officials blamed the PFLP-GC for both failed attacks.

The events of the summer of 1971 prompted El Al to beef up its already tight security screening system at all airline departure points. Check-in luggage as well as carry-on bags would now be searched by hand. El Al was already an airline known for its unreliable schedule, but the new guidelines prompted a joke taken from the El Al acronym: "El Al—Every Landing Always Late." It was hoped that the improved measures would make the PFLP-GC's murderous tasks more difficult. They would not, however, stop Jibril, although it would be a full year before he struck again.

For the first two weeks of August 1972, two eighteen-year-old English girls, Ruth Watkin and Audrey Waldron, were wined, dined, and romanced in Rome by two handsome "Near Eastern" men who told the girls they were Iranian students. A passionate, preplanned affair had blossomed and the foursome decided that they would travel to Israel to see the sights of the Holy Land. Naturally, the two "Iranians" needed to take care of pressing business in Italy, and would have to join the girls at a later date. On August 16, 1972, the two girls boarded El Al Flight 426. Remarkably, they had been able to pass through the new and improved El Al security net, even though they had been given quite a few items to take with them to Israel, including a brand-new record player. Marwan Kreeshat had ingeniously fitted a potent supply of Grade-A Czech-made Semtex into the phonograph, disguising the material and the detonating mechanism brilliantly into the machine's own electronic infrastructure.

Although the El Al security guard who examined their baggage had failed to identify the sabotaged record player as a bomb, El Al's security efforts did, in a roundabout way, prevent the aircraft's eventual destruction. The security checks had caused significant delays for Flight 426, and the plane was still on the ground when the bomb's timer was activated. Although designed to detonate at 20,000 feet, an altitude that would have insured the jet's obliteration, the bomb blew up in the luggage hold as the Boeing jet approached 14,700 feet, when air pressure differential was not as severe.[22] A violent blast rocked the aircraft as a significant gash in the fuselage caused the plane to rock and rattle. Near-panic erupted on board. The flight crew gallantly attempted to settle the jittery nerves of 140 passengers, while the Shin Bet sky marshals clutched their .22 Beretta automatics, fearing the explosion to be an opening signal to an eventual hijacking. Because, according to foreign reports, El Al aircraft were protected by thick sheets of armor plating,* the aircraft and the passengers were spared from midair obliteration.[23] The pilot skillfully turned the limping jet around and landed without incident in Rome. The lives of 154 people were miraculously spared.

Israeli and Italian security officials quickly examined the bomb crater scarring the white, blue, and silver fuselage and were able to pinpoint the explosion as emanating from the bag checked in by the two British girls; there were enough remains of the phonograph to accurately piece together a forensic model of Kreeshat's handiwork. Upon interrogation, the girls recanted their short-lived love affairs with the two Arabs and, to the delight of their Italian and Israeli inquisitors, produced a cheap photo-booth snapshot of the two men taken in a Rome gallery. Cocky in the knowledge that the two girls would soon be dead and their possessions, including the photograph, would soon be at the bottom of the Mediterranean, the two terrorists had foolishly gone against the first rule of security taught in their PFLP-GC training camp. The photograph was checked against Interpol files and supplied to virtually every Italian policeman and carabinieri in the country.

Three days later, a policeman noticed the two men calmly walking along a Rome piazza; he called for reinforcements and twenty-nine-year-old Adnan Mohammad Ali Hasham, from Jordan, and Ahmed

---

* According to this defensive theory never confirmed by El Al but widely reported in the press, much of the outer skeleton of each El Al aircraft was fitted with protective armor plating meant to insure that if a plane was hijacked, the subsequent flying projectiles or possible grenade fragments resulting in the firefight between the terrorists and the Shin Bet sky marshals would not puncture the fuselage and lead to decompressurization and the aircraft's eventual destruction. It was clear, through these defensive countermeasures, that El Al's policy was to fight it out with the terrorists in midair rather than have a repeat of the July 22, 1968, hijacking to Algiers. It is important to note that since that historic skyjacking, no terrorist group has succeeded in seizing an El Al airliner.

Ziad, twenty-four, from Iraq, were immediately picked up. Ahmed Jibril's worst nightmare had come true. Not only had the bomb failed to destroy its target and the only two witnesses, but under questioning, both of Jibril's romantic rogues provided their interrogators with an enormous wealth of information. They told police that they had met Marwan Kreeshat in Yugoslavia (it is believed that he transferred the device from his Sofia safe house to Yugoslavia for security reasons), and were given the bomb, and their instructions, in Belgrade.[24]

Both men were duly tried and provided with lengthy prison terms in maximum security Italian facilities; their sentences, however, would never be served. According to terrorism expert Claire Sterling in her detailed book *The Terror Network*, the two men were secretly released under mysterious terms and deported to an Arab country; perhaps not so coincidentally, the young carabinieri captain who supervised their release was Antonio Varisco, who was assassinated in 1980 by the Red Brigade, a group with extremely close ties to the PFLP-GC.[25] According to several reports, Rome was one of the PLO's most lucrative bases of operations in Europe; Palestinian terrorists received "unique" treatment at the hands of the Italian security services in return for PLO assurances that terrorist attacks would not be carried out on Italian soil. In 1972, the Black September station chief in Rome, Wael Zwaiter, was, according to foreign reports, the first of that organization's leaders to be killed by the infamous Mossad hit teams given the assignment of avenging the September 1972 massacre at the Munich Olympics. Finally, according to several reports, in September 1973, four PFLP gunmen supposedly being deported from Italy for their attempt to blow an El Al jet out of the sky with a SA-7 surface-to-air missile were killed when the Italian Air Force C-47 aircraft ferrying them to Libya was sabotaged by Israeli and Italian intelligence agents.[26]

Interpol was supplied with a transcript of the suspects' testimony and the proper investigative agencies were provided with full-length dossiers with which they were to investigate the PFLP-GC European network and bring the terrorists to justice. But no trace of Jibril or his men were found in Western Europe. Responsible for the destruction of one Swissair plane and the mass murder of forty-seven people, guilty of the attempted bombing of at least four other jets, Ahmed Jibril and his KGB-trained network had slipped back into anonymity. The international airlines could have learned much from the bombing campaign that took place between 1970 and 1972, but instead of enacting stringent security measures to help insure the safety of their passengers, they dedicated their resources to slick advertising campaigns and no-frill promotions. It appeared that only El Al and Swissair (an airline also rumored to employ heavily armed sky marshals and other protective means installed into its planes) had taken the miraculous technical failures of Jibril's and Kreeshat's handiwork as a sign that even greater steps needed to be taken.[27] For Air India, the French-owned U.T.A., and Pan Am, this negligence would have lasting repercussions in the years to follow.

Remarkably, Ahmed Jibril was undaunted by his embarrassing setbacks, viewing them as the risk of conducting such precarious business. Determined to mount a new and, he hoped, bloody offensive, Jibril once again summoned his master demolition team headed by Marwan Kreeshat. The means by which the sophisticated explosive device was brought on board Swissair Flight 330, disguised as an airmail parcel, intrigued the wily terrorist chieftain with its terrifying potential. Even more than international air travel, the mail was a sacrosanct commodity protected by extremely strict laws in most countries. Since terrorism, in its most basic form, is designed to make life so unbearable for the ordinary public that it becomes discontented and demands change, terror via the mail had definite potential. Jibril realized that indiscriminate bombings or killings in Western Europe would, indeed, cause havoc, and would also bring an enormous army of international intelligence agencies down to bear against him; such actions might also displease his Bulgarian and Soviet backers. If, however, he could initiate an indiscriminate campaign against the Israelis, yet make the means an individually targeted device, like a letter, then his East-bloc backers would not pressure him to cease his activities. For this most ambitious scheme, Jibril had the tools and the manpower. He had the infrastructure and, although just barely, the necessary funds. With the success of disguising a bomb as a parcel, Jibril now had his means. The letter bomb was born.

The principle of the letter bomb was simple. A small, though potent, supply of explosive material (believed to weigh no more than one ounce) was placed inside an envelope or package—squeezed into the flap liner with a vice-type device. When the envelope was opened, it released a miniature spring soldered to a percussion striking device that, in turn, struck the detonating mechanism and caused an explosion.[28] Although the letter bomb was not a way to inflict massive loss of life, it could maim or kill the unfortunate person handling it. Jibril had been toying with the idea of a massive letter-bomb offensive for some time. On February 24, 1970, Jibril operatives in Frankfurt and Yugoslavia sent "a few" booby-trapped letter bombs to addresses in

Israel, but they were discovered before being delivered and there were no casualties. On December 28, 1971, Jibril tried once again to inflict a postal reign of terror, when his operatives in Belgrade and Vienna posted approximately fifteen letter bombs to prominent businessmen and institutions in Israel.[29]

One such letter bomb is believed to have arrived in Israel, via surface mail, on February 1, 1972, and was addressed to a senior officer in the Tel Aviv police department; two other booby-trapped packages arrived that day addressed to senior Israeli military commanders, including the OC IDF Central Command, Major-General Rechavem "Gandhi" Zeevi. This was no ordinary letter bomb, however. It was in a large packet, appearing to hold a book, and appeared extremely suspicious; in fact, the Israeli postal authorities notified the police the moment they discovered the package in an incoming mail bag. Tel Aviv's chief bomb-disposal expert, Nissim Sasson, was summoned to head-quarters in Yaffo to disarm the device. Too many people had handled the package before Sasson could successfully defuse it, however, and it exploded in his hands. He received serious wounds, lost several fingers and the hearing in one ear, and was disfigured for life.[30] The fifty-two-year-old Sasson was lucky to have survived Jibril's bomb. Others the world over would not be so fortunate.

Jibril's failed letter-bomb campaign was not lost on a rival Palestinian faction competing for the vanguard role in the revolution: the Black September Organization. Formed in late 1970 by Yasir Arafat as a highly-secretive* commando arm of Fatah to exact bold and bloody revenge against the Hashemite kingdom of Jordan for the treacherous Ailul al-Aswad, Black September soon developed into the most ruthless anti-Israel terrorist faction ever created. Commanded by Salah Khalef (Abu Iyad), Ali Hassan Salameh (the infamous Red Prince, also known by his nom de guerre Abu I'hab), and Muhammad Da'ud O'da (Abu Da'ud),[31] their first action was the assassination of Jordanian Prime Minister Wasfi at-Tal on the steps of the Cairo Sheraton Hotel on November 28, 1971. During this incident, according to eyewitness reports, the attackers lapped up the blood of the mortally wounded premier. Black September's call to fame was Operation Berim and Ikrit, the Munich Olympics Massacre of September 5, 1972, an operation that the Palestinians have forever been linked to in image and interna-

---

* Arafat wanted to create a force whose actions would be so diabolical that it would cause horror and outrage throughout the world, yet he wanted its actions far removed from the moderate image he had been masquerading for the PLO.

tional outrage, and an action that prompted the Israeli government to declare an all-out war against the group. It would be an assassination campaign of hit-teams and spooks that eventually saw to the destruction of Black September. Exactly two weeks after the Olympics killings, however, Black September initiated a letter-bomb campaign of its own (using, it is believed, demolitions technology pioneered by Kreeshat and Jibril), dispatching nearly two hundred letter bombs to Israeli and Jewish organizations throughout the world. Several people were killed in the spree, and letter bombs were even sent to United States President Richard M. Nixon and other American government officials.[32]

Although both Jibril and Kreeshat had soured on the letter bomb as the proper means to continue the war of nerves against Israel, Black September's success in turning the mail into a thing of horror was convincing. In an attempt to bring back some prestige to the PFLP-GC, Ahmed Jibril ordered one final letter-bomb "sortie." In November 1972, PFLP-GC agents dispatched to Singapore mailed a dozen letter bombs to institutions in Israel and on the European continent; the addresses were obtained through the PFLP-GC intelligence-gathering infrastructure inside Israel and in Europe. The bombs did little damage, even though booby-trapped parcels and letters were sent to many diverse locations, including Paris, Geneva, Montreal, Vienna, London, Washington, D.C., Ottawa, Brussels, Kinshasa (Zaire), Buenos Aires, and even Phnom Penh (Cambodia).[33]

Nineteen hundred seventy-two would prove to be a year of embarrassing failure for Ahmed Jibril. Although his forces operating in southern Lebanon and Syria in the Fatahland quadrant succeeded in battling IDF units with considerable skill, his grandiose operations abroad had failed to destroy even one target, or kill even one Jew. Particularly humiliating was the fact that Black September, an entity created by his hated rival Yasir Arafat, had stolen much of his thunder.* Spiritually wounded but resilient nonetheless, Jibril decided to use this period of inactivity to rearm and rethink his strategy. Time, after all, was on the Palestinians' side.

---

* On the morning of July 1, 1973, Colonel Yosef Alon, the IAF attaché in Washington, D.C., was shot to death as he entered the parking lot of his Chevy Chase, Maryland, home. Most Israeli intelligence officials and officers from the Federal Bureau of Investigation (FBI) believe that black militants, hired by Black September to avenge the *Mossad* hit teams, were responsible for the killing. Nevertheless, in his book *Terrorism: From Robespierre To Arafat*, author Albert Parry claims that Alon was killed by PFLP-GC assassins, a claim that, if true, would signal the first-ever PFLP-GC operation perpetrated on American soil.

*   *   *

For the next six months, Jibril consolidated his forces both in Lebanon and especially in Europe. He quietly watched as the Mossad waged a relentless campaign against Black September's European and Middle Eastern networks, and as Israeli intelligence agents destroyed the PFLP's international infrastructure on the streets of Western Europe, Cyprus, and Lebanon. Israel's war against Black September (and the PFLP) culminated on April 9, 1973, when a large-scale IDF commando force, supported by a Mossad support-team and spearheaded by Sayeret Mat'kal, launched a spectacular raid on Beirut known as Operation Spring of Youth. Israel's esteemed security services were less successful against the PFLP-GC, however. Ahmed Jibril's organization, with its intense background checks, counterintelligence training, and well-founded fears that it was the target of "foreign" intelligence-service surveillance, was so secretive—even after the arrests of Ahmed Ziad and Ali Hasham—that the Israelis were unable to penetrate the PFLP-GC. Unmolested by security-service interference, Jibril ran an efficient weapons-smuggling enterprise from the Middle East to his safe houses in Europe. Soviet-bloc arms, shipped from the Polish port of Gdansk and destined for the Iraqi, Syrian, and Libyan militaries, usually found their way into the Syrian port of Latakia, and then through caravan to Turkey and Bulgaria for distribution—usually in stolen vehicles—to the capitals on the Continent. According to several reports, the PFLP-GC vehicles were modified by KGB garages to conceal their illicit cargo.[34]

Jibril, it appeared, was waiting for an opportunity to launch a one-shot offensive in Europe meant to assume uncontested control of the irregular struggle against Zionism. His grand plans would have to wait. A greater threat to the State of Israel had dawned.

On October 6, 1973, at 1340 hours, a flight of Syrian Mi-8 helicopters appeared off the slopes of Mt. Hermon, the strategic Israeli listening post towering above the Golan Heights, and landed a force of heavily armed commandos given the job of capturing the top-secret Israeli position. Ten minutes later, thousands of Syrian artillery pieces opened up a murderous salvo against Israeli defenses along the Golan Heights, while simultaneously, thousands of Egyptian artillery batteries opened fire along the Suez Canal, hammering Israeli defenses in the Sinai with a thunderous eruption. It was Yom Kippur day in Israel, the holiest day in all of Judaism, and Israel's much-vaunted intelligence and military community had been caught completely off guard. The 1973 Yom Kippur War had begun.

Ever since the final smoldering moments of the Six-Day War in 1967, Arab ambitions to launch a bold and successful war of vengeance against Israel had been at the forefront of their national agendas. Both Egypt and Syria, the two most powerful Arab states, realized that if the physical destruction of the Jewish State was no longer a reality, then Israel needed to be taught a humiliating and bloody lesson for its 1967 victory. Vengeance became an Arab obsession, and a thirst almost realized in October 1973. On the Golan Heights, the Syrian blitzkrieg was a mighty combination of overwhelming armor and heavily armed infantrymen, their advance across the Golan Heights supported by a seemingly impregnable gauntlet of Soviet-supplied surface-to-air missiles (SAMs); before mysteriously coming to a halt, the Syrian advance nearly made it to the shores of the Sea of Galilee. In the south, hundreds of thousands of Egyptian troops had crossed the Suez Canal and launched a full-scale bid to recapture the entire Sinai Desert peninsula and push into southern Israel. After overrunning the Bar-Lev Line fortifications, they raced through the desert abyss in an attempt to reclaim the ultrastrategic Mitla and Giddi Passes before Israel could mobilize her reserves and bring her mighty air force successfully into the field. Israel would rebound from her initial setbacks, however, and counterattack—eventually reaching to within artillery range of Damascus and crossing the Suez Canal into the Egyptian mainland, poised for a push against Cairo. Only superpower intervention and the threat of a nuclear confrontation helped bring about a cease-fire.[35]

Although the 1973 Yom Kippur War ended in a decisive Israeli victory, it was one of the most devastating conventional conflicts ever fought between Arab and Jew. In eighteen days of fighting, more than twenty-five hundred Israeli soldiers were killed with more than ten thousand wounded. Arab casualties numbered nearly fifteen hundred dead and nearly fifty thousand wounded. Many people in Israel, Egypt, and Syria understood that the devastation in the next full-scale conventional fray might lead to true Armageddon. A political battle to settle the Arab-Israeli conflict was now under way.

The Palestinians were remarkably absent from the 1973 War. In fact, they almost managed to destroy the intensive and highly sophisticated web of secrecy surrounding the Egyptian and Syrian plans for the surprise attack. In September 1973, Yasir Arafat's deputy commander, Abu Iyad, had been briefed on the impending conflict by Egyptian President Anwar as-Sadat, and was ordered not only to keep absolutely silent concerning the highly classified plans, but also to secretly dispatch a small unit of thirty Fatah fighters to the Egyptian assault force as a symbolic gesture suggesting that Palestinian warriors were in the vanguard effort to push Israel into the sea. Days later, however, Iyad gave an exclusive interview to the Lebanese newspaper *an-Nahar* in which he detailed the Egyptian plans, promising that "Palestine would be liberated shortly."[36] The article was picked up by a special A'man unit assigned the task of obtaining intelligence from open sources, but ignored by superior officers as nothing more than bravado and propaganda.

Militarily, the Palestinians were a nonfactor during the conflict. They did not participate in the military campaign and did not even perpetrate acts of terrorism in Israel or elsewhere in the world to deflect Israeli resolve.* The shuttle diplomacy of American Secretary of State Henry Kissinger that followed the war's end brought about a new era of political mediation to the world's most dangerous deadlock.

It was a period of negotiated compromise toward settlement. It caught the Palestinian movement by surprise and in disarray.

The 1973 war and its aftermath split the ranks of the PLO into two separate and extremely volatile camps. The first, led by PLO chairman and Fatah commander Yasir Arafat, modified their position to meet the realities of their limited (as well as their patron Arab sponsors) abilities in defeating Israel. *All* of what they considered Palestine could never be returned by force; a political compromise, backed by military and terrorist actions, seemed to be their only hope for liberation. Such sentiment emanating from the Fatah camp was tantamount to treason to men like Habash and Ahmed Jibril, prominent members of the second camp consisting of the pro-Syrian groups—the PFLP, the DFLP, and the PFLP-GC. In their opinion, Arafat was more interested in establishing embassies and circulating at nonaligned conferences than in seeing to the destruction of the Jewish State. The more radical groups were working, with covert Syrian assistance, to create a military block to reject Arafat's perfidy. Only a total war could bring about total victory. Only one nation could ensure the continuation of a total war: the Soviet Union.[38]

According to several reports, the Soviet Union realized that a politi-

---

* In a move directed to provide a smoke screen to the Egyptian and Syrian buildups in the days prior to the outbreak of hostilities, Palestinian terrorists from as-Sa'iqa hijacked a train carrying Soviet-Jewish émigrés from Czechoslovakia to the Austrian border and demanded that Chancellor Bruno Kriesky close the Schonau transit camp that assisted Soviet Jews in their emigration to Israel. As as-Sa'iqa did nothing without approval from Damascus, this was a definite terrorist/psychological warfare operation carried out by the Syrians.[37]

cal solution to the Arab-Israeli impasse would seriously weaken its already slipping influence in the region. The Soviets understood that their presence, which began with the signing of the Czech-Egyptian arms deal in 1955, stemmed from the Arab desire to destroy Israel, and Western support for the Jewish State. Should peace suddenly "break out" in the region, the military strength that the Soviets used as an all-important blackmail position would no longer be needed. Already ousted by the Egyptians in 1972, the Soviet's saw Egypt's warming up to America as a clear indication that the largest and most powerful nation in the Arab and Islamic world was heading toward a pro-Western orbit. The Kremlin was terrified by a negotiated peace settlement, and Moscow knew there was one embittered and heavily armed entity in the region it could mold into agents of destabilization.

Toward the end of 1973, in the weeks following the end of the Yom Kippur War, East German and Cuban intelligence* and irregular-warfare experts established a sophisticated terrorist training facility in the South Yemeni desert;[39] the location, so far from the action and Israel, was meant to dissuade the fighter bombers of the IAF from making unwanted visits. The East Germans had for years supported the Palestinian terrorist movements, but Cuba's role was a most interesting development. Although separated from the Middle East by thousands of nautical miles, Fidel Castro had proved his continuous and tangible loyalty to the Arab cause for several years. According to several unconfirmed Western intelligence reports, the Cubans provided the Palestinians in Western Europe with access to their diplomatic facilities and pouches; Cuban MiG-21 pilots, according to these accounts, flew combat sorties with the Egyptian and Syrian air forces. It is, however, confirmed that elite Cuban armored units fought alongside the Syrian Army during the 1973 war on the Golan Heights, and in the bitter war of attrition following the declaration of the cease-fire on October 24.[40] With a history of support for revolution in South America and hands-off assistance to fledgling Communist guerrilla uprisings throughout the Third World, the Cubans had become the most lethal terrorist instructors in the world. Their services were for sale to the highest bidders.

The purpose of the South Yemeni training facility, and several similar sites opened up by Libyan strongman Muammar Qadaffi, was to mold the dedicated Palestinian fedayeen/terrorist into a well-honed

* Cuban intelligence officers were also reported to have assisted the North Vietnamese in interrogating captured American pilots and POWs.

conventional fighter *also* capable of carrying out attacks against heavily defended conventional targets; this training would also make their "routine" terrorist attacks more successful endeavors. The camps were to make the select one thousand or so fighters from the PFLP-GC and the various other pro-Syrian groups into the world's most fearsome warriors capable of executing the most impossible military tasks. They were also trained in intelligence warfare, and taught how to infiltrate both rival and enemy Palestinian groups and assassinate their key figures. The training was incessant and physically brutal. Twenty-kilometer runs in the 120°F desert sun were considered routine, and intimate instruction was given on every type of weapon that could be found in the region. The instructors, old KGB pros, also applied the necessary political brainwashing needed to turn a humble fighter into a fierce martyr. After months of instruction, a new generation of holy warrior was ready for action.

The PFLP-GC was the first to strike.

In the early morning hours of April 11, 1974, Mounir Maghrebi, Ahmed Mahmoud, and Yasin Mouzani, all PFLP-GC soldiers, crossed the fortified frontier separating Lebanon and Israel and marched toward the town of Qiryat Shmoneh. The three PFLP-GC terrorists were armed with Soviet-produced AK-47 7.62-mm assault rifles, PK 7.62-mm light machine guns, and a deadly supply of hand grenades and dynamite. Their objective that spring morning was to seize a school and hold a group of children hostage until their demands that jailed comrades be released were satisfied. If Israel did not acquiesce, the young hostages were to be massacred.[41]

Qiryat Shmoneh was new operational ground for Jibril. Although he had sworn off hostage-taking as a PFLP-GC tactic, Israel's delicate and demoralized national mood following the October Surprise of Yom Kippur 1973 was too tempting a target for him to ignore. But Jibril, a man renowned for his military precision and accurate preengagement intelligence, had grossly miscalculated. It was Passover, and the schools were closed for the holiday spring break. As the terrorists reached the school building and found its doors locked, they panicked. Unable to slip back across the border into Lebanon (where, perhaps, they would risk a PFLP-GC "headbanger" execution for their embarrassing failure), the three men decided to assault a block of flats nearby. Yet instead of taking the residents of the housing facility hostage, the terrorists simply indulged themselves in an orgy of carnage. They went from apartment to apartment and simply killed everyone they saw. It didn't matter if the hapless victim was an old man taking his dog out for a walk or a three-year-old girl playing with her dolls on the staircase—all received a close-quarters burst of 7.62-mm death to the head. In one instance, an entire family was butchered as they sat around the breakfast table. IDF units were summoned immediately at the first sounds of gunfire, as hundreds of residents dialed 100, the Israeli version of 911. The first units to the scene found the town's inhabitants engulfed in panic and outrage. Israel had never seen anything like this before.

The IDF unit assigned to put an end to the ordeal was Sayeret Golani,* the reconnaissance force of the 1st Golani Infantry Brigade. Due to their no-nonsense training, highly selective acceptance procedures, and family-like esprit de corps, it was one of the finest of Israel's commando forces.[42] It was clear to the Sayeret Golani commander, Major R., that his men would be dealing with terrorists who were excellent fighters and not prone to surrendering to superior firepower. The terrorists had accepted the fact that they were dead men, heroes of Palestine—determined to take as many of the enemy with them as possible. Major R. understood only too well and prepared his men for what promised to be a most difficult battle.

The three Palestinian terrorists made it appear as if they were at least a dozen fighters as they raced from apartment to apartment and fired from the open windows. They used their limited supply of ammunition with great skill and discipline, not wasting a single shot and not firing lengthy bursts of automatic fire. The three Palestinians played a cat-and-mouse game with the Sayeret Golani commandos who, wearing heavy flak vests and armed with 9-mm Uzi submachine guns, crawled alongside the building awaiting the opportunity to burst inside in significant numbers and terminate the terrorist squad. It was a daunting task. The reconnaissance infantrymen did not know if the terrorists were holding any hostages, or how many civilians had been killed. Many of the commandos carried stretchers, as they didn't know how many civilians had been wounded.

The battle for one four-story apartment building in a desolate area of Qiryat Shmoneh lasted for more than four hours.[43] The assault force made its way into the building at a methodical pace, "purifying" apartment by apartment, floor by floor. The room-to-room search brought the commandos into close contact with the atrocities that had been committed. These were men from a unit that had conducted countless cross-border forays against terrorist targets in Lebanon and Syria, they

---

* See Chapter Nine for a more complete history of Sayeret Golani.

had fought terrorists in Gaza, and, over half a year earlier, they had spearheaded the recapture of Mount Hermon from Syrian commandos, a battle labeled by many IDF officers as one of the toughest Israel had ever fought. It was a unit that had killed the enemy in lightning strikes, and had seen its own killed in alarming numbers. They were no strangers to blood and suffering, but even these veterans had never seen anything like the slaughter at Qiryat Shmoneh. Seasoned veterans wept openly as they found the bodies of small children destroyed by automatic fire; many commandos threw up in disgust. Perhaps only God could exact proper justice to these murderers, but Sayeret Golani would expedite the process. The cat-and-mouse game continued.

With a desperate situation taking too long to resolve itself and two Golani soldiers already killed in the stand-off, the time to end the debacle was ordered. The Golani commandos had pushed the three terrorists to a top-floor apartment, cornering the heavily armed gunmen in a sure killing zone of fire. As some Golani commandos approached from the nearby staircase already caked in blood, others brought a 106-mm recoilless rifle, a weapon used to destroy tanks, into the courtyard below. The gun's khaki metal barrel was raised toward the targeted flat and readied for action. The gun's blast was deafening, but its results were successful. Seconds after the canister charge ripped through the apartment window and detonated in a thunderous and fiery explosion, the commandos burst into the apartment with their Uzis at the ready. But the Uzis were not needed. The three terrorists were dead.

The final toll at Qiryat Shmoneh was eighteen dead (including eight children and five women) and twenty seriously wounded.[44] The Israeli public demanded vengeance and the destruction of the Palestinian terrorist bases in Lebanon. For the first time since Nazi war criminal Adolf Eichmann was executed in 1961, Israeli politicians silently considered writing a capital punishment law for convicted terrorists. It was the first time in the Arab-Israeli conflict that a terrorist squad had crossed into Israel and perpetrated an indiscriminate bloodbath not meant to achieve publicity or to obtain specific military or political objectives. It would not be the last.*

* On May 15, 1974, a three-man terrorist squad from Nayif Hawatmeh's DFLP crossed the border into Israel from Lebanon and seized a schoolhouse with more than one hundred students in the northern frontier town of Ma'alot. Negotiations with Israeli officials, including Defense Minister Moshe Dayan, failed, and Sayeret Mat'kal was summoned to the rescue. Their bid failed. Twenty-five hostages were killed, and an additional seventy critically wounded.[45]

In Beirut, PFLP-GC spokesman Abu A'bbas called several Western news agencies and, in the name of Ahmed Jibril and the PFLP-GC, claimed responsibility for the massacre, stating that the operation in Qiryat Shmoneh was "the beginning of a new campaign of revolutionary violence and revolutionary suicide inside Israel."[46] The Qiryat Shmoneh melee was a bold move for Jibril. More than any other action he had yet taken against Israel and Israeli interests, Qiryat Shmoneh was a resonant declaration of war that the Jewish State simply could not ignore. In the Knesset (parliament) in Jerusalem, and in the Israeli Defense Ministry and IDF headquarters in Tel Aviv, the name Ahmed Jibril had been ignored for too long. Jibril now joined the ranks of the surviving officers of Black September, George Habash and Wadi Haddad as a marked man. Israel would bring about a war of revolutionary violence against the PFLP-GC.

Retaliation came quickly. The same day that State of Israel buried her latest eighteen victims of terrorism, IDF reconnaissance units attacked southern Lebanese villages that had been used by the terrorists as staging points. In all, six villages were targeted. A total of twenty-four buildings, including a waterworks, were identified by IDF military intelligence as support stations serving Jibril's terrorists and destroyed. Several PFLP-GC gunmen were killed in the raids, and more than a dozen were brought back to Israel for questioning.* Although a lightning-fast response, the operation did little to hamper Jibril's capabilities or intentions. The PFLP-GC commander was determined not to allow Israeli retaliatory—or even preemptive—military action to stop his operations.

On June 13, 1974, four heavily armed PFLP-GC terrorists crossed the Lebanese border at the Mount Hermon crucible (at the base of the Syrian frontier) and headed toward Kibbutz Shamir. Their objective: to seize the school nursery where more than 250 children lived and kill all their hostages should their demands for the release of jailed terrorists not be met.[48] Although a prosperous and heavily populated agricultural settlement, Kibbutz Shamir was a border town well equipped

---

* Two weeks after the raid, the United Nations Security Council condemned Israel for its violation of Lebanese territorial integrity and sovereignty.[47] No mention of the Qiryat Shmoneh massacre or condemnation of Palestinian terrorism was made. At the time of this book's writing in 1992, the United Nations had yet to criticize the Palestinians for any of their attacks against Israel, pro-Israeli installations, or institutions worldwide.

for a terrorist contingency; each resident was armed, and the children slept in fortified bunkers whenever an alert was sounded. Upon entering the kibbutz grounds, the terrorists encountered three women walking from the dining hall—two kibbutz residents and a teenage volunteer from New Zealand. Panicking, the terrorists raised their weapons and shot each woman in the head; the crackling thuds of automatic fire alerted the local civil patrol. Sirens were sounded inside the kibbutz perimeter, and dozens of residents removed their Uzi submachine guns from beneath their beds and hurried outside ready to meet the threat. Suddenly outgunned, the terrorists ran to a deserted toolshed where they blew themselves up with the grenades they carried. Just as they had been taught in the training facilities in South Yemen, they martyred themselves so as not to be captured alive and disclose any information to the Zionist enemy. Near the mangled bodies in the shed, caked with blood, Israeli investigators found leaflets demanding that one hundred Palestinian prisoners be freed within six hours.[49]

Israel did not retaliate immediately, but in the three-day period between June 17 and 20, IAF warplanes conducted a series of incessant air strikes against known terrorist targets in Lebanon, specifically targeting locations where Jibril was believed to be hiding. Although no senior PFLP-GC men were killed, twenty-four terrorists were killed and nearly one hundred were wounded in the aerial assault.

Jibril's much-vaunted revolutionary violence did little more than cause massive loss of life. The PFLP-GC still did not find itself at the vanguard of the sacred offensive destined to liberate Jerusalem, nor did it weaken Israel's resolve to carry on the fight. On the contrary. The dead at Qiryat Shmoneh, Kibbutz Shamir, Ma'alot, and Nahariya galvanized Israel's determination to mount a desperate war of national survival against the terrorists. In fact, Qiryat Shmoneh frightened many Arab leaders—including Hafaz al-Assad—more than it did the Israelis. Other Arab leaders temporarily abandoned Jibril as it was not in their post-1973 war interests to be associated with a man who ordered the deaths of women and children at their breakfast table. Even the Palestinians began to fear Jibril's violent struggle as an uncontrollable storm of rage.

Indeed, a civil war of sorts was erupting in the Palestinian camp. It began during the 1973 war when PLO policy became an ambiguous vehicle of minimized armed struggle and diplomatic legitimacy. It reached a pinnacle on December 13, 1974, when PLO chairman Yasir Arafat addressed the United Nations General Assembly in New York.

The hard-line, pro-Syrian elements in the Palestinian revolution were not about to let compromise-inspired treason extinguish their struggle. On September 26, 1974, Ahmed Jibril became one of the founding members of the Rejection Front, a conglomerate of anti-Arafat terrorist leaders refusing to enter into negotiations with Israel and determined to derail the peace process by attacking all conference participants—especially treacherous Palestinians![50] The Rejection Front included the PFLP-GC, the PFLP, the Iraqi-controlled Arab Liberation Front (ALF),* and the Popular Struggle Front. They were to initiate a civil war, if necessary, to keep the true plight of the Palestinian yearning for justice and revenge alive. Their immediate battlefield would be Lebanon, but Lebanon too would soon be engulfed in civil war.

Ahmed Jibril's PFLP-GC would undergo a civil war of its own, as well. Through circumstances beyond his control, he would be forced to radicalize his politics and ambitions even more and intensify the war against Israel in a most unique fashion.

* The ALF was founded on April 6, 1969, as a means to promote the Iraqi Ba'ath party line into Palestinian terrorist politics. An extremely violent group, the ALF has been since the beginning completely controlled, financed, and supported by Iraq.

CHAPTER FOUR

THE EARLY LEBANON YEARS: CIVIL WAR AND FRATRICIDE

Ein Saheb, Syria January 1975. To the outside eye, the demonstration of military force was awesome. Several hundred men, dressed in full camouflage attire, marched in near-perfect military precision along a sand-caked pathway. As a drill sergeant barked the "left . . . right . . . left" cadence in Arabic, the men and women in the procession clutched their bayonet-adorned AK-47 assault rifles, turned their heads sharply to the left, and then symbolically raised their right arms forward— hitting the banana-shaped magazines of their weapons in a stoic salute toward the flag-draped reviewing stand. Following the marching troops came a procession of men in full battle dress, all carrying Soviet-produced RPG-7 antitank weapons, and all wearing neoprene rubber wet suits.* Pulling up the rear were pretty young Levantine beauties,

---

* In a story relayed to the author by a wire service correspondent stationed in Beirut for several years, most PLO parades were usually held in the main stadium in central Beirut—before it was destroyed in a 1982 Israeli air raid—and usually staged for the foreign press. They sometimes involved extremely embarrassing incidents. During a parade held one year prior to Israel's 1982 Operation Peace for Galilee invasion, frogmen from Force 17, Fatah's elite strike force, and Yasir Arafat's handpicked Praetorian guard were marching in their wet-suit regalia in 100°F heat when they passed out from severe dehydration. When amused Western journalists began photographing the comical sight, heavily armed Palestinian internal security agents began to confiscate cameras and video equipment, and threatened the reporters that mysterious and extremely unpleasant things would happen to them should mention of the debacle ever appear in print or film.

all clutching Soviet-produced commando daggers and mimicking martial-arts exercises.[1] The man receiving this energetic display was Ahmed Jibril. The leader of the Rejection Front was making sure his forces were ready for battle.

ON PAPER, Jibril's army appeared impressive—even though its order of battle had never exceeded more than two thousand men. His forces were organized into one conventional battalion, eventually known as the Sabra and Shatilla Battalion, an artillery unit that included heavy cannons and Katyusha rocket launchers, and a naval frogman unit consisting of Soviet-trained commandos assigned to special operations against Israel. There was even a small air unit equipped with small piston-engine aircraft based in Damascus, and meant to be used as a suicide delivery means against targets in Israel (the unit also possessed several hot air balloons and one or two motorized ultralight hang gliders that were undergoing experimental tests for future deployment).[2]

Although the PFLP-GC was one of the smallest military arms in the Palestinian revolutionary movement, it was by far the most professional. Having an impressive force on paper, however, did not guarantee success on the battlefield. In fact, such displays tended to be nothing more than mere exercises in public relations bravado meant for home consumption: If the refugee camp residents could see Palestinian military assertiveness on Syrian, Lebanese, or Jordanian television news broadcasts, then the fires of hope could still burn in the Palestinian soul. Such displays usually resulted in generous donations to the cause from refugee camp charity boxes, and petrodollars from sheikhs in Persian Gulf states eager to please Jibril and thusly avoid only PFLP–GC operations on their soil. Many times such displays even brought in the odd recruit or two. These parades, however, never managed to accomplish their ultimate goal of frightening or impressing the Israelis in any way. In reality, these forces were Jibril's paper tigers—smartly dressed marching soldiers without any true combat experience or expertise; they were fighting men without a battlefield. In four months, things would change dramatically.

Lebanon's bloody civil war was not an immediate eruption of fanatic violence that was allowed to escalate to unimaginable horrors, but rather a slow and grinding death of a nation used as a battlefield by three of the region's principal powers. Tensions in Lebanon—a mercantile nation that thrived on narcotics, black market smuggling, the flesh trade, and liberal financial shelters for the rich—had been slowly simmering since 1968, when the PFLP used Beirut International Airport as the staging ground for its international terrorist offensive, and when the IDF retaliated with its December 27, 1968, Operation Gift destruction of thirteen Arab airliners on the Beirut tarmac. The Lebanese government and the Christian ruling elite feared that their lovely Mediterranean paradise was becoming an extended killing ground for the Arab-Israeli conflict, and duly dispatched the Christian-led Lebanese Army to check the growing armed Palestinian presence; they openly fought the fedayeen near Beirut and in the south opposite the Israeli frontier. Their efforts, however, were soon checked by the signing of the Cairo and Melkart Agreements, a disastrous pact for Lebanon engineered by Egyptian President Nasser which legitimized an armed Palestinian presence throughout much of the country. Through Nasser's intervention, a Palestinian ministate in southern Lebanon, similar to that which existed in Jordan, was signed into law. After the Ailul al-Aswad of September 1970, the ministate developed into a staging ground for thousands of heavily armed guerrillas.

The armed Palestinians quickly shifted Lebanon's delicate balance of racial power, which had been meticulously arranged by the French and which favored the minority Christians with control of the president's office, into a chaotic dash for alliances based on factional lines. The army and the various Christian militias, with Sheikh Pierre Gemayel's Phalangists in the vanguard, began to consolidate their territory and weapons supplies for the inevitable showdown to come. Kamal Jumblatt's powerful Druze militia in the Shouf mountains also prepared for war, as did virtually every other political and religious faction in the country. Lebanon's vast and diverse leftist groups, including Nasserites, pan-Arabists and Communists, also readied their troops for war, although their alliance with the Palestinians—the only faction to possess an inexhaustible supply of conventional weapons and ammunition—made their voice the strongest in the land; the Shiite Muslim majority, interestingly enough, had yet to awaken and assert itself politically or militarily.

Israel too was a contributing factor in the eventual disintegration of law and order in the land of the cedar. The IDF's pursuit of Palestinian terrorist targets in southern Lebanon throughout the early 1970's, the IDF's execution of numerous preemptive and retaliatory special operations deep inside Lebanese territory,[3] and IAF retaliatory strikes against terrorist targets throughout Lebanon severely destabilized the authority of the central government. Some of the harshest Israeli retributory actions came following the PFLP-GC's Qiryat Shmoneh massacre. Perhaps in fitting fashion, Lebanon would erupt on the first year anniversary of that bloodletting in northern Israel.

Sunday April 13, 1975, was a day of festivities and celebration throughout the slums and refugee camps of Muslim West Beirut. Thanks to Ahmed Jibril, Qiryat Shmoneh had joined Karameh as a victorious battlefield in the quest to liberate Palestine, where the path to freedom was paved with the blood of martyrs. In a typical display of celebration, heavily armed Palestinian gunmen fired their AK-47s wildly into the sunny Beirut sky; emptying magazineloads of 7.62-mm ammunition into the heavens was the camps' version of raising a glass of champagne or throwing confetti. Throughout West Beirut, Palestinian residents proudly displayed the crossed-rifle coat of arms of Jibril's PFLP-GC across their windows and storefronts in a respectful display honoring the first true strike in the age of revolutionary violence. Dozens of cars bearing the PFLP-GC logo raced through the streets of the Lebanese capital, honking their horns and terrorizing the city's non-Palestinians.

One such car full of gunmen celebrating the Qiryat Shmoneh massacre headed from the Mazra'a district toward the 'Ayn al-Rummana portion of the city, and toward a fateful incident that would eventually embroil the entire nation in inescapable violence.

On that same day, the Phalangist's spiritual commander and leader of their *Kata'eb* (Of the Book) political party, Sheikh Pierre Gemayel, was participating in a joyous event of an entirely different nature—the dedication of a new Maronite church in the 'Ayn al-Rummana district. Although traveling in a well-protected motorcade, Gemayel and his heavily armed Phalangist security officials were not expecting trouble that spring day. During the church ceremony the car with obscured license plates and carrying the jubilant PFLP-GC supporters crashed through a defensive barrier outside the church and fired several dozen shots at the crowd. Although Pierre Gemayel was not hurt in the volley of bullets, four men died, including a senior ranking member of the *Keta'eb* party.[4] The audacity of the attack was paramount to the attempted killing of a national leader; with their vast political influence and control over Lebanon's illicit narcotics and smuggling enterprises, the Gemayel clan did, indeed, rule much of Lebanon. The Maronite Christians viewed the volley of bullets directed toward Pierre Gemayel as a serious threat to a thousand-year Maronite presence in the region. Retaliation would be swift.

Throughout Christian East Beirut, news of the shooting in 'Ayn al-Rummana spread like the coming of the plague. Residents closed shops, produced weapons from their closets, and prepared to battle the destructive and divisive Palestinian presence in their land.

Later that day, a bus full of PFLP-GC gunmen* from the Mazra'a district headed toward the sprawling Tel al-Za'atar refugee camp east of the city.[5] The Christians, fearing further Palestinian attacks, were waiting in ambush—their Belgian-produced FN 7.62-mm assault rifles and .30-caliber machine guns were fully loaded, locked, and readied for action. When the PFLP-GC bus approached the ambush position, it was clear to the Phalangist commanders that a *second* Palestinian attack was under way. They ordered their men to fire. After ten minutes of incessant gunfire, twenty-seven Palestinians were dead; a further nineteen were wounded in the melee.

At 1830 hours, as the sun began to set on the shimmering Mediterranean Sea, bazookas and heavy machine guns were used in the close-quarters street battles that now raged between Christians and Palestinian Muslims. Roadblocks soon sprang up on corners opposite exclusive shops carrying the merchandise of Gucci and Pierre Cardin, machine-gun nests were set up adjacent to parked Rolls Royces, and sandbags surrounded the entrance to grand casinos where the rich and powerful had played less than twelve hours earlier. Battles were under way in the northern port city of Tripoli, in the resort town of Byblos, and in the Christian town of Zahle in eastern Lebanon's Bekaa Valley. Full-scale war had now gripped a once peaceful land.

Although a civil war, the bloodletting in Lebanon was clearly a Palestinian-inspired, -instigated, and -dominated conflict. PLO second-in-command Abu Iyad even went so far as to claim that "The road to Palestine leads through Aintoura, Mtein, and Jounieh"—three of the largest centers of Lebanese Christendom.[6] Nevertheless, this was not a war that the Palestinians needed or wanted. It was particularly disastrous for PLO chairman Yasir Arafat. His campaign to make the PLO a legitimate political and diplomatic entity would be a difficult sell in the capitals of Europe while his legions in Lebanon were fighting close-quarter battles for control of street corners and alleyways. In public, Arafat vilified the outbreak of factional fighting as an Arab tragedy and a senseless diversion to the true objective of destroying Israel; in

---

* It has been impossible to confirm whether or not the bus was carrying actual PFLP-GC guerrillas, but several eyewitnesses to the bus shooting were reported as saying that the bus carried "Jibril's men." The vehicle's registration plate number, "95303," belonged to a Jibril lieutenant and PFLP-GC emblems decorated many of the vehicle's windows.

Lebanon, however, he ordered his men to carry out the struggle to its ultimate and bloody end. Perhaps Abu Iyad's sentiments should have never been made public, but his statement accurately depicted Palestinian military strategy. The road to Palestine, indeed, passed through Lebanon, but at what cost?

Ahmed Jibril ordered the 1974 raid on Qiryat Shmoneh to sabotage the Palestinians' flirtation with the peace process. Through such acts, the PFLP-GC was determined to prevent the policy-makers within the Arab world from seeking an agreement that might allow for the establishment of an independent Palestinian state in *only* the territories captured by Israel in the 1967 war; a PFLP-GC communiqué issued sometime after the raid stated, "The operation at Qiryat Shmoneh was carried out to underline that *our* liberation struggle is not limited to the West Bank or Gaza, but covers all Palestinian territory."[7] In ominous fashion, the ghost of Qiryat Shmoneh would not only make Ahmed Jibril a wanted—and hunted—man, but eventually, through acts of Israeli retaliation and the actual outbreak of hostilities on April 13, 1975, plant the seeds for open fratricide in Lebanon, and among the Palestinians as well. Jibril had torpedoed the peace process and, simultaneously, weakened the Palestinians' conventional military potential forever.

In 1975, Yasir Arafat's problems were not only with the Lebanese. Since 1973 and the creation of the Jibril-led Rejection Front, the pieces in the once rock-solid PLO puzzle were quickly falling out of place. In 1973, a young Fatah lieutenant serving out of the PLO's Baghdad office named Sabri al-Banna, better known to the world by his nom de guerre of Abu Nidal, formed the Fatah Revolutionary Council,* an anti-Arafat organization dedicated to ridding the world of all Palestinian leaders about to embark on a peace with Israel. A veteran Fatah officer who had been something of a prodigy in the organization by commanding a station office in ultrastrategic Khartoum, Sudan, Abu Nidal had always displayed a uniquely independent and extremely violent style. When he was transferred to Iraq the close-knit relationship he forged with the Iraqi Muchabarat developed into a full-scale alliance.[8] With Iraqi

---

* The Abu Nidal Faction, as it was also known, also operates under the names Black June (a later reference to the month in which the Syrian Army invaded Lebanon on behalf of the beleaguered Christian forces), the Revolutionary Organization of Socialist Muslims, Black September, Arab Revolutionary Brigades, and Egyptian Revolution.

money, arms, and support, Abu Nidal made the break with Arafat, vowing to rid the PLO of its treacherous leader.

Common sense would have had Abu Nidal and Ahmed Jibril working closely together in pursuit of an Arafat defeat, but the rivalry between Iraq, and Syria, the PFLP-GC's patron saint, made such an alliance impossible. In fact, the Fatah Revolutionary Council's first operations were not against the PLO, nor against Israel, but against the Syrians: on September 25, 1976, three FRC terrorists, operating under the organizational nom de guerre of Black June, seized the Samir Amis Hotel in Damascus and took ninety hostages. They killed four and wounded thirty-four before Syrian commandos assaulted the building. The historic Middle East saying of "The enemy of my enemy is my friend" did not apply with the Palestinians. When civil war broke out in Lebanon, the Palestinians fought as a block against the Christian militias and much of the Lebanese Army, but each organization always looked out for its interests first, and Ahmed Jibril was the most independent minded of all the Palestinian leaders.* Realizing his men had conventional experience but were few in number, Jibril forged an alliance with the Sunni Muslim *Mourabitoun* [or "Ambushers"] militia commanded by Ibrahim Koleilat, and the combined forces launched a fierce offensive against the Christian sections of Beirut.[9]

For the next ten months, Lebanon became hell on earth. The battles waged on the streets of Beirut, inside the Palestinian refugee camps, and throughout the country's principal cities were among the most brutal ever waged in the Middle East—a region beset by violence for well over half a century; the urban melees fought along Beirut's Green Line, the avenue separating Muslim West Beirut from the Christian Eastern half, made the point-blank ferocity of Amman, Jordan, during Black September look like a debutante tea party.[11] Even though the outbreak of the Lebanese civil war caught the Israeli intelligence community largely by surprise, Israel remained a nonparticipant and did not contribute arms or finances to any of the fighting factions; it had dispatched a Mossad fact-finding team to examine the possibilities of an Israeli-Christian alliance in the region.

---

* Just because his group was waging a full-scale war in Lebanon did not mean that operations against Israel had been suspended. On September 4, 1976, the PFLP-GC mounted a unique operation when three gunmen hijacked a KLM aircraft carrying eighty-four passengers from Madrid to Amsterdam and diverted toward Israeli air space, demanding to land at Ben-Gurion International Airport. When Israel refused, the hijackers lost hope and ordered the aircraft to Cyprus, where they surrendered to Libyan authorities.[10]

Syria, however, was another story.

As far as Damascus was concerned, the "troubles" in Lebanon were nothing more than a nuisance and an opportunity, provided that the fighting remained even-handed and one side did not assume dominant control of the country. The Syrian Ba'ath party considered Lebanon to be a mere extension of greater Syria, a land mass including all of Lebanon and much of northern Israel and Jordan; whatever weakened Lebanon, such as the civil war, would prove in the end to be in Syria's national interest. As the fighting intensified throughout the country, however, the Christian-dominated Lebanese Army began to lose more and more ground to the Joint Forces—a loose conglomerate of Muslim forces that included all of the Palestinian organizations (including a loosely established alliance between the 20,000-strong Fatah group and the Rejection Front), the Lebanese leftists and Communists, the Druze Progressive Socialist party and its militia, the National Social party (the ex-Syrian Popular party), the Lebanese Arab Army, and a whole host of small militias, private army and street gangs turned into minimilitary units; all together, these forces exceeded thirty-five thousand combatants.[12]

To the outside world, Syria appeared to play the role of the mediator, pursuing a quick termination of the senseless violence. In reality, however, Syria played an indirect role in the combat when it began to dispatch elements of the Palestine Liberation Army* as well as units from as-Sa'iqa into the fray on December 26, 1975. President Hafaz al-Assad watched the madness from the sidelines and waited with cunning guile until the time was right for decisive action. He observed as the primitive street fighting involving men wearing hoods to conceal their identities evolved into artillery sieges and all-night *Katyusha* rocket barrages. Damascus quietly observed as the conflict dragged into a year-long exercise in butchery. Efforts were attempted to bring the fighting to a halt—particularly by Phalangist militia commander Bashir Gemayel and PLO intelligence chief Ali Hassan Salameh (the infamous Red Prince responsible for planning Black September's Munich Olympics Massacre) who tried to reach lasting cease-fire arrangements; both men, incidentally, were also bankrolled operatives of

---

* The PLA was created in June 1964 in Jordanian East Jerusalem to be the conventional arm of the Palestinian liberation movement. It was to be trained, supported, and part of a patron Arab nation. PLA units existed in the Egyptian, Jordanian, and especially Syrian armed forces. More often than not, however, the PLA was corrupted into a force of mercenaries and cannon fodder sacrificed for special and extremely distasteful military tasks. Its order of battle consists of approximately four thousand troops divided into three brigades (the *Ein Jalut*, the *Alqadisiya*, and the *Hittin*), and three battalions.[13]

the Central Intelligence Agency (CIA).[14] Some infraction, however, usually Syrian-manipulated, always managed to erupt and the guns were never allowed to fall silent for very long. The Palestinians proved to be too formidable a foe for the disorganized, bickering, and poorly led Christian forces. Syria's stakes increased as it meticulously attempted to influence the course of the fighting through its leverage over Lebanese political parties (and their militias), as well as the Palestinian movements under its controlling influence.

Beyond its command over the PLA and as-Sa'iqa, Syrian dominance over the PFLP-GC in Lebanon was absolute: Jibril had proved to be Syria's most potent spark plug in instigating and prolonging the troubles. The PFLP-GC was the first group to go on the offensive against the Christians, and the first to reinstate the Lebanese tradition of kidnapping.

On June 29, 1975, six days after the summer cease-fire was supposed to have gone into effect, Colonel Ernest R. Morgan, the American military attaché in Lebanon, was kidnapped outside the embassy building. Ostensibly he was held by a group calling itself the Revolutionary Socialist Action Organization; in reality, it was the PFLP-GC, using an alias as a means to avoid possible American retribution.[15] Colonel Morgan was kidnapped in order to secure food and supplies to the besieged Palestinian section of Quarantina, which had been hit hard by Christian forces and eventually became a slaughterhouse. The kidnapping, however, marked a serious internal struggle within the Palestinian camp. For two weeks, Arafat had pleaded with Jibril to release his hostage, claiming that taking a hostage, especially an American, did nothing to further the Palestinian cause. Reports even indicate that Arafat had ordered a special unit of his Force 17 Praetorian guard to prepare a rescue assault on a PFLP-GC safe house where Colonel Morgan was believed to have been held. Jibril hated Arafat more than he did the Christian militias and vowed to hold the colonel for as long as the PFLP-GC saw fit. Eventually Jibril was put in his place by Damascus and forced to acquiesce. Colonel Morgan was released two weeks later, unharmed. *

---

* Most kidnap victims in Lebanon were not so lucky. Lebanese hostages, both Christian and Muslim, were usually beaten mercilessly and tortured before either being released (once a hefty ransom had been paid) or executed. Hundreds of individuals simply disappeared off of the nation's streets never to be seen again. Colonel Morgan's lucky fate was best illustrated on June 16, 1976, when Francis Meloy, the U.S. Ambassador to Lebanon, his economic advisor, and his driver were kidnapped by Fatah gunmen and murdered hours later. The men responsible were later promoted by Yasir Arafat and given commissions with conventional PLO units operating in southern Lebanon.[16]

PFLP-GC prowess on the battlefield was nevertheless impressive. During the battles for the D'bayah Palestinian refugee camp (near the Christian port of Jounieh) and the shantytown of Quarantina (which commanded the main road from the Christian area of Beirut toward the Christian heartland in northeastern Lebanon), the small contingent of PFLP-GC fighters proved formidable urban warriors. Trained in Syria, Libya, and South Yemen and instructed by the most capable military minds the Soviets, Cubans, East Germans, and North Koreans[17] could spare, Jibril's legions were as adept in an urban shootout as they were crossing the border into Israel to seize hostages. Trained as commandos, their ability to slink across a no-man's-land with speed and firepower rivaled that of any Arab special-forces unit. They also proved most lethal in the close-quarters house-to-house and room-to-room fighting that typified much of the civil war combat and took a heavy toll on the advancing Christian forces. When the Palestinians assumed the offensive in January 1976, assaulting the Christian-populated towns of Damur and Jiyeh, PFLP-GC units were in the vanguard. Although important centers of Christian life along Lebanon's Mediterranean coast, both towns were quickly overrun and pillaged. The subsequent massacre of more than five hundred Christian civilians in Damur came to symbolize much of the horror of the civil war. The PFLP-GC quickly established a large training facility near Damur, a few miles inland at al-Na'ameh.

Jibril even became an example to his men when, according to the legend, he participated in the fighting for Beirut's hotel district in April 1976. He was wounded in the leg in the close-quarters fighting that gripped the city and had to undergo emergency medical treatment at a Palestinian clinic nearby.

Yet it was during the battle for the Palestinian refugee camp of Tel al-Za'atar (Hill of Thyme), along the eastern half of Beirut, where the PFLP-GC proved its true combat capabilities. Unlike many of the other refugee camps in Lebanon that counted Palestinian, Armenian, Kurds, and Shiites among its population, Tel al-Za'atar was virtually a Palestinian minicity; it was one of the country's most sprawling camps with a population of nearly 35,000 residents. It was once a peaceful camp but had the misfortune of being turned into an armed camp by the PLO in 1970. Due to its location on a strategic plateau controlling a portion of the Beirut-Damascus highway, the most important roadway in all of Lebanon, it also became a Christian objective.

Control of the camp was divided into five autonomous zones, each

managed by a different Palestinian faction. Fatah controlled a neighborhood, as did the PFLP, Hawatmeh's DFLP, as-Sa'iqa, and, of course, the
PFLP-GC.[18] Residents paid a hefty extortion tax to the group controlling the area in exchange for protection against the very real danger of
disappearing, and the various groups recruited heavily from the camp's
residents. Oddly enough, Tel al-Za'atar was a peaceful, though terribly
squalid, camp. At the outbreak of the factional fighting in Beirut, the
Palestinians quickly turned the facility into a fortress. Barricades were
established, and tank traps and gun positions were placed at vital
intersections. Soviet-produced Douchka 12.7-mm heavy machine gun
nests soon appeared on building roofs, including the roof of a nursery
run by Maronite nuns for abandoned babies.

While Fatah and the remaining contingents prepared to fight for the
high ground, the PFLP-GC dug. Perhaps taking a page out of the history
books their North Vietnamese instructors had given them, PFLP-GC
officers ordered their men to dig deep communications and storage
tunnels underneath the camp's streets.* Ahmed Jibril had become
obsessed with tunnels and the prospects of waging a campaign, perhaps
even one day against the Israelis, underground. He had read the stories
of the Vietcong and North Vietnamese Army's success with tunnels as
underground fire bases, arms caches, and staging areas, and their appli-
cation to the Lebanese theater of operations intrigued him. His subter-
ranean fascination would come in most handy.

The siege of Tel al-Za'atar began on January 1, 1976, when 300
militiamen from the *Tanzim*, a small and fanatic Christian group,
manned positions just outside the camp gate and began intercepting
the food supplies. This blockade lasted, on a small scale, for nearly six
months. The Christians' war had not been going well, and safeguarding
their half of the Lebanese capital, as a gateway toward the remainder of
the country, was a final and pragmatic option. Many of the Palestinian
residents tried to leave the impending troubles, but the PLO prevented
them from leaving—often at gunpoint. As the Christian hold on
Lebanon grew more and more tenuous, the siege grew in its intensity
and scope. On June 1, 1976, the Syrian Army "invaded" Lebanon to aid
the Christians by moving into the Bekaa Valley and then advancing on

---

* If several unconfirmed intelligence reports can be believed, then North Vietnamese
advisors supervised the construction of the tunnels in Tel al-Za'atar as well as those
underneath the PFLP-GC's bases in al-Na'amah, Sultan Yaqoub, and several other
locations in Lebanon.[19]

the road toward Beirut; apparently President Assad feared the dawning of a Palestinian-controlled state emerging in his Greater Syria.[20] The influx of eight thousand Syrian troops and two hundred main battle tanks tipped the balance of power to the Christian side with thunderous immediacy. The PLO and their leftist Muslim allies mobilized to meet the Syrian invasion while the Christians moved in for the kill.

Tel al-Za'atar was surrounded by Christian units on June 22, 1976, and a devastating siege was laid for the next fifty-two days. According to several reports, the Christians were able to bring mighty artillery assets to bear in the siege, lobbing in as many as four thousand shells a day into the camp. While the PLO forces decided to engage the Christians head on, the PFLP-GC retreated to its caves, bunkers, and tunnels to wage a deliberate and brutal war of retaliation against the Christian gunners. Emerging from underground shelters,[21] PFLP-GC gunmen ambushed Christian patrols, killing numerous militiamen and taking quite a few prisoners; those captured were usually tortured and interrogated and then murdered—the Geneva Convention did not apply to civil wars. Jibril's men showed considerable discipline in the fighting but, after all, the young men who joined the PFLP-GC were dedicated pursuers of total war against Israel. They were more fighter than revolutionary. It was these martial qualities that Jibril sought.

What made the epic siege of Tel al-Za'atar so tragic—and ironic— was the fact that Syrian gunners assisted the Christians in their merciless bombardment. This situation was even more eerie when one considers the fact that the first of Israel's Mossad/A'man fact-finding tours to Lebanon to establish a close liaison with the Christian forces observed the siege.[22] On August 6, the Christians finally occupied the Tel al-Za'atar refugee camp following the fifty-two-day siege in which a reported 2,500 people were killed. After holding out for as long as their dwindling ammunition supplies would allow, the last PFLP-GC fighters slipped out of the camp under cover of darkness to bases in the Bekaa Valley. The siege of Tel al-Za'atar remains a tragic chapter in Lebanese history. Many attribute the Palestinians' impressive stand to the tenacious, even suicidal, PFLP-GC fighters.

Syrian realpolitik in Lebanon was a severe blow to Ahmed Jibril, who spent much of the civil war in Damascus. It eventually turned Palestinian against Palestinian in a mini-civil war of their own that, in one way or another, continues to this very day.

During the siege of Tel al-Za'atar, for example, Fatah units openly engaged as-Sa'iqa forces throughout West Beirut; Fatah firefights against PLA units were also reported. The most vicious fratricide existed between Arafat's men and the PFLP-GC. Jibril could not hide his loathing of Arafat, and the Syrian invasion prompted the entire Palestinian revolution to draw up sides—those who supported Damascus, and those who did not. It was an extremely bloody mess.

Ahmed Jibril's loyalty to Syria did not sit well with many of his men, especially operations chief and principal spokesman Abu A'bbas. Jibril's prodigy had spent nearly a decade learning the art of terrorism and waging the conflict of revolutionary violence; he had learned that manipulation of the movement by any Arab state was a greater danger to the realization of a Palestinian homeland than the existence of the State of Israel. A'bbas viewed Syrian intervention and the subsequent violent expulsion of Palestinian fighters from their strongholds as treason, a task the Syrians attended to with untold brutality and a level of violence they had never brought to bare even against the Israelis. In their advance through the mountains toward Beirut and then south toward Damur and Sidon, Syrian tank gunners used their 100-mm and 115-mm main cannons in point-blank barrages against Palestinian villages and defensive outposts: In the Ein el-Hilweh refugee camp, the Syrians used multiple barrel ZSU-23s, antiaircraft weapons able to spew out a devastating eight hundred to a thousand rounds of 23-mm ammunition a minute, to root out snipers from crowded buildings. The Syrians had betrayed the Palestinians, and Abu A'bbas would have none of it. With the Iraqis eagerly waiting in the wings, A'bbas decided to do the unthinkable—to break away from Jibril.

On April 24, 1977, Abu A'bbas announced the formation of the Palestine Liberation Front (PLF)—a separate pro-Iraqi Palestinian group that pledged its support to PLO chairman Yasir Arafat.[23] The PLF also had as one of its primary objectives the destruction of Jibril's PFLP-GC; the fact that A'bbas took the name of Jibril's first organization as his own was evidence of the sudden hatred that had emerged between teacher and pupil. A'bbas lured many of Jibril's most capable officers, especially those responsible for special operations, with promises of Iraqi petrodollars and luxurious living conditions for their men and their families. Jibril responded by ordering PFLP-GC defectors killed by the death squads that roamed much of Lebanon. A'bbas had, indeed, owed much to Ahmed Jibril, and the pudgy terrorist chieftain would borrow much from the genius of his master in the years to come. But now the battle lines, in a land already scared by senseless brutality, had been drawn. It was, in effect, a war for the heart and soul of the Palestinian revolution, fought by Iraq and Syria with Palestinian blood.* It was a conflict Ahmed Jibril vowed to win through merciless bloodshed.

Although Palestinian on Palestinian violence was common from the creation of fedayeen in the Gaza Strip and West Bank in the early 1950s, the PFLP-GC-PLF war, which eventually engulfed the remaining Palestinian organizations, was shocking in its brutality. In some cases, the extent of the violence was controlled, such as the PFLP-GC's sinking of the S.S. *Spyros*, a Famagusta (Cyprus)-registered freighter that Jibril believed was carrying Libyan arms headed for A'bbas's men.** Jibril realized that the arms shipment could seriously alter the balance of power, and he sent his Syrian-trained frogmen to plant limpet mines to the ship's hull.[25] The loss of the weapons was a serious blow to A'bbas, as his military campaign against Ahmed Jibril was achieving little other than significant loss of life to his meager legions.

As a course of organizational policy, most PFLP-GC loyalists had been sent behind the Iron Curtain to undergo conventional military courses. The Syrians had seen to it that *their* Palestinians were expertly trained, but so had the Iraqis. Fighting even erupted between the pro-Iraqi Fatah and the PFLP-GC, eventually consuming other Syrian-controlled movements, such as as-Sa'iqa and the PLA. Abu A'bbas attempted to assume command of the anti-Jibril forces, but, like everything else plaguing Palestinian politics, discourse plagued even their own civil war. The Iraqi Muchabarat, through its proxy terrorist army the Arab Liberation Front, attempted to seize the spiritual and military leadership of the Palestinian revolution through veiled promises that the road to Palestine passed through Baghdad.† In the squalid Ein el-Hilweh refugee camp near Sidon, a camp already ravaged by the Lebanese civil war and Syria's summer offensive of 1976, ferocious battles erupted between the ALF and the PFLP-GC. According to U.S.

---

* The Iraqis had already been busily engaged in an anti-Syrian campaign by its financing of Abu Nidal operations worldwide. With a yearly salary of $10 million and 200 expertly trained fedayeen and sleeper-cell terrorists, Abu Nidal became the most lethal instrument of Iraqi revenge against Syrian individuals, and non-Rejection Front Palestinians.[24]

** Most of Jibril's weapon and ammunition shipments came overland via the Beirut-Damascus highway, or via ship, usually through Bulgarian vessels.[26]

† The ALF would eventually make a name for itself on April 6, 1980, when a three-man terrorist squad crossed the Lebanese border and attacked the frontier settlement Kibbutz Misgav Am, seizing the nursery and taking hostage more than twenty infants. The nursery was eventually stormed by a squad from Sayeret Mat'kal and Sayeret Golani. The terrorists were killed.

intelligence reports in summaries published by the Defense Intelligence Agency, the ALF-PFLP-GC battles were the most savage ever fought in Lebanon.

The means of infighting ranged from murder to senseless thievery. PFLP-GC insensitivity—and full-scale larceny—toward their fellow Palestinians was notorious throughout the refugee camps of Lebanon, and frequently documented. In his award-winning book *From Beirut to Jerusalem*, Pulitzer prize-winning journalist Thomas L. Friedman documents one such case where PFLP-GC gunmen, during the PLO's 1983 civil war in eastern and northern Lebanon, systematically looted the homes of Palestinian refugees in the Badawi camp in Tripoli. The women whose life's savings and world possessions were robbed by Jibril's men shouted, "Shame on you! We are not Jews, we are not Jews!" Extortion was the currency of the day as Palestinians and Lebanese businessmen alike paid thousands of pounds a week as protection money. Other times banks, such as the Banque de Syrie et du Liban, which stored Palestinian trust funds and pensions, were routinely looted by PFLP-GC forces.[27]

The Palestinians' internecine struggle reached its zenith on August 13, 1978, when PFLP-GC saboteurs, originally trained for missions inside Israel, prepared a Marwan Kreeshat-designed explosive device inside the West Beirut headquarters of the PLF. The building, a luxurious high-rise in an exclusive Beirut suburb, was the PLF's Pentagon; A'bbas had foolishly concentrated all his commanders and operational planners in one facility. It would be a fatal mistake. Just before noon, a tremendous blast ripped through the building. The explosion was so fierce that most Beirutis believed that a hellish earthquake had engulfed their beleaguered capital. The fireball and plume of black acrid smoke emanating from the crater that was once A'bbas's headquarters was seen for miles around. The death toll was equally horrific. More than two hundred PLF officers and fighters were killed in the explosion.[28] It was the singular most devastating day for the Palestinian terrorist organizations since the inception of the PLO in 1964; even the Israelis, in their incessant and often brutal counterterrorist campaign against the Palestinians, had never achieved such an enormous body count in a single day.

The Palestinians, through years of operations and foreign manipulation, had become too good at their terrorist trade for their own good; it appeared as if there were no boundaries to their violent ambitions and capabilities. The August 13 bombing jolted nearly every faction within the PLO, both Arafat supporters and members of the Rejection Front.

The tragedy was so enormous, the bloody toll so great, and the damage to the Palestinian cause so nearly irreversible, that Ahmed Jibril and Abu A'bbas decided to end their bloody war and resort to nonviolent means to settle internal Palestinian quarrels.

Remarkably, the factional fighting between Jibril and A'bbas was taking place against a unique and dramatic backdrop of large-scale Israeli involvement in Lebanon, a presence that would be a harbinger of things to come.

The spring of 1978 was a tumultuous and aggressive period for the Palestinians. Since November 1977, the historic implications of Egyptian President Anwar es-Sadat's pilgrimage of peace to Jerusalem had forced the PLO to realize that its worst nightmare, an Arab state embarking on a separate peace with Israel, was transpiring before its very eyes. Egypt, the undisputed leader of the Arab world and the most powerful of all Arab military forces, was now the largest traitor to the Palestinian cause. The PLO vowed to assassinate Anwar es-Sadat, instigate a civil war in Egypt that would make the carnage in Lebanon seem insignificant, and, most important, torpedo the peace negotiations. Remarkably, the raid would be led by a woman.

On March 11, 1978, fifteen Fatah terrorists crawled overboard a mothership moored just off of Israeli territorial waters and jumped into two Zodiac motorized rubber dinghies awaiting below. After examining their navigation equipment one last time, the terrorists lowered the motors into the black choppy waters of the Mediterranean and proceeded at full speed toward their target: the Tel Aviv suburb of Bat Yam, where they were supposed to seize a crowded hotel and hold the guests hostage in exchange for the release of hundreds of convicted Palestinian terrorists languishing in Israeli jails. Unfortunately for the terrorists, two members of the group drowned when they were dragged overboard and to the bottom of the murky depths by their heavy equipment. The terrorists had also grossly miscalculated their course, as they found themselves on the shores of Kibbutz Ma'agan Michael, an agricultural collective halfway between Tel Aviv and Haifa, nearly eighty miles from the intended target. Undaunted, the mission commander, a woman named Dalal Mughrabi, ordered the mission to continue ashore. After killing a nature photographer, they commandeered two busloads of Israeli holiday travelers, employees of the Egged national bus carrier, into one vehicle and raced toward Tel Aviv. They would never make it. Israeli security forces, including elite military units and the border guard's antiterrorist commando force, had set up a roadblock at the Country Club junction, approximately eleven kilometers outside the city limits. The subsequent standoff and inevitable bloodshed was shocking. The Country Club Massacre, as it became known, resulted in the deaths of thirty-five passengers and the wounding of seventy-one others; nine terrorists were killed in the fray.[29] It was the singular most devastating terrorist operation ever perpetrated against the Jewish State. It would not go unavenged.

Even though both American President Jimmy Carter and Egyptian President Sadat urged Israeli Prime Minister Menachem Begin to show restraint, Begin did not feel he could bury thirty-five of his fellow citizens without doing something. So on March 14, 1978, the IDF launched a mini-invasion into southern Lebanon, where, according to foreign reports, nearly twenty thousand troops crossed the border to "purify" the frontier area and push Palestinian terrorist bases across the Litani River—out of range, it was believed, of the Israeli border.[30] Operation Litani was primarily an IDF campaign against Fatah. In fact, other groups, especially the PFLP-GC, contributed little to the fighting—with the exception of one foreboding action.

In early April 1978, a PFLP-GC kidnapping squad seized Avraham Amram, an Israeli reservist operating a tractor in southern Lebanon. The objective of the kidnapping was to gain a hostage with which to barter at a later date. Jibril realized that his organization was in a dangerous transitional stage and needed a new direction and some new blood. It just so happened that the Israelis were holding someone Jibril wanted back very badly.

Details of the covert prisoner-exchange talks conducted by the IDF and Jibril's representatives remain classified. It is known that the talks were heated and took more than a year to bring about an agreement in principle; Jibril had originally demanded that Israel release 140 prisoners. In March 1979, the Israeli hostage was finally released in exchange for seventy-six Palestinian prisoners, all hard-core terrorists, including eight who had been sentenced to life in prison. Ten of the freed terrorists, including six women, were allowed to return to their homes in the West Bank; the remainder were flown to Libya. The sticking point in the most difficult of negotiations had been the release of Hafaz el-Dalkamoni,[31] the chief PFLP-GC bigwig in the Israeli high-security prison near Ashqelon and a man whom Jibril viewed as crucial to the expansion and very existence of the PFLP-GC. Indeed, Ahmed Jibril would show remarkable foresight.

The 1979 prisoner exchange was a controversial arrangement and, as dealing with kidnappers and killers went against official governmental policy, was heavily censored in Israel. As a nation of four million, Israel is a small country where the most ardent of leaders are relatively accessible figures. If the mother of an imprisoned soldier wishes to see the Prime Minister, she can obtain an audience. Pressure from the families of POWs can move mountains in political pressure and cause the government to operate with an emotional gun to its head. It was such pressure, according to *Jerusalem Post* defense writer Hirsh Goodman, that prompted Defense Minister Ezer Weizman to release the seventy-six men to Jibril in 1979.[32]

The dangerous precedent of doing business with terrorists had been set.

CHAPTER FIVE

THE WAR IN LEBANON: A SECOND TIME AROUND

THE LEBANESE CIVIL WAR had crippled the PFLP-GC's ability to mount meaningful operations against Israel along the northern frontier. Operations inside the occupied territories decreased in scale and scope, too, with sleeper cells left to wonder if they would ever be called into action. In fact, the PFLP-GC was reduced to carrying out indiscriminate bombing attacks that did little to advertise Jibril's military talents. The deadliest such incident occurred on July 4, 1975. Packed inside a discarded refrigerator outside the Cafe Alaska along Jerusalem's bustling Jaffa street were several kilograms of high explosives connected to a highly sophisticated timing device. The bomb exploded in a thunderous blast: fifteen passersby were killed and sixty-two wounded.[1] The Jerusalem bombing was the target of a massive police and security service investigation; bomb fragments that were recovered from the debris provided invaluable forensic clues. The bombing was the type of operation destined to bring police, army, and Shin Bet "heat" on the territories, security service pressure that Jibril had always tried to avoid inside the occupied territories. His concerns were justified. On February 7, 1977, the squad that carried out the bombing was apprehended by a Shin Bet task force.[2] The Shin Bet, the Hebrew acronym for *Sherut Ha'Bitachon Ha'Klali* (General Security Service), is Israel's version of the American FBI, a force of counterterrorists and counterintelligence agents determined to crush any terrorist cell operating inside Israeli-controlled territory.

The prisoner exchange Ahmed Jibril had managed to engineer with the Israelis helped him to reinstate his precarious position within the PLO, especially since most of the Palestinians released were Fatah terrorists, not Jibril loyalists. Nevertheless, Jibril understood that to place the misery of the civil war and the subsequent fratricidal fighting behind him, he had to make headlines. The PFLP-GC once again attempted to go international, but its networks, had been weakened during its inactive years. On June 20, 1980, Swedish security forces arrested two men at the Danish border who had planned to carry out a hit-and-run machine-gun attack against an El Al air crew at Copenhagen Airport.[3] Much of Jibril's Swedish and Scandinavian network was blown as a result of the botched attempt and subsequent police investigation, and his assets in northern Europe critically weakened.

The Swedish fiasco convinced the PFLP-GC hierarchy that the time was not yet right for overseas operations, and new safe houses had to be established in Malta, Greece, Yugoslavia, and, ominously, Germany for use at a later date. Yet the PFLP-GC continued to train its foreign brethren, primarily Ethiopians, members of the Irish Republican Army (IRA), and the Armenian Secret Army for the Liberation of Armenia in the Lebanese training facilities.[4] There was much work to be done at home.

The year 1980 was a time of dedicated rebuilding for the PFLP-GC. The carnage in Lebanon and the potential for full-scale Israeli military intervention in this, the final base of operations against the Jewish State, convinced the PFLP-GC that Fortress Lebanon needed to be reinforced. With generous Libyan aid, the PFLP-GC was able to assemble a formidable conventional arsenal in Lebanon—primarily in the Bekaa Valley and al-Na'ameh facilities. Beyond its possession of more AK-47s and RPGs than the group could ever hope to deploy in battle, the PFLP-GC began to absorb sophisticated Soviet-bloc arms as well. These included North Korean 122-mm multiple rocket launchers,* AT-3 Sagger wire-guided antitank missiles, and SA-7 Strella handheld surface-to-air missiles.

The Soviets, however, were by far the PFLP-GC's most generous contributor. During Operation Litani, for example, the Soviets began

---

* For one reason or another, the North Koreans attempted to hide their military relationship with the various Palestinian groups. Following Operation Peace for Galilee, Israeli forces uncovered North Korean arms shipments packaged inside crates marked AGRICULTURAL EQUIPMENT.[5]

large-scale open shipments of arms. According to several reports, dozens of Soviet and Bulgarian freighters docked in Lebanese and Syrian ports and unloaded cases of brand-new AK assault rifles, RPGs, and 23-mm antiaircraft guns.[6] Ominously, the Soviets also supplied the PFLP-GC with the most sophisticated infrared and night-scope equipment in its arsenal; some of these scopes and gadgets were top-of-the-line items that had only just entered service with Soviet special forces.

The Soviets also supplied conventional military training to many PFLP-GC personnel in top-secret camps located near Moscow and around the Black Sea. The Soviet installations were far superior to the camps in South Yemen and Libya. An army of well-seasoned *Spetsnaz* (Soviet Special Forces), KGB, and GRU experts taught the Palestinian trainees a wide assortment of military, intelligence, counterintelligence, and Communist instruction. Some of these lengthy and involved courses included incendiary charges and detonators; exploding metals; the do's and don'ts of sabotaging a munitions dump, defended bridges, and combat vehicles; high-speed and evasive driving; evade and escape tactics; how not to crack under Zionist interrogation; urban guerrilla strategy; marksmanship; camouflage and deception; and the A to Z of Soviet-produced weaponry.[7] An important course conducted in the camps was the political value of kidnapping, a tactic Jibril would learn to cherish in the years to come.

The terrorist-training facilities were spread throughout the Soviet Union, Czechoslovakia, East Germany, Poland, and Bulgaria. The recruits were shipped to these diverse areas under a veil of considerable secrecy but, remarkably, they were allowed to enter the surrounding towns on several occasions for rest-and-relaxation furloughs. Many tourists to these regions recall quaint rural areas suddenly flooded with Middle Eastern men speaking Arabic and wearing close-cropped military haircuts. Many Palestinians ended up in considerable trouble with the local authorities following incidents of smuggling foreign currency and narcotics, and practicing Islam, which the atheist Communists ridiculed. Many of the Palestinian "students" also found themselves acquainted for the first time with Russian and Polish vodka and Czech beer. Many got drunk and in serious legal trouble; they were then *conveniently* threatened with dismissal (and possible execution back in Lebanon), or worse, unless they agreed to work for the Soviets as deep-cover intelligence agents. Other Palestinians were entrapped by prostitutes on KGB, *Stasi*, and StB payroll, and recruited—or blackmailed—into spying for the Soviets and the Warsaw Pact.

These semi-conventional courses usually lasted six to eight months.

On graduation, the Palestinian trainee was issued a symbolic military rank, a certificate, and a class photograph. The Israelis learned of this connection in the incredible documentation they uncovered in Lebanon following the 1982 invasion, and found the papers welcome additions to their intelligence archives.

Much of the PFLP-GC's equipment and Soviet training had been paid for by the seemingly endless petrodollar profits of Libya's Muammar Qadaffi. Libya had been the only Arab state outside of Syria to invest large sums of cash and political support in Ahmed Jibril, and a return on their investment consisted of a unique military relationship that, many believed, was a Qadaffi-inspired powerplay designed to challenge Hafaz al-Assad's control of the PFLP-GC. Jibril's men were not only trained in Libya in the fine art of terrorism, but a few dozen PFLP-GC commandos were also offered the unique opportunity to train as combat fighter pilots; they received instruction in the Soviet Union and Eastern bloc, and became on-loan commissioned officers in the *Al Quwwat al Jawwiya al Libiyya*, Libya's Air Force, where they flew MiG-23 Floggers and Tupelov Tu-22 Blinder bombers. The "PFLP-GC pilots for hire" proved to be extremely capable jet drivers, often outperforming their Libyan comrades in air-to-air and ground-strike maneuvers.* According to several reports, these pilots served with considerable success in Chad, as did PFLP-GC special-operations commando squads that Jibril was forced to send to Libya as part of his financial pact with Qadaffi.[9] Libya also provided PFLP-GC units with the then top-of-the-line Soviet-produced SA-9 Gaskin surface-to-air missile system; it is usually seen with a multiple-launcher apparatus and is mounted on a BRDM-2A amphibious scout car. The Soviets, who only provided their client-states of Syria, Iraq, and Libya with the missile, did not really want the SA-9 being handed out to the Palestinians. They feared the secret missile systems would eventually be captured in combat by the IDF and turned over to experts from the North

---

* Yasir Arafat's Fatah also maintains the cadre of Palestinian Air Force in an airborne unit called Force 14. A relatively small element of Fatah, Force 14 consists of approximately two hundred fighters, all equipped with civilian and military pilot licenses. Created in the late 1960s as an aerial-transport service to ferry Palestinian fighters to and from their bases in the Arab world, Force 14 eventually evolved into a combat arm. Palestinian pilots were trained in the Soviet Union, the Eastern bloc, Cuba, and North Korea. Their aircraft included Dutch Fokker 27 transports (ostensibly crammed with explosives to serve as kamikaze craft), American Bell-206 Jet Rangers helicopters, and Soviet-produced MiG-21 Fishbed jet fighters; according to intelligence reports, Force 14 pilots are also MiG-23-proficient. Their principal base is in Yemen, at the outer limits of IAF range.[8]

Atlantic Treaty Organization for further analysis.[10] Qadaffi claimed that the PFLP-GC desperately needed this antiaircraft defense system to protect its Lebanese bases against Israeli air attack, and scoffed at the idea that Jibril's capable commandos would ever allow the Israelis to get their hands on these top-secret weapons.

Jibril's "conventionalization" of his organization showed considerable foresight, because it was obvious to all that Lebanon would soon be the flashpoint of a major conventional Israeli-Palestinian war. By 1981, all the military/terrorist groups within the Palestine Liberation Organization, including the PFLP-GC and the Rejection Front, maintained nearly twenty thousand fully armed fighters in Lebanon (Arafat's Fatah group comprised the largest military bloc, with more than fourteen thousand fighters); they were spread out from positions only yards away from the Israeli frontier to the northern port city of Tripoli and the snowcapped mountains in the northeast. These heavily armed men and women would be desperately needed. Tensions between the Palestinians in Lebanon and the Israelis were coming to a head in spring 1981.

Since March 1978, one of Israel's principal national-security concerns was southern Lebanon. The Country Club Massacre proved to many high-ranking Israeli officials that a highly malignant presence was forming on the northern tier, and unless it were removed altogether, or at least contained, it could eventually unleash untold havoc inside Israel proper. Indeed, the Israeli Defense Ministry had gone to great lengths to insure that southern Lebanon did not become a true staging area for the destruction of Israel. Following Operation Litani, the IDF helped to establish a small, highly motivated Lebanese militia. Commanded by the renegade Christian Major Sa'ad Haddad, the ragtag force included Christian and Shiite residents of southern Lebanon. This Free Lebanese Army, completely trained and armed by Israel,* was assigned not only to protect their own homes, businesses, and lands from marauding Palestinian raiders, but also to provide an armed buffer between the Litani River and the Israeli frontier. When the IDF withdrew to its international border on June 30, Major Haddad's Free Lebanon Zone became a continuous ten-to-fifteen kilometer stretch of terrain from the Mediterranean shore to the base of Mount Hermon in the notorious "Fatahland" quadrant.

The intended compliment to this homegrown remedy to the expand-

---

* Haddad was also supported financially—and spiritually—by evangelical Christian groups, in the United States, including Pat Robertson's 700 Club.

ing Palestinian presence in southern Lebanon was the United Nations Interim Force in Lebanon (UNIFIL). The United Nations' blue-beret peacekeepers were mandated with impartial force separation, but more often than not they openly assisted armed Palestinians heading toward Israel. Bored, lonely, and in a land not known for supporting peace-keepers, many UNIFIL soldiers were courted by the Palestinians, and some were even recruited as active operational agents.[11] In one in-stance, a Nigerian major who had commanded a UNIFIL contingent was arrested inside Israel with a trunkload of weapons destined for terrorist cells on the West Bank.

The face-off between the Israelis and Haddad's army against the Palestinians and U.N. troops was a campaign in which agent running, intelligence-gathering operations, assassinations, and tradecraft dirty tricks were commonplace. It truly was a dirty little war in the guerrilla-infested hills, where incessant violence prevailed. Miraculously, how-ever, the situation had yet to deteriorate into open, all-round fighting. A delicate balance of power with trip-wire tension remained in place for the moment.

Syria was to be a major player in the southern Lebanon sweepstakes too; its flip-flop intervention policy in Lebanon had proved difficult to follow and predict, but it was effective nonetheless. When Syrian mili-tary intervention helped push the balance of power well into the Chris-tians' favor, they once again changed sides and supported the Palestinians. These dramatic developments helped the Israelis and Christian Phalangists to forge a close-knit military relationship; it soon developed into a controversial and unscrupulous military and political alliance. The first contact occurred on April 12, 1976, when an A'man operation helped bring a senior Phalangist officer to Israel.[12] Over the course of the next five years, Israel's investment in the Phalan-gists was remarkable. Both the Mossad and the A'man sent representa-tives to Lebanon, Phalangist officers covertly received IDF training and equipment, and, following the surprise election to power of Prime Minister Begin's right-wing Likud party, *overt* political and military support headed from Jerusalem to East Beirut. Even though the Phalan-gists were just as fratricidal as the Palestinians, and most A'man esti-mates viewed them as unappealing and dangerous allies, Israel pinned its Lebanon strategy on the Christians.

The first true signs of impending conflict came in December 1980, when the Phalangists reclaimed the city of Zahle, the Christian capital of the Bekaa Valley, following heavy fighting with Syrian forces. With its thirty thousand-man garrison in Lebanon, the Syrians were clearly a dominant power in the country, and many believed that the Phalangists attacked Zahle to draw Israel into war. The Syrians duly laid siege to the town, as a punitive measure, not a strategic one, in order to punish the Christians, not to seize it, and they also sent a message to the Israelis that they did not want to fight the IDF. Syrian combat engineers dug out several emplacements for mobile SA-6 Gainful surface-to-air batteries in the Bekaa Valley; the fact that mobile weapons were being placed in fixed positions was a signal to Israel that should Israel intervene on the Christians' behalf, the missiles could be moved in to cover areas of Lebanon frequently flown by the IAF.[13] On April 28, 1981, two IAF F-16 Fighting Falcons blew a Syrian Air Force Mi-8 Hip transport out of the sky over Zahle. Damascus responded quickly by sending the missiles to Lebanon. Only American diplomatic efforts, led by special ambassador Philip Habib, helped avert a full-scale war.

The push for war continued, however. On July 14, 1981, a Syrian Air Force MiG-23 was blown out of the sky as it attempted to intercept IAF fighters bombing PLO camps in southern Lebanon. This time, the Palestinians responded—bombing the northern city of Nahariya with an incessant 130-mm artillery barrage and a slew of Katyusha rockets. Much of the Galilee region of northern Israel was forced to spend tense nights in underground bomb shelters. On July 17, the IAF retaliated with an air raid on the Beirut headquarters of Fatah and Nayif Hawatmeh's DFLP—attacks, in which nearly one hundred people were killed.[14] Palestinian units in southern Lebanon, including PFLP-GC artillery formations operating under Syrian directives, opened up with fierce cannon and rocket barrages against Galilee; the bombardment was incessant and lasted for ten full days. The psychological and physical damage to towns like Qiryat Shmoneh and Ma'alot was ravaging. The situation was so volatile that the United States government sent a special envoy to the region led by Ambassador Habib to arrange a ceasefire and a disengagement agreement in the desperate bid to prevent war.

Yasir Arafat realized that his forces were no match for the IDF in Lebanon. He also realized that Prime Minister Begin and his controversial defense minister Ariel "Arik" Sharon were determined to expel him and his legions from their Lebanese ministate and even take Beirut, no matter what the political cost. To buy time in the event of such an assault, Arafat created an army of last stand in the south, which was meant to stall any Israeli push to Beirut until international pressure could be brought to bear to halt the Israelis. In all, Arafat put together three conventional brigades: the Yarmouk, the Kastel, and the Karameh; a tank regiment consisting of obsolete T-34 World War II-era tanks from Romania and Hungary; as well as artillery batteries with Soviet 130-mm medium-range guns and North Korean Katyusha rocket launchers. The remaining Palestinian factions could field approximately eighty five hundred men in conventional units; the PFLP-GC, according to intelligence estimates, offered only nine hundred of its fighters for "Lebanon's" defense.[15]

All the players were gearing up for action in Lebanon, but Philip Habib's precarious peace was miraculously holding out. Jibril had been one of the few Palestinian leaders vehemently opposed to the cease-fire and, in fact, he tried to sabotage it by initiating attacks against Israel.[16] Jibril's lone-wolf campaign had nearly succeeded, as Israel prepared for a massive assault across the northern frontier right then and there. Remarkably, Arafat exerted the proper pressure on his Palestinian adversary and eventually secured Jibril's promise for acquiescence. He also dispatched heavily armed Fatah military policemen to surround PFLP-GC forward positions.

Israel's eventual 1982 Lebanon adventure was the culmination of three principal events in the region: the movement of the Palestinian base of terrorist operations from Jordan to Lebanon; the Lebanese civil war, with its end result being an apparently permanent Syrian military presence in the area and a resulting controversial and precarious military alliance between Israel and the Phalangists; and the signing of an Egyptian-Israeli peace treaty reached under the Camp David Accords. As far as Israel was concerned, the concentration of virtually all the Palestinian terrorist groups in Lebanon placed them in a position of tactical vulnerability where they could be decisively defeated through a dedicated military campaign. The Syrian presence in Lebanon made Israeli military intervention there a strategic necessity; not protecting this flank against a potential force of thirty thousand Syrian soldiers would have been national security suicide. Israel's newfound Christian allies provided the Jewish State with its first-ever military ally in the region—political and moral joint action that Israel had strived to achieve for nearly four decades. Finally, the new peace between Israel and Egypt allowed Israel to remove the most populated and most militarily potent Arab state from its enemies list. Lebanon was, indeed, poised for war to erupt. All that was needed was a spark.

On June 3, 1982, three gunmen from Abu Nidal's Fatah—the Revolutionary Council—ambushed Shlomoh Argov, Israel's ambassador to the Court of Saint James, outside the posh Dorchester Hotel in London.

In a flurry of gunfire, Argov lay critically wounded. The match had been struck.

It appears that the Abu Nidal attack in London was meant to provoke war, or military mischief of some kind. Abu Nidal's operations were controlled by Iraq, Syria's great rival in the Arab world, and it was in Baghdad's national interest to see a war in which the Israelis, Syrians, and Palestinians were all weakened. Abu Nidal, whose organization was a true anti-PLO/anti-Arafat group, was also keen to see Israel destroy the PLO so that he could emerge as the Palestinians' true leader. It is also believed, according to several Western intelligence sources, that Nidal had the foresight to see that any Israeli intrusion into Lebanon would be a self-destructive conflict much as Vietnam was to the United States. Israel, however, felt obliged to retaliate against the PLO in Lebanon. Prime Minister Menachem Begin, his judgement already usurped by Defense Minister "Arik" Sharon, would not listen to the Shin Bet officials who warned him that the group responsible for the shooting in London was not the regular PLO.

On June 4, at 1500 hours, a flight of IAF aircraft bombed the PLO's headquarters in West Beirut. The destruction was absolute and dozens were killed. Hours later, thousands of Palestinian artillery shells and Katyusha rockets slammed into Galilee. Several Israeli civilians were killed, and tens of thousands of Galilee residents were forced into their shelters. Prime Minister Begin vowed that Katyushas would no longer fall in Galilee.

At 1100 hours on the morning of June 6, the first Israeli armored units smashed across the barbed wire frontier separating Israel and Lebanon; according to foreign reports, the invasion force consisted of sixty thousand men.[17] Operation Peace for Galilee had begun.

Ostensibly, Operation Peace for Galilee was meant to push the Palestinians back to create a forty kilometer buffer zone with Israel. In truth, Israel had intended to push for Beirut all along. The invasion was a full-frontier assault waged along a three-tier axis: the coastal road, through the south-central highlands, and east toward a head-to-head clash with Syrian and Palestinian forces in the Bekaa Valley. At first it appeared as if this campaign was going to be another swift and decisive Israeli victory. The push along the Mediterranean proceeded quickly; many of Arafat's Fatah commanders had run at the first sighting of the Israeli onslaught. But the rank and file stayed behind to fight, sometimes to the last man, and the skirmishes around the Palestinian refugee camps that surrounded the ancient port city of Tyre were fierce and fought at close quarters. On June 7, the IDF/Navy mounted the largest amphibious operation in Israeli history when it ferried a near division-size force of paratroopers to the Awali River tributaries near Sidon.[18] After bitter fighting with Palestinian forces in the Ein el-Hilweh refugee camp (which was originally battered by the Syrians in 1976 and now defended by fanatic elements vowing to fight to the death) and the Casbah of Sidon, major IDF armored units linked up and pushed to seize the Damur and Beirut, while other elements prepared to engage the Syrians for control of the ultrastrategic Beirut-Damascus highway.

In the east, Israeli armored units cautiously pushed into the Bekaa Valley so as not to provoke the Syrians just yet; after all, Damascus still possessed nineteen Soviet-produced and, in many cases, Soviet-manned SA-6 Gainful surface-to-air missile batteries in the Bekaa Valley, which could exact a deadly toll on IAF aircraft. On June 9, however, the IAF mounted one of the most spectacular surprise attacks ever executed in the history of aerial warfare. Utilizing a whole host of electronic tricks, including the deployment of pilotless drones, the IAF was able to activate Syria's electronic battlefield before actually appearing in an engaging posture. They then pounced on the missile sites with devastating skill and effectiveness. When the Syrian Air Force attempted to intercept a seemingly indestructible force of Israeli fighter bombers, an equally devastating garrison of Israeli fighters were waiting for the kill. In epic air battles, in which there were a total of 150 Israeli and Syrian aircraft fighting it out with cannons and missile strikes, the IAF proved masters of the skies, their F-15s, F-16s, Phantoms, and Kfirs destroying dozens of MiGs and Sukhois. Over the course of the next few weeks, the Syrians would lose nearly one hundred aircraft to the IAF's MiG killers; the IAF would only lose two aircraft during the war, and both to Palestinians ground fire.[19]

Within one week of fighting, the IDF was at the gates of Beirut, pushing to cut off the Palestinians and Syrians in the city from reinforcements by slicing through the Beirut-Damascus highway. After much fierce fighting between Israeli armor and Syrian antitank commando units, the IDF laid siege to Beirut. The ultimate military objective of the siege was to oust the fifteen thousand Palestinian terrorists/guerrillas from the Lebanese capital (to Israelis the ultimate icon of PLO terror) and remove once and for all a terrorist presence from Israel's besieged northern frontier. Politically, the siege of Beirut was meant to help install Bashir Gemayel, the military commander of the Phalangists, as Lebanon's next president.[20] In more ways than one, Lebanon was becoming a controversial and deadly quagmire.

For the next two months, Israeli units slowly inched their way into the capital, while artillery and air units increased the pressure with incessant bombardments. It was the first military siege ever filmed live by international television crews, and the damage to Israel's public image as a result of the "via satellite carnage" was enormous. International political pressure too was pushing for a resolution and an end to Beirut's suffering. American Ambassador Philip Habib was once again called into the region to once again perform yet another miracle. Under tremendous political pressure, Habib managed to work out a deal where the Palestinian fighters would be allowed leave Beirut unmolested, as would Syrian troops trapped in the city. No matter how damaged, the PLO would not be physically destroyed, and Israel would achieve what it believed to be a total terrorist departure from Lebanon. Protection for the tens of thousands of Palestinian residents in the capital city would be handled by a multinational force (MNF) of American marines, French paratroops, and Italian infantrymen. It was a hard sell for Arafat, but it was the only workable solution for what remained of the once-formidable PLO military presence.

The decision to evacuate Beirut was a bitter pill for the PLO leadership to swallow. After years of promising to push the Jews into the sea, the Palestinians now found themselves being forced into the Mediterranean. Publicly they claimed that they had been forced to disperse through the failure of their allies to come to their aid.* In reality, all the groups within the PLO, including the PFLP-GC, played a significant role in the decision to withdraw.[21]

Between August 21 and September 1, a total of 14,938 Palestinian terrorists/guerrillas were evacuated from Beirut. Most of the Fatah, Arab Liberation Front, DFLP, and PLF units departed by sea to new exiles-in-training camps in Iraq, South Yemen, the Sudan, Jordan, and Tunisia, where Arafat's entourage would establish its new political and military worldwide headquarters. The Palestinian exodus was protected by the soldiers of the MNF and the watchful eyes of Israeli troops and intelligence officials eager to catch a glimpse of some of the world's

---

* Many would argue that the PLO had really betrayed its constituents in agreeing to the Habib deal. In deciding to withdraw from Beirut, the PLO decided to save itself rather than protect the Palestinian civilians of Beirut.

most-wanted terrorists.* The scene was eerie as tearful Palestinians boarded rusty Greek freighters for trips to nowhere and, in a mock celebration of victory, fired tens of thousands of rounds of small-arms ammunition into the air.

An equally eerie situation existed along the Beirut-Damascus highway, where the Syrian 85th Brigade, which had garrisoned Beirut, was allowed to return to Damascus. Israeli troops lined the busy thoroughfare and watched as tens of thousands of Syrian, PLA, and as-Sa'iqa troopers and terrorists boarded their Soviet-made vehicles for the slow and tortuous drive. Nearly one thousand PFLP-GC personnel were also evacuated to Syria. Most made their way via the land route, but several hundred boarded ships in Beirut and headed for the Syrian port of Tartus; one of those evacuees was a vengeful Ahmed Jibril, who had been in and around the city during the entire Israeli siege.[23]

From its prewar bravado it would have appeared as if the PFLP-GC was more than eager to spill some blood in a fight against the Israelis. In fact, prewar PFLP-GC communiqués proclaimed that the group would be in the vanguard of *all* anti-Zionist operations. Not only had Jibril's agents secured the acquisition of sophisticated night scopes and other bits of high-tech communications gear from the West, but they also commenced serious negotiations with arms manufacturers in Switzerland and Brazil to secure artillery pieces with ranges greater than forty kilometers.[24] Yet when the IDF pushed along the coastal road toward Beirut and into the Bekaa Valley, PFLP-GC units put up an ineffectual resistance. In many instances, units fired their AK-47s only a few times before running away as fast and as far as they could. According to one Israeli intelligence officer who served around the coastal sector, "When the shit hit the fan, the PFLP-GC disappeared into the wind to the protection of the Syrians, or took off their uniforms to blend into the local civilian population." For a group whose self-professed mandate was the dispensing of revolutionary violence, the PFLP-GC's performance during the war was pathetic. Most Fatah, PFLP, PLF, and DFLP officers could not fathom how a group with such an abundant supply of top-of-the-line weaponry and material could simply abandon the fight. In fact, PFLP-GC units even failed to protect the enormous ammunition dumps they had prepared in the al-

---

* According to several accounts, an Israeli sniper team had kept several key PLO officials, including Yasir Arafat, through the cross hairs of their high-powered sniper rifles, as they departed the city. The order to fire was not issued, however, as IDF commanders did not want to be responsible for a dire cease-fire violation that could lead to a resumption of the fighting.[22]

Na'ameh base near Damur. The IDF captured every bit of PFLP-GC equipment—including the SA-9 Gaskins surface-to-air missiles the Libyans had given them. The humiliation was not solely Jibril's, however, as a Libyan liaison officer, Captain Hamduni, had been placed in charge of the air defense weapons in al-Na'ameh with several other Libyan NCOs, but they were the first to shed their uniforms and escape.[25] All of Jibril's booty was taken back to Israel and put on display.

The IDF had expected the PFLP-GC's principal Lebanon base to be a tough fight and had sanctioned a significant force of paratroopers, Golani infantrymen, armor units and engineering and artillery elements to destroy the expected PFLP-GC garrison.[26] IDF intelligence officers had informed battalion and company commanders to expect a fierce and deadly fight; Israeli soldiers were told of Jibril's past track record, especially the Qiryat Shmoneh massacre, and of his group's unique military training. Although the IDF did suffer serious casualties in its June 10 capture of Damur, the Stalingrad-type defense Jibril had promised never materialized.

In the IDF's advance through Damur and the rest of Lebanon, several hundred hard-core PFLP-GC fighters were captured. In intelligence-corps interrogations, they provided invaluable insight into the PFLP-GC's makeup; more often than not, they did not paint a pretty picture. One female terrorist, an attractive brunette, provided an extremely derogatory view of Ahmed Jibril, complaining that the "fearless" leader had never visited his units based in southern Lebanon and that the organization's officers were nothing more than cowards, larcenous fools who embezzled whatever funds they received, routine rapists, and heartless kidnappers.[27] Other PFLP-GC fighters captured by Israeli forces provided similar information, as well as more important details of the group's practices, planned and proposed operations, and strengths inside the West Bank and Gaza Strip. All those captured in Lebanon were detained in the bustling Ansar facility near Tyre, which by the end of the war was home to nearly ten thousand Palestinian and Lebanese known and suspected terrorists.

The PFLP-GC's Lebanon chapter was a paradox. Jibril, the famed international terrorist who prided himself above all else for his military expertise, was a miserable field commander. Although he had for years been a loyal and accessible leader to his men, one who always worried about their welfare and always insured that they were prepared for action, he could not rally them into battle. His men's betrayal was profound. The Israelis were not the only ones to criticize the PFLP-GC combat prowess and Ahmed Jibril as commander.* PLO deputy commander Abu Iyad claimed that Jibril had a failure of nerve during the war.[29]

In fact, the PFLP-GC's contribution to the 1982 fighting could have been considered nothing more than negligible cowardice were it not for the fact that it played decisive roles in two extremely important incidents that sliced through the Israeli psyche in ballistic fashion. Jibril was once again bartering misery and lives in the human bazaar, only this time it was on a larger scale. Many would later view Jibril's intransigence in the following years in dealing with Israeli hostages as a cruel strategy meant to reinstate the PFLP-GC's reputation as an organization to be feared. Indeed, following the 1982 war, he had much to prove to his fellow Palestinians, and his Syrian—and even Libyan—patrons.

* After the 1982 fighting, the PFLP-GC was one of the first Palestinian groups to return to its Beirut offices and installations. It was also among the first military groups to engage American forces, as PFLP-GC snipers "practiced" their trade by harassing U.S. Marines patrolling Beirut International Airport.[28]

CHAPTER SIX

ISRAEL HELD HOSTAGE

On June 11, 1982, IDF tank units advancing into the Syrian-controlled Bekaa Valley were assigned to capture a strategic junction in the gateway to the village of Sultan Yaqoub. In the first five days of the fighting, Israel's armored forces had proved virtually invincible in the wake of Palestinian and Syrian resistance; the war, after all, was the baptism of fire for the *Merkava* (Chariot) main battle tank, an Israeli-designed and produced armored vehicle with a revolutionary configuration that placed crew survivability over speed and firepower. Operation Peace for Galilee also introduced an innovative device into the military vernacular called "Blazer Armor," rectangular boxes crammed with explosive material that exploded on impact and destroyed incoming ordnance rather than allowing missiles and shell fire to penetrate the tank's armor. Blazer Armor kits were placed around the old battlewagons of the IDF to increase their survivability in combat. Blazer had proved to be an ingenious addition to such tanks as the Centurion and Patton. They could not, however, guarantee a tank's survival in a saturated antitank combat environment. Sultan Yaqoub would be one hell of a combat environment!

A battalion of Blazer-equipped Israeli Patton tanks, commanded by Lieutenant-Colonel Ira Efroni, was assigned the job of establishing a defensive perch in the narrow valley hemmed in by the towering hills near the village of Sultan Yaqoub to guard against an expected counterattack by the mighty Syrian 3rd Armored Division. Efroni's men were primarily observant reservists in the *Hesder* program, soldiers who combined military service with religious seminary study.[1] The IDF advance into the Bekaa Valley had been so swift that the IDF's sophisticated intelligence-gathering apparatus failed to reach the surging units in time, and data on the most up-to-date Syrian deployment was unavailable to the advancing armor spearhead. The communications gap would prove fatal. A full brigade of tanks headed straight into the 3rd Armored Division's staging area. The Syrians were just as shocked as their Israeli counterparts. When everyone caught their wits, the killing began.

Sultan Yaqoub will go down in Israeli military history as a close-quarters battle for survival in which courage and confusion reigned supreme. Hemmed in by the steep ravines and cliffs, the Israeli tanks first tried to keep the Syrians at bay by having tank commanders spray the surrounding hillsides with incessant .50 caliber machine-gun fire and accurate bursts of 105-mm cannon fire. But when the overwhelming force of Syrian tanks, including T-72s, and antitank Syrian commandos wielding RPGs and Saggers wire-guided antitank missiles attacked, the carnage was devastating. Within hours, dozens of destroyed and damaged tanks littered the narrow roadway. After a day of fighting, twenty Israeli soldiers had been killed.[2]

One tank hit by antitank fire was an M60 Patton belonging to Captain Zohar Lifshitz, who was killed in the fusillade of antitank fire that pounded his vehicle; the driver managed to escape in the chaos, the communications officer and loader were rescued by friendly forces, but the fate of the gunner, Yehuda Katz, remains a mystery to this day as he is still one of Israel's missing in action. Later that day, Jordanian TV-News displayed video footage of Palestinian guerrillas from as-Sa'iqa parading through the squalored alleyways of the Yarmouk refugee camp in Damascus in a captured Israeli M60 Patton with its top-secret Blazer Armor kit. Most important, the tank was displayed together with several Israeli POWs, much to the delight of the camp's shouting residents.[3] To the frustration of Israeli officials who would later view the tape back in Tel Aviv, the faces of the captured men could not be positively identified from the poor camera angle. This grim portrait of Israeli personnel seized in combat was also seen in Israel, which receives Jordanian television signals with relative clarity. Italian journalists working for the paper *La Stampa* in the Syrian capital claimed that the Israeli POWs (no specific number was ever given) were being held by the elite Defense Brigade in Damascus headed by Rifa'at Assad, the president's brother. Israeli intelligence, however, was able to confirm that the POWs were held by Salah Mi'ani's Sa'iqa.[4] No one can confirm who those men actually were, or if gunner Yehuda Katz was among them.

At about the same time as Captain Lifshitz's main battle tank was fatally struck, another M60 tank was damaged by enemy fire. The armor-piercing rocket that penetrated the vehicle's hull brought about a thunderous blast and a hellish inferno. The crew managed to escape, but they could not evade tragedy. Arik Liberman, the gunner, was eventually captured by the Syrians; Tzvika Feldman, the loader and communications chief, and Ya'akov Baumel, the driver, have not been heard from since, and are still listed as missing in action.* The odyssey of the tank commander would grip much of Israel for years to come.

Chezi Shai, a reservist tank skipper, had left his tank last after it was hit and raced into the surrounding hills before advancing Syrian forces could capture him. Originally he had been teamed with Arik Liberman in the attempt to make it back to Israeli lines, but in the confusion of the smoke and incessant explosions the two men lost contact. It was pitch black, as Chezi recalls, and he crawled through the foliage and underbrush to try and get back to Israeli lines. After descending from a hill perch, he headed to what he thought were the sounds of tank treads churning, but his slow crawl was suddenly interrupted. A voice rang out of the darkness and asked him in Arabic who he was. Since his parents were born in Baghdad, Chezi responded in a heavily accented Iraqi-Arabic, "I am with the Iraqi forces in the area!" The voice in the darkness thought for a moment, and then told Chezi to proceed.[5] Another voice then rang out of the darkness, from a small khaki tent, and ordered the unidentified figure to "wait a minute." Moments later, several armed men wearing camouflage fatigues and carrying AK-47s were examining Chezi. Wearing his olive green Nomex flame-retardant overalls and IDF-issue black combat boots, Chezi Shai realized the masquerade was over. With a still proud voice, he told the group of armed men who had now assembled around him that he was an Israeli soldier. Chezi Shai had unknowingly stumbled across a PFLP-GC forward encampment in the Bekaa Valley; ostensibly, they were there to harass advancing Israeli troops.

The men who had seized their prisoner realized his value and treated him with varying degrees of civility and compassion. He was told not to worry, he was not beaten or assaulted in any way, and he was even offered fresh fruit and water. At dawn, however, Chezi Shai was blindfolded, his hands and legs were bound together tightly with rope and

---

* As will be seen later in this chapter, although Katz, Feldman, and Baumel remain MIAs to this day, a great deal of evidence points to the fact that, if they are still alive, they are more than likely being held by the PFLP-GC.

wire, and he was then dumped into the trunk of a civilian car that transported him to a PFLP-GC facility in Lebanon. There he was kicked a few times, questioned a bit, and then drugged. His final stop would be a small apartment in a PFLP-GC safe house in a Damascus suburb.[6] It would be his home for the next three years.

Ahmed Jibril did not inform the IDF that he had seized one of its soldiers, nor did he inform the International Red Cross. In fact, he even failed to mention it to the Syrians for a while. A student of history, Jibril realized how valuable live Israelis were, and what a hefty price they could bring on the open market. He also realized that there were tens of thousands of Israeli soldiers roaming throughout Lebanon at the time. They were scared, far from home, and in an evil land where only the most ruthless survived. There was very little in the IDF soldiers' training that prepared them for the hell of the Levantine madness.

From his Beirut nerve center, Jibril ordered his operations chiefs to conceive a plan that would turn the PFLP-GC into the most feared entity in the IDF's vernacular.

On September 4, 1982, a force of approximately one dozen PFLP-GC shock troopers, operating under the cover of darkness, assaulted a forward IDF position near Bhamdoun.[7] They had slinked their way through Israeli lines and had stealthily approached their target without attracting any attention. With little struggle and without a shot being fired, eight Israeli servicemen were neutralized and taken into captivity.* Reuven Cohen, Dani Gilboa, Eli Abutbul, Avi Cornfeld, Avi Mintavelski, Rafi Chazan, Nissim Salam, and Yosef Grof were all conscripts, all inexperienced combat soldiers, and all under twenty years old. Jibril had chosen his target well.

The kidnapped soldiers were all from the *Na'ha'l* (the Hebrew acronym for *No'ar Halutzei Lochem*, or Fighting Pioneer Youth), an infantry brigade of soldiers and farmers who split their military service between combat duty and maintaining border agricultural settlements.

---

* The PFLP-GC kidnapping of the eight infantrymen has become one of the most controversial episodes in the history of the Israel Defense Forces. Although Israeli military censorship has forbid the publication of the internal IDF investigation into the incident, there was a general staff outcry over the manner in which the soldiers were seized. According to foreign reports, the soldiers were busy eating oranges and playing backgammon, instead of sleeping in shifts and manning outer defensive positions. In radio interviews given following his tenure as IDF chief of staff, Lieutenant-General Rafael "Raful" Eitan even suggested that the lieutenant in charge of the post, who was not captured, and the POWs themselves be tried in a military court for their failure to follow proper security guidelines in a combat situation.

The essence of an egalitarian fighting man working the land was one of the most treasured dreams of Israeli founding father David Ben-Gurion. The Na'ha'l's sword-and-sickle unit emblem had come to personify Ben-Gurion's dream of dedicated socialists who worked the land while simultaneously defending it. The Na'ha'l was a powerful national icon, one not easily destroyed.

Mysteriously, however, Jibril did not keep all of his prisoners. Six were handed over to Fatah. Perhaps the act was a payback of sorts, perhaps an act of apology for the PFLP-GC's performance in the Lebanese fighting. The intricacies of the deal cut between Yasir Arafat (along with his deputy commander Abu Iyad and Abu Jihad) and Ahmed Jibril remains a mystery to this day. The outcome of the arrangement, however, was not subject to much speculation. Arafat's men now possessed six IDF soldiers; Jibril controlled the fate of two acknowledged Israeli soldiers, Chezi Shai, and, perhaps, the three other Sultan Yaqoub MIAs. One of the most controversial episodes in Israel's war against terrorism had begun. Ahmed Jibril had taken the State of Israel hostage.

The war in Lebanon had already attacked the Israeli psyche in vicious fashion and damaged Israel's sense of invulnerability and duty more than ever before in that nation's history. The war by the end of 1982 had cost Israel more than three hundred dead and nearly one thousand wounded. On September 14, 1982, the Syrian assassination of Lebanese president-elect Bashir Gemayel, Israel's man in Lebanon, destroyed any chances of a peace treaty ever being signed with a Christian leader in Lebanon. Finally, days later, vengeful Phalangist militiamen perpetrated the notorious Sabra and Shatilla massacres, an orgy of killing where Christian Phalangist militiamen butchered nearly eight hundred Palestinian civilians in West Beirut in revenge for the death of Bashir Gemayel. Although the Christians entered the camps on their own with the intended purpose of searching for Palestinian weapon caches, because the IDF allowed them into the camps the world would blame Israel for the actual killings. Yet the question of the missing Israeli servicemen personified the divisive and controversial nature of Operation Peace for Galilee, a conflict that could not be considered settled until every missing Israeli serviceman was accounted for.

One of the fundamental bonds between the Israeli government and its soldiers is that should he or she become a prisoner of war or a captive of any kind, the government and army would do their utmost to secure his or her release. Knowing that the body of even a dead Israeli serviceman is considered sacred, the IDF has as one of its tenets, which every soldier learns, that dead and wounded personnel are *never* left on the battlefield. The practice was learned with horror during the bitter battle for Latrun in 1948, it is religiously upheld to this day.[8]

Kidnapping is as intrinsic an element of the Middle Eastern landscape as are the cedars of Lebanon and the majestic sharp cliffs of the Negev Desert hills. It is a form of business as old as the region itself, and it has always been an effective weapon in the area's countless conflicts. This mode of warfare was not new to the Arab-Israeli conflict either; in fact, kidnapping and hostage-taking has been the currency of virtually *all* of the region's players. In the late 1930s and 1940s, Arab guerrilla bands frequently kidnapped Jewish settlers and bartered for their release, and during the struggle against the British, Jewish terrorists from the *Irgun***** kidnapped three British sergeants and executed them after their demands that Jewish prisoners be released were ignored. In the years of the Palestinian *fedayeen* in the early 1950s, guerrillas were known to kidnap Israeli settlers and soldiers and hold them until the IDF, in particular "Arik" Sharon's Unit 101 commandos, would kidnap their own Arabs to initiate a swap. In 1954, after four Israeli reconnaissance paratroopers and infantrymen replacing a battery on a top-secret A'man eavesdropping device were captured on the Golan Heights by Syrian forces, Israeli reconnaissance paratroopers executed Operation Olive Leaves, the December 11, 1955, raid on Syrian fortifications at the base of the Golan Heights. The IDF assault force killed more than fifty Syrian soldiers and took more than thirty captives. A prisoner exchange followed a few months later.[9] In one of the most famous and spectacular operations designed to secure the release of Israeli captives, commandos from Sayeret Mat'kal crossed into Lebanon to kidnap five Syrian generals touring the south on a terrorist liaison and reconnaissance mission, and held them until the Syrians returned three Israeli pilots captured during the 1967 to 1970 War of Attrition.[10]

More often than not, Israeli prisoner deals were lopsided exercises; the Arab armies realized just how valuable a life (or even a corpse) was to the IDF, and used this national and religious sensitivity as a powerful weapon. Following the 1967 war, Israel *traded* more than five thousand Egyptian soldiers (including several generals and a field marshal) in exchange for a dozen pilots and naval commandos captured in the fighting, as well as a few A'man spies (the legendary Susannah agents) originally arrested in 1954 in Cairo and Alexandria for trying to incite anti-Egyptian sentiment in Washington, D.C., and London by

---

* Menachem Begin's underground army, the *Irgun Tzava Leùml.*

perpetrating bombings of Western interests in Egypt, and then blaming the Moslem brotherhood for the act. Following the 1973 war, similar lopsided deals occurred between the Israelis and the Syrians and Egyptians.

The missing Israeli servicemen presented a difficult challenge to the IDF and the Manpower Branch, which was responsible for such matters. Following the end of the "conventional" aspect of Operation Peace for Galilee in October 1982, there were seventeen Israeli POWs and MIAs: * the five Sultan Yaqoub tank soldiers; the eight Na'ha'l infantrymen; Aharon Achiaz, a Skyhawk pilot shot down over southern Lebanon and seized by Fatah; a reservist truck driver who mistakenly wandered into Syrian lines; and the crew of an IAF RF-4 Phantom shot down over the Bekaa Valley on July 25, 1982, by a Soviet-manned SA-8 Gecko surface-to-air missile (the Palestinians and Syrians also held the bodies of several Israeli servicemen, including a few who fell in Operation Litani in 1978). On August 21, 1982, as part of the deal that allowed the PLO to leave Beirut unhindered, Achiaz was set free, and caskets bearing several soldiers killed in 1978 were turned over to Israeli representatives. It was a start, no matter how small. According to IDF OC Manpower Branch, Major-General Moshe Nativ, "The return of our soldiers was a monumental objective and a stoic statement of our resolve as a military and our character as a nation; to get our boys back, we would bring much of our national resources to bear in this process."[11] There was still much work to be done, however.

Finding the Israeli prisoners (and MIAs), establishing communications with those holding them, and working to secure their release fell to a little known and unheralded force under the command of the Manpower Branch called *Ha'Yechida Le'Itur Ne'edarim* (Unit for Missing Soldiers). Getting the boys back home would be no easy task: Only the Syrians complied by providing information concerning their live prisoners, and eventually permitted International Red Cross visits to the three captives they were holding, Gil Fogel, Yochanan

---

* In April 1983, agents from Nayif Hawatmeh's DFLP kidnapped First-Sergeant Samir Assad, a Druze IDF soldier, in Sidon, and in the years from 1984 to 1986, Shiite gunmen from both the *Amal* (Hope) and *Hizbollah* (Party of God) groups seized or kidnapped three more Israeli soldiers, including Captain Ron Arad, an IAF navigator, and Rechamim Elshayach and Yossi Fink, two *Giva'ati* Brigade infantrymen kidnapped by Hizbollah. Samir Assad's body was exchanged for several hundred Arab prisoners in 1991; Elshayach and Fink are reported to have been killed by Hizbollah torturers; and Ron Arad is believed alive and held by Hizbollah somewhere in eastern Lebanon, or even in Iran.

Alon, and Ariel Liberman (they also provided the Israelis with video-tapes of several grave sites in Damascus where dead Israeli personnel had been buried).[12] At times, Fatah provided sketchy, even tantalizing, clues concerning the missing men they were holding, though only after Israel made a symbolic gesture of sorts, like the release of a few token prisoners. The PFLP-GC, however, would not even acknowledge who it was holding, or what it wanted for their release. Israel's intelligence assets, the Mossad, the Shin Bet, and A'man, scavenged for any tidbit of information regarding the men Jibril was holding. Captured terrorists were questioned incessantly, and foreign liaisons were pressed for any assistance they could provide. According to Lieutenant-Colonel Carmi, a former commander of the Unit for Missing Soldiers, "There are some puzzles with five hundred pieces and some with thousands of pieces. Sometimes you can drown in the information you have, and sometimes you have nothing to go on."[13] Sometimes even the parents and spouses of the missing men were brought into these delicate international negotiations, since they possessed emotional powers of persuasion few governmental agencies could ever hope to muster.

Israel's most important channel of communications and hope passed through the Austrian capital of Vienna, with the help of the Austrian premier, Bruno Kriesky, himself a Jew although one with close leanings to the PLO, and Ambassador Dr. Herbert Amry, the Austrian ambassador to Athens. The Austrians were invaluable to this process, using their diplomatic contacts to nurture trust and hope among the Syrians and the terrorists.

Since the Syrians and Fatah were communicated openly with the Austrians—and then the Israelis—concerning the prisoners, those channels received the greatest initial attention. This angered Jibril, who, though he had yet to confirm or deny that he was holding any POWs at all, felt that by ignoring him Israel was displaying dangerous disrespect. Israel had always suspected that Jibril was holding IDF personnel, but was trying to figure him out, allowing him to make the first move in order to increase its bargaining position. In an interview given to a Jordanian newspaper, Jibril posed a perplexing rhetorical question directed at the Israeli intelligence officers he knew would be reading the article. "Why don't they [the Israelis] turn to us," he asked, "*we* might have two or three prisoners?"[14] In the article, Jibril spoke of a soldier by a fictitious name that sounded too similar to that of Chezi Shai's not to be taken seriously in Tel Aviv. The invaluable initial contact, no matter how indirect, had finally been made.

Israel faced a perplexing dilemma. Three separate groups were holding its people; three separate deals had to be struck. Israel had one trump card of its own, however. Since the first day of the Lebanon invasion, approximately ten thousand Palestinian and Lebanese terrorists and suspects had passed through the sprawling prison minicity at Ansar, near Tyre; the IDF had captured approximately half, and the remainder were seized by several hundred National Police border guards summoned to Lebanon to search and detain wanted terrorists.[15] Clearly the Palestinians also had pressures of their own to retrieve their incarcerated comrades, and Israel felt that it possessed tremendous bargaining leverage of its own. Time, however, was not on Israel's side.

On May 10, 1983, a Palestinian rebellion erupted inside the PLO. A'akid Muhamad Sa'id Musa Marara, better known by his nom de guerre of Abu Musa, initiated a pro-Syrian mutiny in Fatah. Infighting erupted in the ranks of the Yarmouk Brigade in the Bekaa Valley and quickly spread north to Tripoli, where Arafat had established another Lebanon base and headquarters. Desperate fratricidal fighting between the Arafat loyalists and Abu Musa rebels soon broke out. A'man intelligence reports indicated that Fatah was holding the six Na'ha'l infantrymen in Tripoli, the embattled and besieged city where Jibril's forces fought alongside Abu Musa's men and the Syrian Army in this latest campaign against Arafat.

The man initially responsible for coordinating Israel's efforts to bring its personnel home was attorney Arieh Merinski, an ex-Irgun officer and a man brought into the fold at the personal request of Israeli Defense Minister Moshe Arens under the title Advisor to the Defense Minister for Special Tasks.[16] A man not known to mince his words or actions, Merinski was a tough soul whose energetic style rivaled only his dedication and patriotism. He was a man who did not look kindly on bullshit, as one associate said, and who knew how to raise the ante of a confrontation to pressure-cooker levels. During his tenure as troubleshooter for the missing servicemen, his motto epitomized his outlook on this most difficult and emotionally trying task. "It is possible to wage a psychological warfare campaign against the PLO," he said, "because five thousand mothers of terrorists is a tremendous force, and an Arab mother is no pushover!"[17]

Merinski's first objective was determining the fate of the two non-Fatah held Na'ha'l soldiers, Nissim Salam and Yosef Grof; since Chezi Shai's name had come up through the Jordanian press, confirmation on his exact condition was a prerequisite too. To obtain the necessary information, Merinski made a veiled threat, in a most dramatic and dire tone, to be relayed back to Arafat and Jibril by the International Red Cross representatives. Merinski stated that five thousand Palestinians "roughly" equaled the fate of eight Israeli servicemen. Five thousand Palestinian detainees could also be five thousand corpses, however; Merinski threatened to have soldiers of Major Sa'ad Haddad's Free Lebanese Army, notorious for their violence and fanatic loathing of the Palestinians, patrol—and maybe even enter—the Ansar camp. To verify if Salam and Grof were actually alive, the Israelis prepared a list of questions to be completed by the two captured Na'ha'l soldiers; they were intimate inquiries put together by their families. If they were answered correctly, or if Jibril provided proof that he held the men's bodies, Merinski would see to the release of forty PFLP-GC detainees. If Jibril failed this test, the detainees would be isolated and dealt with accordingly.[18]

To increase his chances of obtaining word of Salam, Grof, and possibly Shai, Merinski and his staff turned to a unique channel: Lieutenant-Colonel Salah Ta'amri. A close confidant of Yasir Arafat and the senior ranking Fatah officer in Ansar, Ta'amri was afforded special privileges, including conjugal visits with his wife in five-star Tel Aviv hotels. Adding to the intrigue was the fact that he was married to Dina Abdul Hamed, the first wife of Jordan's King Hussein, a tantalizing woman who the Israelis always referred to as Princess Dina. In the summer of 1983, Merinski, along with Manpower Branch chief Major-General Nativ and Major-General Meir Zorea, the IDF comptroller, traveled to Ansar to speak with Lieutenant-Colonel Ta'amri.[19] Merinski told Lieutenant-Colonel Ta'amri that Israel was interested in one unilateral prisoner exchange involving all of her captives and missing soldiers. The Fatah officer was to select an incarcerated individual in Ansar who could be trusted to carry the message to Arafat and Jibril that Israel wanted to deal.

Israeli officials had always realized that the key to any prisoner deal was the Ansar camp, although it was in Israel's national security interests to keep the thousands of prisoners under lock and key for as long as possible. Ansar was an administrative nightmare and Israeli officials knew it. Privately, the facility was called the IAT, or International Academy for Terrorism, as men trained by the best Eastern-bloc intelligence specialists were now all concentrated together in one teeming and overcrowded facility.[20]

Despite their promises, Lieutenant-Colonel Ta'amri and Princess Dina failed to yield dividends; there was still no sign of life from Salam and Grof, and Jibril still failed to acknowledge that Chezi Shai was in his custody. The Israelis decided to up the psychological ante a level. The *Sha'ba's* (the Hebrew acronym for *Sherut Batei Ha'Sohar*, or Prison Authority) was told to spread rumors inside the various maximum-security prisons containing high-profile terrorists with life sentences that a prisoner exchange was imminent, although delayed by Jibril's intransigence. This tactic increased pressure among the prisoners' families as well, which, in turn, eventually made its way back to Jibril in Damascus. In Israeli maximum-security prisons, the *Sha'ba's* places individuals in cell blocks according to their terrorist affiliations as one method used to buy the peace;[21] prisoners from factions with differing views, factions that could often be at war with one another, were not together in the general prison population. Nobody was more aware of the complicated means of delegating power to the terrorist population inside Israel's prisons than Hafaz al-Dalkamoni. In jail for nearly ten years, he had been a *Shawish* (terrorist representative) in the Ashqelon facility in southern Israel and a liaison among the terrorist population and the authorities. Dalkamoni realized that the prospect of a release would excite and compromise many of the PFLP-GC prisoners, and thus a failure to follow through with the deal—especially if Jibril was blamed—could spark a mutiny among the faithful and perhaps permanently weaken the organization's network inside Israel. The Shin Bet was also brought into the fold and ordered to increase the pressure on areas of the West Bank and Gaza where the PFLP-GC enjoyed significant control. The pressure would always make its way back to Jibril through his agents in the territories.

When Lieutenant-Colonel Ta'amri failed to supply even the faintest bits of optimism to the Israelis, Merinski and the IDF played its "FLA/Haddad" trump card one final time. As the Fatah officer was brought to Tel Aviv for one last meeting, Jibril's personnel at Ansar were separated from the main population and moved to a remote stretch of the sprawling camp. Hours later, jeeps and command cars bearing Haddad's militiamen appeared across the barbed wire concertina for all to see. Heavily armed and cursing the Palestinians in guttural Arabic, the militiamen cocked their weapons and aimed them across the fence. Haddad's men were clearly brought in for psychological pressure—the Palestinians knew that IDF units would never perpetrate a massacre, but the FLA, who had been known to butcher prisoners in cold blood, certainly would. Many of the Palestinians thought that they would soon be dead; some even wrote last letters to their families.

Salah Ta'amri thought he was being taken to a Tel Aviv hotel for a visit with his wife and remained quite calm during his trip from Lebanon. Yet instead of heading for the seaside, the motorcade brought him to a heavily guarded military installation in the area. This time, Merinski was not cordial to Ta'amri, not even civil. Ta'amri was promised that a massacre would soon transpire at Ansar that would make Sabra and Shatilla look like a barbecue at the beach. He was also told that one more double-cross and he could find himself among the dead. After stating that *he* had been a terrorist long before Ta'amri was sucking on his mother's breast, Merinski said in a stern and unflinching voice, "You won't be going back to Ansar because soon it will be a graveyard. You failed to keep your promise of help and now you'll have to pay the price."[22]

The tactic worked. A few weeks later, Princess Dina returned to Tel Aviv after having visited Salam and Grof in one of Jibril's Damascus hideouts, and confirmed that they were alive. Several weeks later, Dr. Herbert Amry traveled to Damascus as well and videotaped the Israeli POWs, although Jibril only agreed to such a visit after the Austrians helped obtain a list of 112 PFLP-GC prisoners that the Israelis were holding. At the same time that Israeli officials were looking at the tape of Salam and Grof, Syrian intelligence officers were beating Chezi Shai during daily interrogation sessions; his safety was not guaranteed since nobody in Israel truly knew his whereabouts and Jibril had yet to confirm that he was a PFLP-GC prisoner.[23]

But Jibril had demands to be met before his business with the Israelis could continue. In order for the negotiations to continue, he ordered Luva Eliav, the government troubleshooter for MIAs, to accompany the parents of Nissim Salam and Yosef Grof to Vienna, where they would be videotaped watching their sons on videotape. This bizarre request was considered the last straw by Merinski, who refused to allow a terrorist to dictate demands, especially when it would devastate the families of the missing servicemen.

Merinski's objective of one deal to secure the release of all Israel's missing servicemen collapsed on two fronts when poor health led to his removal from the government task force, and Fatah struck a separate deal. On the night of November 23, 1983, Israel released 4,500 Palestinian prisoners, all guerrillas seized in Lebanon, from Ansar and an additional one hundred men imprisoned inside Israel for the six Na'ha'l soldiers Arafat was holding in Tripoli.[24] The Palestinians were flown to Tunis, while the Israelis were transferred, via the French Navy, to an awaiting IDF/Navy missile boat in Lebanese waters for the trip back to

Israel.* Although controversial, the prisoner exchange did not spark tremendous outrage in Israel. After all, many of those interned in Ansar were only suspects, and one hundred *convicted* terrorists for six Israeli servicemen was not as lopsided as many would believe.

Dealings with Jibril, however, would not be as straightforward. It was only in the summer of 1984 that Ahmed Jibril finally confirmed that he was holding Chezi Shai. When pressed for information concerning missing soldiers Katz, Feldman, and Baumel, Jibril remained cunningly ambiguous. He also inferred that the time was ripe for more terrorist operations inside Israel. In August 1983, Shin Bet agents, acting on intelligence, seized several Lebanese and Israeli Druze, as well as a car crammed with several hundred kilograms of high-explosives as it attempted to pass through the Lebanese border at the Rosh Hanikra crossing on the Mediterranean coast. The terrorists had been ordered by Jibril to blow up Tel Aviv's Shalom Tower, the tallest building in the city, and perpetrate a Qiryat Shmoneh-type massacre in the city's downtown district.[26] The terrorists would not be in prison for long.

From the onset, the negotiations with Jibril were conducted under a demanding timetable. Israel's staged withdrawal from Lebanon (with the exception of a ten-kilometer-deep security zone opposite the Israeli frontier) was scheduled to culminate in June 1985. In order for the nation to place the debacle and the political damage of the Lebanon war behind it, the conflict needed to end and the prisoners brought home; already there were six hundred IDF dead in the Lebanon involvement. Under the directives of Prime Minister Shimon Peres, elected as part of a national unity government on September 13, 1984, Defense Minister Yitzhak Rabin (IDF chief of staff during the 1967 war, a former prime minister, and, at the time of this book's printing, Israel's current prime minister) began the delicate negotiations to bring the three servicemen back home. The delicate and precarious tap dance with Jibril began on December 14. In the safety of his Damascus nerve center, Jibril would drag out the anguish for another six months.

According to foreign reports, the IDF general staff had at one time considered a military response to the "Jibril situation," including an Entebbe-like commando strike against the house in Damascus where the POWs were being held.[27] Although details of Israeli operational

---

* The Syrians too had cut a separate deal with Israel. In exchange for the six Israelis Syria was holding (three soldiers and three "civilians"), Israel released 291 Syrian POWs (including two colonels) on July 29, 1984; the deal also included the Syrians' returning the remains of several Israeli servicemen killed in Lebanon and during the 1973 war.[25]

plans remain classified, one known, although very hushed up, military response to Jibril's intransigence was actually carried out. In late 1983, Israeli commandos from (according to foreign reports) Sayeret Mat'kal infiltrated back into the Beirut abyss and kidnapped Marwad Bushnak, better known by his nom de guerre of Abu A'ali, a senior PFLP-GC officer and, most important, Ahmed Jibril's nephew.[28] Luva Eliav, the man ultimately responsible for the fate of Salam, Grof, and Shai, thought that the acquisition of Abu A'ali would virtually guarantee the Israelis' quick release. It didn't. Through the office of Dr. Amry, Eliav offered Jibril his nephew in exchange for the three Israeli soldiers. Jibril refused even to respond to the offer. It was an insult. He would not be coerced into accepting anything the Israelis would offer.

Ahmed Jibril realized that he was holding on to much more than three lives. He was now holding a nation of four million hostages. If he so pleased, he could keep his hostages for years, or he could brutally torture them and return the hapless men as cripples. According to reports, when Chezi Shai refused to answer the questions of Syrian Air Force intelligence agents who interrogated him, Jibril, who had been looking on, told the inquisitors: "He is still missing. *Anything* could happen to him."[29]

Through their Austrian intermediaries, Eliav and Dalkamoni conducted tense, sometimes heated negotiations; Eliav had made more than thirty trips to Europe and other regional locations to carry out the talks. Joining in the process was Shmuel Tamir, the official head of the Israeli efforts, and the new OC Manpower Branch Major-General Amos Yaron. An ex-Sayeret Mat'kal officer and Chief Paratroop and Infantry officer during Operation Peace for Galilee, Yaron was a man of decisive action and undisputed courage. His mettle would be tested in the months to come.

The Israelis realized that they would be forced to release a significant number of Palestinians in order to secure a safe and quick return for Salam, Grof, and Shai. Still, they could never have predicted just how outrageous Jibril's demands would be.

In a list handed to the Israelis via their Austrian conduit, Israeli intelligence, military police, and secret service officials found themselves looking at the extortionist's sword pointed straight at their jugular. Even these men jaded by years of combat and covert dealings were taken aback by Jibril's audacity. For the safe return of the three Israelis, Ahmed Jibril demanded that Israel set free 1,150 Palestinians, including an amazing 400 convicted terrorists serving life terms for some of the most spectacular and heinous terrorist operations ever mounted against the State of Israel. Indeed, had a death penalty existed in Israel, it is almost certain that most of these convicted mass murderers would have met the hangman's noose long ago. Jibril's list included the men responsible for planting a car bomb in Jerusalem's bustling Machane Yehuda Market on November 22, 1968, in which twelve people were killed; the two surviving hijackers of a Sabena 707 aircraft to Lod on May 9, 1972; the survivor of the March 5, 1975, seaborne attack on Tel Aviv's Savoy Hotel, in which eight people were killed; three survivors of the March 11, 1978, Country Club Massacre; and one member of a PLF-seaborne squad responsible for the brutal murder of the Haran family in Nahariya, on April 4, 1979.[30] The most notorious man on the list wasn't even a Palestinian. In an audacious move meant to rub Israel's nose in the dirt, Ahmed Jibril demanded that Kozo Okamoto, a Japanese Red Army gunmen responsible for the Lod Airport Massacre on June 30, 1972, be set free. Okamoto was the surviving member of a three-man team working for George Habash's PFLP and responsible for the deaths of twenty-nine people, including twenty-seven Puerto Rican pilgrims, during one of the deadliest attacks ever committed inside Israel. As Okamoto had gone insane in Israeli custody, trying to circumcise himself with a spoon, he possessed negligible publicity value as a returning hero of Palestine and the international revolution; he was, of course, a major embarrassment. He was nevertheless notorious, and Jibril realized that it would pain the Israelis greatly to let him go.

Remarkably, Prime Minister Peres and Defense Minister Rabin agreed to Jibril's demands with little opposition. It would be one of the most controversial decisions ever made by the Israeli government.

Many in the Israeli hierarchy, including Shmuel Tamir, opposed Jibril's take-it-or-leave-it offer. The price was simply too high. But Israel was working against the clock. The country was scheduled to complete its staged withdrawal from Lebanon by June 1985, and it could not leave Lebanese territory until its confirmed prisoners were returned safely. There were other, more pressing, considerations as well. Following a stormy session of the Palestine National Council in November 1984, the PFLP-GC, the PFLP, as-Sa'iqa the Popular Struggle Front, Abu Musa's Fatah rebels, and the Talat Yakoub Faction of the Palestine Liberation Front formed the National Salvation Front (NSF) as a political and military block, supported by Libya and Syria, poised for military action against Arafat. Many Israeli intelligence officials feared that the creation of the NSF on March 25, 1985, could spark a new round of Palestinian infighting that might significantly delay any possible prisoner deal. There were also fears that a rival Palestinian group opposed to the NSF might attempt to kidnap or kill the Israeli servicemen as a means for weakening and disgracing Jibril.

For Israel, the time to act was now, no matter what the price. Jibril and Dalkamoni realized that the Israelis were desperate, and played out the motions of the deal with contemptible cruelty. PFLP-GC spokespersons, using Radio el-Quds as their vehicle, often leaked false dates for the prisoner exchange, manipulating the emotions of the hostages' families. Jibril also insisted that the mothers of the three soldiers be taken to Azur, the town of his birth, and photographed in front of a rundown shack he claimed was the home he left in 1937.[31] While Israeli officials would never have agreed to this outrageous demand under normal circumstances, there was no time for face-saving bravado; the families, anxious to help out their children any way they could, gladly agreed to be photographed. The black-and-white still picture was eventually forwarded to Jibril in Damascus. Receipt of the humbling photograph was proof of his victory.

Finally, according to an Israeli security officer, "Jibril had one final act of ball-busting!" In their excellent book *The Fall of Pan Am 103: Inside the Lockerbie Investigation*, Steven Emerson and Brian Duffy claim that Dalkamoni insisted that each released terrorist receive the following letter prepared by the Israelis: "Dear militant brothers and comrades: The PFLP-GC's members, cadres, and leadership relay their revolutionary compliments to every militant [in his name], highly appreciate your struggles, admire your long-standing patience, your suffering and pains inside the prisons, and would like to convey news of your impending liberation and release."[32] The letter's demand insulted the Israelis. According to one military police officer, "Our men were rotting away in the terrorists' hell, and Jibril was handing out *wedding invitations!*"

Jibril's demands caused many sleepless nights and upset stomachs for the men of the Manpower Branch, the IDF Military Police Corps, and the Sha'ba's. The about-to-be-released terrorists were held in four separate prisons (Nablus, Ashqelon, Ramle, and Neve Tirza), and assembling them into a secure and cohesive environment took quite an effort. The man responsible for locating each terrorist, conducting a security check, and clearing their position in prison with Sha'ba's officials was Lieutenant-Colonel P., head of the operations department in the Military Police Command. He was not given much time to organize and coordinate the tremendous prisoner release.[33] The prisoner swap was tentatively scheduled for May 1985.

Jibril's instructions were meticulous: 610 of the soon-to-be-freed terrorists who were residents of the West Bank and the Gaza Strip would be allowed to return to their homes; buses would simply drive the freed men from prison to their villages and towns; 390 persons held at Ansar and in Israeli jails were to be flown to Geneva, Switzerland, in three separate IAF transports; and 150 released men were to be taken to the Golan Heights for the crossing into Syria at the Quneitra United Nations-patrolled border post.[34] The *actual* exchange would transpire on Swiss soil under the supervision of International Red Cross representatives. Remarkably, there were only 271 PFLP-GC terrorists among the 1,150 about to be freed.

After many false alarms and false gestures given to Salam, Grof, and Shai in Damascus, D-Day was finally scheduled for May 21, 1985. At 1400 hours on May 20, the Palestinian prisoners began the lengthy and bureaucratic process that would transform them from "security prisoners" to freed and liberated heroes of the revolution. They had received their obligatory Red Cross kits, a change of clothes, and several other personal effects, including documentation. They were allowed to shower and shave, and were fed one last warm meal (the Ansar prisoners were given brand-new track suits and, under incredibly tight security, brought to buses that would take them to the airport and the border crossing at Quneitra). Before heading to Ben-Gurion International Airport or to staging grounds from which point they would return to the West Bank and Gaza, Lieutenant-Colonel S., a senior military police officer, addressed the prisoners personally. He requested that they recall the humane and moral treatment each one had received in Israeli custody, and hoped that it would help alter their hate-filled perception of Israel. The Palestinians and international terrorists listened to the speech silently, although several proudly commented that they would soon return to Israel to take over Tel Aviv, Haifa, and Jerusalem. The revolution was about to receive a new and rejuvenated legion of holy warriors.

A fleet of twenty-seven buses would transport the prisoners from their jails to Ben-Gurion International Airport. All the drivers from the Egged national bus company had to have top-secret security clearances, and were all sworn to secrecy; it still remains unclear whether or not they were provided with small arms for personal protection.[35] The security operation to bring the prisoners to the airport was a herculean undertaking. Dozens of vehicles surrounded the bus motorcade, as did hundreds of heavily armed military policemen and snipers. The entire process was supervised by an army of International Red Cross workers, who maintained constant radio communications with their counterparts in Geneva and with Jibril's people in Damascus.

The bureaucratic procession of men and vehicles, from the prisons to the airfield, took all day. Once inside the secured military portion of Ben-Gurion Airport, the prisoners' names were checked off an Israeli list, and then cross-checked off an International Red Cross list. Only when both lists perfectly matched were the terrorists allowed to board the awaiting IAF Boeing 707 transports and await the authorization to take off for Geneva. The last man to board the aircraft was Abu A'ali, Jibril's nephew, a man who frequently made himself available to the Israeli media (including journalists from the IDF's esteemed *Bamachane* weekly newspaper magazine). A'ali raced up the step to the door of the aircraft and raised a "V" victory sign with his fingers.[36]

At about the same time that the military section of Ben-Gurion International Airport was undergoing this chaotic operation, Ahmed Jibril began to revel formally in his victory. At a news conference held in Jibril's Damascus headquarters, the three bewildered Israelis were displayed for the international media. Nissim Salam appeared stoic with his dark eyes and well-kept mustache, as did Chezi Shai, who appeared physically fit. Only Yosef Grof, several teeth missing, bore any physical signs of his ordeal. They all looked emotionally exhausted, perplexed, and dazed by the flashing strobe lights and journalists' questions. They looked humbled and in psychological torment. The terrorists sitting in the background, including Jibril, seemed to be absolutely gleeful.

In the early morning hours of May 21, the three IAF aircraft bearing the terrorists took off from Israel for the four-hour flight to Geneva. At the same time, the 150 terrorists set out from Ansar toward Quneitra, and the some 600 "local" returnees boarded buses inside prison courtyards.

May 21, 1985, was a warm, windy, day in Geneva. The airport was bustling with activity, as heavily armed antiterrorist police from the elite *Stern* and *Enzian* units flooded the airport, patrolling the tarmac with M113 armored personnel carriers. Undercover officers clutched West German Heckler & Koch MP5 submachine guns in specially designed briefcases, and snipers manned rooftop positions. Swiss Army Bell-205 helicopters flew at low level around the airport, maintaining a vigilant airborne command, control, and communications overview of this most delicate operation. International Red Cross representatives, as well as Shmuel Tamir, Luva Eliav, Major-General Amos Yaron, and several other IDF officers were the only officials allowed to mill about the airport; the press was there in force, but it was kept at a safe distance.* Yaron, in fact, was the most visibly nervous of those present. A veteran special operations officer, he understood that dealing with terrorists was, at best, a precarious undertaking. The smallest glitch could torpedo the entire process. Dressed in a smart blue blazer and wearing an uncharacteristic white shirt and tie, Yaron could not remove the look of gut-wrenching anxiety from his face.

The guidelines for the exchange were simple. The Palestinians to be freed from Geneva were to be brought to Switzerland in three separate aircraft, while Jibril's prisoners were to be flown to Geneva in two Libyan and one Austrian Air Boeing 727s; one prisoner, guarded at gunpoint and blindfolded, sat in each aircraft. Each Israeli soldier would be exchanged for a planeload of terrorists, who would then be ferried to the Libyan aircraft for the jubilant flight back to Tripoli, after which he would receive a hero's welcome and personal greetings from Colonel Muammar Qadaffi.

The Israeli aircraft landed on time, but there was a delay in Syria and the aircraft took off late. The Israelis immediately became concerned that some diabolical plot, engineered by Jibril, was about to transpire, and called Jerusalem for further instructions. Even though the International Red Cross officials and other medical officials were on board the three "Jibril" aircraft, it is believed that the IAF pilots had instructions to take off at a moment's notice should the Geneva exchange be a trap—an armed ambush, a military operation meant to "liberate" their own men without relinquishing any of the Israelis, or worse, an operation meant to take the Israeli negotiating team, including several high-ranking officers, hostage! Finally, however, the three aircraft arrived from Damascus (they were parked at a remote corner of the airstrip far from the Israeli aircraft). According to the plans worked out weeks before, the exchange was supposed to take place almost immediately once all the aircraft were on the ground.

In the meantime, Israel was nervously honoring the first stage of the deal. A fleet of buses began to transport the 610 released West Bank and Gaza Strip terrorists back to their homes; some of them even lived inside Israel proper and were repatriated to towns and cities populated by Jews. Throughout the occupied territories, the mass return sparked

---

* According to one former NATO security official, Geneva Airport was crammed with intelligence agents from virtually every principal European, North American, and Middle Eastern intelligence service, eager to photograph the released terrorists for their own top-secret archives.

wild, almost orgasmic, celebrations. Lambs were slaughtered, wild parties were thrown, and residents danced in their drunken joy promising to destroy Israel. It was as if they had decisively won a battle of spiritual salvation, and were now basking in their victorious glory. In essence, a battle had been won, but victory belonged to only one man: Ahmed Jibril. As the celebrations continued throughout the night, IDF units and Shin Bet officials braced themselves for the dawning of a new age of violence in the territories. For security officials in the area, their lives had suddenly become more difficult, their jobs more dangerous.[37]

Ahmed Jibril received word of the release inside Israel and issued the necessary authorization granting Nissim Salam his long-denied freedom. Dressed in IDF class A fatigues supplied to him by the International Red Cross, Salam was escorted across the tarmac by a Red Cross official and then handed over to Major-General Yaron, who issued the corporal a tremendous hug. Finally relieved that his ordeal had ended, Salam offered a tremendous smile back to the Israeli contingent, and quickly boarded the Boeing 707 that would take him home. Shmuel Tamir was elated to finally see Salam face-to-face, and quickly called Defense Minister Rabin, to inform him of the progress; Salam's family was also called. Moments later, the first planeload of terrorists headed to the other half of the airfield.*

At 2200 hours, after the last man from the second planeload of terrorists had been released, Yosef Grof was handed over to the Israeli delegation. He too received an emotional hug from Major-General Yaron. An hour later, the 151 terrorists, who had been sitting inside their buses on the Golan Heights for more than twelve hours, were finally released. They were quickly taken to waiting United Nations minibuses and driven across the one hundred meters of the no-man's-land separating Israeli and Syrian forces. Upon hearing that his men were safely inside Syrian territory, Jibril finally ordered First-Sergeant Chezi Shai to be freed. Shai walked across the tarmac as the last bus brought the terrorists to their waiting aircraft. At 0100 hours on May 22, the operation was complete. The three Israelis were headed back to Tel Aviv, and the two Libyan aircraft were making a course for Tripoli.[39]

At 1930 hours, the government had authorized the IDF Spokesman to

---

* Also loaded, according to several reports, onto that first aircraft were sealed cartons crammed with original copies of highly sensitive files the IDF had captured in Beirut; apparently the IDF advance had been so quick that the PLO hadn't had time to microfilm the files, and since they were originals, they couldn't be burned. Apparently their safe release, no matter how many times Israeli intelligence agencies had photocopied them, was a deal-breaker in the Jibril prisoner swap.[38]

release word of the prisoner deal to the press. News of the prisoner swap outraged and shocked virtually every Israeli citizen. Even though hundreds had gathered at Ben-Gurion International Airport to greet the returning prisoners, most citizens would not believe that their government could release some of the most dangerous men in the world so that they could strike against Israel again at a later date; the fact that 600 convicted terrorists, many imprisoned for murder, were returning to the West Bank and Gaza, within direct reach of the Israeli public, caused desperate pangs of fear.* Many citizens protested outside the Prime Minister's office, others wept openly in the streets.

The release sparked the most painful response from parents who had lost their children or other loved ones in past terrorist attacks. Meir Amrosi, who lost a child in the DFLP's Ma'alot Massacre, yelled: "During the ordeal at Ma'alot, the government refused to trade 270 terrorists for the lives of our children. Chief of Staff Mordechai Gur told us that we cannot succumb to blackmail at the end of a gun, and we accepted this then. But now, as 1,150 animals are set free for only three men, I know that our children died for nothing."[41] Other victims of Arab terrorism, including Smadar Haran, who lost two children and a husband in the PLF seaborne attack on Nahariya, complained bitterly to Prime Minister Peres, wanting to know why the victims and survivors of terrorism were not as important as the families of three captured soldiers. It was, however, hard to argue with the deal after scenes of the three released servicemen being reunited with their families appeared in print and on television. The exchange, no matter how controversial, was a statement written in blood and misery that the State of Israel would do the impossible—and the logically improbable—to bring home its men in uniform.

Ahmed Jibril had done something that no other Arab leader had managed to do. He had caused the Israelis to search their souls and question the morality and loyalty of their government. Perhaps no single action ever taken by the Israeli government has sparked such emotion and public anger. Realizing that he had set a dangerous precedent, Defense Minister Rabin warned Jibril that taking new hostages in order to obtain future grandiose gains from Israel would have dire consequences to all terrorists in the region.[42]

To many in Israel, Ahmed Jibril had become too dangerous, too

---

* The Israeli public would be justified in its fears. Less than one year after the deal, several of those released were rearrested for hostile terrorist activity, including several murders in Jerusalem.[40]

pompous, for his own good. Clearly, after learning how to draw first blood in his much-vaunted war of nerves, he had only just begun his holy struggle. Realizing that the Israelis might seek revenge against him, Jibril is believed by many senior intelligence officials to still be holding the three remaining Sultan Yaqoub MIAs; Jibril, in fact, has often stated that Yehuda Katz, Zvi Feldman, and Zacharia Baumel are still alive, although he claimed that they were not held by the PFLP-GC but rather by Hizbollah.[43] Waving even the faintest of hopes in front of the men's heartbroken families that the three are still alive is a cruel tactic, but one that Jibril believed would guarantee his physical survival.

If the Qiryat Shmoneh massacre inked the wording to Jibril's death warrant, the May 21, 1985, human bazaar signed it into effect. All that was needed was the means and the method. In dealing with the Teflon Terrorist, many in Israel also realized that they would need a fair dose of luck.

CHAPTER SEVEN

A HARBINGER OF WORSE TO COME

ISRAEL DID NOT WAIT LONG in launching attacks against the PFLP-GC, and Ahmed Jibril in particular, to retaliate for the May 1985 prisoner exchange. On October 27, 1985, a flight of four IAF F-15s and F-16s launched an early afternoon air raid on PFLP-GC bases in the Bekaa Valley, including their ultrastrategic Sultan Yaqoub base and forward-staging ground position. The purpose of the raid, as released in an IDF spokesman press statement, was to destroy PFLP-GC gun emplacements, combat vehicles including tanks, and ammunition dumps.[1] It was a "routine" IAF raid, close enough to Syrian SAM sites to rattle their cages, but not threatening enough to warrant military action, either defensive or offensive, from Damascus.

According to several press and intelligence reports, however, the raid was launched because A'man and IAF intelligence had learned that Jibril was conducting an inspection of his personnel at the position that day.[2] The intelligence data was incorrect, however. Jibril was not in the "Bekaa" that autumn afternoon. Had he been there, he would probably have been killed. The IAF pilots recorded accurate hits on all the targets, and aerial photographs of the bomb damage showed much of the facility obliterated.

A thorough pragmatist, Jibril realized that his victory over Israel in the prisoner deal was a flirtation with fate. Not since the days of Black September and the Munich Olympics Massacre had the State of Israel

114

been so affected by a single terrorist action. To deal with Black September Israel had, according to foreign reports, dispatched covert hit teams of Mossad operatives to Europe and the Middle East to kill the organization's top leaders.[3] The campaign was so effective that within a year of the Munich Massacre, Black September no longer posed an operational threat to Israel. All of the organization's top lieutenants had been shot or blown up on the streets of Europe, and their international terrorist network was so compromised by the dedicated Israeli intelligence offensive that it was riddled by informants and double agents, and forever weakened. It had taken then-prime minister Golda Meir less than a month to react to the Munich killings and create a special governmental office known as the Prime Minister's Advisor on Counterterrorism to deal with Black September (the office remains active to this day), and create a mysterious and covert decision making-mechanism known as Committee X to sanction the assassination of top terrorist leaders.[4] Jibril was an energetic student of history—especially when it concerned Israel's counterterrorism policy. The 1,150-for-3 deal had crossed the invisible line from menace to national nemesis. Ahmed Jibril realized that Israel would now be out gunning for him.

Oddly enough, the prisoner deal with Israel had not made Ahmed Jibril a popular, or even respected, leader in the Palestinian revolution. For a man who had succeeded in bringing Israel to its knees in tense and unyielding negotiations, Jibril remained an enigma. Throughout the refugee camps in Lebanon, Syria, and Jordan, posters bearing Jibril's face did not suddenly spring up on the sides of buildings, and few new recruits signed up to join the PFLP-GC. According to several Palestinian officials, it had always bothered Jibril that men like Yasir Arafat, whose military efforts against Israel had usually ended in embarrassing failure; George Habash, who yearned for the dismantling of virtually every Arab state; and even Nayif Hawatmeh, whose fanatic views of Communism were downright impossible to implement in the region, were more accepted, and respected, than he was. Yet it was his fanatic towing of the Syrian line that made Ahmed Jibril a virtual pariah among the Palestinian guerrilla groups. It critically weakened his ability to gain widespread support among the masses, who dreamed not of furthering Syrian policy but of returning to Palestine. His close relationship with the Syrians also made him vulnerable. He realized he was a man who needed allies beyond Damascus, although he did not have to look very far or for very long to find them.

The factional sidelines of Lebanon had always been cut-and-dried except where the Shiites came into play. The most populous religious group in Lebanon were the Shiite Muslims. They had for years constituted the greatest majority among the Christian, Sunni, and Druze population, but their meager economic representation made them a discarded underclass; when the Palestinians began to arrive in 1948, they even surpassed the Shiites in Lebanon's complex and xenophobic social structure. The Palestinian groups in particular took violent advantage of the Shiites, rooting them out of homes in Beirut and forcing them to live as virtual prisoners in their own lands in the south. The worst abuses occurred in the south, where Shiite villages dotted the rugged mountain landscape near the Israeli frontier. Heavily armed Palestinian terrorist units frequently took over Shiite territory so that it could be used for bases against Israel. The terrorists often robbed the Shiites mercilessly, committed untold brutality against their women, including frequent kidnappings and gang rapes, and murdered those who wouldn't pay their extortion. The Palestinians turned the Shiites, a proud and extremely religious people, into slaves and tragic victims; pregnant twelve- and thirteen-year-old girls, raped by PLO personnel and abandoned by their own families, roamed aimlessly through the villages of the south.[5] The Shiites eventually fought back their anger to be Selt in the years to come. The majority of the fighters in renegade Major Haddad's FLA militia were, in fact, Shiites eager to rid their land of the Palestinians. On June 6, 1982, when the IDF invaded Lebanon, the Shiite villagers viewed the advancing Israeli soldiers as liberating heroes, and celebrated their entrance into Lebanon.[6] Members of the Nabih Berri's Shiite Amal militia even handed over their arms to advancing Israeli forces heading into Beirut.

By 1983, the Shiites had even become religious enemies of the Palestinians. The Iranian revolution and the Ayatollah Khomeini's inspiration as a human catalyst for the explosion of fundamentalist Islam had polarized the region, as had the Iran-Iraq war. The Arabs, especially the Palestinians, supported Saddam Hussein and Iraq in its invasion of Iran. Only Syria, the perennial pariah, supported Iran, supplying the purged Islamic army with equipment and military expertise. The Gulf war eventually spread to Lebanon, as Iranian clerics and Revolutionary Guards filtered into Lebanon via Syria and set up camps and representative offices in the Bekaa Valley capital of Ba'albek, the Shiite slums of West Beirut, and the southern part of eastern Lebanon not controlled by the IDF.* In 1983, the Hizbollah movement was created as a result of a merger between a radical element of Hussein Musawi's** Islamic Amal and the Lebanese Shiite *Da'wa* party.[8] *Hizbollah's* fanaticism, fired with meticulous zeal by the group's spiritual leader, Sheikh Hussein Fadlallah, made it a magnet for the disillusioned men of the Beirut slums who saw religious violence and martyrdom as their true spiritual salvation. The political objective of establishing a revolutionary Shiite Islamic state in Lebanon (modeled after Iran) could not tolerate the secular and socialist Palestinians. By 1983 and 1984, open fighting erupted between Palestinian and Shiite groups in several portions of Lebanon.

The one Palestinian group not at odds with the Shiites was Ahmed Jibril's PFLP-GC, and this was a direct result of Syria's close alliance with Iran. Syria had supported the Iranians, permitted Hizbollah to wage its Jihad against the American-led multinational force in Beirut, and wreak havoc against the anti-Syrian Palestinians in the country. Both Jibril and, in many ways, Hizbollah were tools of Syrian policy, and became working allies. The May 21, 1985, prisoner exchange had also elevated Jibril's stock in the eyes of hard-line fanatics in the region, like Hizbollah. In fact, the only Palestinian terrorist group allowed to return to its pre-Operation Peace for Galilee bases in southern Lebanon opposite Israeli forces was the PFLP-GC.[9] While Amal and Hizbollah forces operating in the south had openly engaged Fatah and PLF units heading toward the Israeli frontier (perhaps fearing a return to the barbaric prewar days when the PLO ruled the area), PFLP-GC units were even afforded military honors and logistical support by the local Amal and Hizbollah commanders. The phenomenon of a Jibril-Shiite terrorist alliance worried Israel greatly. For the IDF, the time was ripe to test the waters with decisive action.

On the night of December 2-3, 1985, an IDF infantry force, believed to be from the elite Giva'ati Infantry Brigade, crossed Israel's predesignated security zone along the fifteen kilometer-deep quadrant paralleling

---

* Originally an Iranian Army contingent had been part of the UNIFIL peace-keeping force sent to southern Lebanon in the spring of 1978. When the shah was overthrown in 1979, most of the Iranian soldiers remained behind as loyal agents of the Ayatollah in this most strategic battleground.

** On February 17, 1992, Sheikh A'bbas Musawi, the commander of the Hizbollah terrorist faction, was killed in southern Lebanon when an IAF AH-64 Apache helicopter gunship executed a well-planned airborne ambush on his heavily protected motorcade near Sidon, in southern Lebanon.[7]

the border, and attacked a PFLP-GC forward position at al-Arkub in what was once known as Fatahland; according to IDF intelligence reports, the position was about to be used to launch a strike against a northern Israeli kibbutz or moshav.

Anything past the security zone is known in the IDF vernacular as bandit country, a dangerous and desolate zone of operations where the mountainous terrain and suicidal penchant of the local armed gangs made any military activity a very dangerous undertaking. Taking this into consideration, the infantrymen were heavily armed with a wide assortment of heavy machine guns, RPGs, and grenade launchers, and prepared to engage the enemy with overwhelming firepower. Since forced marches are an IDF training specialty, the attack force managed to negotiate the icy terrain without too much difficulty and approached their heavily defended target with stealth. The Israeli infantry force struck quickly and with a lethal barrage. In a split-second firefight, five PFLP-GC gunmen were killed before most of them could even raise their weapons to firing position; the remaining ten men of the position's garrison were captured before they knew what had happened.[10]

It is doubtful that Israeli intelligence had reports that Ahmed Jibril himself would be in the area that night, or if this operation was a preemptive strike to disrupt terrorist capabilities. The results of the operation were, nevertheless, positive. Ten captured terrorists meant a wealth of information for intelligence corps interrogators, and the raiding force also managed to seize one 60-mm mortar, two light machine guns (a Belgian-produced FN MAG and a Soviet-produced RPK), ten AK-47 assault rifles, one SVD 7.62-mm sniper rifle, several night scopes, and land mines.[11]

Israel was not done in its campaign against Ahmed Jibril. The offensive was no longer a purely military struggle, however. The renowned assets of Israel's espionage services were now brought into play.

The Mossad's campaign against Palestinian terrorism has become an epic tale of a small and dedicated intelligence service, considered by many the world's best, battling a ruthless conglomerate of terrorists and killers. It is a war like any conventional conflagration, but not fought on a field of battle, and not waged with conventional weapons. It is a struggle of the shadows, where the art of the double cross, the false flag, and booby-trapped devices are the most common tools of the trade. The Mossad has been fighting Palestinian terrorism outside of Israel's frontiers since the summer of 1968, when the PFLP's Algiers hijacking extended the conflict well outside the confines of the region.

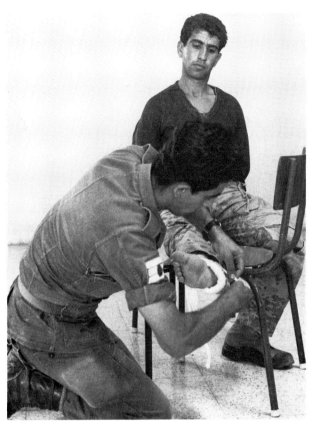

An Israeli paratrooper medic bandages the leg of a Jibril Palestine Liberation Front guerrilla following a successful pursuit in the northern Jordan Valley, circa 1968.

Azur, once a small village and now a Tel Aviv suburb, is the town of Jibril's birth. The parents of the three PFLP-GC prisoners were forced to be photographed in front of Jibril's childhood home before he would consider releasing his prisoners. (*Photo courtesy Sigalit Katz*)

An IDF paratroop NCO stares into the wreckage that was once a school bus. The bus was turned into a death trap by PFLP-GC grenadiers near Avivim, on May 22, 1970. (*IGPO*)

April 11, 1974. Bewildered and grief-stricken residents mill about in front of 15 Yehuda Halevy Street in Qiryat Shmoneh following the *Sayeret Golani* battle with a PFLP-GC suicide squad that infiltrated across the Lebanese frontier and perpetrated one of the worst massacres ever committed inside Israel. (*IGPO*)

November 24, 1983. Two of the 4,500 terrorists released by the IDF make their way onto a Red Cross flight as part of the prisoner swap involving six of the Na'ha'l infantrymen seized by Jibril's gunmen near Bhamdoun. (*IGPO*)

May 20th, 1985. Central Israel. A Military Police senior master-sergeant examines the papers of one of 1,150 released terrorists as he is taken to a transport that will ferry him to his home on the West Bank.

Military airfield—Ben Gurion International Airport, May 21, 1985. In the early morning hours a group of some of the most notorious terrorists that Jibril had demanded be released, including several high-ranking PFLP-GC officers who would feature prominently in the organization's later operations in Europe, prepare to board an IAF Boeing 707 to Geneva.

A nervous IDF OC Manpower Branch Major-General Amos Yaron walks past a Swiss antiterrorist police M113 awaiting the arrival of the Israeli prisoners from Damascus.

Swiss antiterrorist policemen, their Heckler and Koch 9-mm submachine guns at the ready, stand on guard prepared to repel any hostile interruption of the prisoner swap.

Pay dirt. Major-General Amos Yaron clutches Nissim Salam as he is escorted to an awaiting IAF Boeing 707 for the long-awaited flight back to Israel after nearly three years of captivity.

On board the IAF Boeing 707, Yaron telephones Israeli Defense Minister Yitzhak Rabin following the successful—and exhaustive—prisoner exchange. Looking on, center, is Shmuel Tamir, the official head of Israel's exchange efforts.

As a grim reminder of November 25, 1987, the Night of the Hang Glider, Khaled Aker's ultralight still stands stoically outside Camp Gibor.

"Crunch time." In the IDF's Lebanon security zone, soldiers from the Golani Brigade take cover while engaging a force of PFLP-GC terrorists moving from Hizbollah-territory toward the Israeli frontier.

Their faces obscured for security reasons, commandos from Sayeret Golani conduct an antiterrorist patrol inside the security zone.

Two Palestinian terrorists believed to be from the PFLP-GC lie dead a few meters across the Israeli frontier after being killed by an IDF patrol. Their AK-47 assault rifles and packs filled with explosives lie by their side.

An arms cache seized by IDF forces from a PFLP-GC squad attempting to cross into Israel past the security zone. Note field glasses and wirecutters.

Training in the desert, Golani units practice the art of attacking fortified enemy positions.

A Golani infantryman prepares to fire his Glilon 5.56-mm assault rifle. It is fitted with a laser-targeting device that emits a laser beam on the target. During the bitter close-quarters fighting inside the al-Na'ameh caves, this weapon, fitted to the Golani Brigade commandos, would be used with devastating accuracy. (*Courtesy: ITT Lasers*)

Before and after (*facing page*) aerial photographs of a PFLP-GC position in eastern Lebanon's Bekaa Valley after a destructive visit from IAF warplanes in the autumn of 1991.

Lieutenant-Colonel
Amir Meital, Golani
task force commander,
was killed inside the
tunnels of al-Na'ameh
on December 9, 1988.

The intelligence/counterintelligence war has been fought on virtually every continent, in most major cities, and usually with deadly results. From following the "alleged" hit teams that roamed Europe, to manipulating West German prison wardens, to recruiting Tunisian ministers, the Mossad has doggedly pursued the terrorists whose job it is to destroy the Jewish State.[12] Sometimes these efforts have reaped remarkable rewards, like the assassination of Ali Hassan Salameh in Beirut on January 22, 1979.* Sometimes the end results have been disastrous, like the failed hit on Ali Hassan Salameh in Lillehammer, Norway, in 1973 in which a Moroccan waiter was mistakenly killed by a Mossad squad, and virtually the organization's entire Scandinavian network was uncovered, tried, and imprisoned. Sometimes, however, the Mossad's efforts have had the potential to achieve the absolutely breathtaking.

By 1985, the semiofficial Israeli policy against terrorism was based on the conclusion that the most effective means for dealing with the PLO was vigilance and retaliation. The security and military services of the Jewish State would maintain as near to a hermetic seal on the nation's boundaries and around their overseas interests as could be maintained as a way of physically deterring attacks by Fatah and Arafat loyalist groups; of course, intelligence assets would be used to infiltrate these organizations, intercept their communications, and compromise their abilities. If a terrorist attack would transpire, like the Force 17 murder of three Israeli civilians on board a yacht in Larnaca harbor on September 25, 1985, the Israeli military would retaliate with swift and unforgiving destruction; five days after the killings in Cyprus, IAF F-15s and F-16s bombed PLO headquarters in Tunis.[14] The smaller terrorist groups led by one or two men were a different story. They were easier targets, with less political fallout and minimal military risk. If the leader could be removed, the organization ceased to exist, and with one strike a deadly cancer had been eradicated. According to Brigadier-General Gideon Machanaymi, the prime minister's deputy advisor on counterterrorism, assassinating these leaders was a sensible and logical course of policy.[15] A chance to implement that policy would come in Libya.

On February 4, 1986, Tripoli, Libya, was host to a major conference of the world's principal terrorist organizations and their leaders. The

---

* Israel has never officially assumed responsibility for the car-bomb assassination, even though it is widely assumed that a female Mossad agent posing as an eccentric British spinster was behind the operation.[13]

objective of the masterminds' meeting was to formulate a coordinated policy to intensify the struggle against the "conspiracies of Zionism and American imperialism." It was the height of Libyan sponsorship of international terrorism, as many of the world's notorious organizations, from the Provisional IRA to the German Red Army Faction, were all on the Libyan payroll. The terrorists were Qadaffi's foot soldiers with which he waged his holy war against the West. As he convened the conference at a heavily guarded hall in the downtown district of Libya's largest city, Qadaffi looked around a velour-draped table and saw a veritable who's who of the world's most notorious killers: the PFLP's George Habash, the DFLP's Nayif Hawatmeh, the Popular Struggle Front's Samir Ghawshah, the Fatah Revolutionary Council's Abu Nidal, and, of course, one of Libya's most influential—and expensive—servants, the PFLP-GC's Ahmed Jibril.[16] According to intelligence reports, several of the non-Arab world's most influential terrorists were also represented that balmy winter day, including Fusako Shigenobu, the enigmatic female leader of the Japanese Red Army terrorist group.

It was a wild and rhetoric-filled conference. Each terrorist leader vowed to increase the level of violence against Israel, and make America pay for her imperialistic policies and criminal support for Zionist expansionism. One by one the men took the podium, each professing his vow to support Colonel Qadaffi's generous bankrolling of his enterprise. The most energetic speaker that afternoon was Jibril; out of respect for his having engineered the humiliation of Israel in the prisoner exchange, he spoke last. Pounding his fist onto the podium in an angry tirade, Jibril spoke for nearly thirty minutes, claiming that his military forces would soon engage the Zionists in Lebanon and Palestine. Promising to bring the Palestinians' holy war against Zionism back into the international spotlight, he also promised to turn the streets of Israel into a bloodbath.

Following the conference, the participants worked the room for several hours, and then proceeded under heavy guard to the airport for flights to Baghdad, Tunis, and Damascus.

According to several reports, Mossad HUMINT (human intelligence) assets positioned on the ground in Tripoli had prepared the groundwork for a spectacular operation. Once the conference ended in the late afternoon, they would monitor the movements of Habash, Abu Nidal and, of course, Ahmed Jibril and report the details of the men's flight plans back to Syria; IAF aircraft would then intercept the aircraft and force it to land in Israel, where the terrorist warlords would be apprehended and, according to this reasoning, their organizations forever compromised and humbled.[17] There are conflicting reports as to who exactly the Israelis wanted to, or expected to, seize on board the aircraft; several semiofficial versions claim that George Habash was the "wanted man," others say the Israelis intended on capturing Abu Nidal, and, finally, most claim that the day's objective was the 59-year-old Jibril.[18]

The intelligence was just a bit off that day, however. Israeli espionage agents on the ground in Tripoli had relayed a heavily coded message back to their communication breaks in the Mediterranean—or directly in Israel!—that Ahmed Jibril and, possibly, Abu Nidal had boarded a Libyan Arab Airlines Gulfstream II executive jet and was about to take-off for Damascus. The intelligence data *was* received back in Tel Aviv and *immediately* disseminated to IAF headquarters, which, in turn, ordered an F-16 Fighting Falcon squadron placed on full alert; that squadron had, in fact, just returned from a training sortie and was undergoing a debriefing (a sacrosanct postmission function in the IAF) when the unit's deputy commander, Major G., was interrupted with the order to be ready to fly.[19] In all, four planes would be involved in the operation: the two that would physically intercept the Libyan aircraft at a predetermined point as close to Israeli airspace as the Gulfstream traveled, and two that would fly aerial cover—a Mach.2 shield to prevent any interruptions from the Syrian Air Force. The four pilots were quickly briefed as they headed toward their parked aircraft, receiving last-minute instructions as they fastened their G-vests to their chests and checked their survival gear one final time. It was twilight in Israel. The crimson sky was growing dark as the air base readied itself for the afterburner glow of four unexpected takeoffs. Secrecy at the base was absolute, and the officers granting permission to the four Falcons taking off on the illuminated runway did not know what this new mission was, but they know not to ask questions either; even the pilots did not know that they were being launched into the heavens to catch the world's most-wanted terrorists. Although secrecy is the catchword of the IDF, this day's field security was hermetic and unrivaled in its mystery.

Less than sixty seconds after the four birds were authorized for liftoff, the fully armed jets were racing toward the Mediterranean.

The four F-16 Falcons flew at a low altitude, barely skimming the choppy Mediterranean waves in order to avoid Lebanese, Cypriot, and Syrian radar. They headed toward a triangular coordinate between Turkey, Cyprus, and Syria, which would give them room to maneuver while waiting for their target; the two F-16s flying cover flew at high and protective altitudes. The Israeli aircraft would not have to wait very long.

Coming in along a north-northeast heading at 37,000 feet was a small blip on the F-16's radar: the Libyan Gulfstream, and they locked on to the slow-moving target without too much difficulty.[20] The pilots immediately braced for action and headed for the intercept; in order to make sure that the Gulfstream could not make a break for Syrian territorial airspace, the two F-16s continued their low-level flight and they raced upward at a full G-force climb to the aircraft's altitude. Both F-16s pulled up alongside the Libyan aircraft at the dangerously close distance of ten meters from its outer wingtips. According to international law, the procedure for intercepting a civilian aircraft is for the interceptor to wave the wings several times, and then turn sharply to either the right or left sides: the aircraft being snared should, if everything goes peacefully, simply play follow the leader. The two F-16s gave the proper signals but the Libyan pilot appeared dazed by his newfound predicament and continued flying as if nothing was wrong. According to Captain A., the lead F-16 pilot, "I was so close to him that I could clearly read the green letters of the Libyan Arab Airlines logo, as well as seeing the face of the pilot in the illuminated cockpit.[21] After a tense display of patience and an unnerving game of cat-and-mouse, the Libyan aircraft was finally diverted toward Israel, to the Ramat David air base in the north.[22] In order to maintain extraordinary security, the F-16s had to guide the Gulfstream over a section of land that did not cover towns or other civilian settlements.

The Gulfstream was brought to a halt on a remote stretch of the Ramat David air base, which was suddenly turned into an armed camp. The jet was immediately surrounded by approximately one hundred fifty heavily armed IDF commandos.[23] Floodlights were brought around the surrounded aircraft, and a select group of commandos from, according to foreign reports, Sayeret Mat'kal burst their way into the plane as if they were storming an enemy position. The commandos all wore bulletproof Kevlar flak vests, their weapons were cocked and readied, and their trigger fingers were in position to launch a deadly burst of rounds at any sign of armed opposition; if the terrorists were indeed on board the aircraft, their bodyguards would probably put up a suicidal stand. Yet Israeli intelligence had been off—even if by only very little. Ahmed Jibril was not on board the Gulfstream, and neither was Habash or Abu Nidal.* Outraged, the commando group leader

---

* In a press conference in Damascus, Habash would state that the Mossad had not erred by very much. He had intended to fly on board that aircraft, but had changed his travel plans at the last moment for security reasons. The same held true for Ahmed Jibril and Abu Nidal.[24]

stared into the face of each man on board the aircraft, doing double-takes to make sure he had not made a mistake. The faces on board the aircraft did not match the mug shots in his dossier.

The Israelis had inadvertently interrupted the travel plans of a dozen high-ranking officials of the Syrian Ba'ath party, including several confidants of President Hafaz al-Assad. One man, A'bdallah al-Ahmer, was the deputy secretary of the Ba'ath party and occupied a political position similar to Assad's vice-president; he was known by the code name "Red."[25] Embarrassed, the Israeli troops thoroughly searched the aircraft one final time, and then fueled it for takeoff. The local commanders on the scene humbly apologized, but the Syrian officials were none too receptive to kind words or gestures. After twelve hours on the ground, the IAF allowed the Gulfstream to take off for Damascus. A golden opportunity to capture Ahmed Jibril had been lost.

The Gulfstream Incident was an embarrassment to the Israeli intelligence community and, according to American intelligence sources, a severe blow to the Mossad. Yet Israel was not apologetic. In a televised interview the following day, Israeli Prime Minister Yitzhak Shamir stated: "We may be disappointed but are definitely not sorry!" Had Israel's intelligence been real-time, the right aircraft and Jibril might have been seized. But such capabilities were unavailable in a police state like Libya; in fact, most Western nations had even less effective HUMINT assets on the ground in Libya. The attempt was, nevertheless, a noble effort by the Israelis.

The Syrians, however, were enraged by the whole affair. They viewed the way the IDF treated al-Ahmer and the other passengers on board the aircraft, forcing them to stay the night, sleep in military-style squalor, and eat abominable IDF food, as terribly insulting. The Syrian Army Chief of Staff Major-General Hikmat al-Shehabi stated that "Israel would soon learn a lesson it will never forget." The Syrians were not making veiled threats. Nor would the Palestinians.

On March 15, 1986, Libya's Colonel Qadaffi convened yet another terrorist convention in Tripoli—a grand symposium of terrorist masterminds and their international supporters. This time, the gathering of twenty-two Palestinian groups was to formulate a response to the Gulfstream interception. The gathering was billed as an antiimperialist symposium, and the non-Palestinian guests included the Basque Euzkadi ta Askatasuna (ETA, Fatherland and Liberty), radical American Indians, East German experts, Spanish Catalan separatists, Kanaks from New Caledonia, and Moros from the Philippines; observers from dozens of other groups, from Latin America to southern Africa, also attended the conference.[26] The star speaker that winter's morning was Ahmed Jibril. Angered by the Gulfstream incident, especially since he was the intended target of the aerial snare, Jibril spoke in a slow and soft voice. Raising his eyes to the assembled men, he said: "There will be no safety for any traveler on an Israeli or American airliner!"[27]

In the early morning hours of April 17, 1986, Anne-Marie Murphy, a pregnant nineteen-year-old Irish girl, was driven to Terminal One at London's Heathrow Airport by her Jordanian-born boyfriend and fiancé, thirty-two-year-old Nezar Hindawi. The two had known each other for several months and it had been love at first sight. When it was discovered that Ms. Murphy was pregnant, Hindawi promised to marry her, but he wanted the ceremony performed in Israel, together with his family on the West Bank. He convinced her that she should travel alone to Israel, where he would join her a few days later, after he liquidated his assets in London so that he could pay for a memorable wedding in his native village. Ms. Murphy did not want to travel alone, but she faithfully followed her lover's instructions and purchased an economy ticket for El Al Flight 016 to Tel Aviv, a crowded flight that originated in New York's John F. Kennedy Airport.

In the parking lot underneath Terminal One, Hindawi and Murphy said goodbye to one another with a passionate kiss. Before leaving her affectionate embrace, Hindawi handed her a special gift he had purchased for her trip: an expensive overnight bag with some gifts thrown inside for good luck. She kissed him one last time and headed for the departure area and check-in procedures. She had little idea about his politics, or the fact that he was a mercenary terrorist on hire to the Syrian government who had just turned her into a human time bomb.[28] To Ms. Murphy, he was simply Nezi, her handsome and exotic Arab lover.

Ms. Murphy proceeded to the El Al check-in counter, where her ticket was examined and her suitcases were searched; following a brief quiz by the Shin Bet-trained El Al security guard, she was given her boarding pass and wished a pleasant flight and first trip to Israel. She proceeded toward passport control and Heathrow's elaborate security apparatus meant to deter and detect terrorists. Handing her bags to the security guard for inspection, Hindawi's gift bag was placed on the X-ray machine and quickly examined. It passed the scrutiny uneventfully. Ms. Murphy then continued toward the duty-free shop and some quick shopping before making her flight.

Since the first days of hijackings and aerial mayhem, flights going to Israel—especially El Al—have been afforded unique security arrangements by the British transportation ministry. El Al flights from Heathrow were isolated to distant gate Number 23 far from regular traffic, and, ever since Abu Nidal's December 27, 1985, Rome and Vienna massacres, London metropolitan police bobbies from the elite D11 unit armed with West German Heckler & Koch 9-mm submachine guns patrolled and protected the passengers.[29] It was a formidable human and technological gauntlet, but there was one more barrier to cross. Before a passenger would be allowed on board the aircraft, another group of Shin Bet-trained El Al security agents would screen the passengers, X-ray them once again, and perform a body and handbag search. Anne-Marrie Murphy was taken into a small cubicle sealed off by navy blue sheets and questioned by a young male security agent. Politely he asked her some personal questions, including why a single and pregnant Irish woman would be traveling to Israel by herself. Once the words *Arab boyfriend* were mentioned, the well-trained guard searched the travel bag with anxious anticipation. The initial hand check revealed nothing, but on closer examination, the guard discovered a false bottom. Attached to a calculator serving as a timing device was 1.5-kilograms of grade A Czech Semtex.[30] The timer was set to go off at exactly 1304 hours, the time when all the passengers would have been sitting down enjoying a hot lunch and the plane, a Boeing 747 jumbo jet, would be flying high above the clouds over the Austrian Alps. Had the destructive plan succeeded, all 375 passengers and crew would surely have been blown out of the sky. If ever there was a case for human diligence in the fight against terror, this was it.

Without starting a panic, the El Al guard summoned his British police liaison, and Ms. Murphy was quietly escorted to a side room, while her luggage was quickly removed from the 747's cargo hold. The passengers waiting to reboard the flight for the final leg of their trip to Israel were told to wait patiently while a "mechanical" problem was attended to. Security officials from MI5 (the British Secret Service) and the local Shin Bet liaison raced to the airport to question Ms. Murphy. Both the British and the Israelis considered that this could be a false-flag diversion to a more diabolical operation.

Nezar Hindawi did not remain at Heathrow to see if his handiwork had been successful. In fact, he had less than three hours to escape from London altogether. He drove back to the Royal Garden Hotel in Kensington, the principal stopover spot for air crews of Syrianair,* to

---

* According to Western intelligence reports, Syrianair is a principal tool of Syrian Air Force Intelligence, and is used as a legitimized cover; accordingly, most Syrianair employees are potential intelligence operatives.

collect his belongings and then catch the daily Syrianair flight to Damascus out of Heathrow; ominously, Hindawi's flight was scheduled to take off exactly four minutes before El Al Flight 016 would have disintegrated at 40,000 feet over Austria.[31] Hindawi went through the well-rehearsed procedure, and had even boarded a private bus to take him to the airport, but an agent from Syrian Air Force Intelligence who was on call in the hotel lobby and in communication to another agent monitoring developments at Heathrow learned that the bomb had been discovered. Hindawi was physically pulled off the bus and ordered to proceed to the Syrian Embassy. "The Zionists," Hindawi was told, "had complicated matters a bit."

Nezar Hindawi had been told that nothing could possibly go wrong in the El Al bombing. His control officer, after all, was Lieutenant-Colonel Haitham Sayid, a deputy commander of Syrian Air Force Intelligence and chief recruiter for foreign operations, and they had met in the Royal Garden Hotel to discuss the aircraft's destruction.[32] Hindawi was smart enough to realize that he was not working for a small and unreliable terrorist organization, but the principal espionage and internal security service of the Syrian regime. *Idarat Mukhabarat al-Quwwa al-Jawiya*, the Syrian Air Force Intelligence, is the nation's principal domestic and foreign intelligence service, charged with carrying out the most sensitive, and sometimes the most despotic, covert activities, including the apprehension, torture, and execution of Syrian political opponents. Lieutenant-Colonel Sayid's commander was the legendary Brigadier-General Muhammad Khouli, a brilliant and ruthless spymaster who had for years been President Assad's shadowy right-hand man.[33] Brigadier-General Khouli was behind the brutal February 1981 crackdown of the Muslim Brotherhood in Hamma, where a reported twenty thousand civilians were killed, as well as countless other bloody incidents in Lebanon and beyond.* Syrian Air Force Intelligence was an extremely capable organization that even the Israelis grudgingly respected, and Hindawi believed his participation in one of its operations virtually guaranteed his survival. In fact, to see through the successful execution of this mission, Hindawi and Lieutenant-Colonel Sayid, using the name Mr. Kokash, shared a room in the Kensington Hotel.

In the Syrian Embassy, Hindawi was given a lunchtime audience with the ambassador, Dr. Lutof al-Haydar, as well as a pep talk. Three

---

* Syrian Air Force Intelligence is now run by Colonel Ibrahim Huwajy, Khouli's nephew. Brigadier-General Khouli runs the Syrian Presidential Council.[34]

Syrian intelligence agents then took Hindawi to a safe house, where his hair was cut and bleached; obviously Anne-Marie Murphy would have talked, and British and Israeli security officials would be in hot pursuit of "Nezi." Understandably, Hindawi began to fear for his life. He realized that he could very well become the fall guy of the failed operation; to cut their links to the bungled attack, the Syrians might decide to eliminate him. As he was being taken back to the Syrian Embassy on the morning of April 18, he broke free from his escorts and raced to a police station to turn himself in.

For Israel, what soon became known as the Hindawi Affair proved just how safe an airline El Al really was, and how intrinsically involved Syria was with the support and outright perpetration of terrorism. Once in British custody, Hindawi was eager to talk, and he clearly implicated virtually every branch of the Syrian government and intelligence apparatus in the failed bombing attempt. During an extremely detailed court trial in London's Old Bailey, irrefutable evidence of the Syrian connection was made public. Syrian complicity in some of the most horrible acts of terror inside Europe, including the bombing of the La'Belle Disco in West Berlin, which the Americans had mistakenly linked to Libya, was now fact, and Assad's once-impenetrable veil of cloak-and-dagger secrecy had now been shattered forever. In retaliation, Britain broke diplomatic relations with Syria and expelled Ambassador al-Haydar,* and both Washington and Ottawa recalled their ambassadors to Damascus. It was also later revealed that Pierre Marion, former head of France's foreign-intelligence operations, had met with Syrian officials in order to secure guarantees that no acts of Syrian-sponsored terrorism would transpire on French soil.[35]

Nezar Hindawi was sentenced to forty-five years in prison. At Hindawi's sentencing, the judge stated that he saluted the El Al security guard for his vigilance.[36]

The Hindawi Affair remains one of the most mysterious terrorist operations ever attempted, as the true motive behind the failed bombing remains a secret and a source of great speculation. Ostensibly Syria planned to blow up El Al Flight 016 in revenge for the IAF interception of the Libyan Gulfstream. But President Assad, *if* he was informed of the operation, was clearly clever enough to realize that should the destruction of an El Al jet and the loss of 375 innocent lives ever be linked to Damascus, Israel would probably embark on a ferocious, full-

---

* In an attempt to deflect attention from Syria, Ambassador al-Haydar claimed that the Hindawi Affair was a Mossad-orchestrated effort to discredit Syria.

scale war of national retribution against Syria. But Syria was not ready for war against Israel, as its massive rearmament campaign had yet failed to achieve military parity with Israel. Assad simply didn't work that way, according to one American intelligence analyst specializing in Syrian matters: "Assad is the type of man to calculate every move and not take a single risk. He obtains—or removes—his objectives like a professional assassin, not a crazed gunman willing to leave a smoking gun."[37]

The affair could also have been a warning to Israel. The abduction of Ba'ath party officials would *not* be tolerated, and any such future action risked horrendous loss of life.

Remarkably, some observers have suggested that perhaps the disastrous affair was, indeed, engineered by the Mossad to discredit Syria and publicize the evil regime in Damascus for its support of brutal acts of terrorism; after all, if the plot had been engineered by Israel, they certainly would have found the bomb before Ms. Murphy boarded the aircraft. In late 1986, a high-ranking officer in Syrian Air Force Intelligence, Colonel Mufid Akhour, was detained on suspicion of being an Israeli agent. His fate remains a mystery, although many, understanding Syria's historic fears of having its intelligence services infiltrated by Israeli agents,* believe he was quickly executed.

Perhaps, it has also been theorized, the Hindawi Affair was a test conducted by the Syrians on behalf of their Palestinian allies. The operation could have been an examination and in-depth look at El Al's security apparatus, and a probing action meant to determine what El Al guards could and could not detect.

It is also possible that the attempted bombing of El Al Flight 016 was a masterful plan by Syria to discredit, disgrace, or teach a lesson to one of the Damascus-controlled Palestinian terrorist organizations that might have strayed from the official line, or perhaps pursued an alliance with a different Arab state. Should El Al Flight 016 have been destroyed, only one Palestinian terrorist group was known for its bombing of Israeli airliners, and only one group would have been blamed for the disaster: Ahmed Jibril's PFLP-GC.

Most Western intelligence reports claim that Hindawi was a high-ranking terrorist in Abu Nidal's organization, but evidence of this remains sketchy. Although there are no firm facts available to the

---

* In 1965, the Syrian Ba'ath party was rocked by the discovery of one Kamil Amin Ta'abeth, the cover name for Eli Cohen, an A'man/Mossad spy who nearly managed to reach the post of Syrian defense minister. He was executed on May 1, 1965, and the Syrians have vowed never to return his body.

author to directly link Hindawi with Ahmed Jibril's PFLP-GC, the fact that he has claimed to journalists that he will soon be released for the two Israeli "servicemen" Jibril is still holding suggests more than just benign links.[38] Jibril had immediate motive for blowing up an El Al jet, since he was the intended target of the Gulfstream operation, and the PFLP-GC was the only Palestinian terrorist group that had perfected midair bombings and specialized in attacks against El Al; the PFLP-GC was also one of the only groups to have made an art form out of recruiting impressionable young Western women and turning them into sexual slaves and human time bombs. While the Abu Ibrahim's Arab Organization of 15 May* is the only other Palestinian group known for planting bombs on board airliners, it was an organization under firm *Iraqi* control, and almost always attacked *American* airliners, like the April 1, 1986, bombing of a TWA flight en route from Egypt to the United States via Rome and Athens.[39] If the Syrians wanted to pin the bombing on the PFLP-GC for whatever reason, then they would have assistance from the international police agencies that would have surely investigated the incident. The fact that the bomb was timed to explode over land suggests that it was planned for the physical evidence of the blast and the bomb—the data required for prosecution—to have been recovered.

Ahmed Jibril also enjoyed a unique relationship with Brigadier-General Khouli, and the two men briefed each other at least once a week, according to Western intelligence estimates. It is, in the author's opinion, inconceivable that Syrian Air Force Intelligence could have—or would have—undertaken an airline bombing without enlisting the help, or unwitting compliance, of Ahmed Jibril.

Due to the high degree of secrecy maintained by Syria's ruling Ba'ath Party, the truth behind the Hindawi Affair might never become public knowledge. No matter who is directly to blame and what the true motives for the action were, it was an action prompted by the Israeli quest to capture—or kill—Ahmed Jibril and, in the long run, it would also serve the objectives of the PFLP-GC. The attempt to bring a Semtex bomb on board a 747 was a test run—a dress rehearsal meant to insure absolute success the next time an aircraft would be targeted for obliteration.

The next time came less than two years later, over the Scottish hamlet of Lockerbie.

---

* In 1978, the Popular Front for the Liberation of Palestine-Special Operations Group split into three groups: the 15 May, PFLP-Special Command, and the Lebanese Armed Revolutionary Faction.[40]

CHAPTER EIGHT

OPERATION KIBYA, OR THE NIGHT OF THE HANG GLIDERS

ISRAEL'S SECURITY CONSIDERATIONS regarding her volatile northern frontier tended to concentrate on heavily armed terrorists trying to cross the formidable "fence." Although not as imposing and internationally symbolic as the Cold War-era Berlin Wall, the fence separating Israel and Lebanon was a thick and imposing barbed-wire obstacle. Several rows of razor-sharp concertina ringed both sides, as did land mines and electronic sensors meant to signal if a terrorist crossing was under way; the fence was over eight-feet high, so it was virtually impossible for terrorists to climb over it. Yet the fence was far from a hermetic seal protecting the northern frontier. Terrorists resigned to the fact that they were about to become martyrs would risk personal injury and attempt to cut through the barbed wire in order to attack Israel. Once across, the Galilee region was dotted with lucrative targets, like small towns, kibbutzim, and moshavim, which could be attacked in a suicide assault. The IDF and the National Police Border Guards shared responsibility for patrolling the frontier, from Rosh Hanikra at the Mediterranean to the Mount Hermon crucible. The arrangement was known in Israeli vernacular as *Bitachon Shutaf*, or joint security. Heavily armed soldiers, riding in open command cars mounting light machine guns, reinforced the fence, determined to destroy any Palestinian terror squad before it managed to make its way into Israel.

Yet the true gauntlet of deterrents meant to inhibit the Palestinians from even attempting to cross the border is a small force of Bedouin, Druze, and Circassian soldiers whose inherent gifts for the desert allows them to read the land as if it were a holy scripture. The *Gashashim*, or trackers, possess the remarkable ability to gaze upon a stretch of land, stare at the grain of the earth, and determine if it has been tread upon by man or beast. The imprint of the mark can help them determine if a man who walked on that stretch of earth was overweight, or if he had a limp. In a perfect world, this skill, handed down from generation to generation, is used as a tool by the nomadic Bedouins to hunt down wayward sheep or goats. Along the fence, as well as along the fences spread across the Jordanian and Egyptian frontiers, these unique gifts are deployed to hunt humans. The work of the tracker is an intrinsic element to Israeli frontier defenses. In fact, a twelve-foot-wide sand-and-dirt path accompanies the fence from the Mediterranean to the Golan Heights. A tracker accompanies each patrol, his eyes transfixed on the path, and he gazes to see if there are any new marks or imprints in the dirt since the last time the unit passed by; a coiled row of barbed wire is dragged by each patrolling command car to smooth out the sandy strip each time around. It is a tense and demanding task. According to one Border Guard officer assigned the task of securing a portion of the fence, "It is a slow and tedious process requiring a unique patience that no Jewish soldier has, and a force that no terrorist can surpass."[1] Trackers are usually professional soldiers, lifers, who safeguard the frontiers in twenty-year stints.

If a sign of a terrorist crossing is found, the tracker clutches his M-16 5.56-mm assault rifle, a Gashash's favorite weapon, dismounts from his vehicle, and begins his dedicated pursuit. Even if the terrorists have had a several hour head start, the trackers have a bloodhound's ability to find and locate their man; they can even determine if foliage has been stepped on by human feet, and in which direction the target was heading. Once located, the terrorists are usually cornered and terminated in a firefight with IDF or police units. The first into the fray, the trackers usually find themselves in the thick of desperate battles. Hundreds of gashashim have been killed in action.

The terrorists appreciate the effectiveness of the trackers and understand that these men of the desert are, many times, all that stand in their way to repeating the success of attacks, as were seen in Qiryat Shmoneh and Ma'alot. The terrorists hold the gashashim in high esteem, and have gone to remarkable efforts to bypass them. They have coated the soles of their canvas *patauga* boots with goat skins in order to camouflage their tracks, they have rubbed their clothing with various animal wastes to throw the trackers off the scent, and they have crossed the Israeli frontier on all fours, dotting the sandy path with sheep paws removed from dead animals.[2] Most important, the terrorists have attempted more extravagant and spectacular means for infiltrating into Israel.

Because it is so difficult to safeguard and because it is home to two and a half million Israelis, Israel's elongated coastal Mediterranean frontier has been a frequent target for terrorist attack. Since 1974, there have been many massacres along the Israeli coast, from the June 24, 1974, Fatah seaborne attack on an apartment building in Nahariya, in which three family members were killed, to the March 11, 1978, Country Club Massacre, in which thirty-five Israeli civilians were murdered and seventy-one seriously wounded. Through diligence and sheer luck, the *Heyl Ha'Yam* (IDF/Navy) has managed to contain the terrorists' ability to attack the Israeli shore. An elaborate screen of shore-based radar installations, manned mainly by female soldiers, covered the entire Mediterranean coastline; their efforts were supported by radar coverage from IDF/Navy missile boats, and by IDF/Navy IAI Sea Scan 1124N reconnaissance aircraft. If a "skunk," or enemy terrorist vessel, was located off the Mediterranean coast, it was usually destroyed by the *Dabur's* (IDF/Navy [or "Bee"] patrol boats) accurate 20-mm cannon fire.

Since 1980, the Palestinians have failed to achieve a single naval victory, even though they have attempted countless seaborne incursions. On April 16, 1985, Fatah attempted an extremely audacious seaborne assault on the Israel shore when it dispatched more than thirty fighters on board a Panamanian-registered mother ship, the S.S. *Attavirus*, to land on the beaches of the Tel Aviv suburb of Bat Yam. They were to then commandeer a bus and break through the defenses at the IDF Ministry of Defense in Tel Aviv, taking the IDF general staff hostage. This grandiose plan, conceived by Abu Jihad, was torpedoed when the *Attavirus* was intercepted in international waters by an IDF/Navy missile boat and blasted out of the water.[3] On May 30, 1990, the Abu A'bbas Faction of the PLF attempted, perhaps, the most ambitious seaborne attack ever when it dispatched six speedboats loaded with heavily armed terrorists to attack the crowded Tel Aviv beaches during the Shavuot holiday, including one boat destined to attack a Tel Aviv beach with nearly one hundred thousand sunbathers. Four of the boats encountered mechanical and operational difficulties, and both of the remaining attackers were eventually discovered by *Dabur* boats, and the terrorists either killed or captured.[4]

There were, however, other means by which the terrorists could ferry men into Israel.

The PFLP-GC had always searched out unique means by which it could attack Israel. Jibril's amphibious units had an impressive supply of Zodiac rubber dinghies and motorized speedboats by which small forces of men and material could be landed in Israel; these units were primarily trained by Syrian naval commando elements at their principal base at Latakia, on the Mediterranean coast. The PFLP-GC also acquired several motorized remote-control speedboats that could be crammed with several hundred kilograms of high explosives and then guided to their target.[5] The PFLP-GC was the first terrorist faction to invest significant capital in the acquisition of light aircraft for the execution of spectacular operations against Israel. At first, these included small piston-engine civilian aircraft that were to be crammed with explosives and crashed into an Israeli target in a Palestinian version of a kamikaze assault.

A military man always keen to catch the enemy off guard, Ahmed Jibril was also fascinated by the potential for transporting men by truly unconventional means, especially airborne methods such as wind-driven hang gliders and hot-air balloons.[6] Intelligence reports state that Jibril was planning to mount a large-scale aerial offensive at the height of the Lebanese civil war, but that the Syrian invasion and the subsequent mini-civil war that erupted between himself and Abu A'bbas delayed these plans. Hindering Jibril's grandiose operation was the fact that many of the special-operations officers responsible for this type of warfare and terrorism had defected to join forces with Abu A'bbas's new faction of the PLF. Indeed, A'bbas would be the first to attempt this revolutionary means of infiltration.

On March 7, 1981, the PLF launched a unique attack against the Jewish State. Two terrorists equipped with a crude explosive device and side arms were taken to a hill in southern Lebanon, near Beaufort Castle, and launched into the sky on wind-driven hang gliders. The objective of the assault was to fly over the ultrastrategic oil refineries in the port city of Haifa and drop two explosive charges into the facility, initiating a chain reaction of tremendous explosions and uncontrollable blazes which would cripple the Israeli economy for some time. Both sorties failed, however. One terrorist dropped his bomb over a field of flowers and then crash-landed his craft near Kibbutz Afek. He was quickly apprehended by irate kibbutz residents and Israeli security forces. The second hang glider met with even less success. He never left Lebanese airspace. He crashed in territory controlled by Major Haddad's militia and was turned over to Israeli forces.[7]

Many Israeli security officials scoffed at these almost comical attempts by the Palestinians to attack Israel, but IAF commanders were introduced to a new and perplexing operational challenge. The IAF is responsible for all of Israel's air defenses and commands all anti-aircraft units, from American-made HAWK surface-to-air missile batteries to mechanized units sporting the M163 Vulcan 20-mm Gatling gun dynamo.* A hang glider is difficult to spot by a fire-control acquisition radar, and maintaining visual surveillance along the entire Lebanese frontier with World War II-type spotters, the only true means available to detect such a windswept craft, was militarily inconceivable. Nevertheless, a higher state of readiness was implemented along the fence area, and ground units were told to raise their eyes, and gun barrels, occasionally toward the heavens. Remarkably, these extra efforts would pay off as Abu A'bbas opted to raise the ante one notch further.

On April 16, 1981, two PLF terrorists attempted to cross into Israel in a hot-air balloon; the flyby infiltration attempt was carried out at dawn when it was believed IDF preparedness would be at its lowest. The balloon took off from a ravine near the lines of Major Haddad's militia, and proceeded at moderate speed toward the Israeli frontier. Unlike the hang glider, the balloon was a much larger target, both visually and with its radar signature. Alert IAF gunners located the flying bag and laced it with tracer fire. It crash-landed seconds later, but the terrorists survived the fall from the sky. IDF paratroop units crossed the border in pursuit and eventually killed the two PLF gunmen in a firefight.[8] The balloon was brought back to Israel and displayed to the media.

Abu A'bbas's failure was Jibril's gain. The PFLP-GC commander studied the two botched operations and vowed to modify the means of attack as well as the means of delivery. Cunning and patient, Jibril would wait for the opportune moment before dispatching his aerial forces to deliver a deadly blow from the sky. He would wait until the winter of 1987.

---

* This is unique, since in most Western armed forces, like the U.S. military, an air defense network is delegated to land components.

* * *

For the PFLP-GC, 1987 was a perfect time to strike against Israel. Ahmed Jibril had endured nearly two years of incessant Israeli military and espionage-service pressure. From the attack on the PFLP-GC staging area in Fatahland near Hush ad-Dniba, on December 4, 1985, to the failed interception of the Libyan Gulfstream in February 1986, Ahmed Jibril was convinced he was under the gun.[9] Although a self-professed independent, Jibril could not mount any major operation without the permission and logistical support of the Syrians. Historically, President Assad had always succeeded in distancing himself from major terrorist attacks; the smoking gun was *never* to emanate from Damascus. But the April 17, 1986, attempted bombing of El Al Flight 016 changed everything. Hafaz al-Assad was no longer the Teflon supporter of terrorism; he was now linked to attempted mass murder in legal proceedings diligently covered by the mass media. He too felt as if he was being backed against a wall by incriminating public accusations. Yet, when in the spring of 1987 Jibril expressed his plans to strike out against Israel, the Syrians not only sanctioned the operation, they also pledged invaluable support and protection.[10]

At first, Jibril had yet to decide on the exact means by which he would infiltrate his fighters into Israel. Contingency planning included attacks emanating from cross-border forays across the fence, and a seaborne assault in the Haifa area. By early 1987, however, the PFLP-GC had established a serious, however small, airborne component that Jibril called *al-Rawad* (the Pioneers). Completely under the control of Brigadier-General Ali Duba, commander of Syrian Military Intelligence, al-Rawad is commanded by Syrian army officers with PFLP-GC commanders only afforded a limited say in the day-to-day running of the unit.[11] Based in a heavily defended military compound at Di'han, halfway between Damascus and Homs, Jibril's air commandos were trained in the art of airborne infiltration.* Jibril had studied the PLF's two failed 1981 airborne attempts with great interest, and determined that the notion was militarily sound, but that their means was inaccurate and highly precarious. Instead of relying on the wind for power, Jibril chose to equip his airborne raiders with motorized hang

---

* According to Israeli intelligence reports, Jibril's men were also trained in such airborne attacks by "experts from Eastern Europe and Latin America in training camps not only in Syria, but in northern Lebanon, and Libya, as well.[12]

gliders, ultralights, which could be driven like small airplanes to their targets. The first of these aircraft had been obtained from the West German SEEG factory in 1981, but kept in storage in Syria and saved for a special chance to strike at Israel.

Jibril wanted to launch his operation in the summer of 1987, but Syrian Air Force Intelligence and Syrian Military Intelligence were eager to create some distance, at least in terms of time, between themselves and terrorism. Damascus was engaged in a full-fledged public relations and diplomatic offensive throughout Europe meant to mend political relationships burned by the attempted bombing of El Al Flight 016. Through his contacts in Ali Duba's office, Jibril was ordered to delay the operation until the winter. Time was a welcome respite from the pressure. It enabled the men of al-Rawad to train. Ahmed Jibril personally handled much of the training and logistical requirements of the planned operation.[13] Indeed, the planned strike would have Jibril's unique flair for the spectacular. He envisioned the operation as a technical marvel, which would not only insure success but also serve as an example for future operations against Israel. This spectacular raid was code-named Operation Kibya, a reference to the Israeli retaliatory raid on October 14, 1953, conducted by "Arik" Sharon's Unit 101 and a force of IDF paratroopers, in which sixty-nine Jordanian civilians were tragically killed.[14]

Uncontrolled revenge against Israel was clearly the objective of Ahmed Jibril's master plan. So, too, was the symbolism of the carnage he envisioned. The target for his airborne assault was Qiryat Shmoneh, scene of his organization's most impressive operation ever inside Israeli territory.

Jibril's first task was to select the men to carry out the operation. This raid was not meant to serve as a political statement, nor as a hostage-taking ordeal designed to achieve the release of jailed comrades rotting in Israeli prisons; after all, most of the PFLP-GC men the IDF had managed to capture were released on May 21, 1985. The sole military objective of Operation Kibya was a high body count. It was to be a death rampage in which the more Israelis killed the better. Jibril also realized that such an operation was a suicidal undertaking, and that he needed to find men willing to martyr themselves for the cause. After a careful search, which he personally conducted, Jibril found his men: two Palestinians who remain anonymous to this day; a Syrian mercenary, Khaled Muhammad Aker (nom de guerre Abu Rami); and a Tunisian gunman for hire, Maludin an-Naja (nom de guerre Abu Ali).* Although it remains unclear whether or not the four men volunteered for the operation or were designated, reports from Damascus claim that the men attended to their training with fanatic zeal.

Under great secrecy, the men were taken to a special facility near Damascus to learn how to fly the SEEG ultralights. Each terrorist wore race car driver helmets purchased by Syrian intelligence agents in Europe and equipped with high-tech communications gear, including a multiband frequency receiver and a mouthpiece microphone.[16] Recalling the IAF's victory over the Syrian SAMs and the air force during Operation Peace for Galilee, due in part to the Israeli E-2C Hawkeye AWACS and C^3 (command, control, and communications) abilities, Jibril wanted his suicide commandos to keep in constant communication with headquarters in Damascus; according to a Western counterterrorist expert, it is believed that Jibril wanted to listen to the shooting and killings as they took place! The PFLP-GC commander would sit with several Syrian intelligence officers in the Yarmouk refugee camp and monitor the developments from an advanced forward C^3 post equipped with state-of-the-art Soviet-bloc communications gear.

Having witnessed the wanton savagery of the Lebanese civil war firsthand, Jibril realized that four men, heavily armed, determined to kill, and resigned to their own deaths, could exact an enormous human toll on the enemy. Each of the four Operation Kibya commandos would carry an AK-47 7.62-mm assault rifle, complete with twelve 30-round magazines, one dozen antipersonnel fragmentation hand grenades, as well as a Tokarov 9-mm pistol equipped with a silencer. To increase their chances of survival and their ability to kill for as long as they could muster the strength to pull a trigger or hurl a grenade, each commando was also equipped with a Kevlar flak vest. According to several reports, the men were also equipped with booby-trapped vests and belts that could be detonated if one of the men were wounded with IDF troops encroaching. Apparently Jibril envisioned his force exacting a toll on the enemy, even toward the very last breath.

The Operation Kibya commandos trained for nearly four months in the execution of the raid. The preparation was brutal in its intensity,

---

* It remains unclear whether or not Operation Kibya involved three, four, or even five hang gliders and gunmen. Following the raid into Israel, a PFLP-GC spokesman in Damascus issued a statement in which Jibril admitted that four commandos were involved in the operation.[15]

and the men were worked for twelve hours a day, six days a week. In the last week of October 1987, the unit conducted a live-fire dress rehearsal for Jibril. Flying in a tidy and close-knit formation, the four hang gliders sailed into a smooth landing on an empty field (not an easy task considering the tremendous loads each fighter carried); they touched earth silently as their small engines, comparable to that of a lawn mower, were cut in midair. Disconnecting themselves from the aircraft, the men produced their silenced Tokarovs and emptied several rounds into cardboard targets. They then removed the AK-47 7.62-mm assault rifles slung over their shoulders and began a deafening barrage of automatic fire; in a scene reminiscent of the old West, they stopped firing only for the two seconds it took them to discard the depleted 30-round magazine and replace it with a fresh banana-shaped clip. Finally, the men hurled their grenades one after the other. The explosions were deafening, the smoke blinding, and the stench of cordite soon filled the open-air facility. Jibril was pleased. His men were ready to meet their destiny.

Originally, D day was set for November 11, 1987, the opening day of the Palestinian National Council forum in the Jordanian capital of Amman. According to Jibril's calculations, the mayhem that four heavily armed suicide gunmen could cause inside an Israeli city would more than propel his organization and the National Salvation Front's vow never to negotiate with Israel to the forefront of the Palestinian agenda.[17] It was a time when Yasir Arafat's PLO, through a dedicated public relations and diplomatic blitz throughout Europe, was gaining legitimacy, even respectability. It was clear that Arafat was heading toward a compromised approach with Israel; privately, of course, Arafat intensified his military struggle along Israel's Jordanian and Egyptian frontiers, as Fatah incursions escalated in their intensity and frequency. Operation Kibya was envisioned as the Palestinians' true breakthrough—not only as a type of bold and bloody operation mounted against the Jewish State, but in its ability to remove the moderates, and possibly even Arafat, from the PLO leadership. A secondary objective behind timing the operation to coincide with the conference in Amman was to reinstate Syria as the beacon of Palestinian resistance. By supporting the raid against northern Israel, Syria was to replace Iraq as chief military sponsor of the PLO.

In early November, the four hang gliders and their martyr pilots were brought to a staging area in the Syrian-controlled Bekaa Valley. The transfer of the aircraft and men was carried out under a shield of tremendous security. Syrian intelligence agents carried out elaborate deception ploys to keep the convoys secret and away from the prying eyes of villagers, who could be Israeli intelligence agents, as well as the prying eyes of IAF reconnaissance aircraft or remote-piloted vehicle (RPV) drones.* The Syrian desire for revenge against Israel, especially for the Flight 016 debacle, can best be illustrated by the fact that the Syrians allowed the attack to emanate from the central Bekaa Valley, a portion of greater Syria ultrastrategic in its military stance against Israel, and in the poppy-growing fields and narcotics-harvesting center that fund much of the Syrian economy.[19] It was a piece of territory the Syrians did not risk or expose for trivial pursuits.

What Jibril could not control was the weather. The winter's first rains had burst across south Lebanon and northern Israel in the early morning hours of D day. Downpours, in fact, inundated the staging area of the operation, and it became a flooded mess of water holes and mud slides. Visibility was also poor and would be for nearly two weeks. The terrorists were told to sit tight and wait. D day was now set for the night of November 25, when meteorologists in Damascus predicted powerful southern winds and excellent visibility.

November 25, 1987—2030 hours. On top of a hill in Bekaa Valley, the four terrorists assembled with their aircraft under a covering veil of cedar trees. The men had been fed with plenty of sugar and protein and, according to published reports, supplied with impressive doses of amphetamines. They saluted their al-Rawad commander one final time and then, under the watchful gaze of Syrian intelligence officers, checked their gear and their motor-driven hang glider; a reserve motor had been positioned to the cloth and metal ultralight in order to extend its range even farther.[20] After one of the Syrian officers checked with Damascus over a secure frequency, the green light was finally given. The four men stood on a takeoff line similar to that in a civilian airport and awaited the signal, a flashlight's blink. One by one the men

---

* The IAF's fleet of *Ma'z'la'tim*, or remote-piloted vehicles, had scored remarkable success during Operation Peace for Galilee. Not only had they succeeded as miniature aerial (ECM) electronic counter-measures platforms to help knock out the Syrian SAM batteries in the Bekaa in a twentieth-century version of the Trojan horse trick, but the RPVs were also invaluable intelligence-gathering tools, relaying real-time video images back to A'man headquarters in Tel Aviv. The RPVs, especially the Israel Aircraft Industries Scout, also hovered high above Beirut, monitoring locations in which terrorist leaders were known to be hiding so that they could be targeted for IAF attention; in fact, RPVs closely monitored Yasir Arafat's motorcade in Beirut and targeted him for an air strike on several occasions. The RPV's vast potential spooked many terrorist leaders, especially Ahmed Jibril, because it was such a cheap and efficient assassination delivery system.[18]

clutched the hang glider's metal frame and began a gingerly sprint toward the takeoff point. As they gained speed and approached the cliff, they lifted up their legs and began a slow, steady, midair sail. According to Jibril's estimates, the raid inside Israel would begin at approximately 2200 hours.

Unfortunately for Jibril, Operation Kibya encountered initial setbacks. The first two hang gliders had engine failures early on and crashlanded only miles from the Israeli security zone. The third aircraft, piloted by Maludin an-Naja, also suffered mechanical difficulties and landed inside the outer ring of the security zone patrolled by Israeli and South Lebanese Army* units. Only Khaled Aker's aircraft was operating as planned. He flew along the tree line as he had been instructed to do in order to evade Israeli radar, and made a point to evade villages and known IDF forward-observation positions identified by the Syrians. It was a precarious flight.

Israeli radar in the security zone had failed to pick up the slow-moving, ultralight glider. Its small size, few metal parts, and clothwing covering made it a stealth-like creature; because of its low-altitude path, the surrounding trees and hills camouflaged its movement from radar detection as well. The aircraft's small engine, however, did emit a dull, audible noise.

Just inside the Israeli border near Metulla, one hang glider buzzed an IDF armored unit. One tank commander, standing upright in his turret and gazing through his infrared field glasses in search of possible terrorists, heard an oncoming sound that reminded him of a tank's engine. Several other crewmen also heard the noise and assumed defensive positions; they clutched their Glilon 5.56-mm assault rifles, and the commander and loader cocked their turret-mounted .50 caliber heavy machine guns. According to one of the crewmen, "The noise sounded like *tak ... tak ... tak ... tak ... tak*, similar to a small boat engine, even like a tank off in the distance. What made it so mysterious is that it came and went in seconds. In hindsight, I assume that the terrorist saw us and extinguished his motor."[21]

Following standard IDF protocol, the tank commander radioed in the noise and the probability that a light plane was buzzing his position to a forward headquarters post. The young officer didn't sound panicky; after all, it could have been an Israeli drone returning from a mission over Lebanon. It wasn't. Immediately, at 2115 hours, a general alert was

---

* Major Haddad died in 1984; his militia was taken over by General Antoine Lahad and changed its name to the South Lebanese Army.

sounded throughout northern Israel. Units stationed along the fence were placed on their toes and ordered to expect a possible terrorist attack sometime in the night. Tragically, not all the units positioned along the Lebanese frontier took the alert seriously. Forward defensive positions were manned, soldiers donned their flak vests and web gear, and mobile patrols were dispatched to safeguard the isolated kibbutzim and moshavim of the area. Air raid sirens were sounded throughout Galilee, and the residents of Qiryat Shmoneh and Kibbutz Dan were ordered into underground bomb shelters. IAF reconnaissance helicopters, primarily Bell-206 Jet Rangers, and attack choppers were scrambled and dispatched over the security zone, but no sign of hostile terrorist activity was found in the skies. An AH-1S Cobra helicopter gunship, piloted by Captain A., circled Qiryat Shmoneh for nearly half an hour; his ship's forward-mounted 20-mm minigun twisted and turned in search of the one craft reported. Captain A.'s orders were clear: Blow the damn thing out of the sky before it has a chance to land. The orders were too late, however. Khaled Aker had already landed inside Israeli territory.[22]

At 2150 hours, Aker cut his engine and made a smooth landing in a thorny field adjacent to a helicopter landing pad a few hundred yards away from Camp Gibor, a small military encampment near Beit Hillel. Ominously, it was home to a Na'ha'l unit.* Aker removed himself from the hang glider's harness, wrapped the AK-47's sling around his right shoulder and wrist so that it could be fired with one hand, and placed the silenced Tokarov in his left hand; he headed a few yards below to the main Qiryat Shmoneh-Kibbutz Dan roadway and paused for a few seconds to evaluate his situation. Five minutes had passed, and it was still quiet in the area. No one had seen him land.

A short way down the road, the lights of an IDF Peugeot tender ignited the distant backdrop: It was heading from the east toward the Na'ha'l encampment on the top of the hill. The tender's driver, First-Lieutenant Liron Pnini, and his girlfriend, Corporal Tami Arbel, were unaware of the general alert declared throughout Galilee and had not taken any precautions. Hiding in the ditch in a prone firing position, Aker emerged as the tender approached and raked it with a magazine-emptying burst of Kalashnikov fire. The surprise was absolute. The

---

* While Ahmed Jibril's historic obsession with Na'ha'l soldiers stems from the prisoners seized in Lebanon, it has not been confirmed whether Jibril had actually targeted the Na'ha'l base all along, in a cruel statement meant to further tarnish the Zionist icon of the soldier/farmer, or if the attack against the base was a mere matter of coincidence.

fusillade of 7.62-mm ordnance fatally wounded the lieutenant and critically wounded the young corporal.[23] The Night of the Hang Glider, as it became known, had officially begun.

Instead of heading west toward Qiryat Shmoneh, Aker proceeded southward, 150 meters up the hilly road, toward Camp Gibor. The sound of automatic fire should have prompted the base's garrison to drop whatever they were doing and race to perimeter defensive positions. Weapons should have been locked and loaded, full battle kits harnessed, and the front gate sealed by a sizable force of heavily armed infantrymen. In fact, the sight of the lone terrorist racing up the sandy path to the camp's main gate should have ended in a flurry of defensive fire. According to official IDF guidelines, Aker should have never made it to within fifty meters of the front gate.

The hapless gate guard, or *Shin Gimel*, that evening was Corporal Ron Almog, an inexperienced combat soldier who was unfortunate enough to be in the wrong place at the wrong time. Instead of going through the motions of yelling "Stop, identify yourself or I'll shoot," the standard IDF procedure, he froze at his post. When Aker produced a Russian-made F-1 fragmentation grenade from his ammunition pouch and threw it toward Almog, who was standing in the small wooden guardhouse at the front gate, the nineteen-year-old corporal simply ran in a panic.* Aker's luck was absolutely remarkable. There were no obstacles hindering his entrance into the base. Nothing stood in his way from perpetrating a massacre. It was 2156 hours when he crossed the main gate and its large Hebrew sign proclaiming, *Bruchim Ha'Ba'im Le'Machane Gibor*: Welcome to Camp Gibor.

Aker, his body surging with the power of amphetamines and adrenaline, raced into the camp and threw a grenade inside the motor pool building—several vehicles were damaged in the thunderous explosion and subsequent fire. Simultaneously firing both his weapons, he then proceeded toward the base's living quarters, a series of tents and wooden structures arranged in neat rectangular rows. Remarkably, Aker wasn't even challenged in his frantic shooting spree; according to reports to emerge from the official IDF investigation, most of the soldiers were either sleeping or playing cards.[25] Two soldiers, sitting inside the base's canteen preparing for their guard-duty shifts, emerged from the large tent to see what was going on, but were cut down by a

---

* Whether it was an act of cowardice or a terrible case of stress-induced panic, Almog was seen as a scapegoat for the incident. At his court-martial he would say, "I wish I would have been killed by the terrorists instead of sitting in a courtroom."[24]

blinding flash of point blank tracer fire. They died instantly. Two other soldiers who raced out of another tent were also cut down by Aker, who launched over a hundred rounds of ammunition into the campgrounds—the crisscrossing of ricocheting projectiles in the pitch-black night made the camp look like ground zero at an eerie fireworks display. In a little more than sixty seconds, four Israeli soldiers had been killed, and several had been seriously wounded by the flying shrapnel and point-blank firing.

First-Lieutenant Ya'akov Vayar, the twenty-two-year-old deputy company commander, raced to his Peugeot tender the moment the first shots were heard. He got into his vehicle and raced for the base's central compound in order to assume command of what appeared to be a worst-case scenario—a lone man, armed with an AK-47 and a pistol, pumping rounds of ammunition into the surrounding tents. Instinctively, Vayar floored the gas pedal and attempted to run Aker down, but his efforts were unsuccessful. Aker noticed the Peugeot, crouched into a firing position, and emptied a full magazine into the vehicle. Vayar was killed instantly.[26]

Suddenly and miraculously, First-Sergeant Gideon Bashari, the base's maintenance NCO, emerged from between two tents. Aker heard Bashari cock his Glilon assault rifle and turned in his direction. In a split second, both men fired their weapons. Bashari was hit in the legs and shoulder but managed to fire a point-blank magazine-emptying burst of 5.56-mm fire directly into Aker's head. Finally the killing stopped. In less than two minutes, Khaled Aker had killed six Na'ha'l soldiers and wounded seven others. He emptied eight full 30-round magazines in the short spree, and threw five grenades.[27]

Once the killing stopped, the area became a center of bustling activity. Helicopter gunships, responding to emergency calls of gun and grenade fire, raced to Camp Gibor, as did other units from nearby garrisons. Artillery formations stationed nearby fired flares to illuminate the sky, and a general emergency alert, covering all of northern Israel, was immediately declared by the IDF general staff. In fact, Chief of Staff Lieutenant-General Dan Shomron, the hero of Entebbe, had little idea about what was actually going on in northern Israel, and he feared that a large-scale terrorist offensive was under way. Should these fears be true, it would mean that a serious Israeli intelligence *Mechdal* (a Hebrew term indicating absolute negligence) had transpired, and it would also mean that the terrorists would have a won a tremendous public relations victory in the Arab world. Before all the reports from northern Israel could be analyzed, however, Shomron ordered several elite units into the fray to hunt down the terrorists—these included elements of the *Ya'ma'm*, the Border Guard's counterterrorist hostage-rescue force, as well as, according to foreign reports, the top-secret General Staff Reconnaissance Unit, Sayeret Mat'kal.[28]

Throughout the long hours of the night, thousands of Israeli troops mounted a large-scale search-and-destroy mission inside their side of the fence. Armored units, including *Merkava* MBTs with their 105-mm main armament guns, patrolled the northern roadways in search of additional terrorists. The entire area was engulfed in a massive dragnet of confusion and fright. A curfew had been declared and a hundred thousand civilians were forbidden to leave their homes; doors and windows were also ordered locked, and many residents spent a sleepless night gazing out their windows with their licensed Uzi submachine guns in hand. Hundreds of panic-stricken Galilee residents, terrified by the enormous IDF and police presence, began flooding the 100 police emergency lines with reports of hang glider sightings. (Most turned out to be low-flying pigeons!) The Jeep Blazer 4x4 belonging to OC Northern Command Major-General Yossi Peled raced throughout much of the border area that morning, attempting to control and coordinate the desperate search efforts. A freezing chill had broken that dawn, hampering the patrols, and many of the troopers, who hadn't slept the entire night, found their bodies operating on nothing more than the desire to avenge their fallen comrades.

The search operation also crossed into Lebanon, as the possibility existed that additional gunmen had slipped back across the fence to safety. Finally, at 0830 hours on November 26, the Israelis hit pay dirt. A Cobra helicopter gunship hovering over the border area discovered a "suspicious object" which looked like a fallen tent inside Lebanese territory 700 meters north of the fence opposite the village of Yuval; apparently this was the hang glider that the tank crew had discovered.[29] A large force of paratroopers, tanks, armored personnel carriers, and Ya'ma'm commandos crossed the border in pursuit of the terrorist, Maludin an-Naja,* who hid behind a series of boulders waiting for daybreak and an escape back to Syrian lines. He would never make it. In a brief pursuit that lasted fifteen minutes, Maludin was cornered and killed in a quick firefight.

The Night of the Hang Gliders lasted eleven hours, but its repercussions are still felt in the region.

---

* Following the Night of the Hang Gliders, many reports claimed that it was, in fact, Maludin who was responsible for the death of the six Na'ha'l infantrymen.

Later that day, the IDF buried its dead: the young officer Liron Pnini, who was about to be married; Sergeant Daniel Miller, a twenty-one-year-old new immigrant from England who volunteered to serve along the fence; Corporal Binyamin Besterman, twenty, an experienced combat soldier; Corporal Niv Chazon, a nineteen-year-old NCO headed for officer's training; Corporal Guy Netanel; and, First-Lieutenant Vayar. The funerals for the six infantrymen were solemn, grief-filled ceremonies, whose shallow anxiety epitomized the nation's shock at the outrage in northern Israel. Soldiers openly shed tears as the flag-draped coffins were lowered into the ground and honor guard fired one last and respectful volley; female soldiers, many of whom were in Na'ha'l units and many of whom served at the Gibor base, broke down under the tremendous shock and grief. Morale at Camp Gibor echoed the mood of the entire nation. Soldiers wandered about in a daze while military police investigators photographed bloodstains and catalogued evidence. An aura of failure and loss permeated the once picturesque facility, which overlooked the majestic Galilee and southern Lebanese hills. Many soldiers, assault rifles at their side, sat in a crouched position on the muddy floor staring into space, while female soldiers, numbed by the experience, sat at the main gate and chain-smoked cigarettes. A miniarmy of IDF psychologists attempted to alleviate the sense of guilt and loss felt by many of the soldiers.[30]

The failure of the Na'ha'l unit in the Night of the Hang Gliders was considered by many Israelis to be a national disgrace, a disastrous case of negligence and cowardice. A small hobby item that costs a few thousand dollars had exposed an entire nation's vulnerability. The national mood was anxious. *Galei Tzahal*, the IDF radio station, interspersed news accounts of the incident with sad, somber war songs about fallen comrades and lost loved ones. Perhaps to reinforce the national resolve, patriotic songs were also played, such as pop star Gali Atari's tune "This Is My Only Country," which stated that no matter how bad things got, Israel was the only country the people had.[31]

The mood in Damascus was quite different.

Few people were as impressed with the outcome of the massacre in northern Israel as the Syrian defense minister, Major-General Dr. Mustafa Tlas, a man who as former Syrian Army chief of staff and Ba'ath party loyalist has dedicated his entire life to the struggle against Israel. The success of the operation allowed the Syrian hierarchy to openly embrace the PFLP-GC operation. In a Damascus news conference he publicly and proudly admitted that Syrian officers helped Jibril's forces launch the hang glider attack against northern Israel. He went on to say,

"Syria always provides *unlimited* support in the implementation of the violent struggle against Zionist occupation forces." He also said, "The courage of the pilot and martyr Khaled Muhammad Aker, who participated in the operation in northern Palestine and was killed in the battle, *killed* and wounded thirty-seven Zionist officers."[32] Although bombastic, the disclosure marked a semiofficial declaration of war against the Jewish State.

The Syrians were pleased to see the Israelis engulfed in their own humiliation and failure; after enduring countless incidents of military humiliation at the hands of the Israelis over the years, the Night of the Hang Gliders was bittersweet revenge. The Israelis were even forced to admit an Arab victory of sorts, as Israeli defense analysts appeared on television broadcasts and credited the Palestinian Rambo with great skill and determination. IDF Chief of Staff Shomron was also interviewed in a press conference, along with his deputy, Major-General Ehud Barak. Shomron seemed perplexed by the disaster, and rhetorically asked: "How could this happen that one terrorist killed six soldiers and wounded seven others? We cannot live with an event like this!"[33] Colonel Y., the Na'ha'l brigade commander, assumed total responsibility for the failure and even offered his resignation (he was eventually transferred to other duties). An internal IDF investigation, conducted by OC Northern Command Major-General Yossi Peled, disclosed that the Israeli intelligence apparatus had provided the northern units with sufficient warning concerning the potential for an airborne terrorist infiltration attempt, and that the Na'ha'l brigade command failed to disseminate the information properly to its units. The true casualty of the overall command-and-control failure was the hapless gate guard, Corporal Ron Almog, who was eventually court-martialed for failure in face of the enemy and imprisoned for a year.

In Beirut, PFLP-GC* officials were eager to exploit their newfound public relations bonanza. A man claiming to be the commander of the PFLP-GC's airborne unit, using the nom de guerre of Abu Sa'ar, claimed in an interview with the pro-Syrian Lebanese newspaper *al-Shira'a* that the mission had been in the planning for nearly a year, and that *he* had issued strict orders to his men *not* to attack any civilian targets around Kfar Yuval, Kfar Gila'adi, and Halsa (the Arabic name for Qiryat Shmoneh before the 1948 war). Even the enigmatic and publicity-shy Jibril

---

* Interestingly enough, Abu A'bbas's PLF had also claimed responsibility for the attack; from its Beirut office, a PLF spokesman telephoned several news agencies and claimed credit for the "historic operations."[34]

gave an interview to *as-Sfir*, a Lebanese newspaper, in which he vowed: "The future for Israel is dim. The Libyans are now training our personnel to fly heavier aircraft for suicide missions against the Zionist enemy."[35]

To Israel, the present appeared bleak. Yet the Night of the Hang-Gliders would soon loom benign in retrospect compared to what it would inevitably produce: a period of desperate and uncontrolled violence that continues to this day.

All the pundits predicted that Israel would retaliate immediately for the massacre in Galilee. It didn't. Palestinian units throughout southern Lebanon were placed on full alert, and antiaircraft batteries were manned twenty-four hours a day in anxious anticipation of the expected Israeli military response. There was also great fear that Israel would decide to strike against Syria for that country's role in the attack. Such a retaliatory move against Syrian interests could have very well sparked a full-scale Arab-Israeli war. In fact, after attending the funerals for several of the Na'ha'l soldiers, Prime Minister Yitzhak Shamir tried to chair a meeting of his cabinet to discuss military and political contingencies but no-one came.

Khaled Aker's bloody success had mobilized Palestinian public opinion into defiance. Perhaps Yasir Arafat said it best when he praised his longtime rival Ahmed Jibril for the operation in Galilee by stating, "The raid destroyed the *myth* of Israeli security," although he would also state, fearing Israeli vengeance, that his group was not at all responsible for the killings.[36] The myth had, indeed, been badly tarnished. For twenty years, the Palestinians living on the West Bank and the Gaza Strip had been forced to look upon the Israeli soldier not only as an occupier, but also as a supermanlike being capable of spectacular feats. From the Six-Day War to Entebbe, the Israel Defense Forces had continuously humiliated the conventional Arab armies in battle, while at the same time humbling the efforts of indigenous terrorist groups to formulate and intensify an armed struggle into a tangible path toward liberation. The Palestinians looked upon the Israeli soldier with envious respect, a grudging admiration. Massive protests or uprisings were never even attempted by the local Palestinians or urged on by the PLO leadership, since it was feared the IDF would crush the insurrection with fatal efficiency.

The Night of the Hang Gliders changed everything.

Almost overnight, Ahmed Jibril had transformed the Israeli fighting man from an icon into a tangible target. The transformation was most pronounced among Palestinian youth, especially the disenchanted legions living in the squalor of the Gaza Strip and its seven refugee camps. IDF troopers patrolling the strip found themselves the target of verbal insults, curses, and the occasional physical attack. Platoon commanders noticed the sudden change of heart among the strip's residents and duly notified senior commanders about this troubling development.

The first chance for confrontation occurred on November 29, the anniversary of the 1947 United Nations vote to partition Palestine, when demonstrations showed signs of becoming ugly. Then came the murder of an Israeli businessman in the heart of Gaza, the subsequent IDF and Shin Bet search for the killers, and the inevitable curfew and security service clampdowns that quickly ensued. The territories, inundated with Jordanian TV-news coverage of the PFLP-GC attack and Syrian radio reports heralding the PFLP-GC for its actions of revolutionary violence,* soon turned into a pressure cooker. That one fateful night in Galilee provided the Palestinians with new heroes, removed the veil of fear surrounding the IDF, and convinced many of the young men and politically active university students that they were doomed to a future of occupation unless they took matters into their own hands.[37] The move against the Israelis would not come from a coordinated effort directed by secretive leadership cells in the territories, or even in Tunis, but as a result of a combustible mass demonstration of anger. All that was needed was the igniting spark. It would come in a most innocuous form.

On December 8, a fatal traffic accident occurred in the Jebalya refugee camp in which a truck, driven by an Israeli, struck and killed a group of four Palestinian workers. A case of vehicular manslaughter should not have prompted special attention, since tragic traffic accidents in Israel are commonplace. Rumors, however, soon emerged that the truck driver was a relative of the businessman killed in Gaza a few days earlier, and that the killings were a diabolical and government-sanctioned act of revenge.[38] Minor cases of rioting soon erupted, but OC Southern Command Major-General Yitzhak Mordechai didn't view the violence with foreboding. The rioting continued and intensified with desperate speed, however. At first thousands of young men shouted *Jihad . . . jihad . . . jihad* at the vastly outnumbered Israeli forces sent to police the area, but soon rocks and bottles were hurled. In

---

* Although Israeli censorship laws limit news stories of military sensitivities in Arab print and radio reports emanating from the territories, it does not possess the technological means to control and inhibit the airwaves.

an ironic twist of the David vs. Goliath myth, slingshots were used to propel rocks at the IDF troopers. As dusk fell, Molotov cocktails were thrown at IDF and Border Guard vehicles. Tires and inner tubes liberated from nearby garages were placed in the middle of key intersections and set ablaze. Thousands of outlawed Palestinian flags were suddenly displayed across laundry lines and from television antennas. Attempts were even made to assault IDF armored personnel carriers, and seize their mounted machine guns. Law and order had evaporated in one spasm of frustration and rage. The *Intifadah* (Uprising) had begun.

The rioting and chaos soon spread throughout the entire Gaza Strip, and also erupted days later on the West Bank. Israeli forces responded poorly to this new situation, using deadly force to shoot rock-throwers. The killings only increased tensions and raised the level of violence to new and incredibly volatile levels. One of the factors exacerbating the spreading fires of the Intifadah was the absence of a decisive Israeli solution. For an army renowned for solving impossible situations, the absence of a distinctive IDF policy was embarrassing, especially since the PLO had managed to create the illusion that *it* was the sole force directing and manipulating the violence through secret orders it was sending to the area via coded radio broadcasts from Radio Monte Carlo.

Both Defense Minister Yitzhak Rabin and Chief of Staff Lieutenant-General Dan Shomron knew that they had encountered a political struggle that a Western democracy could not crush through military means. As the Army waited for the politicians—or a miracle—to quell the rage, the death toll continued to mount, and Israel's public image nightmare grew in intensity and scope. An international army of television cameramen flocked to the country to film the uprising: The scene of Israeli infantrymen firing into crowds or beating up suspects with clubs or the metal folding stocks from their assault rifles was great drama, worthy of sensational nightly news coverage from Washington to Warsaw. The once-admired IDF was likened to Hitler's SS and the repressive South African security forces. PLO chairman Arafat seized the political initiative in Western countries where his gunmen had once wreaked havoc. His public (though privately refuted) statements accepting Israel's right to exist brought a cavalcade of international support; even Washington gave him gentle nods of approval. It is an initiative that continues to this day with the Middle East peace talks. Never before had Israel's long-term security considerations been so threatened or undermined.

Although it is likely that any spectacular Palestinian terrorist attack in which many Israelis were killed or wounded would have eventually sparked the eruption of some sort of popular uprising against the Israelis, it was the Night of the Hang Glider that provided Israel with a smoking gun. Oddly enough, even the eruption of the Intifadah did little to increase Ahmed Jibril's popularity among the Palestinian leaders or among the residents of the West Bank and the Gaza Strip. Popularity and political support for the various leaders and groups inside the territories were displayed in many different ways. A neighborhood, a block, or even a public institution such as a United Nations school or relief center would usually display a photograph of their leader, or even the group's coat of arms. On the street, however, loyalty was displayed by the color of one's kefiyeh headdress: Those loyal to Fatah wore one with a black design; those loyal to the Islamic Jihad or the *Hamas* movement, a fundamentalist Palestinian terrorist group, wore a green design, and those allied to the Syrian-controlled groups wore a red design. Few of those, it should be noted, were loyal to Jibril; in fact, most of those people supported either George Habash or Nayif Hawatmeh. Ahmed Jibril maintained a small legion of diehard supporters, but mass support for him never came.[39]

Jibril's actions continued to haunt the State of Israel. It soon became apparent to many in the Israeli hierarchy that the PFLP-GC had to be stopped. To kill the snake, the head needed to be chopped off.

On the terrorist front, the Night of The Hang Gliders proved to be a lethal precedent. It prompted the other terrorist factions of the region to think again about their offensive capabilities. The killing of the six Na'ha'l soldiers and the eruption of the Intifadah had proved to be a turning point in the Palestinian revolution, a major transformation for which Jibril was primarily responsible. Immediately, the Abu A'bbas faction of the PLF purchased several motorized hang gliders and ultralights from the French company Latecoere (they were officially purchased by the Iraqi military), as did agents for Hizbollah operating out of Iran and using Nicosia, Cyprus, as their smuggling point to Lebanon.[40] Ominously, the Night of the Hang Gliders became a war cry for many of the world's terrorist factions, far beyond its role as spark to the eruption of the Intifadah. On September 20, 1988, West German terrorists from the Red Army Faction Commando attempted to assassinate Dr. Hans Tietmeyer, a state secretary in the federal Ministry of Finance. The attack failed, though responsibility for the failed hit was claimed by "RAF Commando Khaled Aker"; the lone-terrorist Rambo was now an immortal symbol throughout the terrorist underworld.[41] Also, during the first days of the 1991 Persian Gulf crisis and American deployment to Saudi Arabia, U.S. military officials feared that Palestinian terrorist groups allied with Iraq's Saddam Hussein would attempt to launch a Night of the Hang Gliders imitation raid against American troops positioned in the area. Accordingly, American and allied units were briefed of the Palestinian potential, and the proper defensive responses were duly implemented.

Naturally, Israel vowed suitable revenge for the Night of the Hang Glider and its Intifadah byproduct. In fact, on November 26, 1987, only hours after the IDF buried its six Na'ha'l dead, deputy chief of staff Major-General Ehud Barak vowed, "Jibril's organization will in due time pay the price for its murderous mission." His words were an obvious call for action and the execution of the Bible's eye-for-an-eye edict of revenge.

Eventually, Israel did mount its long-anticipated act of retaliation. On January 2, 1988, the IAF mounted a large-scale, three-pronged air assault on PFLP-GC targets in Lebanon. The air strikes were carried out at night, when the Palestinians' ability to launch effective antiaircraft artillery fire was limited, and three of Jibril's installations were targeted. The first strike hit a PFLP-GC operations center, camouflaged conveniently in the middle of a row of banana trees near the sprawling Ein el-Hilweh refugee camp and Palestinian military bases along the Mediterranean coast; the second wave attacked a principal PFLP-GC base in the town of Jaya in the Bekaa Valley; and the third wave destroyed a series of buildings used by Jibril and his officers in the Bekaa Valley village of Barja. According to Colonel 'A., commander of IAF operations, "Meticulous high-level planning and perfect execution of the missions allowed us to hit exactly what we wanted to hit. The IAF's achievements are not measured in the number of dead and wounded we inflict on the terrorist groups; it is to force the terrorists and their leaders to live in the feeling and knowledge that we will hit them anywhere they might be hiding."[42]

The IAF attack, carried out by several aircraft from one of the *Heyl Ha'Avir's* (Hebrew for IAF) premier bomber squadrons, did encounter stiff resistance. PFLP-GC gunmen, especially around Barja, launched hundreds of 23-mm antiaircraft projectiles at the aircraft diving into their targets from the south. The Palestinian gunners could not see the supersonic jets, but they could hear them diving in a menacing steep descent. All the targets were hit with remarkable precision, all were destroyed. The pilots had been told that this night's mission was of particular significance and that the targets required above-average attention.[43]

Although a success, the January 2 sortie achieved only physical destruction of a few buildings and the loss of equipment: it did not punish the men responsible for the bloodshed in Galilee, nor did it provide the symbolic* preemptive act of deterrence meant to prevent further attacks. Israel's attempt at *true* vengeance would come one year later.

---

* As symbolism is so important to the past, present, and future of the Middle East, the IAF has consistently attacked PFLP-GC bases on anniversaries of the Night of the Hang Gliders. One of the most successful attacks came on the incident's second anniversary, when a flight of IAF aircraft launched a fusillade of air-to-surface missiles at Jibril's Sultan Yaqoub base. A senior terrorist officer was killed, several more were wounded, and a series of installations and weapons stores were destroyed.[44]

CHAPTER NINE

INTO THE DEPTHS OF DESTRUCTION: FOURTEEN HOURS AT AL-NA'AMEH

ISRAEL CIRCA 1988 was a land of despair and turmoil. The Intifadah had scared the Jewish State into a confused nation unsure of its direction and doubtful regarding its future. The question of Palestinian rights, their plea for self-determination, and their yearnings for statehood were now removed from the small stage of a regional conflict and propelled into the international spotlight. The Israeli leadership found itself the target of widespread condemnation, much of its clearly biased, for its handling of the uprising: the firebombing of a Jewish family inside their car was viewed as an end result of tensions allowed to fester for too long, while a rock-throwing Palestinian teenager shot and killed by Israeli security forces became the centerpiece of a United Nations Security Council lambasting and inevitable condemnation. IDF officers and soldiers too soon found their every action examined under the scrutiny of the international press, as well as by Israeli leaders eager to find unwitting scapegoats that would deflect responsibility for the uncontrollable crisis from their shoulders. Muddled and intently vague orders were issued to the front-line personnel combating the uprising, including directives where riot ringleaders were to be beaten with clubs and fists in order to break the bones, literally, of the Intifadah. Inevitably and politically volatile court-

153

martials were carried out for soldiers found guilty of administering undue force in their handling of the uprising. The very moral fiber of the IDF was challenged.

The uprising provided the PLO leadership with a tempting opportunity to assume unchallenged control of a struggle it had no role in initiating. The rock-throwing youths of the camps, the masked men of the *shabab* (the Palestinian youth mob), who had tantalized the world's imagination with their tenacious challenge to Israeli rule in an epic David versus Goliath struggle, were, however, an uncontrolled and unguided force. They needed leadership, and they desperately required direction. Through glory-filled broadcasts via Radio Monte Carlo and fliers distributed throughout the territories, Arafat and his lieutenants in Tunis attempted to blaze the path toward Palestinian liberation. But it was the rock-throwing kids who were in the trenches, not Arafat. It was they who were assaulting Israeli troops, and it was they who were being killed in the ensuing chaos. For the PLO to be able to lay a claim into the soul of the Intifadah, rocks would have to be replaced by AK-47 assault rifles, and Molotov cocktails discarded in favor of five-kilogram loads of high explosives. The man to achieve this difficult task was Abu Jihad—Yasir Arafat's military mastermind and the man in charge of the Western Sector, the body responsible for executing terrorist attacks inside Israel and the territories.

Abu Jihad's career in Fatah had been a stormy and tumultuous tenure of missed glory. One of Fatah's founding fathers, Abu Jihad had assumed a wide array of posts and tasks within the fledgling force of Palestinian liberation since 1964. Not as cutthroat as Abu Iyad, and as a result not placed in charge of the organization's dreaded internal security department, Abu Jihad was instead destined to formulate the organization's military character. Prior to the 1967 war, Abu Jihad had ventured to the far corners of the globe to obtain military assistance and training expertise for his fledgling Fatah liberation fighters; he traveled throughout the Eastern bloc, as well as the People's Republic of China, North Korea, and North Vietnam.[1] Throughout the tumultuous early years of Palestinian armed resistance against Israel, from 1965 to 1973, Abu Jihad had earned a solid reputation as a military planner and as an Arafat loyalist. Yet it was in the aftermath of the joint Mossad/ IDF Operation Spring of Youth, when Sayeret Mat'kal commandos assassinated Abu Yusef, a chief officer in Black September and director of Fatah operations inside Israel proper, that Abu Jihad was thrust into the forefront of the PLO leadership. It was an ironic twist of fate that the unit responsible in a roundabout way for promoting Abu Jihad would eventually be responsible for his elimination.*

For the next fifteen years, Abu Jihad's signature adorned some of the most heinous acts of terrorism ever perpetrated against the Jewish State: the August 1972 takeover of the Israeli Embassy in Bangkok; the June 24, 1974, Nahariya Massacre; the March 5, 1975, seaborne attack against Tel Aviv's Savoy Hotel; the March 11, 1978, Country Club Massacre; and the April 1985 attempted assault on the Israeli Defense Ministry in which the S.S. *Attavirus* was blown out of the Mediterranean waters. Many analysts, in fact, have credited the failed 1985 raid on Tel Aviv as Israel's casus belli for terminating Abu Jihad, since it targeted the Israeli defense minister Yitzhak Rabin for assassination. In retrospect, it was Abu Jihad's failed, though bloody, attempts to raise the Intifadah's level of violence to extraordinary levels that eventually determined his fate.[2]

In early February 1988, Abu Jihad dispatched three heavily laden Fatah terrorists across the Egyptian border into Israel. Their objective: to seize a passenger bus and take hostages inside a Negev Desert cooperative farm. Abu Jihad had personally designed the operation, a bloody undertaking bound to achieve notable media coverage, in order to propel the leadership of the uprising into the PLO's hands. The diabolical task failed miserably, however. The three terrorists managed to cross into Israel but were pursued for twenty-two hours by Bedouin trackers and reconnaissance infantrymen through the desert abyss of southern Israel. On February 11, 1988, the three Palestinians were cornered and, following a brief firefight, forced to surrender.[3] It was a humiliating defeat for Abu Jihad, and one he vowed to avenge.

In the early morning hours of March 7, 1988, three heavily armed Fatah terrorists from Force 17 crossed the Egyptian frontier into Israel, commandeered a car, and raced through the Negev Desert toward the town of Beersheba. Their crossing had been discovered by an IDF unit, and a general security alert had been sounded throughout southern Israel; ostensibly the Israelis believed the terrorists were to attack one of the nearby agricultural settlements, and as a result, all the nearby kibbutzim and moshavim were sealed and secured by armed guards.

* Israel has never assumed responsibility for the assassination of Abu Jihad in Tunis on April 16, 1988, nor have official Israeli sources ever identified the actual units that participated in the lightning operation. As best stated in their book *Israel's Secret Wars*, however, authors Ian Black and Benny Morris claim that these official denials have fooled very few people.

Yet the terrorists hijacked an intercity bus carrying workers from their homes in Beersheba to the top-secret nuclear facility at Dimona. Special police and IDF units were summoned, and the bus was tracked down and subsequently immobilized. A standoff ensued, but after the terrorists murdered one of their hostages, the Ya'ma'm, the border guard's antiterrorist hostage-rescue force, sprung into action. In a matter of seconds the three terrorists were dead, but so, too, were three hostages—all women. The incident, known as the Bus of Mothers Massacre, galvanized the Israeli leadership to act decisively. If Abu Jihad had ascended to the military command of the PLO through an Israeli commando operation, then he could be removed through similar means. On April 13, the Israeli cabinet authorized Abu Jihad's assassination.[4]

In the late-night hours of April 15, 1988, a force of naval commandos from the IDF/Navy's Flotilla 13 landed on the shores of Ras Carthage, off the coast of Tunis. They reconnoitered in the area and were met by a group of Mossad agents in three rented vehicles. Once assured that the coast was clear, the naval commandos signaled to the spearhead of the operation, a task force of Sayeret Mat'kal commandos,[5] to be brought ashore by means of Zodiac craft. The combined Mossad/Sayeret Mat'kal task force drove through downtown Tunis and on to the exclusive Siddi Bouseid suburb where many top PLO officials lived, including Abu Jihad. After staking out the luxurious villa for several hours awaiting the PLO deputy commander's return from a meeting at Arafat's headquarters, the commandos silently eliminated Abu Jihad's security detail, and then quickly raced through the house in search of their target. Abu Jihad was killed in a matter of seconds, destroyed in a flurry of seventy-five bullets. According to several reports, the entire operation was videotaped by one of the Israeli commandos.[6]

The Abu Jihad assassination was a large-scale covert operation involving IDF/Navy missile boats and two IAF Boeing 707 electronic countermeasure and C^3 aircraft; according to foreign reports, the two planes provided an electronic blanket over much of Tunis, rendering Tunisian, as well as Palestinian, military and security communications useless for the duration of the raid. Nearly every aspect of Israel's intelligence community was involved in the operation, and it had been executed with brilliant precision. It was a daring display of a nation's resolve to pay back, with biblical justice, the perpetrators of terrorism. One of the many lethal thorns in Israel's side had been permanently removed. Ominously, however, following the Abu Jihad assassination, a left-wing member of the Knesset (parliament), Yossi Sarid, was quoted as saying, "Abu after Abu can be liquidated but this will not liquidate the Palestinian problem."[7]

Such commando operations proved to be extremely effective—more devastating to the terrorists' overall capabilities than any air raid. According to several reports, the Sayeret Mat'kal commandos assigned to eliminate Abu Jihad had also liberated several top-secret files from his desk, including a comprehensive list of all of the PLO's agents in Israel, the West Bank and Gaza, and Western Europe;[8] it was an indication that such "land" operations possessed unique intelligence rewards that air strikes could not achieve. Israel viewed special-forces operations as the most lethal and effective means of eliminating high-profile and heavily protected terrorist targets. In fact, on the day that the cabinet approved the assassination of Abu Jihad, A'man director Major-General Amnon Shahak, himself a highly decorated reconnaissance paratrooper officer, was interviewed in the pages of *Bamachane*, the IDF weekly newspaper. He said, "I do believe that commando assault operations are highly successful. They do have a strong deterrent impact on terrorists and, therefore, I regard them as a highly important tool. I don't think that the IDF has stopped thinking about them, or that we will stop conducting them."

His words would be prophetic. If the man responsible for stoking the fires of the Intifadah could be hit, then Israel could clearly strike out against the man who was responsible for its eruption. Determined efforts to destroy Ahmed Jibril once and for all were under way.

Although Israel clearly wanted Ahmed Jibril dead, he was not as easy a target as was Abu Jihad. Tunis was, after all, a relatively quiet location. Half Middle Eastern autocracy and half playground for European sun worshippers, Tunisia was a land of luxury hotels, nude beaches, and casinos. The Tunisian military was a small, inexperienced force, and not considered a true deterrent to any threat. Although the PLO did maintain its headquarters in Tunis, the number of Palestinian security units in the capital was not significant enough to ward off any Israeli action. Because of its openness, the Israelis were, according to foreign reports, able to establish an extensive intelligence-gathering infrastructure inside Tunisia including the recruitment of several government ministers.[9] Abu Jihad also helped out his attackers by being a tangible and extremely accessible target. Although a prime assassination figure, the PLO military chief shunned even the most basic security protocols. In fact, his Force 17 security contingent nicknamed him the Wailing Wall, complaining about the scores of people who were allowed to visit him every day to pour out their souls and seek his advice or assistance in a Godfather-type manner.[10]

Ahmed Jibril, on the other hand, rarely ventured outside of Lebanon or Syria, and was never without an extensive shield of bodyguards and Syrian military escorts. The only countries he would visit on official PFLP-GC business were Bulgaria, until 1991 a Communist and Big Brother police state where Israeli operatives were not welcome; the Islamic republic of Iran, where Israel's intelligence operations were extremely limited since the expulsion of the Shah; and, of course, Libya. In his Lebanese and Syrian hideaways, Jibril might have been physically closer to Israel than Abu Jihad was in Tunis, but in reality he was in an envelope of invulnerability. Unlike other Palestinian officials that the Israelis had terminated in the past, such as the Black September officials responsible for the Munich Olympics Massacre,* Ahmed Jibril was not the type of target to be removed by an assassin's—or an intelligence agent's—well-placed .22 caliber bullet; nor did his movements allow his vehicle or living quarters to be booby-trapped with a powerful explosive device. He was a man who did not follow a routine, did not travel to locations where there were large crowds, and never fell victim to the trappings of habit.

The spymasters at Mossad and A'man headquarters in Tel Aviv realized that accurate and timely intelligence would be crucial in any plan to kill Ahmed Jibril, but intelligence work alone would never achieve the task. The work of the intelligence-gatherers and analysts would have to lay the groundwork for some type of hard-hitting lightning military strike. In May 1988, Israel believed it had come across that very lethal combination that would turn a routine operation into a historic undertaking. A'man had learned that Jibril would be conducting an inspection tour of one of his western Lebanon bases south of Beirut. The IDF general staff and IAF headquarters had planned to launch an air strike at the exact time that Ahmed Jibril was walking past his legions and receiving the obligatory honor-guard parade;[12] although not confirmed, it is believed that the IAF dispatched several RPV drones to monitor developments at the PFLP-GC base in Lebanon. At dusk on May 12, six IAF aircraft launched a Stuka-like dive-bombing attack on the PFLP-GC base at Barja, sixteen kilometers south

---

* Israel has never officially acknowledged that it dispatched covert hit teams to Europe to destroy Black September's international network, even though several members of the team were arrested in the sleepy Norwegian resort town of Lillehammer following the mistaken murder of a Moroccan waiter who the Mossad agents believed to be Black September commander Ali Hassan Salameh.[11]

of Beirut, which was situated in the middle of a thick olive grove. Armed with rockets and air-to-surface missiles, the attacking aircraft launched a ten-minute attack on the base, even though Palestinian antiaircraft fire, emanating from 23-mm cannons mounted on flatbed Toyota trucks, was heavy. It has yet to be revealed if Jibril was indeed in the Barja facility, but if he was he miraculously survived, for the Israeli pilots did report that they scored good hits on all the targets.[13]

Clearly the Israelis were disappointed by this latest aerial failure to kill Jibril, even though the IDF spokesman never acknowledged that the objective of the air strike was the assassination of the PFLP-GC commander. It was clear to the IDF chief of staff Lieutenant-General Shomron, his deputy commander Major-General Ehud Barak,* as well as the other members of the general staff that if Jibril was, indeed, to be put out of action it would have to be done on the ground and by a sizable commando force. Such an operation would require an elite force, adept at large-formation conventional fighting as well as lightning assaults deep into the enemy heartland. It would also have to be a force led by the most innovative commanders, known for their unyielding courage and decisive command under fire. In essence, the IDF general staff required the services of its toughest conventional reconnaissance formation in the Israeli Order of Battle.†

That unit was an elite and highly heralded force with the affectionate nickname of the Flying Tigers. The unit assigned to eliminate Ahmed Jibril was the 1st Golani Infantry Brigade's reconnaissance, the Sayeret Golani.[15]

For many years, the 1st Golani Infantry Brigade had been something of an enigma. One of the first truly conventional fighting formations created by the *Haganah* (Defense), the underground pre-independence

---

* On April 1, 1991, *Lieutenant-General* Ehud Barak was appointed the IDF's fourteenth chief of staff. The most decorated soldier in Israeli military history, Barak was at one time the commander of Sayeret Mat'kal, and participated in countless counterterrorist operations, including the May 9, 1972, storming of a hijacked Sabena Belgian Airlines Boeing 707 held by Black September terrorists; the June 30, 1972, kidnapping of five Syrian generals in Lebanon; and the April 9, 1973 Operation Spring of Youth in Beirut.[14]

† There had been quite a bit of speculation in the foreign press, including in Hebrew-language newspapers published abroad, such as *Yisrael Shelanu*, published in the United States, as to why Sayeret Mat'kal, the ultraelite general staff's reconnaissance unit, usually assigned delicate elimination operations, was not called in to al-Na'ameh to deal with Ahmed Jibril.

forbearer to the IDF, in February 1948, the 1st Golani Infantry Brigade was responsible for military operations in lower Galilee. It was a spartan force with few weapons, fewer facilities, and personnel drawn from the area's farming settlements with a few World War II veterans thrown in for good measure. The brigade fought a pitched campaign against irregular Arab forces that had filtered down from Syria to lay claim on Palestine and, following the May 14, 1948, declaration of Israeli independence, it found itself in the middle of a Syrian invasion launched against the infant Jewish State. By the war's end in 1949, the brigade had earned itself an impressive combat reputation, but it would soon be tarnished by the difficulties of nation-building. Drawing from the hundreds of thousands of new immigrants for its recruiting pool, the Golani Brigade found itself a melting pot of immigrants in poor health, many of whom could not speak Hebrew, and whose allegiance to the new Jewish State and its rough-and-tumble army was, at best, a much-tested relationship. There were cases of frustrated NCOs and officers senselessly beating their men to pound them into shape, and other instances where poor soldiers stole the boots from their entire formations to sell them for food for their families.[16] The brigade developed a reputation as a poor military force. This negative calling card was only reinforced in May 1951, when a large-scale skirmish developed along the Israeli-Syrian border near the Sea of Galilee in which forty Golani soldiers were killed.

Like any military formation, there was a cutting edge to the Golani Brigade, and that was its reconnaissance company. Since the first Jewish settlers of Palestine carried Turkish rifles and patrolled their land on horseback, elite units have been the way in which Israel has managed to keep a qualitative balance to the Arab's quantitative superiority. From the Haganah's field companies of the 1936 riots, to Captain Orde Wingate's special night squads, to the World War II-era *Pal'mach* strike companies, small units staffed by exceptionally talented and motivated individuals have been an Israeli mainstay. These small and cohesive formations, whose job has been to conduct reconnaissance deep behind enemy lines as well as execute commando assaults, were seen as the examples the rest of the IDF would emulate. Following Israeli independence and the creation of the Israel Defense Forces on June 30, 1948, virtually each military formation possessed its own Sayeret, or reconnaissance, element—from the Giva'ati Infantry Brigade's elite 54th Battalion (also known as Samson's Foxes) to the Pal'mach's 7th Platoon.

Sayeret Golani too was supposed to act as an example for the rest of the brigade. During the 1948 war a Golani officer named Rafi Kotzer commanded a special reconnaissance platoon in the brigade's Barak (Lightning) Battalion; known as the Commando Force, the unit performed countless deep-penetration operations into Syrian territory.[17] The unit was considered a fine mixture of fighters and crazies who viewed the improbable as highly possible. In the years that followed, several prominent Israeli military men would command the unit, including a young officer named Ariel Sharon. To add to its elite status within the IDF command structure, Sayeret Golani adopted the nickname *Ha'Namer Ha'Me'ufaf* (the Flying Tigers) and devised a Flying Tigers unit insignia to be worn on each commando's class A uniform. But the reconnaissance formation's true emergence as an elite fighting formation came on the night of March 17, 1962, when the Flying Tigers spearheaded a large-scale brigade assault on Syrian positions along the Sea of Galilee at the base of the Golan Heights plateau around the town of Nuqieb. The raid, known as Operation Swallow, developed into a fierce battle as the Sayeret Golani fighters assaulted heavily defended Syrian positions with Uzi submachine guns ablaze; close-quarters hand-to-hand battles lasted for hours inside mud-soaked trenches. Operation Swallow placed the Golani Brigade, and its Sayeret, on the map.[18]

Sayeret Golani spearheaded Israel's assault on the Golan Heights on June 9, 1967, when its commandos, along with the brigade's Barak Battalion* captured the Syrian fort at Tel Fahar, a seemingly impregnable gauntlet of rock and machine-gun nests considered the key to the overall defense of the Golan Heights. Dressed for battle in their lizard-pattern camouflage fatigues, the Sayeret Golani commandos were forced to use their Uzi submachine guns to launch magazine-emptying bursts of 9-mm fire into darkened bunkers at point-blank range, as well as use their compact weapons as metal truncheons in the dozens of brutal hand-to-hand battles that raged throughout the cordite-engulfed fort. The unit's esprit de corps was epitomized by the fact that seriously wounded personnel "escaped" from hospital beds in order to participate in the fighting.

Just as Sayeret Golani would play an instrumental role in the capture of the Golan Heights during the 1967 war, so too would it play an instrumental role in its defense. At 1315 hours on October 6, 1973,

---

* In the all too tragic IDF tradition, the Barak Battalion's commanding officer, Lieutenant-Colonel "Musa" Klein, fell in battle while leading his men, from the vanguard, against a Syrian position.

Yom Kippur day, the Syrians, in conjunction with the Egyptians, who mounted a blitz across the Suez Canal into Sinai, launched a massive surprise attack against Israeli defenses in a bid to recapture the Golan Heights. Initial Syrian successes were impressive. Their blitzkrieg pitted thousands of top-of-the-line Soviet-produced tanks, armored personnel carriers, and surface-to-air missile batteries against one Israeli division-size force, the Golani Brigade was one of the few conscript units responsible for holding the Golan line and defending much of northern Israel from being overrun. Although many of their forward firing positions, or Mutzavim, were surrounded, the Golani Brigade's commander, Colonel Amir Drori, did not order his men to withdraw; in fact, he thought they could execute their duties right from where they were.[19] He was right. Although the Syrians eventually managed to push toward the Sea of Galilee before mysteriously stopping at the B'not Ya'akov Bridge, the Golani Brigade assisted two beleaguered armored brigades in slowing down their advance until the reservist armored formations, the true backbone of the IDF's Order of Battle, arrived. Miraculously, the tide of the war shifted—the IDF snatched victory from the Syrians in a matter of days, and eventually pushed all the way to within artillery range of Damascus.[20]

Once again, the 1973 war was a conflict in which the Golani Brigade's reconnaissance force, with its acts of courage and tenacity, would serve as an example for the entire IDF. Seconds before the Syrians unleashed their thunderous blitz across the Golan Heights on October 6, a force of Syrian commandos was helilifted to Mount Hermon in a dramatic bid to capture the mountain and its ultrastrategic intelligence position. Defended by only a few dozen intelligence corps analysts and thirteen Golani infantrymen from the Gideon Battalion, the Eyes and Ears of Israel, as the position was known, was captured in a matter of hours.* For Israel, the sight of the Syrian flag atop the Eyes and Ears of Israel was the embodiment of the war's initial setbacks and overall failure; the Syrian presence would last for virtually the entire duration of the war. Before allowing the United Nations cease-fire to be implemented, Israel vowed to take back Mount Hermon. It was an objective that the Golani Brigade demanded for itself; on October 8, the third day of the war, two Golani companies attempted to retake the Hermon position, but the attack failed and resulted in twenty-five Israeli dead and fifty-seven wounded. On the night of October 21, three

---

* Syrian and Soviet intelligence specialists were later transported to Mount Hermon to confiscate the top-secret Israeli and American-produced intelligence-gathering gear.[21]

Golani battalions, with the Sayeret in the vanguard, began their treacherous trek up the steep slopes of Mount Hermon to retake the position once and for all. The Syrians, dug in and equipped with inexhaustible supplies of grenades and explosives, were determined to fight to the death. The battle raged without respite for the next fifteen hours, and remains one of the most brutal in the torrid history of the Arab-Israeli wars. By the time the Israeli *and* Golani flags were hoisted to the top of Mount Hermon, fifty-five infantrymen lay dead, with a further seventy-nine wounded. Nearly half the brigade had fallen casualty during the fight.[22]

While its illustrious and bloody history in Israel's conventional battles eventually earned the Golani Brigade a proud combat reputation and the right to wear its own distinctive brown beret, the Flying Tigers earned their calling card as the finest conventional reconnaissance formation in the IDF through its bitterly fought antiterrorist campaigns waged along Israel's frontiers: from Gaza, where Sayeret Golani fought a pitched urban fight against the roaming Palestinian terrorist gangs in 1970, to the mountainous abyss of southern Lebanon's Fatahland. Battling terrorists, in fact, has become a Sayeret Golani obsession. Sayeret Golani commandos, under the command of Colonel Uri Saguy,* played a pivotal role in Operation Thunderball, the July 3, 1976, rescue operation in Entebbe, Uganda, as well as in the hostage-rescue operation in Kibbutz Misgav Am on April 6, 1980, when terrorists from the Iraqi-sponsored Arab Liberation Front seized a nursery full of sleeping infants. Sayeret Golani's most famous operation against Palestinian terrorists, the June 6–7, 1982, capture of Beaufort Castle in the Nabatiyah Heights of southern Lebanon on the first night of Operation Peace for Galilee, was also the unit's most controversial. Because of several logistical delays, the Golani commandos had subsequently lost the element of surprise and attacked almost twelve hours after the war began—when the Palestinian terrorists manning the position were lying in wait for them. The subsequent battle, fought inside the Crusader-era castle, was a close-quarters exercise in the destructive nature of modern weaponry and the courage and tenacity of the human spirit. Before the Israeli and Golani flags were hoisted above the former PLO observation post, six Sayeret Golani commandos lost their lives. It was an unbearable price for such a small and close-knit unit to bear. During the remainder of the war, Sayeret Golani participated in the

---

* Sayeret Golani commander from 1971 to 1972, and Golani Brigade commander from 1976 to 1977, Major-General Saguy was appointed the A'man director in May 1991.

battle for Kfar Sil, a confrontation between Palestinians and Syrians labeled by Chief of Staff "Raful" Eitan as the war's toughest, and captured Beirut International Airport; according to foreign reports, Sayeret Golani also captured the Syrian and Soviet electronic intelligence-gathering post at the top of Jebel Barouk in the Bekaa Valley.[23]

One cynical Sayeret Golani junior officer, commenting on the long-term prospects of his job, once stated, "You know why a Sayeret Golani veteran has never made it to chief of staff? Because they all die at the rank of colonel!"[24] After all, being a Sayeret Golani officer is one of the most challenging posts in the IDF. From their first days in Golani Brigade squad-commanders course to the test period where volunteers, all corporals and sergeants, are allowed to prove their worth in order to be allowed to volunteer into the ranks of the Flying Tigers, Sayeret Golani officers play a role in the day-to-day existence of their men. They eat, sleep, and train together. The Golani, especially Sayeret Golani, officer would rather go without food before his men were denied a meal; the same motherly attention holds true for a leave, or any other facet of the soldiers' day-to-day military existence. Most important, the Sayeret Golani officer would never ask his men to do something he himself would not do. He led from the front, one hand raised and the other on his assault rifle's trigger. The "follow me" ethic of command would become a Sayeret Golani trademark. Tragically, however, many would pay the ultimate price for their inherent leadership-by-example style in combat. Perhaps more than any other officer in the Israel Defense Forces, Sayeret Golani commanders have fallen in action leading their men into combat. Colonel "Tzvika" Ofer, one of Sayeret Golani's founding fathers and a recipient of the I'tur Ha'Gvura, a bravery medal comparable to the American Medal of Honor or Britain's Victoria Cross, was killed in action while leading a pursuit against Palestinian terrorists in the Jordan Valley; Lieutenant-Colonel Reuven "Ruvka" Eliaz, decorated for his command of the Sayeret during the assault on Tel Fahar in 1967, was killed in 1973 while serving as the brigade's deputy commander; Captain Shmaryahu Vinnik, Sayeret Golani's commander during the 1973 war, was killed while leading his men in battle during the pitched close-quarters melee on Mount Hermon; and Major "Gunni" Harnick, a former Sayeret Golani commander, was killed in the fight on Beaufort Castle.[25]

Unfortunately, this fatal tradition would continue to follow Sayeret Golani deep into the caves of al-Na'ameh sixteen kilometers south of Beirut, into the soul of the PFLP-GC's command and military infra-structure where the IDF would attempt to exact its twenty-three years' worth of desired retribution against Ahmed Jibril. From the onset of the general staff's contingencies to deal with Ahmed Jibril through a commando strike, it had been clear to the Israeli generals which unit would be called in to execute the raid. After all, it was Sayeret Golani that had witnessed the savagery of Jibril's handiwork in Qiryat Shmoneh, and it was Sayeret Golani that had vowed to one day take its revenge against Ahmed Jibril and the PFLP-GC.

For any commando assault to work, three basic ingredients are required: accurate intelligence, meticulous preparation, and luck. Israel's elaborate intelligence-gathering apparatus, the Mossad and A'man, was charged with providing an accurate portrait of the PFLP-GC's principal western Lebanon facility: what the position looked like above and below the ground; where the guards mounted their patrols and what types of weapons they carried; where the base's garrison and living quarters were situated; were there any Syrian forces stationed nearby and, if yes, what type of hardware could they bring to bear in a possible engagement. The intelligence supplied to Aga'm, the IDF's operations branch, also had to include accurate information concerning Jibril's whereabouts "around" the targeted date; after all, if Jibril was going to be in Damascus that day going over the organization's accounts, there was little point in mounting such a large-scale and risky operation.* The task force would have to be expertly trained for this most precarious mission, where their close-quarters assault skills would have to be honed to perfection. The commandos would also have to be equipped with the gear necessary to allow them to carry out their mission successfully, and rehearse coordination with the Israel Air Force and IDF/Navy units that would ferry them to their objective. Finally, if the IDF general staff was lucky, all these factors would merge into the successful execution of a most spectacular and effective operation.

Ironically, the true success of such an undertaking would also require symbolism: D day was set for the night of December 8, 1988, the first anniversary of the Intifadah. Much thought and preparation would

---

* Israel has never officially acknowledged that the *true* objective of its operation at al-Na'ameh was the assassination of Ahmed Jibril. In fact, there is great speculation that the Sayeret Golani assault squad was assigned the job of *kidnapping* Ahmed Jibril and trading him off for the three Sultan Yaqoub tank soldiers, Feldman, Katz, and Baumel, still believed held by the PFLP-GC.[26] If ever there was symbolism in a military operation, it would be to take Ahmed Jibril hostage and barter him off in the human bazaar he had helped create.

go into the attack. For several months, since the end of autumn, the IAF mounted tenacious aerial photoreconnaissance flights over the area, including many "mysterious" night flights where, it is believed, infrared photographs of the PFLP-GC positions were taken.[27]

The PFLP-GC facility at al-Na'amah was by no means an easy target—in fact, many considered it virtually impregnable. The once-picturesque suburb of Damur was three kilometers inland from the Mediterranean shore and less than ten miles from the outskirts of the Lebanese capital. The target was in the crux of the Palestinians' post-Operation Peace for Galilee Lebanon ministate, where the various national liberation movements had established staging areas from which the Israeli frontier could be attacked. There were also approximately thirty thousand Syrian soldiers stationed nearby, complete with heavy armor, artillery, and surface-to-air missile batteries. Beyond the *outside* dangers, al-Na'ameh was protected by approximately one hundred fifty well-trained and experienced PFLP-GC foot soldiers from the notorious Sabra and Shatilla Battalion,* and was home to an additional one hundred trainees undergoing terrorist instruction. Complimenting the facility's defenses were several machine-gun nests, dozens of antitank missile emplacements, and antiaircraft guns mounted on crudely armored trucks. Making it a unique challenge to the IDF planners, al-Na'ameh's nerve center, the PFLP-GC headquarters and Jibril's personal living quarters, was situated underground, in a series of bunkers protected by tons of earth and cast-iron doors designed to be impervious to explosive charges; several IDF officers would wryly comment that it was similar to that of Adolf Hitler during the siege of Berlin. The al-Na'ameh facility, which included several two- and three-story buildings that served as administrative centers, was also hemmed in by a series of natural caves and ravines, all connected to the command nerve center by the Vietnamese-designed communication trenches and underground tunnels. According to one IDF operations officer, "It was the type of target that one usually found in an Alistair MacLean novel. Unfortunately for us, there was nothing fictitious about the place. It was only too real."[28]

---

* The Sabra and Shatilla refugee camps in southwestern Beirut were among the largest Palestinian camps in all of Lebanon. Engulfed by squalor and hopelessness, the camps were fertile breeding grounds for future generations of Palestinian terrorists. The camps, of course, received their chilling notoriety in September 1982, when Christian Phalangist militiamen, seeking to avenge the assassination of their leader and Lebanese President-Elect Bashir Gemayel, entered the camps and committed the massacre of more than seven hundred men, women, and children.

Luckily for the Israelis, the IDF had extensive intelligence files on the al-Na'ameh base. Not only had the IDF spent a good portion of 1982 and 1983 milling about the Damur region in the Shouf Mountain foothills, but before withdrawing closer to the Israeli frontier, it had videotaped much of the area for A'man's files.[29] These VIDINT (video intelligence) files would be indispensable in the planning of the operation and the success of its inevitable execution.

Overall planning for the al-Na'ameh Operation fell to Major-General Doron Rubin of the OC Training Branch and a veteran and highly respected paratroop officer, who was also the general staff's man responsible for special operations inside Lebanon and beyond.[30] The objectives for the planned al-Na'ameh Operation consisted of the following:

- Target A: Jibril's headquarters, situated in the underground bunker in the center of the base.
- Target B: Six caves, naturally carved into the base of an adjacent mountain, which served as the living quarters to the al-Na'ameh garrison and the Sabra and Shatilla Battalion.
- Target C: The al-Na'ameh training facilities, which were located a few dozen yards away from the main headquarters compound and included armories, obstacle courses, rifle ranges, and classrooms.
- Target D: A series of antiaircraft positions, including dense pockets of mobile 23-mm cannons and stores of SA-7 Strella handheld surface-to-air missiles, which ringed the entire al-Na'ameh base. This final objective was considered crucial to the success of the operation, since the removal of the antiaircraft positions would afford the Golani commandos virtually unhindered close air support by an armada of IAF helicopter gunships that rode shotgun on the entire operation.

The attack force would consist of a select group of fighters from Sayeret Golani as well as some of the best soldiers from the Golani Brigade's Barak Battalion, one of the brigade's finest. The task forces would be transported to the Damur coastline on IDF/Navy missile boats, and then ferried to shore on Zodiac craft operated by naval commandos from Flotilla 13.[31] The naval commandos, expert in strike assault as well as perimeter defense against vastly superior firepower, would establish a beachhead and then secure the landing zone for the task force's withdrawal from Lebanese territory following the successful execution of the raid. Target A, the most important objective of the

entire operation, was to be personally commanded by Colonel Sh.,*
the Golani Brigade commander. Target B, clearly the most dangerous of
the objectives destined for attack, was the responsibility of Lieutenant-
Colonel Amir Meital, a Sayeret Golani commander for three years who
had recently been given command of the Barak Battalion. The entire
Golani contingent would not consist of more than a few dozen commandos.

In true IDF fashion, where officers are as close to the action as the
men whom they command, a forward command post was to be established along the Damur beachhead—surrounded and secured by the
heavily armed Flotilla 13 commandos—supervised, remarkably, by
IDF Chief of Staff Lieutenant-General Dan Shomron, himself a former
reconnaissance paratroop officer and decorated 1967 war hero, who
demanded to be as close to the action as possible. With advanced
command, communications, and control equipment at his disposal,
Shomron would be able to direct much of the commandos' actions on
the ground, while at the same time coordinating activities with on-call
IDF/Navy and IAF elements; assisting Shomron was the OC IDF/Navy
Major-General Avraham Ben-Shoshan, as well as senior IAF and Operations Branch officers.[32] Very little would be left to chance, as IAF
warplanes would be flying above the battle area, ready to launch deadly
volleys of rocket and missile fire should any element of the task force
encounter unexpected difficulties. An armada of CH-53 transport
choppers, the rotor blade "Mack truck" of the IAF's helicopter fleet,
would also be on call, ready at a moment's notice, should an emergency
evacuation operation be required.

There were few units within the IDF's Order of Battle as well suited
to attack such a gauntlet of targets as Sayeret Golani. Unlike other
Sayerot, Sayeret Golani did not recruit conscripts on their first day of
military service, but rather selected only the best NCOs, all officer
material, within the Golani Brigade. After a Golani trooper had been
with his unit for a lengthy period of time, and if he displayed the
required attributes necessary to become a Flying Tiger, he was *invited*
to volunteer into the reconnaissance force. Here he was subjected to a
grueling week-long indoctrination examination where his physical and
mental faculties were tested beyond all normal limits of endurance.
The week, known as a *Gibush*, was a hellish experience meant to
separate the "mere" infantrymen from commando material; it was a
week in which the discomfort and tenacity of months of basic training

---

* His identity is protected for security considerations.

were concentrated into a seven-day test period. Passing the *Gibush* guaranteed only the beginning of hard work. Harsh combat training unique even to the IDF's standards for excellence and proficiency were administered at a brutal pace. Only after a lengthy training period was the soldier formally accepted into Sayeret Golani by having the Flying Tiger insignia pinned to his chest.

One form of combat in which Sayeret Golani would become expert through incessant and repetitive training was, in the IDF vernacular, *La'ba'b*, the Hebrew acronym for "urban built-up area fighting." Since the bitterly fought battles of Lebanon in 1982, where Israeli infantrymen and paratroopers waged street-to-street, house-to-house, and even room-to-room close-quarters fights involving small arms and grenade fire, the art of purifying urban centers has become an IDF obsession. The close-proximity melee in which men wage battles inside confined spaces is not a practice for which military tactics can be taught on an expansive exercise-training ground to a company of soldiers. It is an individual trial where a soldier's physical ability to turn a corner quickly, then gather his courage in order to burst into a room, weapon ablaze, makes the difference between a victorious engagement and a combat fatality.

Although formation-size urban tactics are difficult to teach, the IDF has managed to help prepare its soldiers to fight and prevail in urban and close-quarters battles. Like many armies, the IDF constructed a special "combat city" training area at an anonymous location in central Israel, where prefabricated houses, city streets, and other items likely to be found in the region were faithfully recreated. These structures were all covered with bullet-absorber plates composed of tin plates meshed together with tar, gravel, and asphalt in order to enable live-fire exercises without risk of injury from ricocheting shrapnel fragments.[33] The facility is known, ominously, as "Hell Town," and is a bullet-ridden testament to a soldier's ability to overcome adversity and confining obstacles in the execution of his duties.

According to foreign reports, the Golani task force had trained incessantly in Helltown for months prior to the al-Na'ameh operation under the close supervision of Major-General Rubin, Colonel Sh., and Lieutenant-Colonel Meital; occasionally the training was also supervised by IDF Chief of Staff Shomron. As the Golani officers stood by the neat rows of prefabricated asphalt single-story huts, with a stopwatch in one hand and a megaphone in the other, the commandos stormed each "position" in neat, single-aisle rows. Each commando carried a Glilon 5.56-mm assault rifle fitted with two 30-round magazines taped together, and wore full battle kit including flak vests, with goggles worn for extra protection. At the commander's signal, the Golani commandos would clutch their weapons aside their chests, and then the lead soldier, the point man, would fall to one knee and prepare his assault. When the commanding officer gave the signal, the point man kicked in the hut's door with a powerful blow, then tossed in a fragmentation grenade. Four seconds later, a muted explosion would be heard, as well as the crisscrossing of hundreds of metal fragments lacing into the walls. The point man would then burst into the room with his weapon ablaze and dedicate his fire around the room, finally concentrating on a predetermined corner. The remainder of the squad would follow suit closely behind, entering through the breached door and peppering a predesignated area with devastating, magazine-emptying bursts of fire. The entire process was to take a matter of seconds and decimate everything in the confined space. Major-General Rubin, Colonel Sh., and Lieutenant-Colonel Meital realized that in this operation, time would indeed be a critical factor in determining the attack's success or failure. The sooner all the terrorists inside the bunkers, trenches, and tunnels were killed, the less likely would be significant Israeli casualties.

In order to familiarize the commandos with the conditions under which they would be operating, much of the training was carried out at night or under the crimson backdrop of dawn. The dramatic light show of thousands of tracer rounds being launched at their targets in utter darkness brought a sharp and foreboding sense of reality to the commandos. Negotiating and overcoming the obstacle course of Helltown at night was hard enough. The fight for al-Na'ameh promised to be absolutely treacherous.

As the Golani commandos became comfortable with their skills and tasks, the training proceeded to a more advanced level according to foreign reports. A wooden mock-up of the al-Na'ameh was constructed "somewhere" in northern Israel,* and served as the task force's home away from home for nearly two months.[35]

---

* Historically, Israeli commando units preparing for special covert operations have been trained on highly detailed mock-ups of the targets they would attack. Prior to launching the epic Operation Spring of Youth in April 1973, the Sayeret Mat'kal and Sayeret Tzanhanim task force trained on a building under construction in an exclusive Tel Aviv suburb that was a virtual carbon copy of the targets they would be assaulting in West Beirut. According to foreign reports, the IDF had built a mock-up of the Abu Jihad home in which the Sayeret Mat'kal commandos trained before being dispatched to Tunis in April 1988.[34]

In fact, nothing was going to be left to chance for this most dangerous operation. The men could be trained to the peak state of readiness, the intelligence could be accurate, and absolute surprise achieved. Nonetheless, waging a minicampaign at night, underground for the most part, against well over a hundred heavily armed terrorists from one of the most fanatical and militarily proficient of Palestinian groups did not sound promising. To compensate for their obvious numerical and tactical disadvantages, the Golani commandos would be equipped with a miniarsenal of top-secret and high-tech equipment meant to turn the fight into a fair one.[36] These indigenously produced gadgets and attachments included IL-7 Mini-Laser IR illuminator goggles, attached to the soldier's Kevlar infantry ballistic helmet and designed turn pitch darkness into optimum visibility. Related slightly was the HIL-40 helmet illuminator, a small, powerful light attached to the soldier's helmet affording visibility in the dark for specialized work such as preparing explosive charges. There were also handheld infrared laser pointers, not much bigger than a Walkman, that field commanders could use to single out a target—i.e., a terrorist—in total darkness and designate its termination by pointing a thin red laser light onto the soldier's head. The Golani commandos also wore the NVG-1 Single-Eye Night-Vision Goggles, a remarkable single-eye vision system that allowed the soldier to operate with one eye in complete darkness while keeping the other eye absolutely unobscured. (There is usually a period of more than one minute during which a pupil dilates after removing "normal" two-eye infrared goggles, and during that period, the soldier is often dazzled and dangerously confused.[37])

Attached to the assault rifles and antitank rockets carried by the Sayeret Golani and Barak Battalion commandos was a wide gamut of low-light and infrared sighting devices. These included AIM-1D laser aiming lights, a beam of red laser light directed to a target and attached below the barrel of an assault weapon such as the M-16, AK-47, and the Galil family; the S-8 minibeam light weapon-mounted target illuminators, which blasts a target with a bright beam of light with a range of up to one hundred meters; SL-1 sniper's spotlights, specifically designed to intensify the image in a sniper's scope in such confining areas as a dark room or cave;[38] and the BL-1 Borelight laser designator for zeroing infrared pointer/markers in on a target. Other low-light sniper scopes, many American-made, would also be carried, as would indigenously produced firing-control systems such as the NVL-11 advanced night sight fire control for RPG-7 and Israeli B-300 antitank rockets. Many of the Golani commandos, especially those given the task of removing the legion of sentries that patrolled the al-Na'ameh perimeter, carried Glilon assault rifles fitted with silencers.[39]

Remarkably, another controversial bit of equipment would also be deployed at al-Na'ameh. Taking a page out of the history books (the Soviet Union in World War II, the United States in Vietnam), the Golani task force, according to foreign reports, would bring with it almost one dozen dogs, highly trained Doberman pinschers and other attack dogs, which were fitted with specially designed backpacks fitted with high explosives, or backpacks loaded with tear gas canisters.[40] The dogs were to be guided to their targets, the dangerous tunnels and communications trenches, by means of laser pointers, and then detonated by remote control. The dogs were to destroy the inner defenses of Jibril's well-protected bunkers, and then flush him out with the tear gas canisters. Even by IDF standards, this was a case of revolutionary, though cruel, innovation.*

According to foreign reports, the Golani task force, along with their Flotilla 13 and IDF/Navy components, performed a dry rehearsal for the IDF top brass in late November. The amphibious landing, assault, and seaborne extraction of the force were performed to split-second precision. The chief of staff was impressed, as was Defense Minister Lieutenant-General (Res.) Yitzhak Rabin, who would issue affirmative authorization for the operation. He would monitor the entire operation from the *Bor* (Pit), the underground nerve center situated underneath the *Kirya*, the sprawling minicity housing IDF headquarters and the Defense Ministry.[42]

The training for the operation went extremely well and D day, set for the night of December 8, came with all the forces at full readiness. Before boarding the IDF/Navy missile boat that would ferry the commandos to the landing zone off the coast of Damur, Lieutenant-Colonel Meital, the low-key and charismatic leader, looked at his men and said, "In my days I have never seen such precise preparation as I have seen for this operation. My feelings for success are *excellent.*"[43] The thumbs-up

---

* Although several of the poor beasts were killed in the raid and their bodies, adorned with explosive and gas packs, uncovered by PFLP-GC personnel, the IDF has refused to confirm or deny that it used, or had ever deployed, dogs as kamikaze bombers in action. Ironically, news of the suicide-dog weapon resulted in animal-rights groups in Western Europe and North America protesting outside Israeli diplomatic facilities. In response, Defense Ministry spokesman Chaim Yisraeli stated, in a quasiconfirmation of the use of the kakimaze dogs, "That the Israeli government is not insensitive to the fate of dogs, but there were exceptional circumstances that required the use of animals in order to save human life.[41]

sign was offered to the commandos. It was a gesture they all returned enthusiastically.

IDF/Navy meteorological specialists had predicted a dark and calm night in the Lebanese waters—there would be little reflection from the moon that evening, and the waves, much to the relief of the Golani commandos unaccustomed to the troubling motions of the sea, would be placid. The journey to the Damur coastline took several hours, and the flotilla of missile boats and patrol craft maintained the highest levels of security in order to avoid detection by Lebanese fishermen or Syrian intelligence agents positioned along the coast. The Israeli armada encountered no opposition. At approximately 2030 hours, the commandos began to lower themselves and their equipment into the Mediterranean waters. There were no more rehearsals, no more in-depth intelligence briefings. This time would be for real.

At 2115 hours, the advance guard of the Flotilla 13 contingent raced through the Damur surf and several yards up onto the shore, established a secure landing zone, and secured the bridgehead for the remainder of the force already in the water. The naval commandos, armed with Soviet-produced AK-47s, fanned throughout the beach in search of any hostile targets. No enemy was found. The task force was radioed in.

Coming ashore in a miniarmada of Zodiac craft, the Golani commandos and Lieutenant-General Shomron's rear command post soon coordinated its activities on Lebanese soil. Already the full naval commando contingent had established a comprehensive defensive position surrounding the beachhead, complete with sniper's positions and anti-tank ambush posts. It was three kilometers to al-Na'ameh, three kilometers through difficult terrain, through villages and towns controlled by a random assortment of Druze militiamen and Palestinian guerrillas. The target commanders assembled their men and quickly began the forced march toward the PFLP-GC base. A three-kilometer march on a training field in northern Israel was considered a brief stroll in Golani jargon, even with a full battle kit weighing in excess of sixty pounds. But in the darkened landscape of this treacherous country, it was a task that had to be attended to carefully, stealthily, and quickly.

At al-Na'ameh, December 8 was proving to be a quiet and uneventful evening, even though Ahmed Jibril was in camp. The men and women had conducted their day-to-day activities as always, although the recent overflights of IAF reconnaissance aircraft had convinced the commander of the Sabra and Shatilla Battalion, Abu Jamil, that an Israeli air raid was inevitable, especially on the first anniversary of the outbreak of the Intifadah. As a result, many of the men were ordered to sleep underground, in what were the caves Lieutenant-Colonel Meital's force was to attack. In fact, since an air raid was expected, guard duty around the base was weakened, so that all available personnel on duty could man antiaircraft positions; all those off duty were all hunkered down, in their pajamas and underwear, in preparation for an air strike.[44] Even Jibril, a man who had prided himself on being a competent military planner, could not have foreseen that Israel would attempt to exact revenge against him through a commando raid.

At 0245 on December 9, the attackers struck. They had managed to slink silently across rough terrain of boulders and thorny weeds and had established a staging area a few yards outside the base's perimeter. Colonel Sh. and his command staff located the PFLP-GC sentries, all wearing camouflage fatigues and carrying Soviet-produced AKMS assault rifles, and identified them with their laser pointers. As the commandos crept closer to the main gate, several Sayeret Golani sharpshooters placed the Palestinians inside their laser-rifle sights and fired quick 5-round bursts of fire. The automatic fire had been muted by the silencers, but the sound of the guards painfully relinquishing their final breaths alerted several additional sentries walking nearby to the developing trouble. As the Palestinian gunmen raced to their comrades' aid, they too were cut down by the silenced Golani fire. H hour was at hand, and the commandos swiftly seized the initiative. Moving quickly in their protective gear and load-bearing equipment, they raced inside the facility, their night-fighting gadgetry turning the darkness into daylight. Colonel Sh. ordered his force to split up into their predesignated groups, but to their surprise the bright lights of a truck soon engulfed the main gate. Since the IAF did not strike, a cautious Abu Jamil had taken a sizable complement of men to conduct one final patrol of the base. The truck bearing Jamil's men slowed down as it neared the bodies of the dead gunmen and, before they could even fire off a round at the attacking Israeli commandos, they were bombarded by a decimating fusillade of automatic fire. They had no chance. Over a secure radio frequency, Colonel Sh. informed the chief of staff that there were already "twenty" dead terrorists in his area. The first report was encouraging. The brigade commander signed off, saying that there would be more news to follow shortly.

The muted sound of gunfire had alerted the terrorists inside the main command building and inside the bunkers. Realizing that something serious was happening, the fortified entrances that surrounded Jibril's underground bunker were immediately sealed shut, and quickly defended by a compliment of more than twenty heavily armed men. A brutal close-quarters firefight developed between the PFLP-GC security detail, also equipped with night-fighting equipment, and the attacking Sayeret Golani spearhead taking cover a few dozen yards away. The concrete-reinforced bunkers that protected the entrances to the facility proved impervious to machine-gun and rocket-propelled grenade (RPG) fire. Several of the Sayeret Golani commandos fired their LAW 66-mm antitank rockets point blank at the fortifications, but managed to inflict only negligible damage. The Palestinians returned fire and relinquished very little ground. A small contingent of Golani commandos managed to get inside one of the reinforced passageways to conduct a firefight in the darkened abyss of an underground PFLP-GC trench. They encountered impassable hails of gunfire, and were unable to inch any closer to Jibril's ironclad bunker. Hand grenades proved ineffective inside the cavernous and heavily fortified vault. Undaunted, Colonel Sh. ordered in the dogs, but the Palestinians managed to kill three of the animals, and the two or three that did explode inflicted little damage. Disappointed, the Golani Brigade commander then instructed his sappers, equipped with C-4 high-explosive charges, to raise the two 3-story buildings sitting atop the bunker.[45] The fighting was so fierce that the attacking Golani commandos weren't even able to enter the building to search for documents.

The moment that Abu Jamil's truck was blasted with several hundred rounds of 5.56-mm fire, Force C and Force D, whose job was to neutralize the training grounds and antiaircraft positions up the road, sprang into action. They too had surprised the sentries (they had just finished a changing of the guard), quickly eliminating them with volleys of automatic fire. PFLP-GC reinforcements quickly raced to the area, but they were cut down by the Sayeret Golani fire. Satchel charges were prepared around both the training base and the antiaircraft guns, and the entire area was soon engulfed in a powerful explosion.

In fact, the entire al-Na'ameh area was soon illuminated by the bright lights of gunfire and by midair flares dropped by a pair of IAF F-4E Phantoms that suddenly appeared over the horizon. The brilliance of the flares engulfed the battle area in a bright glitter, which afforded several AH-1S Cobra helicopter gunships, armed with 20-mm miniguns and TOW antitank guided missiles, the necessary visibility to provide the Golani task force with devastating fire support.[46]

The final force into action, Lieutenant-Colonel Meital's Force B, encountered the most difficult of all tasks: purifying the six earthen caves and PFLP-GC living quarters. Since this attack was mounted a few minutes after the chaos had already erupted, the Palestinian fighters were not only alerted to the Israeli operation; they were dressed, equipped, and waiting in defensive firing positions. Lieutenant-Colonel Meital's Golani fighters encountered an impassable hail of bullets as they tried to advance along the dark cave walls, firing their weapons as they moved. According to First-Sergeant D., one commando involved in the operation, "It was a hellish nightmare of tracer fire and utter confusion. The sound of gunfire was deafening, and the darkness, unrelenting explosions, and unfamiliar surroundings made it the most frightening moments of my life. There were so many sources of fire, exploding muzzle flashes, that it was impossible to fix on one target."[47]

Several small hand-to-hand battles soon erupted, as the commandos fought the Palestinians with their fists, knives, rifles butts, and folding stocks. The battle looked like a scene from the motion picture *Star Wars*, with the streams of thin red laser beams emanating from the commandos' aiming devices, and the glow of crisscrossing tracer rounds ricocheting off of the cave's walls. Lieutenant-Colonel Meital realized that he had led his men into a terrible gauntlet, and that he needed help. He summoned his *Kashar* (communications NCO), Sergeant Guy, and conferred with his brigade commander, when suddenly, a quick burst of Palestinian machine-gun fire ripped through Meital's chest and head. Meital had been the first one in the cave. He had set the tone for the battle and had guided his men with great courage and skill through an impassable hail of heavy fire. The "follow me" method of command that the IDF taught its officers, and that Sayeret Golani practiced until the bitter end, had cost the brigade one of its finest officers.

Sergeant Guy had also been shot in the short volley: the incoming bullets had slammed into his Glilon's banana-shaped magazine and ricocheted off his arm. Although in a great deal of pain, he grabbed the radio handset from the cool cave floor, and frantically yelled out the words "*Kudkud Patzu'a. . . . Kudkud Patzu'a*"—"The crown [a loose IDF term for "commander"] has been wounded."[48] It was clear, however, that Lieutenant-Colonel Meital was dead. The sight of his body took the men aback. They had been in combat before, but losing their commander was a mortal blow. Dr. Tzvi "Tzvika" Sheinberg, the unit doctor, raced to attend to his commander, but he too was cut down by a flurry of Palestinian fire. He was shot in the knee, hips, and elbow, and fell beside Meital. Several other Sayeret Golani and Barak fighters were bleeding from shrapnel wounds, and several others had suffered minor injuries from flying fragments and debris, as well as from the aftermath of the deadly hand-to-hand encounters.

Colonel Sh., hearing the battle inside the cave on the radio, ordered Force B to disengage and retreat. Elements of forces C and D were summoned to provide cover fire, while Meital's men quickly departed the deadly cave. To exit the caves, the fighters had to climb up a steep incline, a topographical nightmare that made carrying the stretchers bearing Meital's body and the two seriously wounded men a most difficult task. PFLP-GC gunmen attempted to follow the Golani soldiers out of the cave, but they were met by the heavy Golani cover fire; several Palestinians were killed in the exchange of gunfire, and several more seriously wounded.

Twenty minutes after the first shots were fired, it was time to retreat back to shore.

Lieutenant-General Shomron, nervously monitoring developments back at the shoreline command post, realized that time was becoming a precious and dwindling commodity. Soon it would be light, and the prospect of a large group of commandos racing through the Lebanese wilderness toward the beach rendezvous, under fire and forced to carry their dead and wounded, was an invitation to disaster. Considering that the Israelis were deep in the heart of enemy territory, Shomron decided to cancel the seaborne extraction plan and call in IAF CH-53 Yasur heavy transport helicopters. The new evacuation point, predesignated prior to the raid, was established a few hundred meters outside al-Na'ameh; it was still desperately close to the fighting, however. Considering these dangerous conditions, the new retreat was carried out in an orderly manner. At 0330 hours, the two CH-53s landed at the newly ordered landing zone and began to evacuate the commandos, as well as the rear command post and the naval commandos.

Suddenly, however, it became clear that four soldiers, a lieutenant and three NCOs, were unaccounted for. This unnerving development caused a series of difficult moral, operational, and political dilemmas for Chief of Staff Shomron, forcing him to make decisions that, even today, are still considered controversial.

The IDF does not abandon its men on the battlefield, and everything that could be done to locate the four soldiers was attempted. At first, several Golani officers tried to reach the missing officer, First-Lieutenant Eli, on the emergency communications frequency, but their calls were pointless. During the pitched battle inside the cave, First-Lieutenant Eli had fired his LAW rocket at a group of Palestinian fighters; the discharge from the portable antitank weapon damaged his

AN/PRC-77 field radio's antenna, and rendered the device virtually useless. Officers with megaphones and high-power beam flashlights then called out to the four men, but there was no response. In fact, First-Lieutenant Eli was only 150 meters from the main force, but he could not make contact because he was pinned down by determined PFLP-GC fire. The sounds of gunfire drowned out his calls for help. A search party, made up entirely of volunteers, was organized and even returned to the heart of al-Na'ameh to search for their comrades. It was, indeed, a courageous undertaking to volunteer and return to the eye of the storm, but the Golani soldiers were adamant about saving their comrades no matter what the price.

Lieutenant-General Shomron could not bear that responsibility, however. Dispatching a search party and allowing them to wander for hours under intense battle conditions risked the safety of all the commandos on the ground. Even with IAF cover, the commandos were extremely vulnerable to Palestinian fire, as well as to a Syrian armored brigade that was based nearby at Kfar Sil.[49] The first rays of light had already emerged over the mountains in eastern Lebanon, and the risk of fighting it out with hundreds of Palestinian, Druze, and Syrian fighters was daunting. Calling in additional units risked the possibility of igniting a battle that could possibly lead to full-scale war. The IDF did not want its al-Na'ameh operation to bring about the seventh major Arab-Israeli conflict, and the chief of staff was forced to make a dangerous and highly atypical field decision. Looking for the four men put too much at risk. Without hesitation, Shomron ordered the *entire* al-Na'ameh task force home. They were to board the CH-53s, which were hovering a few feet above ground and taking fire, and head back to Israel. Several senior officers were breathless with Shomron's dramatic decision; several generals were even rumored to have said, "What are we going to tell our soldiers now?"* Shomron, however, realizing that the buck stopped with him, was at peace with his decision. In an improvised press conference the following day at Haifa's Rambam Hospital, the chief of staff stated: "A unit commander must know that he is forbidden to leave soldiers in the field and he must fight, and even risk his life, to rescue trapped soldiers. But when there is the strong

---

* Many senior IDF officers applauded Shomron for his courageous decision, considering it the right thing to do under the circumstances. Perhaps the greatest words of support came from Lieutenant-General (Res.) Mordechai "Motta" Gur, a former Chief of Staff and Shomron's commander in chief during the Entebbe raid. In a brief statement, Gur commended Shomron, stating: "Even though the decision went against the normal grain of tradition, it was the correct move to make.[50]

possibility of endangering other soldiers, and risking a dire military and political situation, the chief of staff can decide otherwise, just as I did in this instance."[51]

In reality, Shomron did not leave anybody behind: He only delayed their safe return back to Israel for several hours. The extraction operation of the main Golani task force was in itself a dangerous exercise: a test of wills between a helicopter pilot's courage versus the destructive power of terrorist gunfire. At IAF headquarters in Tel Aviv, the senior commanders, including IAF OC Major-General Avihu Ben-Nun, all held their breath while the developing situation was played out over a loudspeaker. The hulking CH-53, low and slow-moving ships, proved to be tempting targets. At 0540 on the morning of Friday December 9, the last CH-53 lifted off of Lebanese territory. At 0545 the sun burst across the smoldering remnants of the al-Na'ameh base. A few hundred yards down a rocky incline, the four trapped Golani troopers prepared a defensive ring in a 360-degree radius. As they watched the last CH-53 lift off in a cloud of dust, they knew that they had to buy time. The IAF would eventually rescue them, but could they hold out? A constant stream of attacking IAF fighter bombers and attack helicopters was keeping the Palestinians at bay while other helicopters flew at low levels in a frantic aerial search for the four men. The sight of the IAF's Star of David emblem was a welcome relief to the besieged Golani commandos.

Under heavy Palestinian fire, however, the fate of the four Golani infantrymen appeared precarious. First-Lieutenant Eli organized his men and took them to a concealed spot a little too close for comfort to the al-Na'ameh base. Hemmed in behind thick foliage, the four infantrymen attempted to obtain the safest form of physical cover from the marauding PFLP-GC gunmen, who, realizing that such an incessant IAF presence after the choppers had lifted off could only mean that there were men left behind, set out to bring a few prisoners back to Ahmed Jibril. In fact, First-Lieutenant Eli and his men could hear the chatter of PFLP-GC gunmen closing in on them through the bush. One group of Palestinians, armed with machine guns and AK-47s equipped with bayonets, approached to within a few feet of the hiding soldiers, and were quickly killed by the four Israelis who popped out from behind a group of boulders launching quick bursts of automatic fire from their Glilon assault rifles. Their shots had to be accurate. They had figured that the IAF would only attempt a rescue under the safety of darkness. If they needed to hide out and survive for another twelve hours, they would need every round of ammunition left in their pouches.

The incredible number of Palestinian guerrillas that emerged from the al-Na'ameh caves was a numbing sight to the four infantrymen; it appeared as if a full army had suddenly materialized in the ruin-filled valley below. Having spent a full night in Lebanon, they had more or less resigned themselves to the fact that they were either going to live through the ordeal or die in battle. According to Sergeant Avi Ben-Kassos, one of the four "missing" Golani commandos, "I personally was not afraid of death or injury, but only of being taken prisoner by Jibril's men."[52]

Three hours had already passed since the Sayeret Golani and naval commandos had departed from Lebanese territory. They were already back in Israel, at an anonymous base in the north, undergoing a personal debriefing by Lieutenant-General Shomron. As the chief of staff listened to the Golani commandos explain each detail of the operation, an aide suddenly burst into the hall and gave Shomron the news he so desperately wanted to hear: an IAF aircraft, strafing Palestinian forces, had established radio contact with the four missing brown berets—and had an approximate fix on their position. First-Lieutenant Eli had managed to fix his radio, and was able to make positive contact with the IAF's protective armada flying above.

Immediately, Shomron and the senior officers present at the debriefing in northern Israel raced to a waiting chopper and flew to the Kirya; they would monitor the rescue operation from the *Bor* where the IAF's C^3 capabilities were the most sophisticated. The al-Na'ameh operation was no longer shrouded in failed mystery and anxious pangs of hindsight. It was now a race against the clock.

The plan to rescue the four men was relatively simple, inspired by an amazing feat conducted nearly two years earlier. On October 16, 1986, an IAF Phantom fighter bomber attacking Palestinian targets in southern Lebanon suffered a mechanical glitch while releasing one of its bombs, and exploded in midair. Both the pilot and navigator managed to eject and parachute safely back to earth. The pilot was located and eventually plucked to safety holding onto the landing skids of an AH-1S Cobra gunship in a dramatic rescue operation conducted at night, under extremely heavy enemy fire.* A repeat performance was ordered, although this time the rescue would be a bit more sophisticated and protected. Two Cobras would fly close cover for the rescue

---

* The navigator, Captain Ron Arad, was captured by Amal Shiite militiamen, and eventually handed over to more radical elements in Hizbollah. As of this book's writing, he is still a prisoner of the Shiite terrorists; several intelligence reports indicate he is even being held in Iran by the Revolutionary Guards.

operation, launching their minigun rounds and rockets at any hostile movements, while two other Cobras would land at a protected spot, situated on an ash road atop a hill, and pick up the stranded Golani commandos. Each Cobra would hold two soldiers, each clutching on to one of the helicopter's two landing skids. The choppers would then fly off toward the Mediterranean, where an IDF/Navy missile boat would be waiting.[53]

It took nearly three hours for the entire rescue to be pulled off. Palestinian fire was so intense that it was impossible for the four trapped Golani fighters to emerge from their hiding spot long enough to signal the choppers, and the Cobra gunships, flying into a gauntlet of antiaircraft—even RPG antitank—fire had to maneuver around the bright explosive lights of tracer fire. Several of the Cobras, in fact, decided to engage the terrorists head on. Instead of firing at the terrorists from a low altitude while making a fast pass over the area, the Cobras simply hovered a few feet above the ground and fought it out with Jibril's men at point-blank range wild West style. According to Brigadier-General R., IAF Chief of Staff, "Fighting it out at close range was the only way the Cobras could prevent the terrorists from reaching the four Golani men. Jibril's men were executing the classic art of infantry attack—advance, take cover, fire to the sides, and advance. They were closing in on the four men quite quickly, and pouring on fire in extraordinary barrages."[54]

According to Major A., the skipper of one of the rescuing Cobras, "The area was an absolute inferno of antiaircraft fire, and dozens of RPG rockets buzzed the air. Then, not fifty yards away, I noticed the four. They had concealed themselves in a kind of trench which provided excellent cover, making them, of course, very difficult to spot from a distance." Both helicopters landed quickly on the ash road, and the Golani commandos, taught to think on their feet, realized what needed to be done. Under enormous enemy fire, they split into two groups; each soldier grabbed a landing skid and held on for dear life. As they left the ground they could see the Palestinian fighters who had attempted to blow the choppers out of the sky taken aback by the dramatic rescue conducted right before their eyes.

Each Cobra pilot flew carefully in order not to throw the soldiers, and attempted to communicate with the dangling men in order to help see them through this most delicate situation. One of the commandos was clutching the skid, as well as holding on to a rucksack filled with personal equipment and his Glilon assault rifle. The pilot, Major A'., could not believe that the soldier was placing so much value on his gear.

Apparently, he was as concerned with having to answer to the base quartermaster as he was with his own safety.

During the entire rescue, the tension inside the *Bor* was nerve-shattering. Several generals, men who had personally led operations deep behind enemy lines, could not stomach the anxiety and had to leave the room to wash their faces. At 1115, when the two Cobras took off from al-Na'ameh with their precious human cargo, a sigh of relief engulfed the smoke-filled command center. No one clapped, and very few handshakes were offered. There was still a chance that the men could fall or slip into the sea. A few moments later, however, when word finally came in that all four commandos were safely on board the missile boat, one "anonymous" general loudly exclaimed, "A tremendous miracle has just transpired."[55] Many of the generals soon found themselves smiling in uncontrollable eruptions of joy.

A while later, the Cobras involved in the rescue operation returned to their landing strip in northern Israel. Standing on the landing pad, in full battle kit and proudly wearing his Golani brown beret, was Colonel Sh., the Golani Brigade commander. The seasoned infantry officer gazed upon the pilots who were emerging from the armored shells of their gunship cockpits, and with a pool of tears in his eyes, simply said *Todah*— "Thanks."[56] After all, those were *his* boys that had been saved.*

Later that day, thousands of mourners attended the funeral of Lieutenant-Colonel Amir Meital, twenty-nine years old, in his hometown of Hadera. One of the most capable commando officers to wear the IDF uniform, he was laid to rest in an emotional ceremony. A man who had helped transform Sayeret Golani into one of the elite among the reconnaissance units in the IDF was, many say, destined to one day assume command of the entire Golani Brigade. He had been given command of Sayeret Golani in 1986, upon his return from a command course in the United States Army Staff College, and he personally had led countless special operations inside Lebanon. One of his comrades stated that Lieutenant-Colonel Meital was one of the true fighters in the IDF, a man who one day might have become chief of staff.[57]

For the IDF, the raid at al-Na'ameh was an uneven mixture of success and failed opportunity. Conservative estimates report that between twenty and thirty PFLP-GC gunmen were killed in the operation, including Abu Jamil, and that a further thirty or forty had been seriously

---

* In an emotional ceremony in Chief of Staff Shomron's office on July 15, 1989, the pilots who participated in the rescue operation received commendations and bravery medals.[58]

wounded; other estimates place the death toll above fifty. Also, the entire facility, with the exception of the command bunker, was destroyed, and much of the PFLP-GC's western Lebanese network was seriously disrupted. Yet Ahmed Jibril was still alive. The Night of the Hang Gliders and the Intifadah, as well as past sins such as Qiryat Shmoneh, had gone unavenged one more day. Now, with a tearful honor guard bearing one final salute to Lieutenant-Colonel Meital, yet another deadly score needed to be settled.

Little is known about what happened to Ahmed Jibril during the raid. American Defense Intelligence Agency communiqués reported that he remained inside the protective confines of his bunker for more than sixteen hours after the first shots were fired, fearing that the IDF had sent in a full brigade to kill him. Moments after the last Israeli aircraft left the area, however, General Ghazi Kana'an, commander of Syrian military intelligence in Lebanon (the *al-Istikhabarat al-'Askariya al-Suria fi Lubnan*), rushed to al-Na'ameh from his Beirut headquarters to see if his Palestinian comrade-in-arms was all right. Later that day, a visibly shaken Ahmed Jibril surfaced in al-Na'ameh to display an extensive assortment of Israeli equipment left behind in the raid, including infrared goggles, sniper rifles, and explosive packs; PFLP-GC guerrillas also displayed the bodies of several dead kamikaze dogs fitted with their explosive packs. Clutching Lieutenant-Colonel Amir Meital's Glilon, fitted with a laser-sighting device and a silencer,[59] Jibril addressed the foreign press corps based in Beirut and Damascus, and claimed that his men had inflicted serious injury to the attacking "Zionist terrorists," and that revenge would soon be exacted.

Also giving a Friday afternoon press conference was U.S. State Department spokesperson Margaret Tutweiler. She said that Israel had violated American agreements by using American-made weaponry in an illegal attack against sovereign Lebanese territory; she also condemned the Israeli raid against Ahmed Jibril's base as a dangerous escalation of violence in the embattled region.

In retrospect, the American attempts to sound a diplomatic chord in the Arab world by condemning Israel's antiterrorist operation against Jibril would appear foolish. Less than two weeks after the al-Na'ameh raid and the U.S. State Department condemnation of Israel, Pan Am Flight 103 disintegrated high above the Scottish hamlet of Lockerbie. Indeed, after the al-Na'ameh raid, the stage was set for one of the most controversial, confusing, highly publicized, and brilliantly conceived terrorist operations ever perpetrated to assume center stage. Ahmed Jibril's "revolutionary violence" was about to hit prime time.

CHAPTER TEN

THE RUSTLING OF AUTUMN LEAVES

ISRAEL'S DRAMATIC RAID on Jibril's al-Na'ameh lair should have prompted the world's police and antiterrorist forces to brace themselves for a multitude of revenge attacks on the four corners of the globe. After all, with the Middle East's bloody penchant for tit-for-tat brutality, an attempt on Jibril's life should have raised red flags in every Western European capital. Exacerbating the obvious need for vigilance against terrorist attack was the fact that the Christmas season, a period of goodwill toward mankind and a time when people traveled home for the holidays, was historically a tinderbox period for Middle Eastern terrorists, and the most common season for Middle Eastern bloodshed, from the PFLP's December 26, 1968, deadly attack on El Al passengers at Athens International Airport, to the December 21, 1985, takeover of the headquarters of the Organization of Petroleum Exporting Countries in Vienna, to the November 23, 1985, hijacking and massacre on board an Egypt Air Boeing 737 in which fifty-seven passengers were killed either by the terrorists or in the botched rescue attempt by Egyptian commandos.

Clearly the most notorious terrorist attack to take place during the holiday season was the December 27, 1985, massacres at the Rome and Vienna airports: the signature of Abu Nidal, random butchery and indiscriminate bloodshed, adorned both attacks. At 0903 hours at the check-in area at Rome's Leonardo da Vinci International Airport, four Palestinians, doped up on amphetamines, produced assault rifles and antipersonnel grenades from travel bags and went on a killing spree around the El Al check-in counter. El Al security guards, trained by the Shin Bet and armed with 9-mm automatics, returned fire and killed all four terrorists, but not before they managed to kill fifteen civilians and wound seventy more.[1]* The sight of the dead, lying on the blood-soaked terminal floor identified by police markers, would come to embody the senseless bloodshed of international terrorism for much of the 1980's. Rome, however, was but an opening salvo for a much more sinister day of carnage. A few minutes after the Rome Airport Massacre, three Abu Nidal terrorists attacked Vienna's Schwechat International Airport; their target, too, was the El Al check-in counter and passengers preparing to board Flight 364 to Tel Aviv. In the brief fusillade of terrorist fire, three persons were killed and forty-seven were seriously wounded.[2]

Ostensibly, the objective of the attack was to torpedo the credibility of Yasir Arafat and the PLO. Both Italy and Austria were two European nations that maintained extremely close relations with the PLO leadership, and both nations had labored hard to bring Israel to the negotiating table with the Palestinians. Since the faintest prospects of peace did exist, Abu Nidal was determined to destroy any hopes for a negotiated settlement, and destroy Arafat's foothold on the European continent.

It is also believed that a third target was singled out for attack that December morning. In a unified attempt by members of the National Salvation Front to weaken the PLO's international standing, Ahmed Jibril had signed a pact with the Fatah Revolutionary Council and agreed to launch a PFLP-GC suicide attack against Frankfurt's bustling airport as the final installment of Abu Nidal's Christmas trilogy of terror.[3] According to the noted journalist Patrick Seale, at the time of the Rome and Vienna attacks both Abu Nidal and Ahmed Jibril were hard at work competing for Colonel Qaddafi's favor and petrodollar millions. Abu Nidal was eager for Libyan cash in order to further his murderous campaign against Israel and the "moderate" PLO, while Jibril, eager to escape the frugal confines of Damascus, was looking to expand his organization into the forefront of the anti-Arafat alliance. But in the typical show of Arab disunity and mistrust, even the consolidated anti-Arafat opposition could not come together. Abu Nidal decided to remove the PFLP-GC from the grandiose operation and go it

---

* According to an Italian carabinieri officer summoned to the airport following the massacre and interviewed later on Italian television, "The death toll could have well exceeded a hundred were it not for the quick response of the El Al security contingent."

alone; either Abu Nidal did not want Ahmed Jibril's popularity to surge in the aftermath of the Rome, Vienna, and Frankfurt bloodbaths and share in the Libyan wealth, or, as it has been suggested, Abu Nidal feared that the PFLP-GC was so penetrated by Israeli (and possibly Jordanian or American) intelligence assets that Ahmed Jibril was a completely compromised entity.[4] The fact that many people, including Jibril, believed that the PFLP-GC was running rampant with spies, informants, and turncoats would play prominently in future operations.

In the end, Abu Nidal won out in the blood-soaked petrodollar sweepstakes. But Abu Nidal's Rome and Vienna massacres, together with the April 1986 bombing of the La Belle Discotheque in West Berlin (an attack perpetrated by two Palestinian brothers working for the Syrians, would prompt President Ronald Reagan to authorize Operation El Dorado Canyon, the April 17, 1986, U.S. air strike against Libya that targeted sensitive military and terrorist positions, as well as Qaddafi's personal "Bedouin-tent" residence. Although Libya was a convenient, albeit incorrect, scapegoat, the American operation, carried out with meticulous Israeli intelligence assistance,[5] convinced the Libyan leader that *his* Palestinian legions had been infiltrated by "counterrevolutionary" spies, and that it was a prudent idea to forgo the support of the much-vaunted international terrorist offensive against the West and Israel—at least on the surface, and at least for the time being. Qaddafi subsequently softened his rhetoric, withdrew overt support for ongoing Palestinian operations in Europe, and began to once again embrace PLO chairman Yasir Arafat for his diplomatic drive for legitimization.

Ominously, these factors would play a significant and symbolic role in the events of Christmas 1988.

True to form, Jibril would strike out in spectacular form during the holiday season, but the attack would have nothing to do with the al-Na'ameh operation.* In fact, the events of Christmas 1988 would have nothing to do with Israel, Lebanon, or the Arab-Israeli conflict, but would find its roots in an expanding new giant in the terrorist game, a nation whose violent hatred for the West, especially the United States and Israel, materialized in the eruption of a jihad waged by martyrs and fueled by religious zeal and the endless revenue from oil production. That country was the Islamic Republic of Iran.

---

* Many Western intelligence officials silently believe that had the Golani commandos succeeded in getting to Jibril's bunker, succeeded in killing or kidnapping him, and subsequently rifled through all the paperwork inside his office, it is likely that Pan Am Flight 103 would have never been blown out of the sky.[6]

Iran's first true contacts with the various Palestinian terrorist factions began the moment the Ayatollah Khomeini deplaned from the Air France Boeing 747 that ferried the spiritual Shiite leader from his French exile to the ascension to power in the chaos of revolution-riddled Iran. For years, the pro-Western Shah of Iran had maintained a close relationship with the Jewish State even though his nation was virtually 100 percent Moslem. The Shah was the sole Near Eastern oil-producing nation to sell its black gold to Israel; the Iranian Army bought Israeli-produced Uzi 9-mm submachine guns; and the much-vaunted Israeli security services, the Mossad and the Shin Bet, virtually built up the dreaded *Savak*, the Shah's security service and secret police. In 1977, Iran's deputy defense minister Hassan Tufanian told the Israeli defense minister Ezer Weizman, "We are the only two countries in the region that can depend on each other."[7] The Jews of Iran, with a population of nearly half a million, thrived under the Shah, and the Israeli flag flew proudly among Tehran's Embassy Row. The Islamic revolution and the ouster of the shah destroyed Iran's relationship with Israel. One of the first world leaders to congratulate the Ayatollah Khomeini for the commencement of the new Islamic age in the region was the PLO leader Yasir Arafat. During the subsequent takeover of the U.S. Embassy and the 444-day hostage ordeal, Arafat even attempted to serve as an honest broker between the West and the Revolutionary Guards that held fifty-two American hostages. To help Arafat, the Ayatollah vowed to send forces to Palestine to help destroy the Zionist infidels and liberate the Holy City of Jerusalem for all Muslims.

Relations between the Iranians and the PLO never developed into a full-fledged alliance that Arafat had so hoped for, however. The Iraqi invasion of Iran truly split the Arab and Muslim worlds, and the PLO, receiving quite a generous stipend from Saddam Hussein, naturally sided with Baghdad. Syria, on the other hand, was the only Arab state to support the Iranians, and the Palestinian groups under Syrian control nurtured contacts with the Iranian Revolutionary Guards and their satellite organizations in Lebanon—principally Amal and, of course, Hizbollah. The bonds forged between the Lebanese Shiites, the Iranians, and Ahmed Jibril's PFLP-GC were particularly productive. In southern Lebanon, the PFLP-GC-Shiite alliance pursued the withdrawing Israeli forces with brutal effectiveness, Shiite forces shielded several PFLP-GC positions from Israeli attack, and, in a rare venture, Jibril's men openly trained with Hizbollah terrorists, even conducting large-scale joint maneuvers together in the Bekaa Valley; according to

Iranian press reports, both Palestinians and Shiites were preparing to liberate Palestine *together*.[8]

Ahmed Jibril's primary case for establishing his close-knit relationship with the Iranians, as well as solidifying his business dealings with the Libyans, was the organization's incessant thirst for cash. From 1986 to 1987, the Syrians drastically cut financial support of the PFLP-GC; this was mainly as a result of the worsening economic situation developing in Damascus, as well as a result of diplomatic—and economic— sanctions imposed against Syria following the failed bombing of El Al Flight 016. According to one Israeli intelligence analyst who wished to remain anonymous, "The PFLP-GC was not an economically vibrant organization with investments in Fortune 500 companies and lucrative real estate and stock portfolios like Arafat's PLO. It was an organization that, like a dog under the table looking for handouts, had to accept whatever endeavor paid cash—no matter how low-down and treacherous, and no matter who offered it." When Syria slashed its allowance, Jibril first turned to Iran, but unlike the Libyans (or Iraqis), the Iranians could not afford to part with their oil profits in order to sponsor PFLP-GC operations against Israel along the Lebanese frontier, or in Europe through its covert deep-cover cells in Western Europe. Iran had virtually bankrupted itself fighting the war against Iraq; it financed its dispatching of fourteen-year-old kids to the front by taking hostages in Lebanon and bartering them off for American and Israeli arms. Nevertheless, Jibril made elaborate efforts to pursue Iranian favors. In December 1987, following the successful execution of the PFLP-GC's Operation Kibya, Jibril met the Iranian foreign minister, Ali Akbar Velayati, in Tripoli, Libya, to convey official PFLP-GC support for the Islamic "revolution," and support of Iranian attempts to form the Islamic Organization for the Liberation of Palestine, aimed at replacing the PLO.[9] In essence, Jibril was hustling for work—promising PFLP-GC organizational know how and destructive discipline in exchange for Iranian cash. The Iranians, however, proved to be shrewd businessmen, and an extremely hard sell.

Jibril was, therefore, forced to pander to Libyan generosity and Libyan cash, the arrangement that carried the most strings attached to it. The Libyans, through the intermediary efforts of Syrian military intelligence commander General Ali Duba (who, undoubtedly, was looking to earn a hefty brokerage fee), hired the PFLP-GC to serve as a proxy to retaliate against the United States for Operation El Dorado Canyon.[10] He had leased a portion of his small PFLP-GC army to the Libyans for their war of national imposition against Chad, and the PFLP-GC's KGB-trained intelligence agents and deep-cover terrorists supported—or even perpetrated—Libyan intelligence operations worldwide. For the arrangement, the PFLP-GC was paid an annual stipend of $20 million to $25 million. But in late 1987, these funds began to dwindle as well.

Just as the Western sanctions had crippled Syrian prestige—and its national economy—following the failed El Al bombing, so too were Western actions disrupting Libya's desire for international recognition and political prestige. By November 1988, when Yasir Arafat's terse and noncommittal renunciation of terrorism in a Stockholm news conference provided Qaddafi with a diplomatic window to escape the American-led stranglehold, the PFLP-GC's desire to raise the ante of violence fell on deaf ears in Tripoli. By supporting Arafat's diplomatic offensive, Qaddafi could return Libya to the fold of mainstream Arab politics and finally be taken seriously by the international community. Yet Arafat's muted recognition of his past sins, as well as conditional PLO acceptance that a nation called Israel did indeed exist, was viewed as a major breakthrough; it failed, however, to earn the PLO chairman recognition in Washington, as well as any reaction from Jerusalem. What it did do was irritate the vengeful souls of the National Salvational Front determined once and for all to rid the Palestinian leadership of Arafat. Discrediting Arafat's promise to repudiate terrorism would not only cancel Arafat's newfound acceptance in the West, but it would also portray him to his beloved Arab masses as a convictionless leader who pandered to American political requirements rather than the legitimate rights of the Palestinian people.

Jibril had seen Arafat's treason coming for years. To destroy Arafat politically and physically, Jibril had just the plan: Perpetrate a diabolical operation inside Western Europe where the death toll would not only be enormous, but would also prove to be a symbolic statement of boldness similar to the 1972 Munich Olympics Massacre, where the fabric of Western security and basic freedoms were to be challenged. The damaging political aftermath of Jibril's attack would force Arafat to run back to Tunis with his tail between his legs, PFLP-GC operatives would then eliminate the PLO's moderates in an exile coup d'etat and Jibril would, finally, assume political and military control of the Palestinian revolution. The PLO realized that Ahmed Jibril had designs on becoming the supreme leader of the movement. Arafat's Force 17 security detail was provided with specific instructions to watch out for *Palestinian* gunmen, perhaps even members of their own entourage, who might make an attempt on Arafat's life. According to one PLO security official, "Jibril, for us, is the most dangerous man in the Arab world."[11]

Indeed, Jibril did maintain an elaborate deep-cover infrastructure in Europe that could carry out such an ambitious terrorist undertaking. For years, Jibril had established an extensive and highly elaborate terrorist infrastructure in Western Europe. Dormant cells existed in Sweden, Denmark, and the Netherlands, and support forces were in place in Yugoslavia. To coordinate and concentrate terrorist activity, two regional headquarters were established where his cells were the largest and their arms caches the most extensive. The first, commanding southern Europe and the Mediterranean region, was in Greece,[12] a pro-Palestinian NATO nation that often turned a blind eye to Middle Eastern terrorist attacks against Western—and especially Israeli—interests; a subheadquarters was established on the island of Malta, home to Libyan naval personnel on liberty, and considered by many observers to be Qaddafi's physical foothold in Europe, used as a base for intelligence and terrorist operations directed against the Continent. The second regional headquarters were in West Germany. Because there were thousands of Palestinians and Arab guest workers in West Germany seeking work or political asylum, the PFLP-GC could easily tap into a large reservoir of recruits and support; also in West Germany, Jibril's contact with the Red Army Faction and the Provisional Irish Republican Army (a group that spent much of its time attacking British military installations) provided him with an intricate network of allies and comrades in arms. Perhaps most important was the historic implications of Palestinian terrorists operating on German soil. It was a nerve slashed open by Black September's 1972 attack on the Olympic village in Munich, and one that Jibril vowed to tease and torture in the coming months. So important was the West German PFLP-GC headquarters that Jibril placed his trusted and loyal lieutenant, Hafaz Dalkamoni, in charge of Western European operations.[13]

What the PFLP-GC's European underground army possessed in determination, training, and desire to act, it lacked in financial resources. Safe houses and covers required money, a lot of it. The PFLP-GC had to struggle just to maintain a European shop. If a large-scale terrorist offensive was to be mounted in order to destroy Yasir Arafat, a large infusion of cash would have to be pumped in urgently. Exacerbating Jibril's financial difficulties was the fact that in 1985 the PFLP-GC had been reinforced by several dozen highly capable bomb-makers from Abu Ibrahim's Arab Organization of 15 May, which had disintegrated earlier that year. Remarkably, much of the rank and file of the May 15 group joined ranks with Fatah, but the officers, European operations officers, and, of course, demolitions experts joined forces with Jibril.[14]

The economically strapped PFLP-GC was now forced to assume responsibility—and provide security—to a Western European network that had been in existence for several years.

Because of its truly bankrupt financial position, the PFLP-GC's grandiose scheme could never have materialized were it not for two important and foreboding factors. One was Jibril's newfound religious fervor, a born-again return to fundamentalist Islam, which placed him in higher regard in Tehran. Jibril has even become a Muslim fundamentalist, a dedication of faith that requires him to pray five times a day, and that has religiously strengthened his determination to destroy Israel. Jibril's fascination with fundamental Islam in his later years has made the PFLP-GC an entity in which the cunning violence of well-trained terrorists has combined with the martyrdom penchant of an Islamic warrior. In fact, when the *Imam* Khomeini issued a death sentence, or *Fatwa*, against Salman Rushdie, author of the "blasphemous" book *The Satanic Verses*, Jibril and Iran's new white knight, the PFLP-GC, offered its assistance (as well as the thirst for the $3 million bounty) for taking care of the matter. The other factor was a fatal technical error in the warm waters of the Persian Gulf, just off the ultrastrategic Strait of Hormuz. Indeed, the formal terrorist alliance that would be forged would have ominous implications for the West. The merging of a highly organized, fanatical group known for its use of wanton violence and a nation-state insensitive to world criticism and sanctions because of its blessing of vast national resources promised to escalate the level of Middle Eastern violence to new extremes.

In the early morning hours of July 3, 1988, Iran Air Flight 655, a French-built A-300 Airbus, took off from the Bandar Abbas military/civilian airport and headed for Dubai across the torrid waters of the Persian Gulf. It was a characteristically hot day, and the events transpiring in the area were even hotter. It was the final days of the Iran-Iraq war, a conflict that had involved the lives of more than a million dead and wounded and accomplished little more than to reiterate the pariah status of both Saddam Hussein's Iraq and the Khomeini's Islamic republic of Iran. The fight on the ground resembled the trenchlike carnage of World War I, complete with gas attacks and horrendous loss of life. Both Iran and Iraq had seized temporary initiative throughout the eight-year bloodbath, from the initial Iraqi invasion to the bogged-down war of the marshes. By the summer of 1988, however, the Iranians were clearly losing the war. Iraq's deployment of ballistic missiles, chemical weapons, and the ability of the Iraqi Air Force's French and Soviet-built warplanes to attack targets deep inside Iran had demoralized the once indomitable fighting spirit of Iran's Islamic holy warriors. The Iranians were attempting one final offensive to consolidate territory and national prestige before United Nations-sponsored negotiations were to bring about an eventual end to the seemingly endless hostilities.

For American naval forces operating in the Gulf, dispatched to the troubled waters in 1987 to protect the free and unmolested passage of Kuwaiti oil tankers, the potential for a wild Iranian offensive, complete with publicity-grabbing assaults on United States interests, was a dangerous reality. At Bandar Abbas, at the gateway to the strategic waterway, the Iranians had concentrated the battered remains of an air force the Shah had once built into the region's most powerful, including several F-4 Phantoms (refurbished with Israeli spare parts no less) and F-14 Tomcats. Bandar Abbas was also the home base to several batteries of lethal Chinese-produced Silkworm sea-to-sea antishipping missiles that could easily strike out against the vast armada of American naval vessels patrolling the Gulf waters. Suicide squads of Revolutionary Guards in small, fast patrol boats and armed with high explosives and RPGs, were even dispatched to the Gulf waters to engage U.S. vessels. On July 3, 1988, at 1010, a helicopter from the USS *Vincennes*, an Aegis-class guided-missile cruiser,[15] drew fire from three Iranian Boghammer fast patrol boats outside the territorial waters off Bandar Abbas; immediately, the *Vincennes* and the USS *Elmer Montgomery* engaged the boats, sinking two of them.

The Aegis class vessel was the most sophisticated warship in the U.S. Navy (and the world, for that matter); its combat information center was a sophisticated, computerized data handling, analysis, and display platform designed to keep track of rapidly changing tactical situations during full-scale combat. The Aegis technology for directing its computer-guided weaponry was touted as foolproof but, according to the noted U.S. naval expert Dr. Norman Friedman, "No system, not even the Aegis, is perfect."[16] That fallibility would soon have tremendous implications.

At 1047, shortly after the sea battle with the Iranian patrol boats, combat information center officers on board the *Vincennes* detected an aircraft, emitting signals from two radio transponders usually transmitted by F-14s, taking off from Bandar Abbas and heading toward the *Vincennes* in a direct and threatening path. It was a day before the July Fourth Independence Day festivities when an Iranian strike against an

American warship would have resulted in enormous publicity for Iran in the Muslim world; it was a fact not lost to astute *Vincennes* skipper Captain Will C. Rogers. Captain Rogers realized the importance of symbolism in the region, and attempted increased efforts for *absolute* IFF (Identification Friend or Foe) verification before any defensive action was taken. The *Vincennes* computer-analysis system identified the aircraft as an Iranian F-14 Tomcat: The possibility for an air attack, or even a suicide assault, was very real. The rules of engagement allowed Captain Rogers to fire upon an aircraft if it approached to within twenty miles of the ship. At 1051 hours, the radar blip breached the twenty-mile envelope. At 1054, Rogers ordered the launching of two Standard surface-to-air missiles to engage the mysterious target.[17] Seconds later the target was destroyed.

Hours later it became clear that the *Vincennes* had made a terrible mistake. At least one of the two Standard SAMs had struck Iran Air Flight 655, shattering it into thousands of fragments and killing all 290 passengers and crew on board, including sixty small children. The filmed clips of lifeless bodies floating in the waters of the Persian Gulf amid the wreckage underscored the senseless tragedy of the accidental destruction of the aircraft. Although President Reagan sent a letter of apology to the Iranian government via Swiss intermediaries on July 4, outrage in Tehran was fervent. Tens of thousands of grief-stricken Iranians flocked to the streets of Tehran in nationally televised funerals where, according to Iranian officials, "the greatest war crime of our era" was mourned.[18] The calls of "Death to America" were deafening.

Although the Iranians, especially those in the ruling elite, usually enjoyed beating the war drums to promote a jihad against the nation it viewed as the "great Satan," *public* calls for revenge against the United States following the destruction of Iran Air Flight 655 were few. The Iranian leadership, led by "moderate" speaker Ali-Akhbar Hashemi Rafsanjani, realized that Iran could not simultaneously fight Iraq, the United States, and, if retribution was significant enough, their allies as well. There were elements in the Iranian government that demanded a way be found to make America pay for its illegal and evil transgression without having the smoking gun being held by an Iranian's hand. The hard-liners included Ali-Akbar Mohtashemi, the all-powerful minister of the interior, and Mehdi Karroubi, a powerful and ruthless politician and key keeper to the lucrative wartime Martyr's Fund; Karroubi is reported to have promised an extremely lucrative premium to any perpetrator of revenge for the destruction of Flight 655.[19]

To Ahmed Jibril, monitoring foreign news reports in his Damascus office, the destruction of Flight 655 was a gift from heaven. He realized that Iran would need to act, although it probably could not strike out on its own. It would need to hire, or subcontract, a third party to make the U.S. pay for its belligerence, and Jibril wanted the PFLP-GC to be that group. According to Western intelligence intercepts, communications at Jibril's Syrian and Lebanese facilities was frantic that July day. He desperately wanted to arrange a meeting between himself, his lieutenant, Hafaz Dalkamoni, and Iranian representatives in the ancient town of Ba'albek in the Bekaa Valley, a fortress-like home to Hizbollah and the Iranian presence in Lebanon; it was conveniently protected by thousands of Syrian soldiers. Apparently Jibril left no stone unturned in his pursuit of Iranian cash in exchange for the taking of American lives. Any *official* Iranian figure, from the chargé d'affairs in Beirut, Hosein Niknam, to any Hizbollah commanding officer Jibril believed possessed a direct line to the bank vaults in the Iranian capital, was contacted. A series of meetings between Jibril and personal representatives of Interior Minister Mohtashemi did, indeed, transpire in the Bekaa. The exchange was simple, short, and terse: Revenge for the Airbus disaster in exchange for cash—a lot of it. According to U.S. National Security Agency (NSA) intelligence intercepts, Jibril is reported to have used a nonsecure telephone line from Lebanon to telephone Mohtashemi personally and outline a long list of possible American targets in Europe that could be hit for a fee.[20] Understanding the Iranians' historic penchant for symmetry, the most important target Jibril promised was an American airliner—preferably a Boeing 747 jumbo jet filled with passengers.

Mohtashemi was himself an old hand at sponsoring terrorist operations. A longtime follower of the Ayatollah Khomeini, Mohtashemi completed religious training at a Shiite seminary in the holy city of Qum before joining Khomeini in his exile to Iraq in 1965, and then to France. Following the ouster of the shah, Mohtashemi was charged with purging Western influences from the state-run radio and television stations, a task he performed with murderous precision: Hundreds of hapless TV and radio personalities, including technicians and stagehands, were tried and immediately executed. His zealous and highly ambitious pursuit of Khomeini's grand vision netted him the coveted post of Iranian ambassador to Syria, where he was to kindle Khomeini's lifelong dream of a Shiite revolution in Lebanon. In 1982, the Iranian embassy in Damascus became Tehran's nerve center for turning the war-scarred Lebanese political landscape into the first true battle in a jihad.[21] It was an objective Mohtashemi attended to with great skill. In less than one year, the Shiites were transformed from a docile majority into the most feared entity in the region. Mohtashemi was behind much of the success attributed to Amal and Hizbollah in its early operations. He was the spiritual and, some say, logistics mastermind behind several Beirut kidnappings, including the deadly bombing of the U.S. embassy and the Marine barracks at Beirut International Airport, in which 241 marines were killed. When, with Mohtashemi's instructions, Hizbollah began to take hostages, including the CIA station chief William F. Buckley,* as well as step up its attacks against Israeli forces in Lebanon, his handiwork became too good for a good many people. With true biblical symbolism, several fingers were blown off of Mohtashemi's right hand when he opened a letter bomb, believed by many people to have had a return address from Mossad headquarters in Tel Aviv.22

Mohtashemi was also Iran's conduit to the Palestinian terrorist groups in Lebanon. From the first days of Khomeini's exile in Iraq to the glorious return to Tehran, Mohtashemi was the man responsible for maintaining the fundamentalist's connection to the various Palestinian terrorist organizations. He had known Jibril for years and respected the PFLP-GC's military prowess. Most important, he trusted Ahmed Jibril.

The covert deal that Jibril, Dalkamoni and Mohtashemi attempted to strike would have remained a diabolical secret—uncovered only after the body bags were filled—were it not for the fact that both the Iranians and PFLP-GC were the targets of massive American and Israeli intelligence scrutiny; according to several reports, the Iraqi Muchabarat, an enemy to the Iranians, the Syrians, and the PFLP-GC, was also keeping tabs on the events unfolding in Tehran.23 According to foreign reports, Israeli intelligence operatives (as well as separate American intelligence assets) had monitored Jibril's movements to Beirut, the Bekaa Valley, and Damascus while he wooed the Iranians, including Iranian diplomats, with his promises for "paid-for vengeance." Although the Mossad had warned the Americans that the Iranians, through possible Palestinian proxy, would attempt to avenge the destruction of Flight 655 by attacking an American airliner,24 Jibril's subsequent appearance in Tehran solidified these concerns into a pretext for outright worry.

The exact figure decided upon in Mohtashemi's Tehran office has yet

---

* Several western intelligence experts believe that Buckley, like Marine Colonel Higgins, was actually tortured to death while under interrogation in Iran.

to be determined. It was reported that the handshake between Jibril and the Iranian minister of the interior resulted in a $2 million advance being funneled to a PFLP-GC account in Damascus;* the balance, believed to be another $8 million, was delivered following the successful execution of the mission.[25]

Jibril's original plan was an ambitious undertaking of a sort his organization had little experience in executing. Several American airliners originating in Frankfurt were to be hijacked and taken to either Syrian-controlled territory in Lebanon, or even to Iran. The American hostages, several hundred of them, would be held until Iran's demands, including "monetary considerations," were met; after all, the Iranians had a remarkably successful track record in seizing hostages, and the Americans had a remarkably poor record in rescuing them.

The true details of the Iranian plans for revenge have never been uncovered, however. It is known that Jibril planned to use his newfound wealth not only to meet his commitment to the Iranian leadership, but also, for good measure, to attack Israeli targets: the raid at al-Na'ameh needed to be avenged. Not only would an American aircraft be bombed, as well as a German nightclub frequented by U.S. servicemen, but flights traveling to Israel would also be hit, including Iberian Airlines Flight 888 from Madrid to Barcelona and then Tel Aviv, as well as two El Al flights traveling from Germany and Spain to Israel.[27] The four aircraft were to be downed over a four-day period before Christmas when they would be filled to capacity with holiday travelers, and sensitivities to acts of terror would be at their highest.

In September 1988, Dalkamoni traveled from the PFLP-GC's forward base of European operations in the Yugoslavian town of Krusevac to West Germany, in order to awaken his deep-cover cells and prepare them for action. A Krusevac apartment was used as a PFLP-GC arms cache, and it possessed enormous supplies of weapons, ammunition, and, most important, Czech-produced Semtex plastic explosives. Dalkamoni would arrive in the Federal German Republic ready for action.

---

* Another theory, among the countless concerning the destruction of Pan Am 103, claims that Iran paid Syria the $10 million to destroy an American airliner. Assad kept half of the contract sum, and paid Jibril the remainder to carry out the mission;[26] eager to deflect blame from affecting either his government or Iran's, Assad's intelligence people ordered Jibril to use a Libyan connection as a convenient scapegoat. Because so much mystery continues to engulf the Pan Am bombing, the incident will join the November 22, 1963, assassination of President John F. Kennedy as a never-ending source for conspiracy theories.

In all, there were thirty-four members of the PFLP-GC's West German operation. It was a considerably large force to be concentrated in one country, and a presence that posed a serious security risk because it was likely to gather the unwanted attention such a large group of men might warrant from the security services. Increasing the danger of detection, Dalkamoni's cell also maintained contacts and armed support with operatives based in Sweden, including former members of *Jabhat al-Nid'al el-Sha'abi el-Filastini* (the Palestinian Popular Struggle Front), an obscure and vehemently independent Palestinian terrorist group commanded by Dr. Samir Ghawshah, which changed its allegiance to either Syria or Libya.[28] Two members of the Swedish operation, Muhammad Abu Talb and Martin Imandi, would feature prominently in the events to follow. Dalkamoni had brought with him enough weapons to arm three times the number of men he had on his payroll.

Dalkamoni entered West Germany on a Syrian passport (provided to him, it is believed, by General Khouli's Air Force intelligence) and maintained the proper security protocols of a wanted man, always making sure to use pay phones for important communications and traveling in a roundabout fashion to disrupt surveillance. Yet West German police had been covering Dalkamoni's movements since January, when he initially arrived in Neuss, a picturesque suburb of Dusseldorf, the regional headquarters for his cell, and, like any foreigner, registered with the authorities. Dalkamoni was no anonymous Arab visitor to Germany, however. His pronounced and unmistakable limp, as well as his appearance in Interpol files following his time in Israeli prison, made him a "blown" man. In fact, the Germans had known about Dalkamoni's connection to Ahmed Jibril and the PFLP-GC since his release from Israeli custody in 1979.[29] Cynics have argued that the Germans paid little attention to Dalkamoni's movements because of a tacit agreement between the Syrians and the Germans concerning Palestinian terrorist activities on German soil ("Don't blow up anything in our jurisdiction, and we won't hassle you!"), but it appears as if the Germans thought Dalkamoni was on a "routine" high-tech weapons and equipment shopping spree and wouldn't harm anything or anyone. It appeared as if only the Mossad, which, according to foreign reports, maintained a sizable intelligence-gathering operation in West Germany, was following Dalkamoni's movements with any interest. It has been reported that the Mossad liaison in Bonn attempted to get the Germans to act, but Israel's pleas fell on deaf ears even though the Germans had known of Dalkamoni's role in a most

atypical PFLP-GC operation in 1987, when he is believed to have masterminded the bombing of two U.S. troop trains near Frankfurt.[30]

From the onset, Dalkamoni's German operation was doomed to detection and disruption—either by fate, foreign intervention and infiltration, or, possibly, internal self-design. When, in September 1988, the
German Red Army Faction's failed assassination attempt on the life of
Hans Tietmeyer, the state secretary in the Finance Ministry, was credited to the Khaled Aker Commando, the West German *Bundeskrim-
minalamt* (federal police, or BKA), cross-checked their computerized
files and Middle Eastern liaisons; after all, Khaled Aker was an Arab
name and strongly suggested Palestinian involvement. When the tele-
type from Tel Aviv matched Khaled Aker to the Night of the Hang-
Gliders and the PFLP-GC, Ahmed Jibril, and a roaming Hafaz
Dalkamoni, the potential for a new terrorist offensive sent chills of fear
and anxiety through the halls of the West German government and the
defense ministry. The timing of the Khaled Aker Commando was
ominous. An Iranian airliner had been blown up only months before;
Arafat was embarking on his diplomatic offensive in order to recognize
Israel without actually saying the magic words, so he could appease
American demands; and terrorist leaders from Ahmed Jibril to Abu
Nidal vowed to disrupt any peace process with pools of blood. The time
to act was now—*before* the streets of Germany looked like a mere
extension of the seventh Arab-Israeli war. A surveillance operation
code-named Operation Autumn Leaves was sanctioned.

For the next month, more than seventy BKA agents, supported by
elements from *Grenzschutzgruppe 9* (GSG-9), the Federal Border
Guard's elite antiterrorist hostage-rescue force, as well as agents from
the *Bundesamt fur Verfassungsschutz* (BfV), the domestic intelligence
service, and the *Bundesnachrichtendienst* (BND), the foreign
intelligence-gathering espionage organization, conducted an elaborate,
high-tech, around-the-clock electronic surveillance of Dalkamoni.[31]
Suburban Neuss became the sight of one of the largest West German
counterintelligence/counterterrorist operations ever mounted, including the bloody and treacherous campaign against the Baader-Meinhof
Gang in the early 1970's. The nerve center was 16 Isarstrasse, home to a
greengrocer named Hashem Abassi, a pleasant and low-key man who
was playing host to Dalkamoni, who just happened to be Abassi's
brother-in-law.

In fact, Dalkamoni's movements throughout Europe had been followed all the way from Sofia, Bulgaria, to the PFLP-GC's Krusevac,
Yugoslavia, safe house, into Germany by a large force of BKA intel-

ligence agents; several foreign reports have indicated that the Mossad was also monitoring Dalkamoni's movements quite closely. When Dalkamoni entered the Federal Republic of Germany on October 5, the long line of visitors to the Abassi household—all members of the PFLP-GC's West German cell—began to arrive, as one intelligence agent would say, "like guests to a wedding."[32] They included Ahmed Abassi, the grocer's youngest brother, who was acting liaison with the Swedish cell, as well as other members from the Swedish unit, including Martin Imandi and Mohammed Moghrabi. The German intelligence agents, taking hundreds of surveillance photographs, could not believe the size of the cell that was materializing before their very eyes at 16 Isar-strasse. It was highly unusual for so many "suspicious" characters to move about together, since it was considered a poor execution of even the most basic of counterintelligence/countersurveillance tradecraft techniques ostensibly taught to every terrorist worthy of working on the European stage. Other visitors to the Neuss grocer included Ramzi Diab, a PFLP-GC courier and a most mysterious figure who had brought with him several components for constructing an explosive device; and Marwan Kreeshat, the famed bombmaker. Kreeshat had developed quite a reputation for himself over the course of twenty years. His signature, the barometric bomb, had adorned several terror-ist attacks in Europe in the 1970s, especially the February 21, 1970, bombings of the Swissair and Austrian Air jets en route to Israel, as well as the failed attempts to blow up several El Al jets heading from Europe to Tel Aviv. The Germans, through their Israeli intelligence liaison, had extensive dossiers on the master bomb-maker, and his entrance into the PFLP-GC cell in Neuss had ominous overtones. It was obvious that this was no simple terrorist operation being established on German soil, and this was no ordinary terrorist cell. It soon became apparent to the German investigators executing Autumn Leaves that the Arabs under surveillance were preparing for a major operation.

Another target of intense German surveillance was an apartment located in Sendweg 28, in the middle of Frankfurt's Arab quarter, The comings and goings of dozens of secretive Arab men, loosely following security protocols to shake off intelligence-service surveillance, was highly suspicious. The proximity of this Frankfurt safe house to both the Frankfurt airport and its adjacent, sprawling Rhein Mein American Air Force base, was reason enough to raise a few eyebrows at BKA and BfV headquarters.

For the next week, the combined investigative force of the BKA, BfV, and BND was engrossed trying to figure out what Dalkamoni's cell was up to. On October 16, Dalkamoni was followed as he drove to the town of Hockeneim, where he picked up plastic bags and storage boxes. On the night of October 19, Dalkamoni's silhouette was seen through the shades of Abassi's Neuss flat. He was holding the telephone with one hand and clutching a cigarette with the other. He first called a take-out grilled-meat restaurant in Nicosia, Cyprus (where Jibril maintained one of his forward staging areas for Mediterranean operations), and spoke in some sort of cryptic code (one that the BfV's Arabic-speaking technicians taping the phone call could not decipher) to a man not identified by name. Moments later, Dalkamoni was once again on the phone, this time calling Damascus. The man on the other end of the phone has yet to be identified, but Kreeshat picked up an extension in Abassi's apartment and stated that he had made some changes to the *medicine*, and that it was now "stronger and better than before."[33]

The German police officers playing back the tape of Kreeshat's ominous statement knew that the Jordanian-born bomb-maker was not a pharmacist, and he wasn't talking about something to ease Dalkamoni's migraine headaches or his own stomach problems due to the rich German food and beer. He could only be talking about explosives. German fears were reinforced over the course of the next several days when they followed Dalkamoni and Kreeshat as they shopped in and around Neuss, buying electronic odds and ends including wires and batteries; they also made several impromptu visits to the apartment at 28 Sendweg; they never stayed there for more than a few minutes. On October 24, the two men traveled to the Huma-Market department store in Neuss, where they bought alarm clocks (both mechanical and digital), and then went on to Kaufman's department store, where they picked up over a dozen 1.5-volt batteries, electronic switches, nuts and bolts, and industrial-strength adhesives.[34]

The Germans were getting edgy at these developments. The warm autumn days had brought out hundreds of citizens to the city's streets and parks in preparation for the Oktoberfest celebrations. Although the German intelligence agents hadn't a clue about the cell's true target, the prospect of carnage on the streets of Germany was daunting. Bombs planted in a department store, beer hall, or train station could kill hundreds of people. German officials were also losing their resolve. They were ready to wrap up the Palestinians in one major sweep and get them off the nation's streets as soon as possible.

The Germans' casus belli for action came later that night when Marwan Kreeshat telephoned an unknown location in Amman and stated that he'd be "done in a few days," and he'd "see him [the individual in Amman] on Friday."[35] The police could not wait in good conscience any longer. The time to wrap up Autumn Leaves was at hand.

At 0745 hours on the morning of October 26, 1988, units from the federal police, covered by BfV agents and GSG-9 commandos, stormed more than a dozen apartments in six German states and cities, including Hamburg, Mannheim, and Berlin. In all, seventeen men, all Palestinians or Arabs, were arrested.

The apartment at 28 Sendweg yielded paydirt. In a closet police found several dozen automatic weapons, including Hungarian AMD-65 7.62-mm assault rifles, handguns, mortar rounds, ammunition, explosives (including six strips of TNT), more than thirty antipersonnel fragmentation hand grenades, night-vision equipment, and other bits and pieces needed to equip a company of soldiers; they even uncovered an American 66-mm LAW antitank rocket, stolen, it is believed, from NATO stores in Germany.* The cells were, indeed, paramilitary in nature and organization, and they also possessed enough material to equip a conventional military formation. Ominously, the West German police uncovered five kilograms of grade-A Czech-made Semtex—the weapon of choice when blowing an airliner out of the sky. At a hastily assembled press conference in which a hearty congratulation was offered to all participants in Operation Autumn Leaves, a government spokesman told reporters: "This is the largest terrorist weapons and explosives cache we have ever found in the Federal Republic."[37]

Also seized at 28 Sendweg was one Abdel Fatah Ghadanfar, a forty-seven-year-old Palestinian who was a boisterous and, according to one German police officer, obnoxious captive. Perhaps hoping to be afforded the diplomatic honors of a man who had moved about in the political and espionage circles of Syrian government officials, Ghadanfar claimed to be a personal representative of Ahmed Jibril's PFLP-GC, and commander of its external-operations sector responsible for foreign operations. From his imposing, even condescending, attitude toward his arrest, it was clear that he was a man who thought that he would be released shortly. For the first time, PFLP-GC personnel in captivity were not only talking but boasting.

---

* According to several reports, a sizable portion of the weaponry supplied to the various pro-Syrian terrorist factions operating in Western Europe was part of a bargain struck with the Italian Mafia, where Lebanese narcotics, mainly pure heroin and hashish, were traded for weapons. The Mafia allegedly diverted enormous supplies of weapons, via Spain and Nigeria, to Syria (including more than one million antipersonnel and anti-tank land mines and radar guidance systems for missiles), in exchange for drugs from the Syrian-controlled Bekaa Valley.[36]

German police captured both Dalkamoni and Kreeshat last. The police had followed both men through the streets of Neuss, and when they parked Dalkamoni's green Ford Taurus to make a call at a bank of public pay phones in the town center, nearly a dozen heavily armed German officers emerged from their BMW and Mercedes surveillance cars and pounced, with guns drawn, upon the two Palestinian terrorists. Outnumbered and surrounded, the two did not offer any resistance; neither seemed particularly surprised. Inside the trunk of Dalkamoni's car the police found several blank Syrian and Spanish passports (ostensibly to be used for the attacks against the flights emanating from Madrid to Tel Aviv), as well as a Toshiba Model 453 Boombeat radio-cassette player. The evidence was taken to BKA headquarters, and Dalkamoni and Kreeshat were ushered into custody.

Moments before Dalkamoni and Kreeshat were arrested, German police swooped in on Abassi's flat at 16 Isarstrasse.* There they found several stopwatches, batteries, detonating devices, and several more Syrian passports; among Dalkamoni's personal effects was a Syrian diplomatic passport issued by the Syrian Ministry Of Religious Affairs.[39]

None of the men seized by the Autumn Leaves task force were talking. Ostensibly, the Germans believed the PFLP-GC's target was an Israeli handball team from *Ha'Po'el Ramat Gan*, a major sports club, on a goodwill tour of Germany and playing a match in Dusseldorf, a few kilometers from Neuss. The prospect of Palestinian terrorists seizing Israeli athletes on German soil was, indeed, symbolic and brought back the nightmare scenario of the 1972 Munich Olympics Massacre. It would soon become clear, however, that the Israeli athletes were not the cell's actual target; it is likely that Dalkamoni had no idea that such a lucrative target was housed only a few hundred yards away from his command and control headquarters.[40] As the German police officers began to examine the weapons and material they had uncovered in the operation, they finally learned the true objective of Dalkamoni's cell: the destruction of civilian aircraft, probably in midair. With Kree-

---

* Six months later, while conducting a more thorough search of the Abassi flat in the wake of the investigation into the bombing of Pan Am 103, German police would find a Sanyo computer monitor in Abassi's home complete with 400 grams of Semtex, a barometric triggering device, and a timer. Abassi seemed shocked by the discovery of the bomb in his house, and he told German, American, and British investigators that his small son had even played with the television screen in the apartment. It is doubtful, however, that Abassi could not have known the true nature of his brother-in-law's business.[38]

shat's presence in the gang, this aspect of the terrorists' capabilities should have been clear from the start. But only two days later police decided to take a closer look at the radio found in Dalkamoni's Ford Taurus. A BKA and BfV computer check of known PFLP-GC operations had revealed Kreeshat's barometer-bomb rap sheet, and the information that all his bombs had been camouflaged inside the inner workings of radios, tape players, and phonographs. Police officials called in the bomb squad and decided to give the Toshiba radio a closer look.

On October 29, the seized Toshiba Boombeat radio-cassette player was finally dissected by police experts. First, the model number 453, "Boombeat," was a design only sold in the Middle East and North Africa; the player found in Dalkamoni's Ford is believed to have been purchased in the notorious Smugglers market in the old city of Damascus in the summer of 1988.[41] On the outside, the tape player seemed normal: it was the usual size and weight. In fact, it was the typical radio-tape player that most people owned and took with them to the beach or on picnics. It was there that the innocence of the tape player ended, however. Inside the "Boombeat" was an ingenious explosive device. Shaped smartly into a cylinder was 300 grams of grade-A Czech-made Semtex, attached to an electronic detonator and two activating devices. The first activator was a barometer-sensitive indicator hidden beneath the tape player's motor; the other was a more conventional "sizzle"-type mechanism that detonated the explosives once it was dissolved by the charge's incendiary timing device.[42]

The bomb's sophistication was designed to fool the most advanced airport defenses. Since Jibril's destruction of the Swissair flight to Tel Aviv in 1970, major airports had developed a pressurized examination chamber in which luggage was placed to simulate midair conditions: If there was a barometer-triggered bomb inside the suitcase, the pressure chamber would cause the device to explode. To fool this final line of airport security, Kreeshat's Boombeat bomb needed to be pressurized for more than thirty-five minutes before its timer—which could be set for seconds, minutes, or even hours—was set. As airports did not have the time to subject any piece of luggage inside a pressurized chamber for more than a couple of minutes, these security procedures would not have uncovered Kreeshat's masterful device.[43] Upon further investigation, German police would retrieve three more Kreeshat barometer bombs inside Toshiba Boombeats, as well as the *fifth* Sanyo television monitor device seized several months later.

With their Autumn Leaves operation, the Germans had pulled a major coup and, it was believed, saved countless lives by thwarting a massive terrorist offensive before it had a chance to go into action. But the German judicial apparatus had mysteriously let all but three of the PFLP-GC cell members, including Ramzi Diab, walk; incredibly, eleven of the men, all suspected terrorists, were released on their own recognizance due to insufficient evidence. Within three days of the Autumn Leaves arrests, six of the seized men had escaped Germany altogether. Dalkamoni and Abdel Fatah Ghadanfar were remanded to German custody and arraigned for trial, but Kreeshat, the bombmaker and the man with the most to fear from legal authorities, was acting like a man who was sure of his salvation. In early November, Kreeshat asked to make a phone call and promptly telephoned a man identified as a senior Jordanian Muchabarat official, to whom he spoke at length about the need to "expedite the legal matters in Germany at once." It soon became clear that Kreeshat was an agent for King Hussein's intelligence service, and the Jordanians were not about to let languish in prison one of their deep-plant operatives, a man who had no doubt provided intimate data on a Palestinian terrorist group that had often targeted the pro-Western Jordanian monarchy. Days later, Kreeshat was released. He immediately flew to Jordan, where he lives under Jordanian security service round-the-clock protection. Published reports also indicate that Kreeshat was a German BND agent, while other reports claim that Jibril's principal bomb architect was a longtime operative for Israel's Mossad.[44]

In fact, the Mossad was the sole voice of reason throughout this entire affair. Israeli intelligence was responsible for alerting the Germans to the threat of a PFLP-GC terrorist cell developing in Germany, and had long been skeptical as to the true nature of the cell uncovered in Autumn Leaves. Dalkamoni, to use a Yiddish word uttered by several of the Mossad investigators who conducted their own private look into the events of December 1988, was said to be too much of a *Macha* (big shot) to be dispatched into Germany to build up a cell and personally command a large-scale covert terrorist operation. After all, he was too close to Jibril to be risked on an overseas assignment. Should he be caught, he could compromise the entire organization—he knew everything about the PFLP-GC, including whether or not the three missing Sultan Yaqoub tank soldiers were alive and in PFLP-GC custody, and he had firsthand knowledge of the financial infrastructure of Jibril's organization. There was something very suspicious about Dalkamoni's capture, about the immediate release of the eleven cell members, and about Kreeshat's hasty return to Jordan.

In late November 1988, the Mossad warned the British foreign espionage service, MI6, that it had information that there was a possibility that a Middle Eastern terrorist group, probably one of the anti-Arafat pro-Syrian groups, would attempt to sabotage a civilian airliner flying out of Europe around the Christmas holiday season.[45] The British dismissed the Israeli fears as alarmist rubbish. In truth, MI6 (British Foreign espionage) was suspect about anything the Mossad supplied to it. Their once close-knit liaison was badly damaged on June 17, 1988, when the British government ordered the expulsion of Arieh Regev, the Mossad station chief in London, together with four other Israeli diplomats believed to be intelligence agents; the move virtually shut down the Mossad's London station.[46] Regev, according to British accusations, had been running a vast network of intelligence operatives and operations on British soil—concentrating, primarily, on infiltrating the extensive Fatah and PFLP infrastructure throughout the United Kingdom. Since the Palestinians often maintain close links to the various Irish terrorist groups, Regev's activities and his liaison with MI5 and MI6 should have benefited both countries. But revelations about a Force 17 terrorist that MI5 had arrested in 1987 being, in fact, a double agent working for the Mossad, together with several other controversial incidents in which Mossad participation was suspected, outraged the policymakers in Whitehall and forced them to take decisive action. They apparently felt that Israel had turned Great Britain into its own intelligence-warfare playground. Five months after the diplomatic snafu, British intelligence commanders thought that the Mossad's warnings concerning Arab terrorists planning to blow up an airliner were self-serving publicity designed to repair the damaged relations between MI6 and the Mossad, the Shin Bet, and Israeli military intelligence. London could not believe that the Mossad was being sincere. In retrospect, it was a fatal error.

Over the course of the next month, warnings from Israel would continue to flow to many European capitals, as well as to Washington, D.C., and to CIA headquarters in Langley, Virginia. Experts in Israel realized that the time was ripe for some sort of Palestinian action and that dramatic preventive measures needed to be taken. The downing of the Iran Air flight had yet to be avenged, Arafat's Stockholm roundabout proclamation of "accepting" Israel's right to exist had yet to receive the violent reaction much of the Arab world promised to express in response to this selling-out of the Palestinians' cause, and, of

course, there was Israel's large-scale raid on al-Na'ameh. Several warnings were, in fact, heeded, but preemptive defensive action was never
taken. In the end, when Jibril did strike, it would be against an extremely vulnerable target and directed against a nation not used to
having its citizens targeted for mass murder.

CHAPTER ELEVEN

SUBCONTRACTING TERROR: THE DESTRUCTION OF PAN AM 103

DECEMBER 21, 1988, might have been the winter solstice, but it was a hectic day at Frankfurt's bustling international airport. Pan Am Flight 103, a flight to London utilizing a Boeing 727, and then on to New York and Detroit in a connecting Boeing 747 jumbo jet, was scheduled for takeoff at 1630 hours. Because of increased holiday travel, the passengers were told to be at the airport ninety minutes prior to takeoff, and they were subjected to the most routine of security examinations. Security at Pan Am's gate at Frankfurt, like all other Pan Am gateways, was delegated to the Alert security firm.* Realistically, Pan Am had no security at Frankfurt. In 1986, the airline had hired a security consultant firm called KPI to conduct a study of Pan Am worldwide; KPI's director and the man who conducted much of the investigation was Isaac Yefet, a man who had directed El Al Israel Airlines security for more than six years. After an extensive examination of Pan Am security procedures throughout the airline's gateway hubs on three continents, Yefet concluded, in a detailed report he sent to Pan Am executives, that Pan Am, in essence, didn't have any security. It was a

---

* A private joke had commented that the security the firm provided was not Alert but, in fact, Inert.

vulnerable airline and, as an American carrier, a tempting target. If Pan Am wanted to prevent a tragedy, it would have to build a security apparatus and infrastructure based on KPI's recommendations."[1] Pan Am executives were outraged by Yefet's disclosures, and quickly fired him and KPI. They also instituted a $5 security surcharge which, according to Pan Am management, would make Pan Am's security the best of any airline. In Frankfurt, Alert staffers received little training; many of those placed among the passengers to search luggage didn't speak English; and the Frankfurt station chief, Ulrich Weber, had a criminal record and primarily hired only beautiful women on whom he had sexual designs.[2] At 1640 Flight 103 took off from Frankfurt with 125 passengers. Also on board was a bomb, hidden in a Toshiba Boombeat tape player camouflaged inside a copper-colored Samsonite suitcase.

A total of forty-nine passengers from Flight 103 continued on to New York and Detroit at Heathrow; they boarded the 747, dubbed the *Maid of the Seas*, at Heathrow's refurbished Terminal 3 along with 194 additional passengers, mostly American businessmen and exchange students from Syracuse University heading home for the holidays. The luggage from Frankfurt was quickly transferred from the Boeing 727 into a cargo hold inside the *Maid of the Seas* without undergoing a security examination—neither X-ray search, hand examination, nor a pressure chamber test. The luggage was not checked off against the passenger list—a virtual invitation for terrorist attack—and Pan Am security had no way of knowing if all the suitcases belonged to all of the passengers. Nevertheless, Pan Am 103 was scheduled for takeoff at 1800 hours. Congestion on Heathrow's bustling runways was intense that evening, however. The Boeing 747 was forced to sit and wait for its place on the takeoff line. The passengers, all 243 of them, prepared for the eight-hour flight by fastening their seat belts, removing their shoes, and anticipating emotional reunions with their families in the States. The sixteen crew members braced for takeoff after giving the required emergency-situation speech where the proper use of all the aircraft's survival equipment is quickly demonstrated.

At 1825 hours, after nearly a thirty-minute delay, the *Maid of the Seas* was airborne, lifting off from runway 27L, and headed westward toward the windswept skies over Scotland. Once airborne over central England, *Maid of the Seas* was monitored by Alan Topp, in the Scottish air-traffic control center in Pretwick, who took control of the aircraft the moment it entered Scottish airspace at 1856 hours; on Topp's radar screen was a blip with the flight number, 103, the aircraft's altitude,

310 (the abbreviation for 31,000 feet), and the number 59, the city code for Pan Am 103's final destination, New York's Kennedy Airport.[3] The aircraft was flying at 365 miles per hour. Sipping his coffee, Topp gazed across his busy screen, realizing that the aircraft was about to turn westward for the trans-Atlantic portion of its flight. But at 1702 hours he saw the radar image of Pan Am 103 suddenly disintegrate into several sections and then disappear altogether from his screen. Pangs of anxiety overtook the air-traffic control center. Topp tried to raise Flight 103's skipper, Captain James Bruce MacQuarrie, on the emergency frequency, but there was no response. Topp suspected the worst, and the watch supervisor confirmed his fears. A Glasgow to London shuttle had noticed a huge fireball on the ground over a small Scottish hamlet. Death had come to Lockerbie.

The bomb that ripped through Pan Am Flight 103 had blown the plane into five separate sections. The debris of the 747,000 pound aircraft, its passengers, and their belongings, rained down over the picturesque Scottish town of Lockerbie in a sudden and terrible fashion; parts of the town was reduced to rubble in scenes reminiscent of the blitz during the early days of World War II. The crimson night's sky assumed an eerie orange glow as fires emanating from the debris rained down on the small town like falling bombs—both wings landed close to one another, and their 80,000 pounds of jet fuel exploded on impact. The 120-mile-per-hour crosswinds at 31,000 feet had spread the debris for 845 square miles, from the center of Lockerbie at ground zero all the way to the North Sea. A huge crater marked the center of the town as a sudden and unforgiving graveyard. Nineteen homes were destroyed, and eleven people in them were killed; the bodies of several Pan Am passengers had fallen from the sky and were dangling in macabre fashion from Lockerbie rooftops and ledges. The main fuselage section of the aircraft, and the sixty-one bodies it held, slammed into a courtyard in a residential area. Two miles away, the battered shell of the cockpit, with the crew's mangled bodies still inside, rested silently in an empty pasture. It was obvious that none of the plane's passengers had survived the destruction. Hundreds of bodies littered the hillside in land usually grazed by sheep. Many of the nearby farmers wept openly as they witnessed the absolute horror that had befallen their sleepy town. Police, fire, and medical emergency crews that rushed to the scene could not fathom the extent of the incredible destruction before their eyes. In all 270 people died that evening.

The *Maid of the Seas* was a nineteen-year-old aircraft, and initially it was thought (hoped!) that a terrible mechanical malfunction had caused the aircraft's destruction. Immediately, however, it became apparent that this tragedy was no accident. It was murder. Mass murder had destroyed the season of goodwill toward mankind. The small and unheralded Scottish constabulary, headed by Peter Fraser, the lord advocate of Scotland, immediately opened an investigation into the catastrophe with the chilling premise that this was a pure and simple case of murder.[4] It was clear to Scottish investigators, as well as British Ministry of Defense technicians and specialists, that the aircraft's destruction was not due to depressurization caused by an accident, but had been blown out of the sky by a powerful bomb.

The British Ministry of Defense dispatched thousands of soldiers from the British Army and Royal Air Force to Lockerbie to sift through the countryside in search of physical evidence to be used in any criminal investigation. Although the tragedy was a diabolical example of the barbarity of terrorism, there was a golden forensic lining to the incident. The bomb that had ripped through the cargo area of the Pan Am Boeing 747 was designed by its makers to explode over the Atlantic Ocean; that way, the aircraft and any information concerning the means of its destruction would have remained a secret locked away under the frigid depths of the Atlantic. But because Pan Am Flight 103 was delayed for twenty-five minutes on the tarmac at Heathrow, the bomb's timing device, which had activated during the first leg of the journey from Frankfurt to London, had been fooled into blowing up early. Had the flight been delayed another half-hour, the explosion, which would have taken place on the tarmac, might not have killed a single person. Fate, however, had dealt the investigators a painful, though appreciated, spot of luck.

The British servicemen who roamed through the grassy, rolling hills of western Scotland crawled on their hands and knees in search of small bits of metal or cloth that might provide investigators with clues or forensic evidence; hundreds of policemen and soldiers would walk in line to cover an area the size of ten football fields in order to comb the area. The main objective of the investigators, now headquartered at an incident control center in central Lockerbie, was to reconstruct the remnants of the aircraft and provide the legal authorities—assisted by the intelligence communities of nearly a dozen nations—with the evidence needed to open criminal proceedings in a court of law. The efforts of these dedicated men and women, urged on by an emotional and heartfelt responsibility to exact justice for the victims and their families, reaped enormous dividends. Policemen crawling on all fours and wearing face masks so as not to breathe on the items they came across, found the lock of the suitcase that had held the bomb.[5] By February 1989, the bomb that brought down the aircraft was rebuilt by British forensic scientists and demolitions experts. It was a Toshiba Boombeat bomb, model 453. Immediately the PFLP-GC became the prime suspect. According to several reports, special agents from SO 13, Scotland Yard's antiterrorist investigative and counterterrorist force, were also called to Lockerbie to help solve the Pan Am 103 puzzle.

The Lockerbie investigation involved thirty-five nations and the police and intelligence forces of dozens more. It would last 1,059 days and cost in excess of $29 million[6] yet its inconclusive findings would satisfy very few people.

Relatives of the 270 people killed at Lockerbie have had to wrestle with the painful question of how several Western governments that had touted their stern opposition to terrorism in countless news sound bites for so long could have allowed their loved ones to perish in such an avoidable tragedy. Had the warnings of an attack been taken seriously, had Pan Am been more concerned about its own security instead of the egos of its own operating officers who insisted that existing preventive arrangements were sufficient, Pan Am Flight 103 might have never become immortalized.

Tragically, the uncovering of Dalkamoni's PFLP-GC cell in Neuss, and the discovery of the four Boombeat bombs, seemed to have convinced just about everyone—including the West Germans, Interpol, and the Americans—that a tragedy in the making had been averted. The Israelis, however, had not been fooled. Through their liaisons to the CIA, the DIA, and the State Department, the Mossad and, it is believed, A'man continued to supply intelligence data concerning the potential for a terrorist bombing of an American airliner, somewhere in Western Europe over the Christmas holiday travel period, probably to be perpetrated by the PFLP-GC. The Americans, and Pan Am, ignored the warnings, even though they continued as little as twenty-four hours before the destruction of Pan Am 103.[7]

There had been ample warning to several European security agencies, and their country's respective airlines, for them to have taken preventive measures against one of Jibril's Kreeshat-built barometric bombs. The devices seized at Neuss were virtual blueprints for the ingenious bombs. They were photographed and dissected, and information concerning their infrastructure, detonating mechanism, and telltale features had been passed on to dozens of airlines and intelligence services. A December 19 memo from the British Ministry of Transport, for example, explicitly warned British carriers and airports, as well as some foreign carriers, of a new terrorist bomb recently uncovered, packed with Semtex, that was hidden inside a radio-cassette player; the British provided special and detailed warnings to El Al (which received its own up-to-date intelligence regarding terrorist threats), Air India, and South African Airways, the likeliest targets for any sophisticated terrorist bombing attempt.[8] The memo detailed the design and appearance of the Toshiba Boombeat model 453 radio-cassette player captured at Neuss, as well as the methods to be deployed to detect such a device, including the fact that if the "play" button was depressed, the machine would not operate (even with its batteries inserted), and the inner workings were fitted with far too many wires for an ordinary radio and tape player.

The British alerts came a full month after the U.S. Federal Aviation Administration (FAA) issued its own series of memos and alerts warning of the Toshiba bomb. The FAA warning came weeks before the now-famous "anonymous" caller warned the U.S. Embassy in Helsinki, Finland, that a man named Abdullah would pass a sophisticated explosive device to an unwitting female passenger, a Finnish woman, on board a U.S.-bound aircraft in Frankfurt. The call was made at 1145 hours on the morning of December 5, and the mysterious caller was later identified as Samra Mahayoun, a Palestinian born in Lebanon who was in Finland on a student's visa; according to Finnish police reports, Mahayoun was in his late twenties and heavily involved in drug trafficking.[9] The call was dismissed as a hoax, but it should have raised a series of red flags in Washington, Bonn, and London. Samra Mahayoun claimed that the attack was going to be perpetrated by terrorists from Abu Nidal's Fatah Revolutionary Council. Since terrorists rarely stray from their *modus operandi*, it should have been apparent to the Finnish security services that investigated Mahayoun's call, as well as to the security officers in the Helsinki embassy and the FAA in Washington, that though Abu Nidal might have hijacked an aircraft and murdered passengers preparing to board passenger jets, his organization had never used a bomb to blow up a flight in midair. It cannot be dismissed that the call in Finland was a red herring designed to confuse any security force from concentrating on a PFLP-GC grandstand operation. It is difficult to say if this false-flag approach worked, but several Western intelligence agencies did, indeed, initially attribute the destruction of Pan Am 103 to the Fatah Revolutionary Council.

Although the phone call was publicly dismissed as nothing to be taken seriously, the FAA did issue warnings, which were held back from public knowledge, and posted in American embassies and consuls warning against travel on Pan Am to the United States, especially on flights emanating out of Frankfurt around Christmas. The FAA warning, taped to the bulletin board in the American Embassy in Moscow, caused several diplomats and embassy officials to change their travel plans and make reservations on non-American airlines. The fact that many American diplomats were booked on Pan Am Flight 103 and then canceled their reservations opened the flight to many of those eventually killed over Lockerbie. Naturally, the Helsinki phone call and its subsequent FAA memo derivative remain a Pandora's box of guilt and finger-pointing by the families of those killed on Pan Am 103. After all, the diplomatic community was spared death, but the ordinary traveling public was not.

What did happen at Lockerbie? Perhaps the world will never really know, as only the terrorists themselves are able to provide the true story, and most of them take their secrets to their graves. It is believed, however, that the West German cells commanded by Dalkamoni and subdivided to Sweden under the command of Muhammad Abu Talb were simply throwaways—extra baggage, so to speak, that was discarded and used to deflect attention from Jibril's real plan to exact revenge for the downing of Iran Air Flight 655. When asked to reason why Ahmed Jibril, a man in the business of terror and secrecy, would purposely give up over a dozen of his own men, including one of his most trusted lieutenants and his master bombmaker, an Israeli intelligence officer simply said: "Money. If he was to collect on the remainder of his Iranian windfall, he had to successfully destroy an American airliner, and he couldn't destroy an American airliner with an organization infiltrated by foreign intelligence agents."[10]

Jibril had known of his organization's poor security for sometime. Typical PFLP-GC treatment for a traitor was not kind. It usually consisted of brutal interrogation sessions conducted with the assistance of Syrian intelligence officers, in which a verbal confession was extracted. Once "I am guilty" was uttered by the remnants of the individual, he was taken behind a building and put out of his misery with a single shot to his head from an AK-47 assault rifle. Jibril, however, had been semi-active over the course of several months, and there were no operations compromised by the men he "suspected" as working for the Israelis, the Americans, one of the European intelligence services, and even the Syrians; eager to know exactly what was going on inside the inner sanctums of the PFLP-GC, the Syrians would routinely plant informants inside Jibril's command circle. In fact, Jibril believed Dalkamoni to be a Syrian agent. The Iranian connection had resulted in a minimutiny in the PFLP-GC, with many of Jibril's lifelong comrades openly objecting to the new Teheran Connection and the forgoing of the old-time relationship with Damascus. Dalkamoni is reported to have openly opposed any attack that did not target solely Israeli targets, and to have felt that the risk in avenging the Iranian airbus was too great for the PFLP-GC to take.[11] Dalkamoni's newfound political awareness might have aroused suspicions in Jibril that could cause years of comradeship to evaporate in the anxiety of mistrust. Why kill Dalkamoni, possible traitor, if he could be used as a tool to secure $10 million from the Iranians? Other intelligence analysts also suspect that Jibril, already undergoing the transformation from Ba'ath party loyalist to fundamentalist Muslim, decided to purge his organization of its atheist, pro-Syrian elements, of which Dalkamoni certainly was a leader, in favor of a close-knit and trusted cadre that supported the organization's shift to Iran.

Marwan Kreeshat was another one Jibril suspected of double-dealing. Not active since the late 1970's, Kreeshat may have been responsible for some of the PFLP-GC's early successes in the bombing of Israeli and foreign airliners traveling to the Jewish State, but he hadn't been used properly since 1979 when, it is believed, he designed the device that turned Abu A'bbas's Beirut headquarters into a killing field. If Kreeshat was, indeed, working for the Jordanian Muchabarat (or anyone else), Jibril would find it hard to kill him, too. Eliminating a man with such an esteemed international reputation for constructing sophisticated explosive devices would have a ripple effect through the terrorist underworld. "Technicians," as bomb experts were known, were not routinely killed, since it tended to deter others from filling their shoes. It should have been obvious to the German intelligence agents monitoring Dalkamoni's PFLP-GC cell in Neuss and Frankfurt in Operation Autumn Leaves that there was something suspicious about Kreeshat's appearance on the scene. His subsequent release by the Germans should have confirmed the skeptic's fears that the terrorists seized were plants in a false-flag operation.

Kreeshat remains an enigma to this day. It is known that he did not construct the sixth Boombeat barometric bomb that, in the end, destroyed Pan Am 103. Through liaisons with Jordanian intelligence, however, it is believed that Kreeshat did help West German, British, and American investigators reconstruct the bomb, and assisted in the investigation.[12] According to most reports, he lives in Jordan under constant protection by Muchabarat bodyguards. He has not been seen since his return to Jordan in November 1988.

The Talb cell is also the source of intense mystery and circumstantial evidence. In fact, most of the existing physical evidence implicates Muhammad Abu Talb, the Egyptian-born terrorist who chose bombing as a profession rather than a conviction, of being the individual responsible for planting the bomb on board Pan Am 103. In October 1988 he had traveled from Stockholm to Cyprus, where it is believed he met Dalkamoni one final time, and then moved on to Malta. Fragments of clothing discovered in the suitcase that housed the PFLP-GC's barometer bomb that did obliterate the Pan Am Boeing 747 did, indeed, originate in Malta. But when Swedish police arrested Talb in his Uppsala home, they discovered four different passports, including Talb's genuine and legal Swedish papers, which indicated that he had departed from Malta on October 26. The clothing found in the suitcase, according to the testimony of the shopkeeper from Mary's House Boutique in Sliema, were purchased only in November or late December;[13] the shopkeeper, who today is under the constant protection of the Malta police, would disclose only that a "young Arab" had purchased an assortment of clothes without too much concern about their style or size. Having Dalkamoni meet Talb in Malta was a convenient tie-in, perhaps engineered by Jibril. He probably realized that an army of international investigators would pursue the perpetrators of the Pan Am bombing, and so threw them a few bones: a suspect, a motive, and the invaluable prime suspect seen "at the scene of the crime," which might keep them from pursuing a direct link between Jibril and the Lockerbie bombing. After all, all of Jibril's German network was either in prison or in the Middle East, and Muhammad Abu Talb was not a PFLP-GC regular. Talb did, indeed, meet Dalkamoni in Cyprus in early October 1988, but it is unlikely that he was the one responsible for placing the booby-trapped radio in to a piece of luggage and then onto Pan Am 103. More likely than not, Muhammad Abu Talb was a diversion, or even a fall guy. He might have known about the attack—the date December 21 was circled in a calendar in his Uppsala home—and clothes bought in Malta were found in his home.

In the early morning hours of May 18, 1989, more than one hundred heavily armed security agents, policemen, and antiterrorist commandos from the Swedish *Sakerhetspolis* (known by its acronym SAPO) raided several apartments in Stockholm, Göteborg, and Uppsala, and arrested fifteen members of the Palestine Popular Struggle Front.[14] Although the BKA had informed their SAPO liaisons concerning the movements of Palestinians driving Volvos registered in Sweden following Operation Autumn Leaves, the German information was not the reason behind the arrest of the Palestinians. From 1985 to 1986, there had been dozens of minor acts of terror perpetrated by Arab terrorists in Scandinavia and other countries of northern Europe, including the bombing of a synagogue, a Northwest Airlines office, and failed bomb attacks against the Copenhagen and Amsterdam ticket offices of El Al. The link between the German and Swedish PFLP-GC and Palestine Popular Struggle Front cells had been known for some time, and it has never been explained why German authorities waited so long before making the connection and pursuing it further. It is known that the effort to expand on the German-Swedish connection came in 1989 only after the Sanyo barometric bomb was uncovered from Abassi's flat. Subjected to further examination at BKA headquarters, the booby-trapped device exploded, killing Hans Jurgen Sonntag, a police demolitions officer, and seriously wounding his partner, Thomas Ettinger.[15]

Muhammad Abu Talb has yet to provide his inquisitors with any information. He remains stoic and silent in his Swedish jail cell—an incarceration that, if Swedish legal concerns are implemented, will last his entire lifetime. On December 21, 1989, one year after Pan Am 103 disintegrated into a fiery ball over Lockerbie, Scotland, Muhammad Abu Talb was convicted of hostile terrorist activity and sentenced to life in prison; in Sweden that sentence usually means only twenty years.[16] It is unlikely, however, that he will serve even that long. It is virtually guaranteed that in his movements throughout Europe and Malta while orchestrating the charade of being a prime suspect, Abu Talb was promised that he would be included in the next Jibril-engineered prisoner exchange. If he informed on Jibril, it is likely his life wouldn't be worth a penny.

There is also the case of Ramzi Diab—the most mysterious member of Dalkamoni's cell to be released—as a potential suspect for planting the bomb on board Pan Am 103. According to several reports, he was an Israeli citizen, a Druze Arab, and, it had even been suggested, a former IDF soldier; other reports claim that his real name was Salah Kwikas, and that he had been captured by Israeli troops while on a terrorist mission inside Israel in 1980, and then freed in the prisoner exchange of May 21, 1985. Diab/Kwikas is believed to have transported Kreeshat's fifth barometer Toshiba Boombeat bomb to Vienna before disappearing. There have been countless reports speculating on whether or not Diab was a loyal PFLP-GC courier killed for his eternal silence, or if he was a spy in Jibril's organization, executed for his treason. There are many reports that indicate that Diab was, in fact, working for the Mossad, although this has never been confirmed. Since he was a Druze, with ties to family members in Syria, there are also those who believe he might have been a Syrian intelligence plant meant to spy on Jibril; other reports indicate that he was a paid agent working for the German BND. As Ramzi Diab returned to PFLP-GC headquarters in Damascus sometimes in November via Vienna and Belgrade (through what was known as the Adriatic Back Door), Jibril had concluded that Diab was definitely an enemy agent. Upon his arrival in Damascus, PFLP-GC security men seized Diab at Damascus International Airport and ushered him off to an interrogation center, believed to be used primarily by the Palestine Branch (*Fara' Falastin*) of the Syrian military intelligence. After a complete search of all his belongings, two forged Israeli passports were found among Diab's possessions. These findings reinforced Jibril's long-held suspicion that Diab was an agent for the Mossad. According to reports, Diab was held in Syrian custody until after Pan Am 103 was destroyed. He has not been seen or heard from since.[17]

There have been many theories concerning the destruction of Flight 103, ranging from an American-sponsored Drug Enforcement Administration sting operation gone sour to reports, printed in the respected Munich newspaper *Abendzeitung*, claiming that a terrorist working on the ground in London's Heathrow Airport attached the bomb to the outside of the aircraft shortly before its takeoff.*

Some of the more interesting theories, coincidences, and possibilities regarding the Pan Am 103 bombing include the following:

• The bomb that destroyed Pan Am 103 was brought on board, unknowingly, by Khalid Ja'afer, a twenty-year-old Lebanese-American student who was returning from a family visit to Lebanon; he was sitting in seat 53K when the aircraft was destroyed. It is believed that Ja'afer, a handsome young man who mysteriously traveled to Lebanon frequently (even though the State Department had warned against such travel), and whose family in Lebanon was heavily involved in the narcotics trade, was slipped the bomb in a copper-colored Samsonite suitcase, believing it to be a shipment of heroin; apparently, he was used to carrying packages without asking any questions. According to the theory, Ja'afer was involved in a sting operation being run by the

---

* Terrorist plants, working as maintenance workers, caterers, and cleaning crews at major international airports, have often assisted with attacks against civilian air targets, and terrorist operational planners consider these sympathetic workers instrumental in their schemes; plants were used to assist in the 1976 Entebbe hijacking, and the Shiite's 1985 hijacking of TWA Flight 847.

DEA to see how Middle Eastern heroin is smuggled through Frankfurt to the thriving Arab community in Detroit.[18] Interestingly, Khalid Ja'afer was a Shiite muslim whose family came from Ba'albek—home to the Iranian Revolutionary Guards and a major PFLP-GC training and logistics center in eastern Lebanon. The DEA, however, has denied any links to the incident, as have spokespersons from the FBI.

• Another theory also centers on the Middle Eastern narcotics trade, and a rumored deal between Monzer al-Kassar, a Syrian arms and narcotics merchant, and the CIA.[19] In exchange for assisting the United States in its efforts to free the American hostages held by Hizbollah in Beirut, al-Kassar was permitted to ship drugs through a protected route via Frankfurt to the United States; ostensibly the bomb that destroyed Pan Am 103 was hidden inside one of these shipments. According to this theory the German BKA was also aware of this operation, as well as of how the drugs were smuggled into the luggage area of the Frankfurt airport.[20]

• Another plot involving the CIA, and the possible rescue of American hostages held in Beirut, concerns four passengers on board the doomed flight who just happened to be senior American intelligence agents in the Middle East. They were Daniel Emmet O'Connor, a State Department regional security officer based in Cyprus; Ronald LaRiviere, a regional security officer in the Beirut Embassy; Matthew K. Gannon, believed to be a senior CIA officer assigned to Beirut; and Major Charles McKee, U.S. Army Intelligence (G2) and, perhaps, a serving officer in the Army's Intelligence Support Activity, a covert, or "black," special operations unit dedicated to counter terrorism. McKee was the most mysterious of all the American intelligence operatives on board the aircraft. His highly classified military record shows that he was fluent in Arabic, expert in counterterrorist and irregular-warfare tactics, and was used to being deployed to extremely hostile environments.[21] Both Gannon and McKee flew from Beirut to Cyprus on December 20, and then on to London. Apparently, these CIA men were in Lebanon to arrange a covert Delta Force/U.S. Navy SEAL (Sea, Air & Land) Team 6 rescue operation of the American hostages held by Hizbollah in Beirut. They were in Lebanon's embattled capital in order to gather invaluable HUMINT and lay the groundwork for the planned spectacular rescue operation; they were forced to carry out this dangerous mission personally because, according to several reports, Israel's destruction of the PLO in Lebanon had destroyed many of the CIA's assets in Lebanon, since an elaborate CIA-PLO relationship had existed for some years prior to 1982.[22] Following the destruction of Pan Am 103,

Scottish police received urgent communications from the American Embassy in London that there were four CIA agents on board the doomed flight, and that they were carrying extremely sensitive documents the agency was anxious to recover before they fell into the wrong hands. Those who believe that Pan Am 103 was destroyed in order to assassinate the four CIA men blame the affair on the Iranians. The initial suspicions concerning this theory held that a suitcase containing the Boombeat bomb was switched with McKee's bag (which contained the extremely sensitive documents) in either Beirut or Larnaca, Cyprus (convenient, considering that both Dalkamoni and Abu Talb had visited both island nations in the fall of 1988). Yet, even if the true reason behind the aircraft's destruction should turn out to be an assassination operation against one, or all, of these intelligence officers, we know that the explosive device was not in any of their personal possessions. The four agents flew directly to London to connect with Pan Am 103. They did not fly to Frankfurt, where the bomb began its deadly journey to London and then Lockerbie.

• There were also several speculative inquiries into the remote possibility that the Provisional Irish Republican Army was responsible for the destruction of Pan Am 103, since the Libyans had supplied them with enormous supplies of the Czech-produced Semtex plastic explosives. This theory was popular within British circles for a while, yet the notion that any Irish terrorist attack would target Americans seems exceedingly farfetched.

Even though the U.S. government, with the apparent support of both the British and French governments, eventually handed down their indictments against the two Libyan intelligence agents, charging them with being the sole perpetrators behind the bombing of Pan Am 103, the flow of charges claiming a governmental cover-up and conspiracy abound. One of the most incredible—and controversial—of such media-designed fingerpointing came on April 27, 1992, when *Time* magazine published as a cover story, based on the accusations of several suspected witnesses and experts, that the bombing was the work of a Syrian drug dealer, who had double-crossed the DEA in order to assassinate intelligence agents employed by the CIA.

The centerpiece of this *Time* claim is the so-called investigative work of Pan Am's law firm, Windels, Marx, Davies & Ives, and the work of their controversial investigator, Yuval Aviv, (It is believed that "Avner" is an alias that Yuval Aviv uses, and many believe that Aviv first tried to sell his services to the bereaved families of those killed on board Pan Am 103, and then, when these efforts failed, sold his "expert" services to Pan Am.) chairman of Interfor, an investigative firm specializing in intelligence and security matters, based in New York. Pan Am and its legal representation hired Aviv and Interfor to limit the liability the airline would eventually be responsible for in civil court. As a means to deflect the claim of poor security as the major contributing factor behind the destruction of Pan Am Flight 103, Pan Am and Interfor pointed the finger of blame toward the U.S. government, stating that the bomb that brought the Boeing 747 down over Lockerbie did not originate in Malta on board Flight KM 180 but had been smuggled on board Flight 103 in Frankfurt. This rogue bag was supposedly placed on board the aircraft by one Monzer al-Kassar, a Syrian arms and drugs merchant with close ties to Syrian intelligence (his brother-in-law is with Syrian military intelligence); his wife, Raghda, is reported to have close family ties to Syrian President Assad. According to this theory, the U.S. intelligence agents previously mentioned as killed on board Pan Am 103 were targeted by Iranians and the PFLP-GC because they were close to working out the final details of a hostage-rescue operation to free U.S. citizens held by Hizbollah in the slums of West Beirut and Lebanon's Bekaa Valley. Motives and means aside, the objective of the Pan Am bombing, according to this theory, was the assassination of the intelligence officers to prevent them from implementing a U.S. special operations assault on Beirut.

From the moment the *Time* issue hit the newsstands, its assertions were the subject of immense scrutiny and virtually unanimous dispute. According to most Western intelligence sources, the theory that Ahmed Jibril destroyed Pan Am Flight 103, at the Iranians' behest, with intelligence double-dealing from Monzer al-Kassar, appears ridiculous. In fact, national-security journalist Steven A. Emerson, one of the most knowledgeable experts in the Pan Am case, calls it ludicrous. First, Yuval Aviv, Interfor's chairman and a man Pan Am hired because he claimed to be a former Mossad officer (amazingly he had claimed to have headed Israeli hit teams hunting down Black September terrorists in Europe in 1972), although these claims appear to be a self-serving attempt at grandiose fiction. Israel and the Mossad claim, as stated in a stinging expose in Israel's daily newspaper Ma'aviv, that Aviv was never a paid agent, and his only connection to security work stems from brief and unsuccessful employment with El Al as a junior security officer. Second, a DEA informant by the name of Lester Knox Coleman, III, the person whose claims *Time* based much of its thesis on, now appears to be nothing more than a journalist rogue who not only duped the magazine but also helped send false signals—signals that were eventually accepted as fact to ABC and NBC about the Pan Am bombing. According to an expose in *New York Magazine*, Lester Coleman was a low-level informant for the DEA in Cyprus and, according to many accounts, a high-level bullshit artist with a history of spinning tales. All these negative and questionable factors about Yuval Aviv, as well as al-Kassar's role as set-up man for a PFLP-GC Iranian/DEA/CIA double-cross sting and assassination attempt, were hardly enough to convince the American people or the American justice and intelligence communities that they were worthy of further attention.

Through all the theories, no matter how reasonable or inconceivable, Jibril continued to be the primary suspect; the Iranians and, of course, the Syrians also were implicated in this act of airborne mass murder. According to Noel Koch, former American assistant secretary of defense, "There is no question that the PFLP-GC was involved in it too, and there is no doubt that the Syrians are involved in it."[23] These views were shared by current officials, such as State Department official Frank Moss: "The bottom line is that I can't believe the PFLP-GC could have done it without someone high in the Syrian government knowing about it."[24]

The Israelis too remained absolutely convinced that the PFLP-GC was behind the attack. Even after political pandering toward Syria managed to deflect American interests from prosecuting Jibril, Israeli security officials had no doubt that the destruction of Pan Am Flight 103 was masterminded, logistically handled, and even possibly carried out by Jibril and the PFLP-GC.[25]

So how did Ahmed Jibril execute his blood contract with the Iranians to destroy an American airliner? Enter a sixth Toshiba Model 453 Boombeat bomb, enter a secret and trusted terrorist squad, and enter—according to intelligence reports, forensic evidence, and pure deduction—the helpful hand of Colonel Qaddafi's intelligence service and a nation eager to exact inexpensive vengeance for the April 1986 American attack against Libya. Perhaps never in the history of international terrorism has a diversionary counterintelligence operation, run by a small terrorist faction, succeeded so brilliantly in throwing some of the world's most efficient intelligence services completely off the track of an incredibly involved and sophisticated international criminal investigation. Just as the brilliance of a terrorist is not judged by skill or technique but by the final body count of the executed operation, so the destruction of Pan Am 103 would be Ahmed Jibril's true masterstroke.

As documented, in highly-detailed ABC-TV news accounts following a special investigation, to carry out the destruction of an American airliner, it is believed that Jibril recruited three Palestinian terrorists whose anonymity and allegiance would, in the end, secure the operation's success. The men were known in Israeli circles as the Kenya Three (Mohammad al-Makousi, Ibrahim Tawfik-Yousef, and Hassan Hadi al-Ahar),[26] three terrorists seized by Kenyan security agents on January 18, 1976, with a tip-off from the Mossad, in a failed attempt to blow an El Al jumbo jet out of the sky with a handheld SA-7 Strella surface-to-air missile as it made its landing approach to Nairobi Airport; 110 passengers were on board the aircraft. Kenya, a staunch ally to Israel in an otherwise hostile African continent, wanted nothing to do with the three terrorists, and they were secretly smuggled from a maximum-security facility in Nairobi to Israel. On May 21, 1985, they were included in the prisoner exchange between the PFLP-GC and Israel and flown to Geneva, and then on to Libya. They were men who owed Ahmed Jibril a great deal.

According to this theory into the destruction of Pan Am 103, Jibril had absolute faith in these three men (apparently, there was no suspicion that they had been turned while in Israeli custody). There is no evidence of their operating in Europe or in the Mediterranean from the time of their release to the uncovering of the Dalkamoni cell in Germany; it is more than likely that they were kept under wraps in one of the PFLP-GC's Syrian facilities, well out of the spotlight. Jibril is reported to have told them only to report to him personally, and never admit their allegiance to the PFLP-GC.[27] With the Kenya Three, Ahmed Jibril would possess perfect deniability—a crew (similar to those employed in organized crime families) that was publicly independent of the PFLP-GC but that privately did his personal bidding.

The sixth bomb, destined to be planted on board Pan Am 103, was built in Damascus, probably by one of the Abu Ibrahim bombmakers who joined the organization in 1985 or 1986, and was shipped to Tripoli in December of 1988; the Kenya Three were responsible for transporting the device to Libya, although some reports even indicate that they constructed the bomb themselves. In Tripoli, the device was handed to two senior Libyan intelligence operatives who, in the end, would be responsible for planting the bomb on board the Pan Am flight. The Libyan connection is an interesting one and, if the theories are correct, displays the true and absolutely terrifying genius of Ahmed Jibril. Already paid a handsome fee by the Iranians to down an American airliner, Jibril, it is believed, began to play the part of savvy businessman and turned to Libya's Colonel Qaddafi with an opportunity to obtain cheap revenge for Operation El Dorado Canyon. The offer came in September 1988, during a major international terrorist conference in Tripoli, where plans were also discussed for revenge against the French for the overt military support of Chad in its war against Libya.[28] It is not impossible to conceive that by subcontracting minor Libyan assistance, Jibril received *two* payments for the destruction of Pan Am 103.[29]

Libyan involvement in the bombing of Pan Am 103 was compelling, and only discovered after the most exhaustive investigation. British, German, and American investigators, intelligence agents, and security officials searched for clues in fifty-two nations and interviewed close to fourteen thousand witnesses.[30] Clearly this was a high-profile case, an instance of state-sponsored mass murder, and to alleviate the traveling public's fears, as well as to provide justice to the victims and their families, immense resources were invested to find and prosecute the individuals responsible for the murders. The tireless search for clues involved the FAA, the DIA, the FBI (and its elite crime lab), and the CIA (including its Counterterrorism Center, a world command post for thwarting and responding to terrorist movements); the British MI5, MI6, and Scotland Yard Special Branch; the German BKA, BfV, and BND; and, to a lesser extent, the French *Service de Documentation Extèrieure et de Contre-Espionnage* (SDECE); the Italian *Ufficio Centrale per le Investigazioni Generale e per le Operazioni Speciali*; the Swiss national police; and the Israeli Mossad and Shin Bet.[31] Some of the investigative findings, especially those involving forensic evidence, were simply remarkable.

Tons of debris and aircraft fragments were recovered from the 845-square-mile area of the crash and taken to a special hangar in Farnborough, England, where the skeleton of the aircraft was meticulously reconstructed so that the exact location and situation of the blast could be determined. One piece of evidence recovered from the high Scottish grass included a fingernail-sized bit of electronic circuitry, a miniaturized computer chip, with Semtex residue on it. It was clear that this bit of wire and metal was instrumental in identifying the bomb, but its connection to Colonel Qaddafi's Libya would not come from pure detective work, but rather from another aircraft blown out of the skies by terrorists.

On February 20, 1988, two Libyan intelligence agents, known only by their aliases of Mohammed al-Marzouk and Mansour Omran Saber, were arrested by Senegalese police in the capital of Dakar. The two had taken an Air Afrique flight from Togo en route to Abidjan, Ivory Coast, when they were apprehended. In their luggage, Dakar policemen found nine kilograms of Semtex* plastic explosives, several blocks of TNT, and ten timer-activated detonators.[33] It appeared as if these men were laying the groundwork for a massive terrorist offensive, but six months later, the two men were mysteriously released from Senegalese custody.

On September 19, 1989, U.T.A. Flight 772, en route from Brazzaville to Paris, blew up over the Ténéré Desert in Niger shortly after taking off following a brief stop in N'Djamena, Chad. When the aircraft had reached a moderate altitude, a powerful blast ripped through the DC-10's cargo hold; the thunderous explosion caused the aircraft to crash like a missile onto the desert floor. All 171 passengers and crew were killed instantly. The similarities between the destruction of U.T.A. Flight 772 and Pan Am 103 were too glaring not to be connected somehow. French investigators were rushed to the North African desert in an attempt to retrieve as much of the wreckage as possible that remained intact from the force of the desert winds; the remaining physical evidence was brought to Paris for extensive forensic examination. It was discovered that the bomb that destroyed Flight 772 was also a Boombeat barometric device, and was linked to the explosives and detonators found in the possession of the Libyan agents in Senegal a year before. The French SDECE and DST (*Direction de la Surveillance du Territoire*) opened an immediate criminal investigation into the U.T.A. bombing, and, several months later, four Libyan intelligence operatives were indicted. They were Abdallah Senoussi, Colonel Qaddafi's brother-in-law and deputy commander of the External Security Agency, the Libyan intelligence group in charge of foreign operations; Abdallah Elazragh, an employee in the Libyan People Bureau in Brazzaville; and two low-level Libyan agents, Ibrahim Naeli and Musbah Arbas.[34] Ostensibly the French believed that the Libyans had destroyed the U.T.A. DC-10 to protest French military involvement in Chad. Several intelligence reports, however, have theorized that the Iranians contracted the PFLP-GC to carry out the bombing. Before the U.T.A. bombing, PFLP-GC commanders held talks with pro-Iranian

---

* Czech President Vaclav Havel stated that the former Communist government in Prague shipped more than one thousand tons of Semtex to Libya, which, in turn, shipped the material to several terrorist organizations, including the Palestinians and the Provisional Irish Republican Army. Czech assistance to the world's terrorist forces was enormous, and there were so many different terrorist factions undergoing training inside Prague, as well as arms merchants plying their goods, that the Red Berets, the Czech Army's elite antiterrorist unit, spent much of its time protecting hostile factions from one another.[32]

elements in Beirut and discussed schemes and potential operations to deter France from activating its naval forces deployed off the Beirut coast from being used against Syrian forces striking out at the Christian Lebanese renegade general, Michele Aoun. The Iranians also wanted revenge against France for its alleged failure to fulfill its part in a deal where Paris was to forward several million dollars to Tehran in exchange for the 1987 release of French hostages held by Hizbollah in Beirut.[35] According to one anonymous Israeli intelligence analyst knowledgeable in Middle Eastern terrorism, "It is inconceivable that the Libyans would be foolish enough to perpetrate a terrorist act, especially such a high-profile operation such as an airliner bombing with great loss of life, in North Africa, so close to Tripoli where Qaddafi would be the obvious prime suspect. *Obviously*, another party must have been responsible."

The FBI and Scotland Yard, too, had analyzed bits of the device responsible for bringing down U.T.A. Flight 772, as well as the two living models seized in Dakar. They matched it to the fingernail-sized computer-chip fragment recovered from Lockerbie, and tracked the timer to the Swiss electronics firm of Meister and Bollier, Inc. According to Meister and Bollier director Ed Bollier, the company manufactured computerized circuit boards for use in household appliances and sold them throughout the Middle East; Meister and Bollier only manufactured twenty timers capable of detonating bombs, however, and had sold quite a few of them to the Libyan government in the mid-1980's. The Libyan purchasing agent responsible for obtaining the circuits was identified as Izzel Din al-Hinshiri, a former assistant director of the Libyan intelligence service.[36]

The Meister and Bollier computer chip, as well as the clothing fragments that originated in Malta from garments produced by Yorkie Clothing and sold only in the Mary's House Boutique in Sliema, linked the Boombeat bomb that destroyed Pan Am 103 to a piece of unaccompanied interline luggage loaded onto the doomed flight. In cargo pallet 14L, where the bomb was held, there were fifteen pieces of interline luggage: nine were from connecting flights inside Germany, two belonged to U.S. government officials and originated in Vienna, one belonged to a Swedish diplomat and originated in Brussels, and two belonged to the Americans Gannon and McKee.[37] One bag, a copper-colored Samsonite with no passenger identification attached to it, was also in 14L. It was that bag that carried the bomb that destroyed Pan Am 103 and the lives of so many innocent people.

On November 14, 1991, U.S. prosecutor Robert Mueller, III, publicly

disclosed the results of the three-year investigation of the destruction
of Pan Am 103 by indicting two Libyan intelligence agents, Abdel
Basset Ali al-Megrahi, a Libyan spy whose cover was chief of security
for Libyan Arab Airlines, and Lamen Khalifa Fhimah, the Libyan Arab
Airlines station manager at Luqa Airport in Malta, as the men responsible for the aircraft's destruction; according to several reports, the two
men were identified by a high-ranking Libyan defector working for the
Americans.[38] According to the American (and British) version of
events, Fhimah stole several Air Malta baggage tags from Luqa Airport
on December 15 and handed them to Megrahi, who arrived from
Zurich several days later (after, it is believed, a surveillance stop in
Frankfurt). The two men traveled to Libya, where they received the
bomb from "unknown" individuals, wrapped it in bundles of clothing
that Megrahi had purchased in the Mary's House Boutique in Sliema,*
sealed shut the copper-colored Samsonite suitcase, and then adorned it
with a destination tag belonging to Air Malta Flight KM 180 between
Malta and Frankfurt. On December 20, after, it is believed, meeting
with PFLP-GC liaisons in Tripoli, the two men returned to Malta. On
the morning of December 21, both men checked in the Samsonite
suitcase as *unaccompanied luggage* on Flight KM 180 to Frankfurt.[39]
The two-staged timer was activated in midair on board the Air Malta
flight, and then timed to detonate approximately nine hours later when
Pan Am 103 was to be flying high over the Atlantic Ocean. As Pan Am
interline security at Frankfurt was nonexistent, a bag traveling to the
United States with no passenger claiming it as their own was not even
subjected to X-ray examination.

In pointing a finger of blame only at Libya, the Americans were going
solely on forensic evidence. According to Richard Boucher, a State
Department spokesman, "This was a Libyan government operation
from start to finish."[40] Libya's motive behind the Pan Am 103 bombing,
according to American beliefs, was to avenge the 1986 Tripoli bombing.
But that argument is weak. It went against traditional *modus operandi*
that the Libyans, in their support of the entire gamut of international
terrorists, had maintained for nearly two decades. The Libyans never
perpetrate acts of terror against Israeli or Western targets utilizing
Libyan personnel, since the first rule of state-sponsored terrorism was

---

* To many Western intelligence agents, the connection between the clothing purchased
by Megrahi in Sliema and those found in Muhammad Abu Talb's possession in his
Uppsala home was but a small indication that the entire Libyan operation was designed
as deniable cover for the PFLP-GC.

to always use a third party in the actual act. A sovereign government was never to be caught holding the smoking gun. The fact that the Swiss-produced timers, purchased by the Libyans, were used to destroy Pan Am 103 proved absolutely nothing. Ze'ev Schiff, Israel's leading military journalist, cited Mossad and A'man agents when he said: "The Swiss timers might have been ordered by the Libyans, some of them had been transferred to other parties. *It is not impossible* that these were also transferred to Ahmed Jibril's PFLP-GC."[41]

In a *New York Times* article, an American security official wishing to remain anonymous stated that evidence linking Libya to the Lockerbie disaster did not clear Iran, Syria, or Ahmed Jibril and the PFLP-GC of complicity in the Pan Am bombing.[42]

Colonel Qaddafi has refused to turn over his two intelligence officers so that they might stand trial in either an American or a British court for the mass murder of 270 civilians. The Libyan leader understands that any trial, with its international implications, would unleash a Pandora's box of Libyan, Syrian, Iranian, and Iraqi support for international terrorism over a twenty-year span, and probably result in some sort of decisive military action. Both the United States and Great Britain have sponsored United Nations-imposed sanctions against Tripoli, including a civilian air embargo and the possibility of military action. At the time of this book's writing, the clash between Libya and the United States and Great Britain over custody of the two Pan Am 103 bombers has been litigated in the World Court in The Hague, Netherlands, with the Libyans ordered to relinquish their men. A standoff continues with United Nations sanctions achieving absolutely nothing.

The Israelis, however, were convinced that Syria—in its permanent support for the PFLP-GC—was behind the Pan Am bombing, and not just Libya, although Tel Aviv has never refuted a Libyan connection to the incident. Because of Qaddafi's relative military weakness, the United States has historically found it easier to strike out against Libya rather than against other (more dangerous) sponsors of Middle Eastern terrorism such as Syria and Iran. According to a headline in the daily newspaper *Ha'aretz*, considered by many to be *The New York Times* of Israel, "Syrian Terror? America Does Not See It or Hear It!" America is unwilling to pin any act of terror to Damascus. Although the Americans dismissed Israel's claim that Syria, Iran, and the PFLP-GC were behind the Pan Am bombing as nothing more than political posturing to make Syria look bad, Washington has gone out of its way to deflect blame from Damascus. By the autumn of 1991, when evidence of the

Libyan involvement was leaked to the press, President George Bush found it politically correct to exonerate Syria, since a Syrian role in the delicate anti-Saddam Hussein Operation Desert Shield coalition became a linchpin in American military policy, as well as its political prestige and influence in the region. America's remarkable disregard for Syria's complicity in the Pan Am bombing clearly stems from Syria's minimal participation in the Arab coalition against Iraq's Saddam Hussein during Operation Desert Storm and for Syrian agreement to participate in the subsequent Middle East peace conference. Outside Madrid's Royal Palace at the opening installment of the Middle Eastern peace process in October 1991, John Root,* a New York lawyer, protested with a sign stating: "ASSAD MURDERED MY WIFE ON PAN AM 103;" Root's wife, Hanna-Marie, was killed over Lockerbie.[43]

Just as the United States had traditionally found Libya to be a useful and accommodating scapegoat, so Syria proved to be at the opposite end of America's retributive spectrum. The United States did not retaliate against Syria following the bombings of the American Embassy in Beirut, or against the Marine barracks in 1983 when 241 marines were murdered. Perhaps Washington was not willing to risk a fight against a determined and capable Arab military entity, or perhaps, realizing that Syria is the nerve center and command post for many of the region's dangerous terrorist forces, the United States did not wish to promote Damascus as the worldwide mecca of anti-American terrorism. As a result, Syria's support for international terrorism has made it a state of true deterrent power reaching to the four corners of the globe; with a track record of terrorist attacks and airline bombings, Syria need not even threaten its adversaries, but merely bring up past incidents. With foot soldiers like Ahmed Jibril, Syrian President Hafaz al-Assad, the sphinx of Damascus, has truly won this war of nerves against the West.

In fact, American efforts to remove suspicion from Syria in the Pan Am bombing has caused great friction with traditional allies, as well as

---

* John Root managed to obtain press credentials from a local New York newspaper, *The Jewish Press*, and sat in on the numerous press briefings the Israeli, American, Soviet, Jordanian-Palestinian, and Syrian delegations provided following each negotiations session. Determined to vocalize his heartfelt anger over the murder of his wife, Root asked several hard-hitting questions of Syrian foreign minister Farouk al-Shara'a. He was forcibly removed from the press hall, however, after asking U.S. Secretary of State James A. Baker III about the criminal irony in the warming of relations between America and Syria.

concerns regarding the course of America's present Middle Eastern policy.

Following the destruction of Pan Am 103, a baffled United States attempted to find circumstantial or physical evidence that would link the PFLP-GC to the Lockerbie bombing. Its most tangible link to the terrorists was inside Syria itself, and American intelligence-gathering efforts inside the dictatorial state were increased markedly. Attempts were made to locate informers, tap into classified communication lines, and obtain any tidbit of evidence that might conclusively link Jibril to the Pan Am disaster. On March 3, 1989, however, the American military attaché to Syria, Colonel Clifford Roberts, and his deputy, Major Robert Segal, were apprehended by PFLP-GC security agents outside one of the organization's logistics centers north of Damascus.[44] They were caught red-handed photographing the base with extremely sophisticated photographic equipment, and they were handed over to Syrian security forces, detained, and expelled. According to Radio Damascus, "It was not the first time that the CIA had spied on Syria on behalf of the Israelis."

The United States, at a loss on how to obtain accurate information on the PFLP-GC, quickly turned to Israel, the most reliable ally in the area. According to several reports, the Israelis responded by turning over extremely sensitive intelligence documents that, it is believed, conclusively linked Syria and the PFLP-GC to the destruction of Pan Am 103. The data, considered by Israeli intelligence to be state secrets of the highest order, were handed to Washington on the condition that it be seen by only a handful of trusted CIA and DIA officials.[45] On September 14, 1990, during a meeting in Damascus meant to secure Syrian participation in the anti-Iraq coalition, U.S. Secretary of State James A. Baker III confronted Syria's President Assad with the Israeli intelligence data in hand about the alleged role of Syrian and Palestinian forces in the destruction of Pan Am 103. Sharp debates existed between American intelligence officers and Bush Administration officials over how strongly Assad should be confronted with firm evidence linking Syria to terrorism. Officials from the Bush Administration were told that President Assad should be given an unusually detailed briefing about the actions of Syrian-based terrorists to impress on him the weight of the evidence against his government. Administration officials had been warned that such disclosures would place human intelligence assets on the ground in extreme danger, but the order to supply Syria with the information was still issued.[46] President Assad would, indeed, use this information well. Later that month, the PFLP-GC executed two or three undercover agents inside the organization believed to be working for the Mossad.*[47]

These tragic events were viewed with great contempt in Israel and severely weakened the once close-knit intelligence service relationship that existed between Washington and Jerusalem. The deaths of the two agents prompted the Israelis to release news that the Bush Administration was hiding irrefutable evidence linking Syria and the PFLP-GC to the Pan Am bombing.[49] Sadly, politics in the Middle East remain a more important landmark of the region than the pursuit of justice.

American efforts to remove the veil of guilt from Iran stemmed from the failed efforts of past administrations to secure the release of eight American hostages held by the pro-Iranian Hizbollah in Beirut. In order to secure their release and place the tragic twelve-year chapter of Americans as hostages to the back pages of history, the United States was willing to overlook its volumes of intelligence intercepts in which Iran and Jibril were conclusively implicated in planning an operation that targeted an American airliner for destruction.

The bombing of Pan Am Flight 103 remains yet another one of Jibril's terrorist undertakings for which he has remained impervious from persecution or even retribution. Ominously, there have never been official calls for justice against Ahmed Jibril and the PFLP-GC, even when they were the public suspects in the Pan Am bombing. The Teflon Terrorist and his organization, through guile, sheer luck, and the criminal pandering of politics, remains untouchable. The PFLP-GC commander was steadfast in his denials to any connection with the Lockerbie disaster, even though evidence concerning his covert relations with Iran, from Dalkamoni's statements to West German police to U.S. intelligence intercepts, seemed to implicate him more than any other suspect. His most passionate denial came on January 9, 1990, when he held a news conference in the Mar Elias refugee district in southern Beirut. Flanked by heavily armed bodyguards (including several Iranian Revolutionary Guards) carrying assault rifles and sophisticated communications equipment, Jibril stated: "Our relations with the Islamic revolution of Iran started before the Pan Am accident. Reports of our engagement in the blast were mere media fabrications

---

* In an attempt to lessen the controversy over the tragic American error, the Bush Administration announced that it believed the executed spies to be agents for the Jordanian Muchabarat and not the Mossad.[48] Apparently, they believed, the deaths of two Arab agents would not be as explosive an issue.

that were not based on facts. Anyway," Jibril wryly added, "Iran would not need Palestinian forces in its war against imperialism."[50]

The attack on Pan Am 103 solidified Jibril's standing with the Iranians and is certain to have promised him opportunities for greater financial rewards. In January 1989, following clandestine meetings between Jibril and Mohtashemi, the Iranians dispatched several hundred Revolutionary Guard commandos to PFLP-GC installations in Lebanon to solidify the "united Islamic front against Zionism" and help protect Jibril and his installations from attack."

Between 1968 and 1988, 1,120 persons have died as a result of bombs going off on board airliners.[51] The practice of targeting the traveling public has developed into an international epidemic that most countries vehemently vow to fight but few actually do. In fact, by failing to indict—either legally or publicly—Iran, Syria, or the PFLP-GC, the United States, Great Britain, and France have simply turned their backs on a problem they pray will disappear into the benign reaches of history. By failing to act decisively and militarily, they assume a portion of the responsibility in one of the most heinous criminal acts to have occurred since the emergence of international terrorism in 1968. Following Syria's failed bombing of El Al Flight 016, Prime Minister Yitzhak Shamir stated that if the bombing had succeeded in killing the 375 persons on board, Israel would have had no choice but to punish Syria in an all-encompassing fashion by launching a full-scale war of retribution.[52] Massive revenge can sometimes be the most effective deterrent.

Only time will tell if the world has learned its lesson from the Lockerbie disaster. New means for making civilian aircraft bombproof are being tested, including the use of blowout panels for cargo holds; preventive measures, including the deployment of thermal neutron-analysis systems designed to detect odorless plastic explosives which are being tested at major international airports. Yet, tragically, the inaction of the governments most affected by the destruction of Pan Am 103 only insures that such outrages will be repeated by terrorists in the coming years.

In June 1991, Hafaz Dalkamoni was sentenced to fifteen years' imprisonment for his role in terrorist attacks against American troop trains in Germany; Abdel Fatah Ghadanfar, received an eight-month sentence. Both men, serving time in the maximum-security facility in Wuppertal, Germany, remain confident that they will not be held for very much longer. Apparently eager to end the plight of their own two German hostages still held by Hizbollah in Beirut, the Germans have discussed trading Dalkamoni and Ghadanfar in any future prisoner exchange the PFLP-GC, Abu Nidal, or the Iranians might arrange.[53]

The West's war against terrorism, especially that waged by a master like Jibril, remains a losing battle. Even when the Israeli Air Force launched its successful February 16, 1992, air strike against a convoy carrying Hizbollah warlord Sheikh Abbas Musawi, a man responsible for hostage-taking and the 1983 destruction of the U.S. Marine Corps barracks at Beirut International Airport, the media seemed to concentrate more on Israeli terror rather than the killing of a man with the blood of hundreds on his hands. Many in the American media, for example, like syndicated columnist Robert Novak, severely criticized Israel's killing of Musawi on the February 21, 1992, edition of the CNN show, *Crossfire*, remarkably claiming that Musawi was *instrumental* in securing the release of the American hostages in Lebanon (never bothering to state that Musawi had ordered the hostages seized in the first place). Weeks later, however, the topic of terrorism was removed from the media and back to the trenches when Hizbollah agents in Argentina blew up a powerful car bomb in front of the Israeli Embassy in Buenos Aires; more than twenty people were killed in the attack, and hundreds seriously wounded.

POSTSCRIPT

PERHAPS THE UNITED STATES and Great Britain have relinquished their pursuit of Ahmed Jibril and the PFLP-GC for its role in the destruction of Pan Am 103, but Israel still views the wily terrorist chieftain as one of the greatest threats to the safety of the Jewish State today. According to Jerusalem, he is a man who needs to be punished for his past crimes in order to ensure that future outrages will not be perpetrated. Lockerbie, and the skeletal remains of Pan Am 103, were but stoic reminders to the Israeli defense establishment that Jibril is a man that must be stopped.

The Golani Brigade's December 8-9 commando assault on Jibril's al-Na'ameh lair may have failed in achieving its ultimate and true objectives, but the Israeli military has maintained incessant aerial pressure against the PFLP-GC ever since. From the destruction of Pan Am 103 over Lockerbie through January 1992, the IAF has mounted more than thirty air strikes in which the PFLP-GC was solely targeted. Some of the air raids have been extremely successful, such as the March 24, 1989, bombing runs against a PFLP-GC base in the northeastern Bekaa Valley in which fifteen terrorists, including several officers, were killed and several dozen wounded. Many believe the attack, deep into Syrian-controlled and -protected territory, to have been a statement directed against both Jibril and Syria's President Assad: In light of the Lockerbie incident, both men were considered fair game.[1] Indeed, the IAF was willing to go to incredible risk and effort to hinder the PFLP-GC's ability to wage its war of revolutionary violence against Israel. On March 17, 1990, a force of IAF fighter bombers strafed and bombed a PFLP-GC naval facility in Khan Khayat, north of Tripoli, in the *farthest* raid into Lebanon since 1987.[2] In the air strike, Israeli warplanes blew several fast attack craft out of the water with bombs and rockets, and then proceeded to obliterate several ammunition dumps in which, it is believed, abundant supplies of Libyan-supplied Semtex were stored.

233

One of the largest raids took place on June 4, 1991 when, in the largest Israeli air operation over Lebanon since the 1982 invasion, more than twenty IAF aircraft struck PFLP-GC targets throughout southern and eastern Lebanon.[3] Sometimes Jibril's camps were being hit as frequently as twice a month.

As has usually been the case, Ahmed Jibril was undaunted by the aerial attention his forces were receiving courtesy of the IAF. In fact, he remained cocky, almost taunting the Israelis to try and destroy him. After al-Na'ameh and Pan Am 103, he had good reason to feel confident. It appeared as if he could not be touched. Not by the Swiss, the Germans, the British, or Americans. Not even by the Israelis. Perhaps he was right.

On the night of February 4, 1990, a bus ferrying Israeli tourists from Cairo toward the Suez Canal area was ambushed by several PFLP-GC gunmen armed with antipersonnel fragmentation hand grenades and automatic rifles.[4] Acting in concert with the terrorists was the driver, a Palestinian-born Egyptian citizen, who stopped the bus at the predesignated ambush site along the desert road and leapt out his window as the terrorists pummeled the tour bus with hundreds of rounds of ammunition, tossing several grenades into the fray for good measure. Convinced that all of the Israelis were dead, the terrorists simply disappeared into the dark desert abyss. The final death toll was nine, with more than twenty critically wounded. The objective of the brief outburst of fire was to damage the already strained "cold peace" that existed between Israel and Egypt. The attack signaled an ominous increase in PFLP-GC activity in North Africa,* which coincided with increased attempts by Jibril to launch terrorist attacks against Israel across the Jordanian frontier. Several intelligence reports consider these moves by Jibril as inspired purely by Iran, and the final consolida-

---

* The once-docile North African segment of the region has recently been rocked by a mini-invasion of Iranian-inspired Islamic fundamentalism, particularly in Sudan. Looking to branch out, Iran has offered Sudan, a nation returning to fundamentalist Islam and fighting a civil war against the nation's Christian minority, with massive military and political assistance. In December 1991, Iran's President Rafsanjani visited Sudan; he was accompanied by Defense Minister Akbar Torkan and the commander of the Revolutionary Guards, Major-General Hussein Radhair; also accompanying this contingent to Khartoum were several senior officers from the Iranian intelligence community.[5] One of the objectives of the Iranian visit, beyond providing money and arms, was to establish terrorist bases in Sudan from which groups like the PFLP-GC and Abu Nidal could use to strike out against Egypt and strategic Western interests in the horn of Africa. Sudan is also believed to be a prime supporter of the Hamas movement inside the Gaza Strip and the West Bank.

tion of a terrorist alliance forged with the bombing of Pan Am 103 and sealed into fact in July 1989, when Jibril paid a state visit to Iran to confer with Ayatollah Ali Khamenei, the successor of the Ayatollah Khomeini, in Tehran.[6]

Jibril's close ties to Iran have provided him with something few Palestinian leaders have ever enjoyed: political leverage. The Islamic Republic of Iran has developed into one of the most feared nations on earth, and clearly a force to be reckoned with in the shaping of the Middle East and Persian Gulf region. With Syrian military and security support and Iranian money, Ahmed Jibril was poised to solidify his military power within the Palestinian community as no leader had ever done before. With Iran behind him, (Jibril even claims to have been given access to Capt. Ron Arad, a prisoner held by the Iranian-backed Hizbollah) and the Syrians at the vanguard, Jibril could bear one million soldiers against Israel, as well as provide spiritual support to the Islamic holy warriors of the Palestinian Hamas terrorist group operating on the West Bank and the Gaza Strip.[7] The PFLP-GC also escalated its war against Israeli forces in Lebanon, consolidating their positions opposite the IDF security zone, and assisting Hizbollah in strikes against Israeli forces along the Lebanese border. On November 25, 1990, in "celebration" of the third anniversary of the Night of the Hang Gliders, Ahmed Jibril attempted to launch a major seaborne attack against northern Israel. Five heavily armed PFLP-GC gunmen, equipped with assault rifles, machine guns, and antitank weapons, departed the Sidon area of southern Lebanon in a motorized speedboat and raced toward the Israeli coast; their assignment was to carry out a suicide raid against one of Israel's coastal cities. Yet before they could reach Israeli territory and possibly carry out a massacre, an IDF/Navy patrol boat blew the terrorist's vessel out of the water. All five terrorists were killed.[8]

In his lifelong campaign to destroy Israel, Ahmed Jibril and the various groups he has commanded have come a long way in the execution of their sacred holy war against the Jewish State. The conflict has taken Jibril from the frustration of anonymity to being one of the most wanted men on earth. As the State of Israel nears its fiftieth year of existence, it appears as if Ahmed Jibril is attempting to escalate the struggle into one final zenith of destruction before it is too late. The PFLP-GC has acquired several dozen hang gliders,* motorized

* Oddly enough, many armies the world over have studied the PFLP-GC's success with hang gliders in the Night of the Hang Gliders, and have begun to deploy them in the field. Ultralights and hang gliders are now used by the elite British Special Air Service and American Special Forces.[9]

ultralights, and remote-piloted vehicles from several British, French, and German companies.[10] The prospect of a terrorist fleet of silent airborne warriors launching a suicide attack against a northern Israeli settlement is daunting. Even more frightening to Israeli security concerns is the fact that the PFLP-GC, with Syrian and Iranian assistance, has begun to invest in the services of microbiologists, commissioned to produce biological agents that will be used in future terrorist attacks in Israel.[11]

To prove the seriousness of its future war of revolutionary violence against the Jewish state, the PFLP-GC has vowed to use spectacular acts of terrorism to strike against the hundreds of thousands of Soviet Jews leaving the remnants of the Soviet Union and immigrating to Israel. Ahmed Jibril realizes that Jewish migration to Israel is the essence of Zionism, and the influx of more than two hundred thousand Soviet Jews into Israel is a phenomenon that can only be stopped through armed resistance and wanton bloodshed.[12]

In a rare interview granted to the American journalist Richard Cheznoff, Ahmed Jibril stated: "We [the Palestinians] *must* continue in the armed struggle at any price. *We* fought for 150 years against the crusaders until we won, and we are now only fighting Israel for a little over forty years."[13] Ahmed Jibril, however, might not have one hundred years remaining in which to wage the holy struggle against Zionism. The IAF remains dedicated to ending Jibril's career by waging an incessant war of revolutionary violence of its own against the PFLP-GC. The latest and most effective aerial offensive has targeted the al-Na'ameh caves, a symbolic landmark of Israel's desire to terminate Jibril. From December 1988 through April 1992, IAF warplanes mounted timely strikes against the PFLP-GC's al-Na'ameh base that, according to foreign reports, are designed to assassinate Jibril as he is visiting the facility. Realizing that the al-Na'ameh caves are impervious to "ordinary" ordnance, the IAF has attempted to guide smart bombs, launched at 8,000 feet by some of the most experienced pilots in the IAF's Order of Battle, through the front of the caves with laser guidance systems.[14] Although the air strikes did indeed, once and for all, destroy the al-Na'ameh caves,* Jibril was never harmed.

It appears that time, not the IDF, the CIA, or even the Mossad, is now

---

* Just to make sure the sprawling underground and cavernous facility never returned to fully operational form, the IAF continues to make al-Na'ameh a priority target. On January 10, 1992, an IAF air strike against the remnants of the PFLP-GC position killed twelve terrorists and destroyed several installations and arms caches under repair.

Ahmed Jibril's greatest enemy. In 1990, several reports suggested that Ahmed Jibril suffered a serious heart attack in Damascus and was close to death; in order to continue the PFLP-GC's legacy, Jibril is believed to have named Talal Naji, his deputy, as his successor.[15] Ahmed Jibril is a man with many enemies operating in a business where old age is an extremely rare commodity: Terrorists simply don't retire on pension plans. He may end up like Ali Hassan Salameh or Abu Jihad, killed by the Israelis, or Abu Iyad, murdered by his own fellow Palestinians loyal to Abu Nidal; he might even end up like his old mentor Dr. George Habash, and be forced to beg the West for medical assistance even if it meant a risk of arrest and incarceration as was the case in January 1992, when George Habash was mysteriously whisked into a Paris hospital with heart-failure. Or Ahmed Jibril will join his bitter rival Yasir Arafat, and spend the remainder of his life as a man humbled by age and defeat, and be forced to die in the exile of a foreign land. Perhaps his greatest punishment will be to never again set foot in his sacred land of Palestine. The Palestinian peoples' inability to further their national aspirations of independent statehood (as well as seeing to Israel's destruction) is, perhaps, the greatest tragedy of the Palestinians' terrorist revolution that has engulfed the region since the end of the 1967 war. Perhaps this senseless display of violence has been the great tragedy of the Palestinian people.

The final battle between Ahmed Jibril and his hated enemies has yet to be fought. His war, Israel's war, and the world's war, has yet to end.

ENDNOTES

INTRODUCTION

p. 2 Arieh Hasabiyah, *"Milion Chayalim Neged Yisrael,"* *Bamachane*, November 13, 1991, p. 25.

p. 3 As discussed on the TV news documentary *Frontline*, titled "The Bombing of Pan Am 103," WGBH-TV, Show #802, which aired January 23, 1990.

p. 3 Arieh Hasabiyah, *"Milion Chayalim,"* p. 25.

p. 5 Boaz Ganor, *"Sartan U'Shmo Terror: Ha'Irgunim Ha'Palestina'im Ha'Pro'Surim,"* *Matara*, No. 13, 1990, p. 47.

CHAPTER ONE

p. 8 This message was conveyed to the local inhabitants of the region's nations not only through propaganda in the government-controlled press and radio, but also in a dedicated and highly convincing campaign presented in newsreel footage. Moviegoers in Cairo, Damascus, and the refugee camps of the Gaza Strip were shown entertaining films that were carefully prepared in a Goebbels-like fashion. One movie depicted Syrian paratroopers in war maneuvers simulating the destruction of an Israeli kibbutz; in the same film, the Syrian troopers skinned a live snake and then ate the flesh. Another movie showed Egyptian assault forces practicing judo to background music that said they would liberate Jerusalem, Haifa, Yaffo, and Akko with their fists and weapons. And another showed a staged Palestinian guerrilla attack on an Israeli position in southern Israel, where masked fedayeen assaulted a heavily fortified military installation, with deadly results.

p. 9 Helena Cobban, *The Palestinian Liberation Organisation: People, Power and Politics* (London: Cambridge University Press, 1984), p. 31.

p. 9 *Ibid*, p. 24.

p. 10 Eilan Kfir, *Tzanhanim Chi'r Mutznach: Tzahal Be'Heilo Entzyklopedia Le'Tzava Ule'Bitachon* (Tel Aviv: Revivim Publishing, 1981), pp. 74–75.

p. 10 One of those "patients" was young Nayif Hawatmeh, a man who would go on to become the commander of the Democratic Front for the Liberation of Palestine, one of the most violent and hard-line Communist of all Palestinian groups. See Yuval Arnon-Ohana and Dr. Aryeh Yodfat, *Asha'f: Diyukno Shel Irgun* (Tel Aviv: Ma'ariv Library, 1985), p. 50.

p. 10 Helena Cobban, *The Palestinian Liberation Organisation*, p. 141.

p. 10 *Ibid*, 142.

p. 10 Steven Emerson and Brian Duffy, "Pan Am 103: The German Connection," *The New York Times Magazine*, March 18, 1990, p. 84.

p. 12 Guy Bechor, *Lexicon Asha'f* (Tel Aviv: Israel Ministry of Defense Publishing, 1991), p. 123.

p. 12 Sharon Segev, "*Ha'Chatifa Ha'Rishona*," *Biton Heyl Ha'Avir*, No. 63-64, July 1988, p. 100.

p. 12 There were many people inside IDF operations who were trying to work out a military solution to the PFLP hijacking, including the landing of commandos from Sayeret Mat'kal in Algiers and rescuing the hostages. There were also plans for the IDF to hijack several Arab airliners and barter off the hostages with the terrorists. See Samuel M. Katz, *The Elite* (New York: Pocket Books, 1992), p. 63.

p. 13 Jibril's part in the hijacking of Flight 426 has never been officially confirmed, although most intelligence service studies on terrorism list Jibril as a force behind Habash's operation.

p. 13 Guy Bechor, *Lexicon Asha'f*, p. 73. It must be noted that many sources have credited the July 23, 1968, hijacking to Algiers to Jibril's group within the PFLP. See William B. Quandt, Fuad Jabber, and Ann Mosely Lesch, *The Politics of Palestinian Nationalism* (Berkeley: University of California Press, 1973), p. 62.

p. 13 Steven Emerson and Brian Duffy, *The Fall of Pan Am 103: Inside the Lockerbie Investigation* (New York: G.P. Putnam's Sons, 1990), p. 112.

p. 14 Guy Bechor, *Lexicon Asha'f*, p. 73.

p. 14 Yocheved Weintraub, ed., *Irgunei Ha'Mechablim* (Tel Aviv: IDF Chief Education Officer/Israel Ministry of Defense Publishing, 1974), p. 15.

p. 14 Helena Cobban, *The Palestinian Liberation Organisation*, p. 161.

p. 14 Neil C. Livingstone and David Halevy, *Inside the PLO* (New York: William Morrow, 1990), p. 219.

p. 15 IDF spokesman's office press release, *Syria and the PLO: 1964–1982* (*Background Information*), 1983, p. 2.

p. 15 *Ibid*, p. 4.

p. 15 Middle East Watch, *Syria Unmasked: The Suppression of Human Rights by the Assad Regime* (New Haven: Yale University Press, 1991), p. 50.

p. 16 Boaz Ganor, "*Sartan U'Shmo Terror: Ha'Irgunim Ha'Palestina'im Ha'Pro-Surim,*" *Matara*, No. 13, 1990, p. 45.

p. 17 Interview with former A'man officer, May 29, 1990, Ramat Aviv, Israel.

p. 17 Claire Sterling, *The Terror Network* (New York: Berkley Books, 1982), p. 255.

p. 17 Helena Cobban, *The Palestinian Liberation Organisation*, p. 143.

p. 18 Abdallah Frangi, *The PLO and Palestine* (London: Zed Books, 1982), p. 110.

p. 18 Uri Milshtein, *Ha'Historia Shel Ha'Tzanhanim: Kerech Gimel* (Tel Aviv: Schalgi Publishing House, 1985), p. 1276.

p. 18 Samuel M. Katz, *Follow Me! A History of Israel's Military Elite* (London: Arms & Armour Press, 1989), p. 94.

p. 19 Helena Cobban, *The Palestinian Liberation Organisation*, p. 144.

p. 19 John K. Cooley, *Payback: America's Long War in the Middle East* (Washington, D.C.: Brassey's (U.S.), 1991), p. 163.

p. 19 Neil C. Livingstone and David Halevy, *Inside the PLO*, p. 203.

p. 19 William B. Quandt, Fuad Jabber, and Ann Mosely Lesch, *The Politics of Palestinian Nationalism*, p. 68.

p. 20 Most sources, such as Helena Cobban's *The Palestinian Liberation Organisation*, list the creation date of the PFLP-GC as October 1968. Guy Bechor's *Lexicon Asha'f* gives the founding date of the PFLP-GC as April 24, 1968.

p. 20 David Tal, *Inter: International Terrorism in 1989* (Jerusalem: Jaffe Center for Strategic Studies, 1990), p. 62.

p. 20 Yocheved Weintraub, ed.,*Irgunei Ha'Mechablim*, p. 31.

p. 21 Guy Bocher, *Lexicon Asha'f*, p. 23. The reader should not confuse Ahmed Jibril's nom de guerre of Abu Jihad with that of Khalil al-Wazir, the PLO's deputy commander killed in Tunis on April 16, 1988.

CHAPTER TWO

p. 23 Steven Emerson and Brian Duffy, *The Fall of Pan Am 103: Inside the Lockerbie Investigation* (New York: G.P. Putnam's Sons, 1990), p. 114.

p. 23 *Ibid.* p. 114.

p. 24 *Ibid.* p. 114.

p. 24 Brian Michael Jenkins, "Terrorist Threat to Commercial Aviation, *IDF Journal*, Spring 1989, p. 12.

p. 25 Claire Sterling, *The Terror Network* (New York: Berkley Books, 1982), p. 256.

p. 25 Interview with Israeli Intelligence Corps officer, June 1, 1991, Tel Aviv.

p. 25 U.S. Defense Intelligence Agency, *Intelligence Appraisal Libya: Terrorist Apparatus (U)*, DIAAPPR 160-81, October 15, 1981, p. 1.

p. 26 Edgar O'Ballance, *The Language of Violence: The Blood Politics of Terrorism* (San Rafael: Presidio Press, 1979), p. 70.

p. 27 Marvin G. Goldman, *El Al: Star in the Sky* (Miami: World Transport Press, 1990), p. 81.

p. 27 David Tal, *Inter: International Terrorism in 1989* (Jerusalem: Jaffe Center for Strategic Studies, 1990), p. 72.

p. 28 Claire Sterling, *The Terror Network*, p. 257.

p. 28 Edgar O'Ballance, *The Language Of Violence*, p. 79.

p. 29 Steven Emerson and Brian Duffy, *The Fall of Pan Am 103*, p. 115.

p. 29 Zeev Schiff and Raphael Rothstein, *Fedayeen: Guerrillas Against Israel* (New York: David McKay, 1972), p. 140.

p. 30 Various editors, *Tzava U'Bitachon B'* (*1968–1981*) (Tel Aviv: Revivim Publishers, 1984), p. 42. For some unexplained reason, there are numerous variations as to the actual date of this attack in countless periodicals and book accounts of Israel's war against terrorism. Several accounts list the date as May 22, 1970, while others list it as "May 1972." According to official Israeli records, the date listed in the text is accurate.

p. 30 *Ibid*, p. 42.

p. 31 Edgar O'Ballance, *Arab Guerrilla Power: 1967–72* (London: Faber and Faber, 1974), p. 112.

p. 31 Eilan Kfir, *Tzanhanim Chi'r Mutznach: Tzahal Be'Heilo Entzyklopedia Le'Tzava Ule'Bitachon* (Tel Aviv: Revivim Publishing, 1981), p. 131.

CHAPTER THREE

p. 33 Guy Bechor, *Lexicon Asha'f* (Tel Aviv: Israel Ministry of Defense Publishing, 1991), p. 113.

p. 33 United States Department of Defense, *Terrorist Group Profiles* (Washington, D.C., 1988), p. 29.

p. 33 For the best accounts of the tumultuous and bloody events leading up to full-scale civil war in Jordan, see Brigadier S.A. El-Edroos, *The Hashemite Arab Army 1908–1979* (Amman, The Publishing Committee, 1980); David Hirst, *The Gun and the Olive Branch* (London: Future Publications, 1978); John Laffin, *Fedayeen: The Arab-Israeli Dilemma* (New York: The Free Press, 1973); Peter Snow, *Hussein: A Biography* (Washington, D.C.: Robert B. Luce, 1972); and Yisgav Nakdimon, *"Ha'Melech Hussein Bikesh Siyu'a Me'Heyl Ha'Avir Ha'Yisraeli,"* *Biton Heyl Ha'Avir*, No. 65, October 1988, pp. 19, 20, 21, and 47.

p. 34 Eilan Kfir, *Tzanhanim Chi'r Mutznach: Tzahal Be'Heilo Entzyklopedia Le'Tzava Ule'Bitachon* (Tel Aviv: Revivim Publishers, 1981), pp. 113–114.

p. 34 Various editors, "Fedayeen Activity in Jordan," *Defense Intelligence Digest*, October 1970, p. 13.

p. 35 Uri Dan, *Etzba Elohim: Sodot Ha'Milchama Be'Terror* (Ramat Gan: Masada, 1976), p. 32.

p. 36 David Hirst, *The Gun and the Olive Branch*, p. 307.

p. 37 *Ibid*, p. 309; and, Yisgav Nakdimon, *"Ha'Melech Hussein*, p. 20.

p. 37 Edgar O'Ballance, *The Language of Violence: The Blood Politics of Terrorism* (San Rafael, California: Presidio Press, 1979), p. 132.

p. 38 Riad el-Rayyes and Dunia Nahas, *Guerrillas for Palestine* (New York: St. Martin's Press, 1976), p. 50.

p. 38 Various editors, *Tzava U'Bitachon B' (1968–81): Tzahal Be'Heilo Entzyklopedia Le'Tzava Ule'Bitachon* (Tel Aviv: Revivim Publishing, 1984), pp. 42–43.

p. 39 Guy Bechor, *Lexicon Asha'f*, p. 131.

p. 39 Uzi Benziman, *Sharon: An Israeli Caesar* (New York: Adama Books, 1985), p. 115; and Ron Ben-Yishai, *"Ha'Shitot Shel Sharon Lo Hayu Ovdim A'achshav," Yediot Sheva Yamim*, January 22, 1988, p. 8.

p. 39 Ron Ben-Yishai, *"Ha'Shitot,"* p. 8. For the best account of the Shin Bet's counterintelligence campaign against Palestinian terrorists in the Gaza Strip during the bloody years of 1970 and 1971, see David Ronen, *Shnat Sha'ba'k* (Tel Aviv: Ministry of Defense Publications, 1990). For a look at the PFLP-GC's unyielding influence in Israel's prison population, see Roni Daniel, *"Model 71," Matara*, No. 13, 1990, p. 5.

p. 40 Boaz Ganor, *"Beit-Kele Bitchoni: Beit Sefer Le'Terror," Matara*, No. 23, 1991, pp. 10–19.

p. 40 For a description of the Popular Struggle Front, see Guy Bechor, *Lexicon Asha'f*, pp. 121–122. For a description of the European operations, see Dr. Ariel Merari and Shlomi Elad, *The International Dimension of Palestinian Terror* (Tel Aviv: Jaffe Center for Strategic Studies, 1986).

p. 42 Uri Dan, *Etzba Elohim*, p. 35.

p. 42 Edgar O'Ballance, *The Language of Violence*, p. 131.

p. 42 Eli Cohen, *"Etzel Palestinai Be'Tisat 'El Al' Gam Kubiat 'Lego' Me'oreret Chashad," Yediot Aharonot*, March 28, 1988, p. 8.

p. 43 Edgar O'Ballance, *The Language of Violence*, p. 131.

p. 43 *Ibid.*

p. 45 Steven Emerson and Brian Duffy, *The Fall of Pan Am 103: Inside the Lockerbie Investigation* (New York: G.P. Putnam's Sons, 1990), p. 115.

p. 45 Edgar O'Ballance, *The Language of Violence*, p. 132.

p. 46 Steven Emerson and Brian Duffy, *The Fall of Pan Am 103*, p. 116.

p. 46 Claire Sterling, *The Terror Network*, p. 258.

p. 46 Shapi Gabay, *"Me'Tikei Asha'f: Kach Chisel Ha'Mossad Et Abu Shrar,"* *Ma'ariv*, September 18, 1987, p. 5.

p. 47 John Moody, "Keeping Fear at Bay," *Time* magazine, January 6, 1986, p. 28.

p. 47 Edgar O'Ballance, *The Language of Violence*, p. 165.

p. 48 Dr. Ariel Merari, *The International Dimension*, p. 132.

p. 48 Chen Kotas, "*Ha'Met Ve'Ha'Chai*," *Bamachane*, January 27, 1987, p. 19.

p. 48 Guy Bechor, *Lexicon Asha'f*, p. 247.

p. 49 Dr. Ariel Merari, *The International Dimension*, p. 133.

p. 49 Claire Sterling, *The Terror Network*, p. 257.

p. 50 *Ibid.*

p. 51 For the most comprehensive—and *accurate*—account of the 1973 Yom Kippur War, see Chaim Herzog, *The War of Atonement* (London: Weidenfeld & Nicolson, 1975).

p. 52 Oded Granot, *Heyl Ha'Mode'in: Tzahal Be'Heilo Entzyklopedia Le'Tzava Ule'Bitachon* (Tel Aviv: Revivim Publishers, 1981), p. 105.

p. 52 Ian Black and Benny Morris, *Israel's Secret Wars* (London: Hamish Hamilton, 1991), p. 293.

p. 52 For a complete history of the Soviet Union's relationship with the various international terrorist groups, see Roberta Goren, *The Soviet Union and Terrorism* (London: George Allen & Unwin, 1984).

p. 53 Claire Sterling, *The Terror Network*, p. 263.

p. 53 Joseph S. Bermudez, Jr., "The Syrian Tank Battalion," *Armor*, November-December 1984, p. 17; and Jerry Asher, with Eric Hammel, *Duel for the Golan: The 100-Hour Battle that Saved Israel* (New York: William Morrow, 1987), p. 54.

p. 54 Edgar O'Ballance, *The Language Of Violence*, p. 230.

p. 55 Motta Har-Lev, *Golani Sheli* (Tel Aviv: Avivim Publishing, 1991), p. 151.

p. 55 Various editors, *Tzava U'Bitachon B'*, pp. 134–135.

p. 56 *Ibid*, p. 134.

p. 56 For an examination of the Ma'alot Massacre, see Samuel M. Katz, *The Elite* (New York: Pocket Books, 1992), pp. 180–188.

p. 57 Edgar O'Ballance, *The Language Of Violence*, p. 230.

p. 57 *Ibid*, p. 230.

p. 57 Steven Emerson and Brian Duffy, *The Fall of Pan Am 103*, p. 116.

p. 58 Albert Parry, *Terrorism: From Robespierre to Arafat* (New York: The Vanguard Press, 1976), p. 574.

p. 59 Guy Bechor, *Lexicon Asha'f*, p. 123.

p. 59 *Ibid*, p. 131.

CHAPTER FOUR

p. 61 According to an IDF report provided to journalists by the IDF Spokesman's office in September 1985, the Ein Sehab facility is the PFLP-GC's largest training and operations base, and its principal headquarters in the region.

p. 61 Various editors, *"Emtza'im Metuchkamim Be'Yadei Ha'Mechablim,"* *Ma'ariv*, June 1, 1990, p. 3.

p. 62 These raids included Operation Basket, the June 21, 1972, kidnapping of five high-ranking Syrian intelligence officers in southern Lebanon by *Sayeret Mat'kal*; Operation Turmoil 4 Expanded, the September 17, 1972, large-scale purification of southern Lebanese villages harboring Palestinian terrorists following the Munich Olympics Massacre; Operation Hood 54-55, the February 21, 1973, amphibious commando raid against PFLP and Black September training camps in the northern Lebanese city of Tripoli; and, of course, the April 9, 1973, Operation Spring of Youth. For the best description of Israel's deep-penetration raids against Lebanon, see Uri Milshtein, *Ha'Historia Shel Ha'Tzanhanim Kerech Daled* (Tel Aviv: Schalgi Publishing House, 1987); Yosef Argaman, *Ze Haya Sodi Be'Yoter* (Tel Aviv: Ministry of Defense Publishing, 1990); Samuel M. Katz, *Follow Me! A History of Israel's Military Elite* (London: Arms & Armour Press, 1989); and Eilan Kfir, *Tzanhanim Chi'r Mutznach: Tzahal Be'Heilo Entzyklopedia Le'Tzava Ule'Bitachon* (Tel Aviv: Revivim Publishers, 1981).

p. 63 Jillian Becker, *The PLO: The Rise and Fall of the Palestine Liberation Organization* (London: Weidenfeld & Nicolson, 1984), p. 116.

p. 64 Janet Wallach and John Wallach, *Arafat: In the Eyes of the Beholder* (Rocklin, California: 1992), p. 263; and Joseph G. Chami and Gerard Castoriades, *Days of Tragedy, Jours de Misère: Lebanon/Liban 75-76* (Nicosia, Cyprus: J. Chami—G. Castoriades, 1978), p. 36.

p. 64 *Ibid*, p. 384.

p. 65 Steven Posner, *Israel Undercover: Secret Warfare and Hidden Diplomacy in the Middle East* (Syracuse, New York: Syracuse University Press, 1987), p. 41.

p. 65 Guy Bechor, *Lexicon Asha'f* (Tel Aviv: Ministry of Defense Publishing, 1991), p. 65.

p. 66 Robert Fisk, *Pity the Nation: The Abduction of Lebanon* (New York: Touchstone/Simon & Schuster, 1990), p. 79.

p. 66 IDF spokesman, *Palestinian International Terrorist Activities 1968–86* (Tel Aviv: IDF spokesman's office, 1986), p. 19. In *The International Dimension of Palestinian Terrorism*, the comprehensive study of terrorist acts perpetrated by the various Palestinian groups overseas and published by the prestigious Jaffe Center for Strategic Studies at Tel Aviv University, Dr. Ariel Merari and Shlomi Elad attribute the September 4, 1976, hijacking to the Palestine Liberation Front, an indication that perhaps the aircraft seizure was perpetrated by PFLP-GC gunmen loyal to Abu A'bbas and eager to perform an action that would weaken Jibril's organization. Indeed, 1976 was a year that saw the Lebanese civil war reach ferocious dimensions, and also saw the various Palestinian terrorist factions known for their overseas exploits attempt to bring attention away from the civil war by executing spectacular feats directed against Israel. These included the January 25, 1976, abortive SA-7 attack on an El Al airliner in Nairobi by Wadi Haddad Faction terrorists; the June 28, 1976, hijacking of an Air France jetliner to Entebbe by Wadi Haddad Faction terrorists; the abortive attack on El Al passengers in Istanbul on August 11, 1976, by PFLP terrorists; and the November 17, 1976, seizure of the Intercontinental Hotel in Amman by Abu Nidal gunmen.

p. 66 For the best and most insightful examination of the Lebanese civil war, see Robert Fisk, *Pity the Nation: The Abduction Of Lebanon* (New York: Touchstone Books/Simon & Schuster, 1990); Naomi Joy Weinberger, *Syrian Intervention in Lebanon* (New York: Oxford University Press, 1986); Jonathan C. Randal, *Going All the Way: Christian Warlords, Israeli Adventurers, and the War in Lebanon* (New York: Vintage Books, 1984); Lina Mikdadi Tabbara, *Survival in Beirut: A Diary of Civil War* (London: Onyx Press, 1977); and Joseph G. Chami and Gerard Castoriades, *Days of Tragedy, Jours de Misère: Lebanon/Liban 75-76* (Nicosia, Cyprus: J. Chami—G. Castoriades, 1978).

p. 67 Joseph G. Chami and Gerard Castoriades, *Day of Tragedy*, p. 387.

p. 67 Guy Bechor, *Lexicon Asha'f*, p. 292.

p. 68 For a discussion of the relationship between Ali Hassan Salameh and Bashir Gemayel, see Michael Bar-Zohar and Eitan Haber, *The Quest for the Red Prince* (New York: William Morrow, 1983), p. 209. For a mention of their CIA connections see Yossi Melman and Dan Raviv, *The Imperfect Spies: The History of Israeli Intelligence* (London: Sidgwick & Jackson, 1989), p. 286; and Bob Woodward, *Veil: The Secret Wars of the CIA 1981–1987* (New York: Pocket Books, 1987), p. 222.

p. 68 Albert Parry, *Terrorism: From Robespierre to Arafat* (New York: Vanguard Press, 1976), p. 465.

p. 68 Robert Fisk, *Pity the Nation*, p. 83.

p. 69 Joseph S. Bermudez, Jr., *North Korea: The Terrorist Connection* (London: Janes, 1988), p. 111.

p. 70 Jillian Becker, *The PLO*, p. 133.

p. 70 For North Vietnamese involvement with the Palestinian terrorist groups based in Lebanon, see Raphael Israeli, *PLO in Lebanon: Selected Documents* (London: Weidenfeld & Nicolson, 1984), pp. 53, 79, 82, and 293.

p. 71 Daniel Asher, *Ha'fa'alat Koach Me'Shurian Behar: Ha'Me'urevet Ha'Tzva'it Ha'Surit Be'Levanon (1975–1976)* (Tel Aviv: Ministry Of Defense Publishing, 1985), p. 51.

p. 71 Jillian Becker, *The PLO*, p. 133.

p. 71 Ian Black and Benny Morris, *Israel's Secret Wars* (London: Hamish Hamilton, 1990), p. 366.

p. 72 Guy Bechor, *Lexicon Asha'f*, p. 133.

p. 73 Jillian Becker, *The PLO*, p. 199.

p. 73 Robert Fisk, *Pity the Nation*, p. 117.

p. 73 Claire Sterling, *The Terror Network*, p. 261.

p. 74 Jonathan C. Randal, *Going All the Way*, p. 103; and Thomas L. Friedman, *From Beirut to Jerusalem* (New York: Farrar, Straus & Giroux, 1989), p. 60.

p. 74 Helena Cobban, *The Palestinian Liberation Organisation: People, Power and Politics* (Cambridge: Cambridge University Press, 1984), p. 162.

p. 76 Yechiam Fadan, ed., "*Bitachon Yisrael—40 Shana Luach Iru'im*," *Skira Chodshit*, No. 3–4, Volume 35, April 25, 1988, p. 77.

p. 76 *Ibid.*

p. 76 Steven Emerson and Brian Duffy, *The Fall of Pan Am 103: Inside the Lockerbie Investigation* (New York: G. P. Putnam's Sons, 1990), p. 118; and Ze'ev Schiff, "*Heskem Metaskel*," *Ha'Aretz*, May 21, 1985, p. 9.

p. 77 ABC News *Nightline*, "Israeli Prisoner Deal: Too High a Price?" May 23, 1985, Show #1044.

CHAPTER FIVE

p. 78 Edgar O'Ballance, *Language of Violence: The Blood Politics of Terrorism* (San Rafael, California: Presidio Press, 1979), p. 238.

p. 78 Yechiam Fadan, ed., "*Bitachon Yisrael—40 Shana Luach Iru'im*," *Skira Chodshit*, No. 3–4, Volume 35, April 25, 1988, p. 74.

p. 79 Jens Møller, "*Beviser Mod Terror-Gruppe I Sverige*," *Politiken*, July 19, 1980, p. 2.; Tim Johnson, "Planlagde Terrorist-angreb I København," *Politiken*, July 16, 1980, p. 3; and IDF Spokesman, *Palestinian International Terrorist Activities 1968–86* (Tel Aviv: IDF Spokesman's office, 1986), p. 26.

p. 79 United States Department of Defense, *Terrorist Group Profiles* (Washington, D.C.: U.S. Government Printing Office, 1988), p. 26; and various editors, *Inter: International Terrorism in 1989* (Jerusalem: Jaffe Center for Strategic Studies, 1990), p. 86.

p. 79 Claire Sterling, *The Terror Network* (New York, Berkley Books, 1981), p. 261.

p. 80 Following the war, the IDF displayed much of this material in a three-week-long display in Tel Aviv's Exhibition Gardens. Many of the North Korean crates were displayed intact.

p. 80 Claire Sterling, *The Terror Network*, p. 262.

p. 81 Various editors, "*Shevu'on Italki: 'Le'Asha'f Yesh Heyl Ha'Avir She'bo 10 Metosei Mig,'*" *Yisrael Shelanu*, May 14, 1987, p. 11; and Guy Bechor, *Lexicon Asha'f*, p. 174.

p. 81 For a mention of PFLP-GC personnel undergoing aerial instruction and service in Libya and in Chad, see Defense Intelligence Agency (DIA) report on the PFLP-GC; various editors, *Inter: International Terrorism*, p. 68; and Steven Emerson and Brian Duffy, "Pan Am 103: The German Connection," *The New York Times Magazine*, March 18, 1990, p. 84.

p. 82 In an interview, an American intelligence analyst claimed that the first antiaircraft missiles the Afghan Mujahadin received were SA-7 Grails the Palestinians sold or gave them; apparently, Muslim bonds were stronger than ideological or political ties to the Soviets. According to these unnerving facts, the Soviets issued directives to their Arab state allies that the Palestinians were not to be equipped with generous supplies of these sophisticated missiles. Several Soviet transport planes flying VIP tours of the Afghan battlefield were reported to have been blown out of the sky in 1980 and 1981 by SAMs once owned by the Palestinians.

p. 83 Ian Black and Benny Morris, *Israel's Secret Wars* (London: Hamish Hamilton, 1990), p. 203.

p. 83 Ze'ev Schiff and Ehud Ya'ari, *Israel's Lebanon War* (New York: Simon & Schuster, 1984), p. 11.

p. 84 *Ibid*, p. 33.

p. 84 *Ibid*, p. 37.

p. 85 General Dr. Mustafa Tlas, ed., *The Israeli Invasion to Lebanon* (Tel Aviv: Israel Ministry of Defense Publishing, 1991), p. 458.*

p. 85 Helena Cobban, *The Palestinian Liberation Organisation: People, Power and Politics* (Cambridge: Cambridge University Press, 1984), p. 162.

p. 86 Richard A. Gabriel, *Operation Peace for Galilee: The Israeli-PLO War in Lebanon* (New York: Hill & Wang, 1984), p. 65.

p. 87 For the most accurate account of the amphibious operation, see Naval Captain (Res.) Mike Eldar, "The Amphibious Assault at Sidon," *IDF Journal*, Vol. III, No. 3, July 1987, pp. 47–51. For information concerning the disposition and designation of the units involved, see Richard A. Gabriel, *Operation Peace for Galilee*, p. 48.

p. 87 For the best account of Israel's blitz on the Syrian SAMs in Lebanon's Bekaa Valley, see Arieh Avneri, *Ha'Mahaluma* (Tel Aviv: Revivim Publishing Ltd., 1983); and Eliezer "Cheeta" Cohen and Tzvi Lavi, *Ha'Shamayim Einam Ha'Gvul* (Tel Aviv: Sifriat Ma'ariv, 1990).

p. 88 Although this has never been confirmed as a written matter of fact, the political desire to place the Gemayel clan in the Lebanese presidential palace in Ba'abda was clear. For the best description of the political relationship between the Israelis, especially Defense Minister Sharon,

---

* A Hebrew translation of the original Hebrew published in Syria by the current Syrian defense minister and former military chief of staff.

and the Christian Phalangists, see Shimon Shiffer, *Kadur Sheleg: Sodot Milchemet Levanon* (Edanim Publishers, Yediot Aharonot Books, 1984).

p. 88 Rashid Khalidi, *Under Siege: P.L.O. Decision Making During the 1982 War* (New York: Columbia University Press, 1986), p. 180.

p. 89 Ze'ev Klein, ed., *Ha'Milchama Be'Terror: U'Mediniut Ha'Bitachon Shel Yisrael Be'Shanim 1979–1988* (Tel Aviv: Revivim, 1988), p. 73; and Neil C. Livingstone and David Halevy, *Inside the PLO* (New York: William Morrow, Inc., 1990), p. 264.

p. 89 Robert Fisk, *Pity the Nation: The Abduction of Lebanon* (New York: Touchstone Books/Simon & Schuster, 1990), p. 568.

p. 89 Ze'ev Schiff and Ehud Ya'ari, *Israel's Lebanon War*, p. 84.

p. 90 Helena Cobban, *The Palestinian Liberation Organisation*, p. 163; and Raphael Israeli, *PLO in Lebanon*, pp. 170–171.

p. 90 Major-General Yoram "Ya-Ya" Yair, *Iti Me'Levanon: Chativat Ha'Tzanhanim Be'Milchemet Sheleg* (Tel Aviv: Ministry Of Defense Publishing, 1990), pp. 53–70.

p. 90 Rashid Khalidi, *Under Siege*, p. 82.

p. 91 United States Department of Defense, *Terrorist Group Profiles*, p. 27.

p. 91 Raphael Israeli, *PLO in Lebanon*, p. 297.

CHAPTER SIX

p. 92 Ze'ev Schiff and Ehud Ya'ari, *Israel's Lebanon War* (New York: Simon & Schuster, 1984), p. 174.

p. 93 Amos Lavo, *"I'm Bo Ha'Shkacha," Yediot Sheva Yamim*, June 10, 1987, p. 18.

p. 93 *Ibid*, p. 20.

p. 93 *Ibid*.

p. 94 Sarit Yeshai-Levi, *"Shavui," Chadashot Shel Shabbat*, April 22, 1988, p. 35.

p. 95 *Ibid*, p. 35.

p. 95 Ze'ev Klein, ed., *Ha'Milchama Be'Terror: U'Mediniut Ha'Bitachon Shel Yisrael Be'Shanim 1979–1988* (Tel Aviv: Revivim, 1988), p. 124.

p. 97 Dr. Reuven Gal, *A Portrait of the Israeli Soldier* (New York: Greenwood Press, 1986), pp. 143–165; and Ariel Sharon, with David Chanoff, *Warrior: An Autobiography* (New York: Simon & Schuster, 1989), p. 58.

p. 97 Eilan Kfir, *Tzanhanim Chi'r Mutznach: Tzahal Be'Heilo Entzyklopedia Le'Tzava Ule'Bitachon* (Tel Aviv: Revivim, 1981), p. 39.

p. 97 Yosef Argaman, *Ze Haya Sodi Be'Yoter* (Tel Aviv: Ministry of Defense Publishing, 1990), pp. 31–42.

p. 98 Interview with Major-General (Res.) Moshe Nativ, New York City, January 1988.

p. 99 Ze'ev Klein, ed., *Ha'Milchama Be'Terror*, p. 124.

p. 99 Barbara Sofer and David Rudge, "Missing Sons," *Jerusalem Post International Edition*, week ending June 29, 1991, p. 9.

p. 99 Ze'ev Klein, ed., *Ha'Milchama Be'Terror*, p. 124.

p. 100 Interview with Brigadier-General Gabi Last, Border Guard headquarters, Lod, January 1986.

p. 100 Arieh Merinski, "*Im Jibril Lo Yeshachrer Et Ha'Shelanu, Ish Lo Yetze Chai Me'Ansar*," *Yediot 24 Sha'ot*, April 19, 1989, p. 4.

p. 100 *Ibid.*

p. 101 *Ibid*, p. 5.

p. 101 *Ibid.*

p. 101 According to Lieutenant-Colonel Y., an intelligence corps officer and an expert in Palestinian terrorism, during a radio interview on *Galei Tzahal*, April 22, 1984.

p. 102 Boaz Ganor, "*Beit Kele Bitchoni—Beit Sefer Le'Terror*," *Matara*, No. 23, 1991, p. 13. For the most insightful view of Israel's prison system, see David Perry, *Yoman Ramle: Reshimot Shel Mefaked Kele* (Tel Aviv: Sifriat Poalim Publishing House, 1986).

p. 103 Arieh Merinski, "*Im Jibril Lo Yeshachrer*," p. 19.

p. 103 Sarit Yeshai-Levi, "*Shavui*," p. 37.

p. 103 Yosef Walter, "*6 Shveyei Tzahal She'Be'Yedei Asha'f Huchlafu be-4500 Mechablim*," *Ma'ariv*, November 24, 1983, p. 1.

p. 104 Colonel Yehuda Weinreb, "Prisoners," *IDF Journal*, Spring 1988, p. 41.

p. 104 Various editors, "*Ha'Mechablim Me'Irgun Jibril Zamemu Le'Fotzetz Et Migdal-Shalom Ule'Vatze'a Pigu'im Be'A'arim*," *Davar*, January 21, 1985, p. 1.

p. 104 Eliezer Whartman, "How Many More Killers Will Now Go Free?" *Jerusalem Post International Edition*, week ending September 9, 1989, p. 9; and Ze'ev Klein, *Ha'Milchama Be'Terror*, p. 127.

p. 105 Various editors, "Enough Is Enough," *Time* magazine, August 14, 1989, p. 20; and, Shapi Gabay, "*Ben Achot Jibril*" Lo Yiyachen Shalom Bli Ha'Palestina'im Me'Haifa, Yaffo Ve'Lod," *Ma'ariv*, May 21, 1985, p. 15.

p. 105 Steven Emerson and Brian Duffy, *The Fall of Pan Am 103: Inside the Lockerbie Investigation* (New York: G. P. Putnam's Sons, 1990), p. 118.

p. 106 Eiran Shenker and Baruch Ron, "*Sof Tov, Ha'Kol Tov?*" *Bamachane*, May 30, 1985, p. 4.

p. 107 Yosef Walter, "Jibril Ratza Tzilumim Shel Mishpachot Ha'Shvuyim," *Ma'ariv*, p. 2; and Steven Emerson and Brian Duffy, *The Fall of Pan Am 103*, p. 119.

p. 107 *Ibid*, p. 118.

p. 107 Eiran Shenker and Baruch Ron, "*Sof Tov*," p. 4.

p. 108 *Ibid.*

p. 108 *Ibid*, p. 6.

p. 109 *Ibid.*

p. 111 Yehuda Goren, Meir Rarevuni, and Ezra Yaniv, "*Ha'Mechablim*

She'Shuchraru Hitkablu Be'Fantaziot Be'Kfarim A'ravim," Ma'ariv, May 22, 1985, p. 2.

p. 111 Eliezer Whartman, "How Many More Killers," p. 10.

p. 111 Various editors, "Boeing Ha'Shichrur," Biton Heyl Ha'Avir, No. 45, Volume 146, June 1985, p. 3; and Eiran Shenker and Baruch Ron, "Sof Tov," p. 6.

p. 112 Eilan Becher, "Me'Shuchrarei Jibril Hinhigu Et Knufiat Ha'Retzach Be'Mizrach Yerushalayim," Ma'ariv, May 6, 1986, p. 9.

p. 112 Yehuda Litani, "Nidbach Nosaf Le'Terror," Ha'Aretz, May 22, 1985, p. 7.

p. 112 Yosef Walter, "Naasor Ha'Meshuchrarim Im Yichtafu Chayalim," Ma'ariv, May 22, 1985, p. 2.

p. 113 According to Barbara Sofer and David Rudge in their article "Missing Sons," (Jerusalem Post International Edition, week ending June 29, 1991, p. 10), in a letter intercepted by West German security officials in 1988, Nizar Hindawi, a Syrian agent with loose ties to Ahmed Jibril, convicted in London of attempting to blow an El Al airliner out of the sky, wrote to his brother in German custody for a bombing that he hoped he would soon be exchanged for the "two soldiers held by Jibril." Ahmed Jibril himself said that three Israeli servicemen were still alive. See Ron Ben-Yishai, "Jibril: 3 Shvuyim Chaim; Yisrael Doreshet Hochachot," Yediot Aharonot, August 14, 1991, p. 1.

CHAPTER SEVEN

p. 114 Tali Zelinger, "Heyl Ha'Avir Hiftzitz B'sisei Irguno Shel Jibril Be'Biqa'at Ha'Levanon," Davar, October 28, 1985, p. 1.

p. 114 Steven Emerson and Brian Duffy, The Fall of Pan Am 103: Inside the Lockerbie Investigation (New York: G.P. Putnam's Sons, 1990), p. 119.

p. 115 Christopher Dobson and Ronald Payne, Counterattack: The West's Battle Against the Terrorists (New York: Facts on File, 1982), p. 88.

p. 115 Yossi Melman and Dan Raviv, The Imperfect Spies: The History of Israeli Intelligence (London: Sidgwick & Jackson, 1989), p. 204.

p. 116 Interview with Israeli National Police Border Guard officer Zichron Ya'akov, January 1986. Also see Jillian Becker, The PLO: The Rise and Fall of the Palestine Liberation Organization (London: Weidenfeld & Nicolson, 1984), p. 143, p. 266.

p. 116 In many Shiite villages, the entrance of the advancing Israeli armored columns signaled the first signs of freedom that the villagers had experienced since 1970. Many international network news teams covering the initial Israeli invasion were shocked to see elderly Shiite women standing on the banks of roads and throwing flowers and rice at IDF tank crews; many Israeli commanders were even invited to attend village Chaflas, or celebration and feasts, in thanks for liberation.

p. 117 Arieh Egozi, *"Ha'Mechasel," Yediot Aharonot 24 Sha'ot,* February 18, 1992, p. 1.

p. 117 U.S. Department of Defense, *Terrorist Group Profiles* (Washington, D.C., U. S. Government Printing Office, 1988), p. 15.

p. 117 Shapi Gabay, *"Tnu'at Amal Ishra Le'Jibril La'Chzor Le'Bsisav Be'Drom Levanon," Ma'ariv,* December 4, 1985, p. 1.

p. 118 For the number of PFLP-GC killed, see Shapi Gabay, *"Tnu'at Amal Ishra,"* p. 9. For a discussion of men and equipment captured, see a declassified DIA document dated 12/12/85, pages 0060-0061, from the U.S. Defense Attaché's office in the Tel Aviv embassy to the headquarters of the DIA, Washington, D.C. The DIA document, it should be noted, was labeled as an information report, and not as evaluated intelligence.

p. 118 *Ibid,* p. 0061.

p. 119 Samuel M. Katz, *Guards Without Frontiers: Israel's War Against Terrorism* (London: Arms & Armour Press, 1990), pp. 53–67.

p. 119 Michael Bar-Zohar and Eitan Haber, *The Quest for Red Prince* (New York: William Morrow, 1983), pp. 215–222.

p. 119 Yechiam Fadan, *"Bitachon Yisrael—40 Shana Luach Iru'im," Shira Hodshit,* No 3–4, Volume 35, April 25, 1988, p. 89.

p. 119 Yossi Melman and Dan Raviv, *The Imperfect Spies,* p. 34.

p. 120 *Ibid.*

p. 121 In his book *By Way of Deception: The Making and Unmaking of a Mossad Officer* (New York: St. Martin's Press, 1990), failed Mossad agent-turned-telltale-author Victor Ostrovsky claims that he was in a Nicosia, Cyprus, hotel room that fateful February day, relaying a signal to IDF/Navy missile boats moored off Cypriot shores, which would, in turn, relay the coded coordinates of the plane bearing Jibril to IAF headquarters so that fighters could be scrambled for the intercept. It is impossible to confirm his personal claim, however, and it should be treated as suspect at best. For an intelligence officer given so sensitive a counterterrorist assignment, Ostrovsky makes several factual errors no operatives "in the know" could possibly make: He claims that Jibril was responsible for the *Achille Lauro* affair: he wasn't. The Abu A'bbas Faction of the PLF perpetrated the operation. He also claimed that Ahmed Jibril was the reason Lieutenant-Colonel Oliver North, a senior staff member of the White House National Security Council and the eventual Iran-Contra fall guy, was forced to install a sophisticated security system outside his suburban home. This too is false. Lieutenant-Colonel North was forced to take extra protective measures after being threatened by Abu Nidal.

p. 121 Ian Black and Benny Morris, *Israel's Secret Wars: The Untold History of Israeli Intelligence* (London: Hamish Hamilton, 1991), p. 434; and Steven Emerson and Brian Duffy, *The Fall of Pan Am 103: Inside the Lockerbie Investigation* (New York: G.P. Putnam's Sons, 1990), p. 119.

p. 121 For discussion of the squadron's notification, see Ariel Golar and Elina'ar Ben-A'akiva, *"Kach Yiratnu Et Ha'Gulf Stream Ha'Luvi,"* *Biton Heyl Ha'Avir*, No. 50-51, pp. 151–152), April 1986, p. 14. For the squadron being identified as an F-16 squadron, see Yossi Melman and Dan Raviv, *The Imperfect Spies*, p. 34.

p. 122 Ariel Golar and Elina'ar Ben-A'akiva, *"Kach Yiratnu Et Ha'Gulf Stream Ha'Luvi,"* p. 15.

p. 122 *Ibid.*

p. 122 Victor Ostrovsky and Claire Hoy, *By Way of Deception: The Making and Unmaking of a Mossad Officer* (New York: St. Martin's Press, 1990), p. 170.

p. 122 Shapi Gabay, et al., *"Habash: A'amadeti Latus I'm O'zrav Shel Abu Nidal Be'Matos She'Yurat,"* *Ma'ariv*, February 5, 1986, p. 9.

p. 122 *Ibid*, p. 1.

p. 123 *Ibid.*

p. 124 Rod Nordland and Ray Wilkinson, "Inside Terror, Inc.," *Newsweek*, April 7, 1986, p. 26.

p. 124 *Ibid.*

p. 124 ABC News Nightline, "Terrorism: Syrian Involvement," Show #1415, October 24, 1986, p. 2.

p. 125 Yochanan Lahav, *"Mechabel A'ravi Hafach Et Chaverato Le'Ptzatza Chaya,"* *Yediot Aharonot*, April 18, 1986, p. 1.

p. 125 *Ibid.*

p. 126 ABC News Nightline, "Terrorism: Syrian Involvement," p. 3.

p. 126 *Ibid.*

p. 126 Ian Black and Benny Morris, *Israel's Secret Wars*, p. 435.

p. 126 Human Rights Watch, *Syria Unmasked: The Suppression of Human Rights by the Assad Regime* (New Haven, Conn: Yale University Press, 1991), p. 51.

p. 127 Bill Smolowe, "Questions About a Damascus Connection," *Time*, October 20, 1986, p. 53.

p. 127 Yochanan Lahav, *"Ha'Shagrir Ha'Suri A'lul Le'Shalem Be'Rosho,"* *Yediot Aharonot 24 Sha'ot*, October 26, 1986, p. 2.

p. 128 Interview, New York City, January 3, 1987.

p. 129 Yochanan Lahav, *"Ha'Shagrir Ha'Suri,"* p. 1.

p. 129 U. S. Department of Defense, *Terrorist Group Profiles*, p. 9.

p. 129 Guy Bechor, *Lexicon Asha'f* (Tel Aviv: Ministry of Defense Publishing, 1991), p. 51.

CHAPTER EIGHT

p. 131 Interview with Border Guard superintendent Nachum Mordechai, northern Israel, January 11, 1986.

p. 132 Interview with a Druze Border Guard tracker, Sergeant-Major Y.,* January 11, 1986.

p. 132 Sigal Buchris, *"Ka'ashe Le'Ta'er Ma'Haya Koreh Eilu,"* *Bein Galim*, No. 180, April 1990, p. 47.

p. 133 Shani Payis, *"Eize Chag Yachol Haya Le'hiot Lanu,"* *Bein Galim*, No. 182, January 1991, p. 8.

p. 133 Various editors, *"Emtza'aim Metuchkamim Beyadei Ha'Mechablim,"* *Ma'ariv*, June 1, 1990, p. 3.

p. 133 Various editors, *"Mize Shana Yadua'a She'Jibril Mefateach Ve'Boneh Gilshonei-Avir,"* *Yisrael Shelanu*, December 4, 1987, p. 4.

p. 134 Neil C. Livingstone and David Halevy, *Inside the PLO:* (New York: William Morrow, 1990), p. 251.

p. 134 *Ibid*, p. 252.

p. 135 Uzi Machnayami, *"Ha'Mechablim Hitamnu Be'Hatasat Ha'Galshanim Be'Bsisam She'Ba'Suria,"* *Yediot Aharonot*, November 29, 1987, p. 2.

p. 135 *Ibid*.

p. 135 Haim A. Raviv, *"Me'Achorei Ha'Dvarim,"* *Bamachane*, December 2, 1987, p. 8.

p. 135 Or Kashti, *"Ha'Chashash: Chadira Avirit,"* *Bamachane*, October 9, 1991, p. 11.

p. 136 Uzi Machnayami, *"Ha'Mechablim Hitamnu*, p. 2.

p. 136 Shapi Gabai, *"Asha'f: Ha'Terror Ha'Shmaymi,"* *Ma'ariv Sof Shavu'a*, January 19, 1990, p. 20.

p. 137 Uzi Machnayami, *"Ha'Mechablim Hitamnu,"* p. 2.

p. 137 Various editors, *"Tatzlum Acharon Lifnei Ha'Yetzia Le'Pigu'a Be'Galil,"* *Yediot Aharonot*, December 4, 1987, p. 3.

p. 138 *Ibid*, p. 2.

p. 139 For a description of the RPVs, especially in Lebanon, see Danny Shalom, *Kol Metosei Heyl Ha'Avir* (Tel Aviv: Ba'Avir Aviation Publications, 1990), p. 144; and Eliezer "Cheetah" Cohen and Tzvi Lavi, *Ha'Shamayim Einam Ha'Gvul: Sipuro Shel Heyl Ha'Avir* (Tel Aviv: Ma'ariv Book Guild, 1990), pp. 604–633.

p. 139 Yonah Alexander, "Syria: Still a Terror Master of All These Years," *Jerusalem Post International Edition*, week ending January 12, 1991, p. 10. The article by esteemed professor Alexander also claims that Rifa'at Assad and the various Palestinian groups under Syrian control main-

* Identity is concealed for security considerations.

tain intimate business dealings and drug-trafficking connections with the Sicilian Mafia and the Colombian Medellin drug cartel. The article continued to claim that a remarkable 20 percent of the heroin illegally distributed into the United States comes from the Syrian-controlled Bekaa Valley. There are also claims that the Syrian drug fields in the Bekaa Valley are cultivated and protected by PFLP-GC (and as Sa'iqa) personnel. See James Adams, *The Financing of Terror* (New York: Simon & Schuster, 1986), p. 232.

p. 139 Various editors, *"Ma Be'Emet Kara Be'Leil Ha'Galshanim,"* *Yisrael Shelanu*, December 4, 1987, p. 2.

p. 140 *Ibid.*

p. 141 Various editors, *"Be'Rega'a Ha'Acharon: Milchemet A'atzabim Be'Mechablim,"* *Biton Heyl Ha'Avir*, No. 60 (161), November 1987, p. 14.

p. 142 Emanuel Rosen, *"11 Ha'Sha'ot Shel Leil Ha'Galshanim Be'Galil,"* *Ma'ariv Shabbat*, November 27, 1987, p. 3.

p. 142 Eitan Mor, *"A'adif Haya Le'Hiraheg, Amar Ha'Shin Gimel, Ke'She'Nishlach Le'Kele Ve'Paratz Be'Bechi,"* *Yediot Aharonot*, March 28, 1988, p. 3.

p. 142 Thomas L. Friedman, "Syria-Based Group Says It Staged Israel Raid," *The New York Times*, November 27, 1987, p. A14.

p. 143 Emanuel Rosen, *"11 Ha'Sha'ot Shel Leil Ha'Galshanim Be'Galil*, p. 3.

p. 143 Steven Emerson and Brian Duffy, *The Fall of Pan Am 103: Inside the Lockerbie Investigation* (New York: G.P. Putnam's Sons, 1990), p. 119.

p. 144 Danny Sadeh, *"Ha'Chayalim Sichku Shesh Besh, U'Pitom Hitchilu Ha'Yeriot,"* *Yediot Shabbat*, November 27, 1987, p. 3; and see Various editors, *"Be'Rega'a Ha'Acharon,"* p. 14.

p. 144 Emanuel Rosen, *"11 Ha'Sha'ot Shel Leil Ha'Galshanim Be'Galil*, p. 3.

p. 145 Merav Arlozorov, *"Lefachot Ha'Layla Hem Lo Yehyu Levad,"* *Bamachane*, December 2, 1987, p. 5.

p. 145 Thomas L. Friedman, "Syria-Based Group Says It Staged Israel Raid," *The New York Times*, p. A14.

p. 146 Various editors, *"Mustafa Tlas: 'Siya' anu Le'Hatkafat Ha'Galshanim,"* *Yisrael Shelanu*, December 10, 1987, p. 5.

p. 146 Various editors, "Death From the Skies," *Time* magazine, December 7, 1987, p. 33.

p. 146 Jonathan Broder, "Shamir Blames Syria for Raid," *New York Daily News*, November 27, 1987, p. 3.

p. 147 Shapi Gabai, *"Asha'f: Ha'Terror,"* p. 20.

p. 147 Various editors, *"Kibalnu Hora'a Lo La'Tkof Yishuvim Ezrachim,"* *Yediot Aharonot*, December 4, 1987, p. 4.

p. 148 Ze'ev Schiff and Ehud Ya'ari, *Intifada* (New York: Simon & Schuster, 1989), p. 77.

p. 148 *Ibid*, pp. 17-18.

p. 150 Robert Rosenberg, "Intifadeh," *Penthouse*, May 1988, p. 140.

p. 150 Yonah Alexander and Dennis A. Pluchinsky, ed., *European Terrorism: Today and Tomorrow* (Washington, D.C.: Brassey's (U.S.), 1992), p. 71.

p. 151 Sharon Sadeh, *"Gam Hizbollah Rochshim Gilshonim,"* *Bamachane*, October 25, 1989, p. 5; and Shma'aya Kider, *"Kafrisin: Mercaz L'Aspakat Gilshonim Le'Mechablim,"* *Ma'ariv*, May 28, 1990, p. 2.

p. 151 Dror Merom, *"Heyl Ha'Avir—Ha'Emtza'ei Ha'Ya'ail Ve'Ha'Meduyak Be'Yoter Le'Milchama Be'Mechablim,"* *Biton Heyl Ha'Avir*, January 1988, No. 61 (162), p. 10.

p. 152 *Ibid*, p. 11.

p. 152 Danny Sadeh, *"Hutkafu Be'Sisei Jibril,"* *Yediot Aharonot*, November 25, 1989, p. 1.

CHAPTER NINE

p. 154 Jerusalem Post staff, "Father of the Holy War," *Jerusalem Post*, April 17, 1988, p. 4.

p. 155 Neil C. Livingstone and David Halevy, "Israel Commandos Terminate PLO Terror Chief," *Soldier of Fortune Magazine*, December 1989, p. 76.

p. 155 Emanuel Rosen, *"Ha'Mechablim She'Chadru Mi'Gvul Ha'Shalom Tichnenu Lizro'a Mavet,"* *Ma'ariv*, February 12, 1988, p. 4.

p. 156 Ian Black and Benny Morris, *Israel's Secret Wars* (London: Hamish Hamilton, 1991); p. 470.

p. 156 Samuel M. Katz, *The Elite* (New York: Pocket Books, 1992), p. 288.

p. 156 Marie Colvin, "Abu Jihad Knew Hit Team Was in Town," *London Sunday Times*, April 24, 1988, p. A15. It is believed that the video camera in question was a special device, produced by the Israeli firm IT Lasers Ltd., which can record in virtual darkness with uncanny clarity.

p. 157 Jim Smallow, "Assignment Murder," *Time* magazine, May 2, 1988, p. 37.

p. 157 Various editors, *"Yisrael Tafsa Be'Tunis Reshimat Sochnei Asha'f Be'Aretz U'Be'Shtachim,"* *Yediot Aharonot*, May 8, 1988, p. 1.

p. 157 Ron Dagoni, *"Sarim Be'Tunisia Hufa'alu Be'Sherut Ha'Mossad,"* *Ma'ariv*, November 8, 1988, p. 1.

p. 158 *Jerusalem Post* staff, "Father of the Holy War," p. 4.

p. 158 For the best description of the hit teams, see Michael Bar-Zohar and Eitan Haber, *The Quest for the Red Prince* (New York: William Morrow, 1983); and David B. Tinnin and Dag Christensen, *The Hit Team* (New York: Dell Publishing, 1976).

p. 158 Shapi Gabai and AP sources, *"Heyl Ha'Avir Chipes Et Jibril: Takaf Mifkeda Be'Levanon Be'A'at She'Rav Ha'Mechablim Biker Sham,"* *Ma'ariv*, May 13, 1988, p. 1.

p. 159 *Ibid*.

p. 159 Ron Ben-Yishai, *"Ra'Mat'Kal Chadash Le'Tzahal, Yediot Aharonot,*

April 1, 1991, p. 2. Also see Uri Milshtein, *Ha'Historia Shel Ha'Tzanhanim Kerech Daled* (Tel Aviv: Schalgi Publishing House, 1987); and Yosef Argaman, *Ze Haya Sodi Be'Yoter* (Tel Aviv: Israel Ministry of Defense Publishing, 1990), pp. 31–42; pp. 259–276; pp. 357–368.

p. 159 The true size of Sayeret Golani remains classified. In his semiofficial history of the Golani Brigade, Motta Har-Lev indicates that the unit is designated the *Plugat Siyur Golani* (Golani Reconnaissance Company), and is therefore a company-strength force; several foreign reports, however, indicate that the unit might be of full battalion strength.

p. 160 Major (Res.) Louis Williams, "The Golani Brigade," *IDF Journal*, Vol. III, No. 2, Spring 1986, p. 12.

p. 161 Motta Har-Lev, *Golani Sheli* (Tel Aviv: Avivim Publishers, 1991), p. 163.

p. 161 Avi Battleheim, *Golani—Heyl Ha'Raglim: Tzahal Be'Heilo Entzyklopedia Le'Tzava Ule'Bitachon* (Tel Aviv: Revivim Publishers, 1981), pp. 60–61.

p. 162 Major (Res.) Louis Williams, "The Golani Brigade," p. 19.

p. 162 For the best description of the Golani Brigade's operations during the 1973 Yom Kippur War, see Avi Battleheim, *Golani Mishpachat Lochamim* (Tel Aviv: Golani Brigade Command/Israel Ministry of Defense Publications, 1980).

p. 162 Yossi Melman and Dan Raviv, *The Imperfect Spies: The History of Israeli Intelligence* (London: Sidgwick & Jackson, 1990), p. 213.

p. 163 Avi Battleheim, *Golani Mishpachat Lochamim*, pp. 168–181.

p. 164 For an examination of Kfar Sil, see Ze'ev Schiif and Ehud Ya'ari, *Israel's Lebanon War* (New York: Simon & Schuster, 1984). The Jebel Barouk reference came from an interview with an American intelligence officer, New York, June 1990.

p. 164 Interview, New York City, December 1991.

p. 164 Motta Har-Lev, *Golani Sheli*, pp. 162.

p. 165 Barbara Sofer and David Rudge, "Missing Sons," *Jerusalem Post International Edition*, week ending June 29, 1991, p. 9.

p. 166 Dafnah Vardi, "*Nichshal Ha'Nisayon Shel Tzahal Le'Fotzetz Mateh Jibril Be'Emtza'ut Klavei Nefetz*," *A'l Ha'Mishmar*, December 11, 1988, p. 1.

p. 166 Interview, Tel Aviv, June 1, 1990.

p. 167 Baruch Ron and Yair Silbersheleg, "*Le'Hakdim Tmuna Le'Maka*," *Bamachane Chu'l*, August 1984, p. 16.

p. 167 Emanuel Rosen, "*Ha'Koach Chiletz Et Ha'Ptzu'im Ve'Gufat Ha'Ma'ga'd Ve'Lo Sam Lev She'Arba'a Chayalim Notru Me'Achor*," *Ma'ariv*, December 11, 1988, p. 4.

p. 167 For the IDF/Navy's naval commando force being identified as Flotilla 13 (its Hebrew designation is *Shayetet Shlosh-Esrai*), see Neil C. Livingstone and David Halevy, "Israeli Commandos Terminate PLO Terror

Chief," p. 77. For Flotilla 13's role in the al-Na'ameh operation, see various editors, *"Ma'Ga'd Be'Golani Neherag Be'Pshita No'ezet Shel Tzahal a'l Mifkedet Jibril Be'Levanon,"* Yisrael Shelanu, December 16, 1988, p. 9.

p. 168 Emanuel Rosen, *"Ha'Koach Chiletz Et Ha'Ptzu'im,"* p. 4.

p. 169 Various editors, "Built-Up Area Warfare," *Defense Update International*, No. 54, 1984, p. 2.

p. 170 For a mention of the Sayeret Mat'kal training prior to Operation Spring of Youth, see Michael Bar-Zohar and Eitan Haber, *The Quest for the Red Prince*, p. 156. For discussion of a mock-up prior to the Abu Jihad assassination, see Neil C. Livingstone and David Halevy, "Israeli Commandos Terminate," p. 77.

p. 170 Various editors, *"Ma'Ga'd Be'Golani Neherag,"* p. 9.

p. 171 It is clear that were the al-Na'ameh raid to have been a total success, news of the equipment carried by the Golani commandos *would never* have been made public—the IDF military censor's office clearly would have seen to it that no mention of such equipment ever would have been made. But because of the ferocious fighting and Israeli casualties, several bits of equipment were left behind by the attacking Golani commandos and later captured by PFLP-GC personnel. Much of this classified gear was later displayed by Ahmed Jibril in an al'Na'ameh news conference.

p. 171 Interview with representative from IT Lasers, New York City, December 16, 1989.

p. 171 *Ibid.*

p. 172 Photograph with Jibril holding Lieutenant-Colonel Amir Meital's Glilon show it fitted with a long silencing device.

p. 172 John Blosser, "Shocking Cruelty," *National Enquirer*, January 9, 1989, p. 18.

p. 172 Various editors, "Questions After Lebanon Raid," *Jerusalem Post International Edition*, December 24, 1988, p. 3; and Emanuel Rosen, *"Ha'Koach Chiletz Et Ha'Ptzu'im,* p. 4.

p. 172 Emanuel Rosen, *"Ha'Koach Chiletz Et Ha'Ptzu'im,"* p. 4.

p. 172 *Ibid.*

p. 174 Army correspondent, *"Shomron Lakach Ha'Chlata Amitza,"* Yediot Aharonot, December 12, 1988, p. 3.

p. 175 Various editors, *"Ma'Gad Be'Golani' Neherag,* p. 10.

p. 175 IAF magazine staff reporters, "Cobras, Cobras: A Strike or Two and You're Out," *Israel Air Force Magazine*, 1990 Annual, p. 35.

p. 176 Interview, Haifa, May 24, 1991.

p. 176 Chan Kotas, *"Pa'am Natanu Lo Chalva,"* Bamachane, December 14, 1988, p. 5.

p. 178 Emanuel Rosen, *"Hachlata Amitza U'me'ureret Machlukot,"* Ma'ariv, December 11, 1988, p. 3.

p. 178 Tali Zelinger, *"Tzanhanim Vatikim: Paga'a Be'E'rech Yasod; Motta Gur: Hachlata Kasha—Va'Nechona,"* Davar, December 11, 1988, p. 1.

p. 179 Arieh Kozel, *"Shomron: Horiti A'l Pinui Ha'Kochot Mi'Chashash Le'Histabchot Tzvait U'Medinit,"* Yediot Aharonot, December 12, 1988, p. 2.

p. 180 Aharon Lapidot, "Battle by Night, Rescue by Day," *Israel Air Force Magazine*, 1990 Annual, p. 34.

p. 181 Chan Kotas, *"Hotzeinu Et Kol Ha'Arba'ah, Bamachane Chu'l,"* September 1989, p. 67.

p. 181 Aharon Lapidot, "Battle by Night, Rescue by Day," p. 34.

p. 182 Emanuel Rosen, *"Hachlata Amitzah,"* p. 3.

p. 182 Chan Kotas, *"Hotzeinu Et Kol Ha'Arba'ah,"* p. 67.

p. 182 Various editors, *"Ha'Ma'Gad She'Neherag—Echad Ha'Lochamim Ha'No'azim Ve'Ha'Muvcharim Shel Tzahal,"* Yisrael Shelanu, December 16, 1988, p. 2.

p. 182 Yehuda Goren, *"Ha'Ra'Mat'Kal: Mekablei Ha'Tza'La'Sh He'I'difu Ha'Klal A'l Yatzar Ha'Kiyum,"* Ma'ariv, July 16, 1989, p. 4.

p. 183 As per an Associated Press photograph that appeared in *Ma'ariv*, December 11, 1988, page 3, under the headline: "Jibril and a Galil." For the weapon's identification as belonging to Lieutenant-Colonel Meital, see interview with IT Lasers representative, New York City, December 16, 1989.

CHAPTER TEN

p. 185 Ed Magnuson, "Ten Minutes of Horror," *Time* magazine, January 6, 1986, pp. 74–76.

p. 185 *Ibid*, p. 75.

p. 185 Patrick Seale, *Abu Nidal: A Gun for Hire* (New York: Random House, 1992), p. 243.

p. 186 *Ibid*, p. 244.

p. 186 Neil C. Livingstone and David Halevy, "Bombs Over Benghazi," *Soldier of Fortune Magazine*, January 1990, p. 24.

p. 186 Interview, New York City, December 10, 1990.

p. 187 Yossi Melman and Dan Raviv, *The Imperfect Spies: A History of Israeli Intelligence* (London: Sidgwick & Jackson, 1990), p. 90.

p. 188 Philippe Perinet, *"Le DC10 D'UTA: Piege Pour La France,"* Raids, No. 43, December 1989, p. 6. For mention of the PFLP-GC Shiite alliance in southern Lebanon, see Ihsan A. Hijazi, "Israel Raids Base in South Lebanon," *The New York Times*, December 18, 1991, p. A6.

p. 188 Various editors, *Inter: International Terrorism in 1989* (Tel Aviv: Tel Aviv University/Jaffe Center for Strategic Studies, 1990), p. 67.

p. 188 *Ibid*, p. 68.

p. 189 John K. Cooley, *Payback: America's Long War in The Middle East* (Washington, D.C.: Brassey's (U.S.), 1991), p. 164.

p. 190 Various editors, *Inter: International Terrorism in 1989*, p. 74.

p. 190 *Ibid.*

p. 190 *Ibid*, p. 76.

p. 192 William P. Grunner, "No Time for Decision Making," *Proceedings*, November 1990, p. 39.

p. 192 Interview, New York City, December 1990.

p. 193 William P. Grunner, "No Time for Decision Making," p. 40.

p. 193 John K. Cooley, *Payback*, p. 160.

p. 193 *Ibid*, p. 162.

p. 194 Steven Emerson and Brian Duffy, *The Fall of Pan Am 103: Inside the Lockerbie Investigation* (New York: G.P. Putnam's Sons, 1990), p. 202.

p. 194 Stephen Engelberg, "U.S. Calls Iranian Cleric Leading Backer of Terror," *The New York Times*, August 27, 1989, p. A9.

p. 195 *Ibid.*

p. 195 Neil C. Livingstone and David Halevy, *Inside the PLO* (New York: William Morrow, 1990), p. 214.

p. 195 Various editors, " 'Ha'Mossad' Hi'Zhir Et Ha'Americanim: Ha'Mechablim Mit'konenim Pitzutz Matos," *Yisrael Shelanu*, July 20, 1990, p. 8.

p. 196 For mention of the $2 million advance paid to the PFLP-GC, see Neil C. Livingstone and David Halevy, *Inside the PLO*, p. 215. For mention of the final payment to Jibril for the destruction of Pan Am 103 being $10 million, see "The Bombing of Pan Am 103," *Frontline*, WGBH-TV, Show #802, January 23, 1990.

p. 196 John Frick Root, "U.S. Stupor on Pan Am 103 Report," *The Jerusalem Post*, May 17, 1990, p. 4.

p. 196 John K. Cooley, *Payback*, p. 166.

p. 197 Guy Bechor, *Lexicon Asha'f* (Tel Aviv: Israel Ministry of Defense Publishing, 1991), p. 122.

p. 197 Steven Emerson and Brian Duffy, "Pan Am 103: The German Connection," *The New York Times Sunday Magazine*, March 18, 1990, p. 32.

p. 198 *Jerusalem Post* staff and agencies, "Germany Sentences Two Jibril Terrorists," *The Jerusalem Post*, June 4, 1991, p. 1.

p. 198 Steven Emerson and Brian Duffy, "Pan Am 103: The German Connection," p. 32.

p. 199 Interview, Frankfurt, May 19, 1991.

p. 200 Steven Emerson and Brian Duffy, "Pan Am, 103: The German Connection," p. 34.

p. 200 *Ibid.*

p. 201 *Frontline*, WGBH-TV, Show #802, January 23, 1990.

p. 201 *Ibid*, p. 35.

p. 201 Yossi Bar, *"Ha'Mafia Me'Saya'at La'Mechablim Ha'Palestinaim Tmurat Samim,"* *Yediot Aharonot*, September 6, 1987, p. 3.

p. 202 "Frontline," WGBH-TV, Show #802, January 23, 1990.

p. 202 Steven Emerson and Brian Duffy, *The Fall of Pan Am 103*, p. 208.

p. 202 Shlomoh Shemger, *"Anshei Jibril She'Nilkadu Be'Germania Lo Tichnenu Lifgoa'a Be'Ha'Po'el Ramat Gan,"* *Yediot Aharonot*, October 30, 1988, p. 1.

p. 203 John K. Cooley, *Payback*, p. 166.

p. 203 Steven Emerson and Brian Duffy, *The Fall of Pan Am 103*, p. 168.

p. 203 *Ibid*, p. 169.

p. 204 Melissa Ludtke, "Keeping Lockerbie Alive," *Time* magazine, November 27, 1989, p. 33.

p. 205 Yisrael Rosenblat, *"Shalosh Shanim Be'A'aqavot Me'Fotzetzei Matos Pan Am,"* *Ma'ariv Sof Shavu'a*, November 22, 1991, p. 7.

p. 205 Yochanan Lahav, *"5 Sochnim Shel Ha'Mossad Nitztavu La'Tzeit Mi'Anglia,"* *Yediot Aharonot*, July 24, 1988, p. 1.

CHAPTER ELEVEN

p. 208 *Frontline*, WGBH-TV, Show #802, January 23, 1990.

p. 208 ABC News, *Prime Time Live*, November 30, 1989.

p. 209 Steven Emerson and Brian Duffy, *The Fall of Pan Am 103: Inside the Lockerbie Investigation*, p. 16.

p. 210 ABC News, *Prime Time Live*, January 23, 1989.

p. 211 *Ibid*.

p. 211 Boaz Ganor, *"Luv: Shagrirut Ha'Retzach Ve'Ha'Chabala,"* *Matara*, February-March 1992, No. 24, p. 37.

p. 211 Stephen Engelberg, "Warning on Bomb Hinted by Pan Am," *The New York Times*, November 2, 1989, p. A4.

p. 212 Jim Smolowe, "Late Alarms, Failed Alerts," *Time* magazine, March 27, 1989, p. 28.

p. 212 ABC News, *Prime Time Live*, November 30, 1989.

p. 213 Interview, Jerusalem, June 4, 1991.

p. 214 John K. Cooley, *Payback*, p. 164.

p. 214 *Ibid*, p. 167.

p. 215 ABC News, *Prime Time Live*, November 30, 1989.

p. 215 Steven Emerson and Brian Duffy, *The Fall of Pan Am 103*, p. 238.

p. 216 *Ibid*.

p. 216 Various editors, "Pan Am Bombing Suspect Convicted of Other Attacks," *The New York Times*, December 22, 1989, p. A8.

p. 217 ABC News, *Prime Time Live*, November 30, 1989.

p. 218 Michael Wines, "D.E.A. To Study Claim of Role by Agent in Pam Am Bombing," *The New York Times*, November 1, 1990, p. A14.

p. 218 Melissa Ludtke, "Keeping Lockerbie Alive," *Time* magazine, November 27, 1989, p. 33.

p. 218 Shmaya Kider, " 'Ha'Moach' Ve'Ta'alumoto Ha'Rasis Me'Matos Pan Am, *Ma'ariv Shabbat*, January 5, 1990, p. 2.

p. 218 *Frontline*, WGBH-TV, Show #802, January 23, 1990.

p. 219 John K. Cooley, *Payback*, p. 85.

p. 221 *Frontline*, Show #802.

p. 221 Steven Emerson and Brian Duffy, "*The Fall of Pan Am 103*, p. 245.

p. 221 Emanuel Rosen, "*Yisrael: Ha'Ish Hu Jibril*," *Ma'ariv Shabbat*, November 22, 1991, p. 7.

p. 222 ABC News, *Prime Time Live*, November 30, 1989.

p. 222 *Ibid.*

p. 223 Youssef M. Ibrahim, "Libya Denies Link to Airline Blasts," *The New York Times*, June 28, 1991, p.A 13.

p. 223 Michael Wines, "Portrait of Pan Am Suspect: Affable Exile, Fiery Avenger," *The New York Times*, December 24, 1989, p. A11.

p. 223 Michael Wines, "Libya Now Linked," *The New York Times*, p. A8.

p. 223 Michael Wines, "Pan Am Blast—An Inquiry in Hot Pursuit," *The New York Times*, January 1, 1989, p. A4.

p. 224 Craig R. Whitney, "Havel Says His Predecessors Sent Libya Explosives," *The New York Times*, March 23, 1990, p. A5; and Kenneth W. Banta, "The Arms Merchants' Dilemma," *Time* magazine, April 2, 1990, p. 29.

p. 224 Alan Riding, "Four Libyans Charged by France in Air Bombing," *The New York Times*, October 31, 1991, p. A9.

p. 224 Various editors, *Inter*, p. 78.

p. 225 Eloise Salholz and Bob Cohn, "Who Paid for the Bullet," *Newsweek*, November 25, 1991, p. 28.

p. 225 *Frontline*, Show #802.

p. 225 David Johnston, "Plane Blast Still Open Case, U.S. Says," *The New York Times*, November 26, 1991, p. A12.

p. 226 *Ibid.*

p. 226 Andrew Rosenthal, "U.S. Accuses Libya As 2 Are Charged in Pan Am Bombing," *The New York Times*, November 15, 1991, p. A1.

p. 226 Clyde Haberman, "Israelis Remain Convinced Syrians Downed Flight 103," *The New York Times*, November 21, 1991, p. A14.

p. 227 Michael Wines, "Libya Now Linked," *The New York Times*, p. A1.

p. 227 Allison Kaplan, "Terror Victim's Husband Rejected," *Jerusalem Post International Edition*, week ending November 9, 1991, p. 7.

p. 228 Uzi Machnayami and Arel Ginai, "*Anshei Jibril A'tzru Be'Damesek Shnei Diplomatim Americanim*," *Yediot Aharonot*, March 12, 1989, p. 3.

p. 229 Tzadok Yechezkeli, "*Ar'Hab Chasfa Sochnei 'Ha'Mossad' La'Surim—Ve'Hem Hutzu Le'Horeg*," *Yediot Aharonot*, February 8, 1991, p. 6.

p. 229 Michael Wines, "2 or 3 Agents Are Believed Killed After Rare U.S.-Syrian Contacts," *The New York Times*, February 7, 1991, p. A1.

p. 229 *Ibid*, p. A18.

p. 230 Michael Wines, "Jordan Link Reported for Spies Slain in Syria," *The New York Times*, March 12, 1991, p. A8.

p. 230 Ted Klemens, "Report: U.S. Hid Syria Bomb Link," *New York Daily News*, November 21, 1991, p. 30.

p. 230 Various editors, "Palestinian Radical Denies Link to Flight 103 Bombing," *The New York Times*, January 10, 1990, p. A10.

p. 231 ABCNews, *Prime Time Live*, November 30, 1989.

p. 231 Brian Michael Jenkins, "Terrorist Threat to Commercial Aviation," *IDF Journal*, Fall 1990, p. 14.

p. 231 Yisrael Rosenblat, "*Shalosh Shanim Be'A'aqavot*, p. 7.

p. 231 Douglas Davis, "Lockerbie Terrorist Holds Key to German Hostage Release Plan," *The Jerusalem Post*, May 21, 1990, p. 10.

POSTSCRIPT

p. 233 Kenneth Kaplan, "Syria Was Target in Attack on Jibril," *Jerusalem Post International Edition*, week ending April 1, 1989, p. 4.

p. 233 Joshua Brilliant and David Rudge, "IAF Hits Jibril Base," *Jerusalem Post International Edition*, week ending March 24, 1990, p. 2.

p. 234 Danny Sadeh, "*Heyl Ha'Avir Halam Pa'amayim Be'Bsisei Mechablim Be'Levanon*," *Yediot Aharonot*, June 5, 1991, p. 1.

p. 234 Steven Emerson and Brian Duffy, "Pan Am 103: The German Connection," *The New York Times Magazine*, March 18, 1990, p. 84; and Alan Cowel, "Attack on Israelis Upsets Palestinians in Egypt," *The New York Times*, February 7, 1990, p. A6.

p. 234 Jane Perlez, "Sudan Is Seen as Safe Base for Mideast Terror Groups," *The New York Times*, January 26, 1992, p. A 12.

p. 235 Stephen Engelberg, "Terror and Iran: Links Still Seen," *The New York Times*, November 12, 1989, p. A6.

p. 235 Arieh Hasabiyah, "*Million Chayalim Neged Yisrael*," *Bamachane*, November 13, 1991, p. 25.

p. 235 Joel Brinkley, "10 Die in Three Clashes Along Israel's Borders," *The New York Times*, November 26, 1990, p. A12.

p. 235 Douglas Davis, "10 Die In Three Clashes," p. 5.

p. 236 Douglas Davis, "Arab Terrorists Said Acquiring Heavily-Armed Hang-Glider Fleet," *The Jerusalem Post*, May 28, 1990, p. 5.

p. 236 Yochanan Lahav, "*Ha'Mechablim Rachsu E'srot Galshonim*

Ve'Maz'La'Tim Ve'Hem Ma'asikim Microbiologim," Yediot Aharonot, May 10, 1990, p. 5.

p. 236 Jerry Lewis, *"Jibril: 'Ha'Matara Ha'Ba O'lim Mi'Bri'hm,"* Yediot Aharonot, June 10, 1990, p. 9.

p. 236 Richard Cheznoff, *"Shum Davar Eino 'Batal Ve'Mevutal',"* Ha'aretz, October 27, 1989, p. 3.

p. 236 Yisgav Nakdimon, *"Ma'arot Ha'Mechablim: Ha'Cheshbon Nisgar,"* Biton Heyl Ha'Avir, No. 74, July 1990, p. 38, and various editors, *"Metosei Heyl Ha'Avir Hishlichu Tilim Le'Minharot Mifkedet Jibril Be'Na'amah,"* Yisrael Shelanu, September 29, 1989, p. 5, and, Ihasan A. Hijazi, "Israeli Air Raid Near Beirut Kills 12," The New York Times, January 11, 1992, p. A3.

p. 237 Guy Bechor, *"Jibril Chai O' Met,"* Hadashot, May 14, 1990, p. 3.

CHRONOLOGY

MAJOR TERRORIST OPERATIONS BY THE POPULAR FRONT OF THE LIBERATION OF PALESTINE GENERAL COMMAND (PFLP-GC) AND GROUPS CONNECTED TO AHMED JIBRIL

23 July 1968	El Al plane hijacked en route from Rome to Tel Aviv and landed in Algeria. First true successful hijacking of plane by Arab/Palestinian terrorists.
26 December 1968	El Al plane attacked at Athens Airport, one Israeli tourist killed.
21 February 1970	Swissair plane en route from Zurich to Lod (Israel) blown up in mid-air by altimeter bomb. Thirty-eight passengers killed.
21 February 1970	Explosion in baggage compartment of Austrian Airlines plane en route from Frankfurt to Vienna. Bomb causes minimal damage, and plane makes an emergency landing.
24 February 1970	Letter bombs sent from Frankfurt to addresses in Israel; devices are deactivated by Israeli bomb-disposal officers.
22 May 1970	Eight Israeli schoolchildren and four adults are killed when PFLP-GC guerrillas infiltrate into Israel from southern Lebanon, and launch antitank grenades at a school bus near Avivim. In the attack, twenty-nine schoolchildren are seriously wounded.
6 October 1970	Letter bombs addressed to El Al and Israeli embassy personnel discovered in London.
6 November 1970	Two bombs explode in Tel Aviv's Central Bus Station, killing two men.
28 July 1971	Attempt foiled to blow up El Al plane en route from Rome to Tel Aviv by means of a booby-trapped device in a suitcase.

265

1 September 1971	Abortive attempt to blow up El Al plane en route from London to Tel Aviv by means of a booby-trapped device in a suitcase.
28 December 1971	About 15 letter bombs sent from Yugoslavia and Austria to businessmen in Israel. A police bomb-disposal officer is critically wounded.
29 April 1972	Letter bombs sent to Israeli pavilion, Hanover Fair, West Germany.
16 August 1972	Abortive attempt to blow up El Al plane en route from Rome to Tel Aviv. Device, hidden in baggage, explodes in midair, but does not cause fatal damage; pilot skill and El Al jet's reinforced fuselage allows the flight to land safely.
7 December 1972	Letter bombs sent from Singapore to public institutions in Israel.
April 11, 1974	A four-man PFLP-GC terrorist squad infiltrates into Israel from southern Lebanon, and launches an attack against an apartment building in the frontier town of Kiryat Shemona; the terrorists had originally intended on seizing a school, but the facility was empty on the Passover holiday. Before a force of *Golani* Brigade commandos kill the terrorists in a ferocious battle, the terrorists kill sixteen civilians in cold blood. One year later, the Lebanese Civil War erupts when PFLP-GC supporters, celebrating the Qiryat Shmoneh massacre, attack Christian leader Pierre Gemayel's motorcade.
29 June 1975	US military attaché kidnapped in Beirut, and later released.
20 June 1980	Abortive attack on El Al personnel in Copenhagen.
20 January 1985	Abortive plan to kill PLO representative in London.
20 May 1985	After brutal and lengthy negotiations with the PFLP-GC through the auspices of the International Red Cross, State of Israel releases 1,150 convicted Palestinian terrorists (including mass murderers) in exchange for three Israeli soldiers Jibril seized in Lebanon in 1982.
25 November 1987	A PFLP-GC terrorist crossing into Israel on a motorized hang-glider attacks a frontier IDF post along the Lebanese border, and proceeds to kill six Israeli soldiers and wound seven before being gunned down. Days later the attack, known as *Night of the Hang-Glider*, prompts the eruption of violent protests in the Gaza Strip and the West Bank and the beginning of the Palestinian *Intifadah*.
21 December 1988	Pan AM 103, a Boeing 747 aircraft, erupts into a fire ball over the hamlet of Lockerbie, Scotland. Two hundred-seventy people are killed (259 on board the aircraft, 11 on

	the ground). Two Libyans are later indicted for this act of terror.
19 September 1989	French UTA airlines DC-10 destroyed by bomb planted in baggage compartment over the desert in Niger. All 171 passengers on board the aircraft are killed.
4 February 1990	Five Israeli tourists are killed and nearly one dozen wounded when PFLP-GC gunmen ambush a tour bus in Egypt.

GLOSSARY

ELITE AND COUNTER-TERRORIST UNITS OF
THE ISRAEL DEFENSE FORCES

Ha'Kommando Ha'yami: The IDF/Navy's naval commando element, also known by its designation, according to foreign reports, of *Shayetet 13*, or "Flotilla 13." Created in 1948, the IDF/Navy's naval commandos have participated in dozens of counter-terrorist operations, including the infamous February 21, 1973 raid against PFLP bases in Tripoli, Lebanon, and the April 9, 1973 "Operation Spring of Youth" raid against Black September and *el-Fatah* targets in the heart of Beirut. According to foreign reports, naval commando forces secured a beachhead for a force of *Mossad* agents and *Sayeret Mat'kal* commandos on April 16, 1988, on the shores of Tunis, prior to the assassination of PLO deputy commander Abu Jihad. According to reports, naval commandos secured the beachhead for the *Sayeret Golani* force tasked with attacking Jibril's lair at al-Na'ameh on December 9, 1988.

Ha'Mista'aravim: Figuratively "The Arabists," this unit, formed during the Palestinian *Intifadah*, was tasked with apprehending and neutralizing key— and heavily armed!—elements of the Palestinian uprising. One unit, known as *Duvdevan* [or "Cherry"] operates in the West Bank, and *Shimshon* [or "Samson"] operates in the Gaza Strip. The men of this unit all masquerade as local Arabs, and produce weapons from their indigenous clothing before striking out at their targets.

Sayeret Golani: Known by their affectionate military nickname of *Ha'Namer Ha'Me'ufaf,* or "Flying Tigers," the reconnaissance force from the 1st *Golani* Infantry Brigade is one of the more effective conventional commando forces in the IDF's order of battle. Excellent shock troops in battle against Syrian commandos on top of the Golan Heights in 1967 and 1973, and against Palestinian guerrillas in Lebanon in 1982. They are also a unit with a rich counter-terrorist heritage. During the dark days of the 1967–70 War of Attrition, the "Flying Tigers" fought a bitter counter-insurgency campaign against Palestinian guerrillas in the notorious *Fatahland* region between the

269

Lebanese, Syrian and Israeli frontiers. In 1974, *Sayeret Golani* commandos fought back Jibril's suicide commandos in Qiryat Shmoneh, and along the beaches of Nahariya; the unit also played a significant role during the IDF's spectacular "Operation Yonatan" rescue of 103 hostages from Entebbe, on July 4, 1976. One of *Sayeret Golani*'s most infamous operations was the December 9, 1988, raid on Ahmed Jibril's lair at al-Na'amah.

Sayeret Mat'kal: The highly classified, ultra-top-secret, General Staff Reconnaissance Unit was formed in 1957 as a super elite reconnaissance force to be dispatched deep behind enemy lines to conduct intelligence-gathering operations; they were to be a mission impossible-type force known to only a select few in the IDF General Staff. Their special talents, however, also landed them a unique role as counter-terrorists. In 1968, a *Sayeret Mat'kal* force launched a retaliatory raid against Beirut International Airport, in which thirteen Middle East Airlines aircraft were destroyed. *Sayeret Mat'kal* also participated in the May 1972 rescue of a hijacked Sabena airliner to Lod (in which the commandos dressed up as mechanics in white coveralls); the assassination of three of Black September's top commanders in "Operation Spring of Youth;" the rescue bids at Ma'alot and at the Savoy Hotel in Tel Aviv; and, of course, spearheading the rescue operation at Entebbe under the command of Lieutenant-Colonel Yonatan "Yoni" Netanyahu. According to foreign reports, the unit was responsible for the April 1988 assassination of PLO deputy commander Abu Jihad, and the July 1989 abduction of *Hizbollah* commander Sheikh Abdel Karim Obeid.

Sayeret Tzanhanim: The reconnaissance force of the IDF's conscript paratroop brigade, *Sayeret Tzanhanim* has participated in some of the most bitterly fought battles in Israeli history—from the Golan Heights to the urban squalor of Suez City and Beirut. They have participated in their share of spectacular counter-terrorist operations, including the 1968 raid on Beirut International Airport, "Spring of Youth," "Entebbe," and other operations that are still classified to this day.

Ya'ma'm: Acronym for Special Police Anti Terrorist Unit, the *Ya'ma'm* is the National Police Border Guard's specialized hostage-rescue unit, built much like Germany's infamous GSG-9.

THE PALESTINIAN TERRORIST GROUPS

Fatah The largest and most important group, commanded by Chairman Arafat under his nom de guerre "Abu Amar." Most closely identified with the Palestinian desire for a national homeland, it has traditionally opposed Syrian attempts to dominate the Palestinian effort for Syrian ends, including behind the scenes efforts to limit a Syrian manipulation of the American-sponsored peace talks. Arafat's organization is divided into the following divisions:

I: *Political*
   (A) The Central Committee—the decision-making political body.
   (B) The Revolutionary Council—the miniature "parliament in exile"
II: *Security & Terrorism*
   (A) The Western Sector—led by "Abu Jihad" before his assassination on April 16, 1988, in Tunis, deals mainly with targets in the West Bank, and inside Israel proper.
   (B) United Security—led for over two decades by Salah Khalaf (better known by his nom de guerre of "Abu Iyad") prior to his Janaury 1991 assassination at the hands of Abu Nidal gunmen; it is the offensive operations branch.
   (C) Security and Information responsible for internal security and intelligence. *Force 17*, Arafat's elite personal bodyguard, is part of this branch.
III: *Military*
   (A) The Central Operations Room—led by "Abu al-Ma'tassem;" coordinates military operations by *Fatah* units in the field. *Force 14*, the nucleus of a "future Palestinian air force," is controlled by this branch; originally established with suicide air attacks in mind, it is mainly stationed in South Yemen, with over 20 aircraft including MiG-21s, Fokker transports, and French helicopters.

The largest of the Palestinian terrorist groups and parent-organization to the infamous Black September Organization in the 1970s, *Fatah's* operations included: the 1972 Munich Olympics Massacre (carried out with East German secret service assistance); the December 1972 seizure of the Israeli embassy in Bangkok, Thailand; the March 1973 seizure of the Saudi Arabian embassy in Khartoum, Sudan, and the assassinations of the American and Belgian ambassadors; the failed September 1973 missile attack against an El Al jet in Rome; the June 1974 Nahariya massacre; the March 1978 "Country Club" Massacre in Tel Aviv where 35 civilians were killed; the April 1985 attempt to land on the coast of Tel Aviv and seize the IDF Ministry of Defense; and, the September 1985 murder of three Israeli civilians on a yacht in Larnaca harbor (the attack prompted Israel's air raid on PLO Headquarters in Tunis). *Fatah* terrorists have also been responsible for hundreds of acts of terror (ranging from bus bombings to random stabbing) inside Israel; and the Occupied Territories, as well as revenge killings against fellow Palestinians in the *Intifadah*.

The Popular Front for the Liberation of Palestine (PFLP): Commanded by Dr. George Habash, this pan-Arabist Marxist group is structured, like most Third World national liberation movements, along the lines of "democratic centralism." The second-ranking member of the Palestine National Council, it is vocally pro-Syrian. Most PFLP terrorist elements are stationed in Syria, while its military guerrilla forces (one artillery and five "commando" battalions) are based in Lebanon. A special group known as "Subjugated Lands" is responsible for *Katyusha* attacks on northern Israel. Best known for his hijacking operations in the late 1960s and early 1970s. In 1991, Habash caused a minor political uproar in France, when the convicted terrorist with a "journal" of extradition orders was admitted to a Paris hospital for emergency medical care.

The Democratic Front for the Liberation of Palestine (DFLP): Commanded by Nayif Hawatmeh, the DFLP, together with *el-Fatah* and the PFLP, belongs to the authentic core of the PLO-charter members prior to the Karameh battle. Marxist-inspired and fiercely independent, it has nevertheless mediated during rifts between various guerrilla factions. Military strength is estimated to be 1,000 fully-trained fighters, deployed as units throughout Lebanon. Training facilities mainly located in Syria. Operations sections include a "Subjugated Lands" unit, central military intelligence, and a small "Special Forces" unit.

The Popular Front for the Liberation of Palestine—General Command (PFLP-GC): Together with *As-Sa'iqa*, the PFLP-GC acts as the most vocal supporter of Syrian policies within the PLO. Primarily military, the group enjoys little political or ideological support. Led by Ahmed Jibril, it numbers about 1,000 fighters. Its headquarters are in the Rehan district of Damascus, and it enjoys the use of many offices and training facilities throughout Syria, foremost among these being "Camp 17th September" at Ein Saheb, which houses the PFLP-GC operational staff. Its military organization is the single "Sabra & Shatilla Battalion" with supporting artillery, rocket and special forces units, including a frogman element.

As-Sa'iqa: (The lightning-bolt), formed in 1968, is the terrorist arm of the Syrian Ba'ath Party, being an integral part of the Palestinian section of the Syrian Ba'ath. Led by Assam al-Qadhi, it has some 1,300 fighters, and serves as a loyal instrument of Syrian policy within the various Palestinian movements (though during the 1983 rebellion within *el-Fatah*, many *as-Sa'iqa* fighters joined the Arafat loyalists). Its organizational command is located in the Susa district of Damascus, and is responsible for five "battalions" in Lebanon, mainly in the Beka'a Valley, northern Lebanon, and the Mount Lebanon region. There is a "security department" run in cooperation with the Syrian *Muchabarat*.

The Popular Struggle Front (PSF): is a small Marxist group, numbering approximately 600 fighters, working in close cooperation with the PFLP-GC and *As-Sa'iqa*.

The Palestinian Liberation Front (Abu A'bbass Faction): is a small but innovative group, several hundred strong, led by Abu al-A'bbass; it is politically split, allying itself with Arafat or the Syrians depending upon circumstances. It is most famous for several attempts to infiltrate Israel by air; an attempt by hot air balloon and another by hang-glider, both in 1981, met with failure. Its greatest claim to fame was the 1985 hijacking of the Italian cruise ship *Achille Lauro*, and the murder of an elderly man in a wheelchair. Flown out of Egypt under safe conduct, the terrorists were taken into custody after their airliner was forced to land in Sicily by U.S. Navy F-14 Tomcats; Abu al-A'bbas himself was on board, but escaped being taken prisoner by an awaiting contingent of American naval commandos from SEAL Team 6 when Italian authorities bowed to pressure. His last attempted act at a major terrorist attack (at the time of this book's writing) was the failed *Shavuoth* holiday beach massacre along the Tel Aviv shore in May 1990.

The Abu Ibrahim Arab Organization of May 15: A pro-Iraqi terrorist faction known for its bomb-making capabilities. Behind a series of airline bombings, included the January 1982 bombing of a Kosher restaurant in West Berlin in which one child was killed and forty-six civilians wounded, the August 1982 bombing of an American airliner destined for Hawaii in which one passenger was killed, and a bombing of a TWA jet. The group has now splintered into different sections.

The Arab Liberation Front (ALF): is commanded by Abd al-Rahim Ahmad; it was established by the Iraqi Ba'ath Party, and receives its orders from Baghdad. Its positions shift according to Iraqi policy; at the time of this book's writing it sides with Arafat against the Syrians. Offices and training facilities for its 400 fighters are in Iraq, although it has substantial representation in Beirut and Tripoli. The group is mainly known for a vicious attack on Kibbutz Misgav-Am in February 1980, resulting in the death of an infant girl.

The Abu Nidal Faction (Fatah-Revolutionary Council): was founded at the end of 1973 by Sabri al-Bana ("Abu Nidal"); before 1981 it enjoyed full Iraqi patronage, though its infrastructure today lies in Syria, Iran and Libya. Its 500-800 fanatical terrorists are stationed throughout the world, mainly in Western Europe and in moderate Arab countries. It specializes in assassinating Palestinian officials whose indirect dealing with Israel brand them as "traitors to the revolution"; and Sabri al-Bana has been under sentence of death by a PLO court for years. By terrorist acts such as the attempted murder of Israel's UK ambassador (touching off the 1982 Lebanon War), the Rome and Vienna airport massacres of December 1985, and the hijacking of the Egyptian Boeing 737 to Malta, the Abu Nidal Faction has developed the reputation of the world's most dangerous and ruthless terror organization. Responsible for countless "revenge-killings" among noted Palestinian leaders seen as too pro-western and pro-peace, including, remarkably, the assassination of PLO deputy chief of Abu Iyad in January 1991.

The Naji Alush Faction (Popular Arab Liberation Movement): is a small group whose eponymous leader broke away from the Abu Nidal Faction in 1979. It consists of only 100 terrorists, but maintains excellent networks throughout Europe, providing weapons and explosives to European terror groups such as the Red Brigade and the IRA.

The Salim Abu-Salem Faction (Popular Front for the Liberation of Palestine— Special Command): is another small, though internationally operational group, whose main bases of support lie with Iraq and South Yemen. They have been quite active in assassinating PLO leaders, though not in operations which might seem to advance the revolution.

(Pro-Palestinian, Anti-Israeli, Anti-Western Arab terrorist factions)

Amal, Hizbollah, and Jihad al-Islami The religious zeal of the Shiite revolution in Iran, together with the power vacuum in Lebanon, has polarized Lebanon's Shiites, the majority ethnic group long exploited by the wealthier Sunni community. Proud, independent and militant, the Shiites first embraced the invading Israelis as saviors from harsh PLO occupation, but later turned against the Israelis and Americans for their support of the Christians. Their struggle against the IDF in southern Lebanon developed into a three-year guerrilla war which cost Israel almost 400 dead. Shiite fanaticism— expressed in three successful car-bombings which killed over 350 people, including 241 U.S. Marines—forced American withdrawal from Lebanon. Today they are the most powerful military force within Lebanon and, led by Nabih Berri's *Amal* militia, are battling to prevent a renewed PLO build-up in the refugee camps. The ultra-militant *Hizbollah* ("Party of God") and *Jihad al-Islami* ("Islamic Holy War") groups are closely tied to the Iranian Shiites, and the Ayatollah Khomeini's Iranian Revolutionary Guards train their members for terrorist missions at their Ba'albek headquarters near the Syrian border. The exact strength and structure of these groups remain clouded, however, due to extreme secrecy, deliberate disinformation, and a degree of spurious identification with them sometimes claimed by quite different elements in Lebanon's murderous chaos of competing gangs. The last major terrorist operation that *Hizbollah* was responsible for is believed to be the 1992 bombing of the Israeli embassy in Buenos Aires, Argentina. *Hizbollah* maintains extremely close ties with the PFLP-GC; according to reports featured in the October 17, 1992, issue of the Jerusalem Post, Jibril has even had access to Captain Ron Arad, an Israel Air Force navigator captured by *Hizbollah* in 1986, and (at the time of this book's writing) a hostage ever since.

INDEX